Coffeetime in Summer

Bible-based Reflections for Each Day of the Season

MY COFFEE-CUP MEDITATIONS

Coffeetime in Summer

Bible-based Reflections for Each Day of the Season

ROGER ELLSWORTH

This edition 2022 Coffeetime in Summer
ISBN 978-1-63342-283-4

Shepherd Press
P.O. Box 24
Wapwallopen, PA 18660

www.shepherdpress.com

www.mycoffeecup meditations.com

www.rogerellsworth.org

Purpose

My Coffee Cup Meditations are short, easy-to-read, engagingly presented devotions based on the Bible, the Word of God. Each reading takes a single idea or theme and develops it in a thought-provoking way so that you are inspired to consider the greatness of God, the relevance of the good news of the life, death, resurrection, and coming-again of Jesus, and are better equipped for life in this world and well prepared for the world to come.

www.mycoffeecupmeditations.com

https://www.facebook.com/MyCoffeeCupMeditations/

We hope you will enjoy these Bible-based meditations. We would love to hear from you, so please send us a note to tell us what you think—which ones you liked most, and how they made a difference in your life or in the life of a family member, friend, or work associate.

To reach us online, go to
www.mycoffeecupmeditations.com/contact

We offer quantity discounts for bulk quantity purchases.
Contact us for more details.

Be sure to collect each of the four volumes in this series!

Coffeetime in Winter: 978-1-63342-281-0
Coffeetime in Spring: 978-1-63342-282-7
Coffeetime in Summer: 978-1-63342-283-4
Coffeetime in Autumn: 978-1-63342-284-1

About the Authors

Roger Ellsworth is a retired pastor, active in ministry and writing, who lives in Jackson, Tennessee. He and his wife, Sylvia, love the message of the Bible, and they enjoy sharing the wonderful counsel of the Word of God in language that ordinary people can understand and appreciate. Roger has written numerous books on the Christian faith, and has exercised a preaching ministry for over fifty years.

Roger and Sylvia have two sons, Tim and Martyn, who have also contributed devotions to this volume.

Introduction: All About this Series

From God's Word, the Bible...

O Lord, You have searched me and known me.
You know my sitting down and my rising up;
You understand my thought afar off.
You comprehend my path and my lying down,
And are acquainted with all my ways.
For there is not a word on my tongue,
But behold, O Lord, You know it altogether.
You have hedged me behind and before,
And laid Your hand upon me.
Such knowledge is too wonderful for me;
It is high, I cannot attain it.

Psalm 139:1-6

What you have here is the third part of what was produced as a big book—twelve books all in one, in fact. The idea of connecting enjoying coffee and reading the Bible devotionally happened early in 2017 when I wrote the first book in what became a series of *My Coffee-Cup Meditations*.

God's knowledge of us is wonderful; there is nothing about us that He does not already fully know. The psalmist celebrated this in Psalm 139. It is a wonderful thing that God knows all about us. But how much of God do we know? We must read His Word, the Bible, if we are to learn of Him and to grow in His grace. Without reading and reflecting on the Bible regularly and prayerfully, we will be destined to a life of stunted growth.

Early mornings are very predictable for lots and lots of Christians. Roll out of bed, turn on the coffee pot, pour a cup, settle into a favorite chair and enjoy what is called "the daily devotional." This usually consists of reading a passage from the Bible and a selection from a devotional book. It concludes with prayer.

Christians who follow this pattern can go through a good bit of devotional material as the years go by. So they are always looking for new material—something to go along with their Bible and their coffee.

Hoping that I could be helpful in supplying the need for more devotional material, I gathered up some articles I had written and put them in a book—*A Dog and a Clock*. The idea was to supply brothers and sisters in Christ with enough devotions to carry them through one month. That quickly led to another book—*The Thumbs Up Man*—to carry "devotion-doers" through another month and then another.

You can guess what happened after three or four books came out. There are twelve months in the year. So why not provide enough books to cover a year? So off we went and out the books came until there were finally twelve books, each with thirty-one readings! Since these books were designed to go with the Bible and a good cup of coffee, it seemed right to call them *My Coffee-Cup Meditations*. Thanks to my good friends Jim and Sue Holmes for that suggestion! And thanks to my wife, Sylvia, and my sons, Tim and Martyn, for contributing some chapters along the way.

Then came the idea of producing the books together, so that there would be enough readings for a whole year, and with some left over, as not all months have thirty-one days. So the result is that we combined all twelve of the books into one big one: *The Big Book of Coffee Cup Meditations*! That way, people would be able to read from whichever month they wished to at any time in the year—and never have too few days in the month, because there would always be thirty-one readings in each month!

As we thought and prayed about how to present these books in yet another format, the idea of Bible readings for each of the seasons of the year came to mind: Coffeetime in Winter, Spring, Summer, and Fall. And so it is that you are holding the third of the set of four books in your hand!

One of my main concerns in writing these books was to cause the gospel of our Lord Jesus Christ to shine. It's wrong to think that the gospel is for unbelievers only. Believers need the gospel! We need to be reminded again and again of the greatness of what our Lord Jesus Christ did for us in His life, death, resurrection, and ascension. The more we ponder the gospel and the more deeply we ponder it, the more we will find our hearts flooded with gratitude, and the more willing we will be to faithfully serve Him.

My Coffee-Cup Meditations are published for you with the hope that you will read the devotions, enjoy them, and, most of all, find that you are inspired to consider the greatness of God, the relevance of the good news of the life, death, resurrection, and coming-again of Jesus, and are better equipped for life in this world and well prepared for the world to come.

And don't forget to pour that cup of coffee!

THE MONTH OF JULY

Sure Signs of Heavenly Hope

... And 30 Other Bible-Based Meditations

After we sang our closing song and prayed our closing prayer, these wonderful people began coming to me one after the other to bid farewell. I couldn't speak their language, and they couldn't speak mine, but I soon discovered we didn't need an interpreter as we had a common language after all. It was the language of smiles, tears and uplifted index fingers. Yes, as they said their goodbyes to me, these Brazilian brothers and sisters in Christ would point upward. That was each one's way of saying: "I will meet you in the air."

Contents

July 1

Sure Signs of Heavenly Hope

From God's Word, the Bible...

And if Christ is not risen, your faith is futile; you are still in your sins! Then also those who have fallen asleep in Christ have perished. If in this life only we have hope in Christ, we are of all men the most pitiable.

1 Corinthians 15:17-19

The time had come for my eighth and final sermon in a conference for Brazilian pastors and their wives. Organized and promoted by Missionary Richard Denham, it was a well-attended conference with approximately 800 registrants.

The Scripture I chose for this final sermon was 1 Thessalonians 4:13-18, the passage in which the Apostle Paul gloriously wipes away the concerns of his readers about their loved ones who had died in faith in the Lord Jesus Christ.

I divided the sermon into three parts—two kinds of sorrows, four blessed events, and one crucial condition. The two kinds of sorrows Paul indicates in verse 13 are sorrowing with hope and sorrowing without hope. The four blessed events he lays out in verses 14-17 are the return of the Lord, the resurrection of dead believers, the rapture of living believers, and the meeting in the air. The one crucial condition is stated by Paul in these words: ". . .if we believe that Jesus died and rose again. . ." (v. 14). The glorious future Paul lays out in this passage is only for those who trust in the redeeming work of the Lord Jesus Christ.

As I brought the sermon to a close, it occurred to me that it was very doubtful that I would ever see any of my hearers again in this life. So I closed with these words: "It's very likely that I will never see you again in this life, but I *will* see you again." As I made that closing statement I pointed upward with my index finger, indicating that marvelous meeting in the air.

After we sang our closing song and prayed our closing prayer, these wonderful people began coming to me one after the other to bid farewell. I couldn't speak their language—Portuguese—and they couldn't speak mine, and my interpreter was nowhere to be seen. But I soon discovered that we didn't need him as we had a common language after all. It was the language of smiles, tears, and uplifted index fingers. Yes, as they said their goodbyes to me, these Brazilian brothers and sisters in Christ would point upward. That was each one's way of saying: "I will meet you in the air."

I remember very well the loud, boisterous singing of those precious people. I recall how their love for the preaching of God's Word seemed to make them hang on every word. I haven't forgotten their warmth and friendliness. But the memory I treasure most is those uplifted fingers. Those fingers were signs of the common hope that Christians share.

How much the Scriptures make of that hope! It is our "blessed" hope (Titus 2:13). It is "sure and steadfast" (Heb. 6:19). It is our "living" hope (1 Peter 1:3). It is the hope of "eternal life" that has been promised to all believers by the God "who cannot lie" (Titus 1:2).

The hope of Christians puts a wide, yawning chasm between them and unbelievers. When unbelievers speak of hope, they are probably referring to a desire or yearning for something that may or may not come true. They hope that life will bring them health, happiness, and material success, and that they will be free from difficulties and calamities. And, of course, they hope for the same for their children and grandchildren. But such things are by no means certain. Christians most certainly share this kind of hope and the uncertainty that comes along with it. But that kind of hope is limited to this life. The great hope of Christians lies beyond this life, and it is a sure and certain hope. It is the hope of that meeting in the air and of eternal life in heaven.

Unbelievers consider that great hope to be as unsure as all other hopes. They think Christians believe it merely because they want it to be true, and that there is no foundation for it. A twentieth-century American philosopher once said of faith that it may be defined briefly as "an illogical belief in the occurrence of the improbable."[1]

Christians laugh at that definition and look to the resurrection of Jesus as the foundation for their hope. If Jesus arose, we shall arise, and if He lives, we shall live (John 14:19). On that basis, I will lift my finger and point upward.

1 H.L. Mencken, https://www.goodreads.com/quotes/4690-faith-may-be-defined-briefly-as-an-illogical-belief-in

July 2

A Doctor Thanks a Sick Man

From God's Word, the Bible...

But we are bound to give thanks to God always for you, brethren beloved by the Lord, because God from the beginning chose you for salvation through sanctification by the Spirit and belief in the truth, to which He called you by our gospel, for the obtaining of the glory of our Lord Jesus Christ.

2 Thessalonians 2:13-14

When I went to the conference mentioned in the previous reading, I had some concern about eating. Some of my friends, who were quite experienced in the area of foreign travel, told me that it could be very difficult to suddenly transition to eating a different kind of food. So when I arrived at the conference center, I began to ask the few English-speaking people I could find about what I should and should not eat. One told me to refrain from eating the meat. Another told me that I should not eat the vegetables. Yet another told me to stay away from the fruit. It occurred to me that I was quickly running out of things to eat! I decided that the best strategy was to eat a little bit of the same food each day. So I did, and I got sick—very sick! I began to wonder if I would be able to fulfill each of my preaching assignments.

When I conveyed my situation to Richard Denham, the missionary who engaged me to come to Brazil, he told me that he knew a doctor who was attending the conference and would ask her to see me. A more gracious lady one could never expect to meet. When I thanked her for making time for me, I was much surprised by her response. With tears welling up, she said: "You don't need to thank me. I need to thank you for coming to preach the Word of God to us."

Preaching is to be done with the eye trained on God's approval and not on the listener's. But if a hearer is blessed by the preaching, there certainly isn't anything wrong with him or her conveying that to the preacher. Preachers need that kind of encouragement, and most of us would say that we have often been blessed to receive it. In the area of favorable responses I have received, this doctor's was in a class by itself. It was more heartfelt and genuine than any other. It wasn't because of any spectacular ability that I possess as a preacher; it was rather due to what I was preaching—the Word of God.

This doctor made a connection that appears to be increasingly rare. She understood that if we value God's Word, we must also value the preaching that declares it.

Preaching has fallen into disfavor. Some pastor search committees reflect this by openly advertising for candidates who will preach short, humorous sermons. Many preachers seem themselves to be in full flight from preaching. While they would tell us that they have been "called to preach," they oftentimes seem to not want to preach. Imagine a fisherman not wanting to fish or a golfer not wanting to play golf!

How are we to explain such things? Some say preaching is necessarily in decline because people have shorter attention spans than those of previous generations. Others argue that we live in an entertainment culture. We may not like it, they argue, but it's a fact. Instead of resisting it, we must find ways to go along with it. If we don't, there is no future for the church. And some tell us that preaching was once an accepted mode of communication, but it's now outdated.

The root of the modern distaste for preaching is ignorance. We don't know who God is, who we are, and what the Bible is. Who is God? He is our Maker and our Sustainer, and He will eventually be our Judge. Who are we? We are rebels. We don't live the way our Maker intended us to live, we don't appreciate what He does to sustain us, and we don't concern ourselves with His judgment. What is the Bible? It is God speaking to us about these very issues. It is God telling us the truth about Himself and about us. Moreover, it is God revealing to us the only way that rebels can stand safely before Him when He judges. That way is Jesus, the God-Man, who lived the life we have refused to live and who received on the cross the wrath we deserve.

Knowing these things prompted my doctor in Brazil to express thanks. If you know them, thank God. And while you are at it, thank Him for faithful preachers.

July 3

The Tent of Meeting

From God's Word, the Bible...

Moses took his tent and pitched it outside the camp, far from the camp, and called it the tabernacle of meeting. And it came to pass that everyone who sought the Lord went out to the tabernacle of meeting which was outside the camp.

Exodus 33:7

Here's a very important question: When can we expect to see God moving in extraordinary ways to achieve extraordinary things? Or we can put it this way: When can we expect to see a season of God's mercy and power?

And here, I suggest, is the answer to those questions: when God's people so feel the burden of the times that they are willing to take special measures to seek God's face.

We can find in Moses an example of this answer. Moses certainly felt the burden of his time. He and the people of Israel were camped at the foot of Mt. Sinai. While Moses was on the mount to receive God's laws, the people were cavorting and carousing around a golden calf (Ex. 32).

It was a case of flagrant, full-throttled idolatry deserving of severe judgment. And severe judgment is what Moses meted out. Moses realized that it wasn't enough to eliminate the idol. The people must be encouraged to wholeheartedly turn back to God. So he set up a tent for that purpose. This tent was not the tabernacle, which had not yet been constructed (Ex. 35-40). It was a tent of meeting set up outside the camp, and "everyone who sought the Lord" went out to this tent of meeting.

We may assume that many Israelites, also feeling the burden of their situation, took advantage of this tent of meeting. We know that they had "mourned" when they heard the "grave tidings" that the Lord was withdrawing from them (Ex. 33:1-4). And we know that the tent of meeting achieved its purpose as God promised to be present with His people again (Ex. 33:14).

This episode in the life of Israel should prompt us to ask ourselves some very searching questions. Are we guilty of idolatry? Are we aware how such idolatry grieves God and drives Him from us? Are we taking any special measures to seek God?

If we don't answer the first question in the right way, we can't answer the other questions in the right way. In other words, if we don't see our idolatry, we can't see God withdrawing from us. And if we don't see God as withdrawn, we certainly won't be taking any special measures to seek Him.

We don't seem to be guilty of idolatry. After all, we're not dancing around a golden calf as the Israelites did. But if idolatry is more subtle than blatant, it is still idolatry, and idolatry, whether subtle or blatant, drives God away. The truth is that anything that receives from us the time, the attention, the allegiance, and the love that belong to God alone is idolatry. Anything that keeps us from loving, worshipping, and serving God as we ought is an idol, and every idol grieves God.

Many churches used to have what they called "revival meetings." We know that having a meeting isn't the same thing as having a revival, but it was easier for these churches to say "revival meetings" than to say "meetings to seek revival."

These meetings were intended to be like Moses' tent of meeting. They were intended to call the people of God to go outside the camp to seek God; that is, they were intended to urge God's people to lay aside as much of their ordinary routine as possible and give attention to God.

Such meetings have all but died out. The reason? Church members became increasingly unwilling to lay anything aside so they could seek God. It became clear that church members had become so comfortable inside the camp (their normal lives) that they wouldn't go outside the camp.

Is this a plea for churches to return to having revival meetings? No, it is rather a plea for us to feel the burden of our idolatry and the absence of God. The sad truth is that most Christians have little or no interest in seeking God because they don't even realize that He is missing! As long as the church machinery is running, they assume that God is present with His people and blessing them.

If we have been saved, we would do well to remember that it is because Jesus went outside that camp to die on the cross for us (Heb. 13:12-13). There, the sinless Son of God took upon Himself the sin and disgrace of all who would ever turn from their sin and trust in Him.

July 4

"But God" (1)

From God's Word, the Bible...

But God, who is rich in mercy, because of His great love with which He loved us, even when we were dead in trespasses, made us alive together with Christ (by grace you have been saved), and raised us up together, and made us sit together in the heavenly places in Christ Jesus, that in the ages to come He might show the exceeding riches of His grace in His kindness toward us in Christ Jesus.

Ephesians 2:4-7

Two little words consisting of six letters! But what words! Enfolded in them is our only hope for eternal life in heaven. Those two little words come from the pen of the Apostle Paul. Blessed pen that wrote these blessed words: "But God"!

The first three verses of Ephesians 2 present us with a scene of unrelieved gloom. They place us in a graveyard. Somber place! This is not the typical graveyard with bodies resting beneath the sod and headstones marking the resting places. This is a much sadder graveyard. It is the graveyard of souls. This is the graveyard of spiritual death.

It may seem to be lunacy, but the fact is we are all born into a graveyard. We're born dead. We're living physically, but we're dead spiritually—dead toward God! We come into this world in a state of living death. Physically alive! Spiritually dead!

Why are we in this state? What is it that produces spiritual death? It's all due to sin. Sin has killed us spiritually. It has made us dead toward God. By nature we have no interest in Him. We're not interested in knowing Him. We certainly don't love Him. We have no desire to serve Him.

Do you need proof of your spiritual deadness? Paul supplies it. He tells us to look at the course we follow, the god we obey, and the cravings we fulfill. The answer is plain, isn't it? We follow the course of this world. Just as the water in a river follows the course dictated to it by the riverbed, so we follow the course dictated to us by this world. We think, talk, and act the way the world wants.

We obey the god of this world—Satan. He is the ruler of the invisible kingdom of darkness, a kingdom that permeates this world just as the atmosphere does.

And the cravings we fulfill are those of the flesh. Spiritual deadness so enslaves us to our physical appetites and desires that we find it virtually impossible to say "no" to these things. While we're dead in regard to God, we're very much alive in regard to sin.

This horrible state of spiritual deadness isn't only true of one person here and a few others over there. It's true of all of us. Paul's phrase "even as the rest" (v. 3) could be translated "just like everyone else."

Think of physical death for a minute. While there are degrees of decay among the dead, there are no degrees of deadness. The person who died a hundred years ago is more decayed than the one who died five minutes ago, but they are both equally dead. In the spiritual realm, some sinners are worse than others, that is, they go deeper into sin than others. But a great sinner is no more spiritually dead than other sinners.

Is there any hope for dead sinners? There is! That hope is bound up in those words: "But God."

We're all by nature in the spiritual graveyard, and there we would have stayed were it not for this—God comes into that graveyard and raises the dead. He grants spiritual life to spiritually dead sinners.

Why does He do this? It's certainly not because those spiritually dead sinners do anything to earn it. How can a dead person earn anything? It's rather because God is "rich in mercy" (v. 4). It's "by grace" that we're saved (v. 10).

Would you see the greatness of God's mercy toward dead sinners? You must look to the cross where Jesus died. God's mercy toward us is always channeled through Christ (v. 7). He died that we might live.

"Surely, there is something I must do to earn that grace," says the sinner. Then it's not grace any more. Mix one element of human merit in with God's grace, and you no longer have grace (Rom. 4:4; 11:6).

But doesn't our faith earn salvation for us? No, faith—which is itself the gift of God—merely receives the salvation God provides. The hands of grace are the working hands in salvation while the hands of faith are simply the receiving hands.

I was in the spiritual graveyard, but God brought me out. Let me now go along life's way rejoicing in those two little words—but God!

July 5

"But God" (2)

From God's Word, the Bible...

But as for you, you meant evil against me; but God meant it for good, in order to bring it about as it is this day, to save many people alive.

Genesis 50:20

Quite often in the Bible we find those blessed words "but God." Oftentimes those words put before us dire circumstances from which there seems to be no escape only to have God step in and reverse things.

In the previous reading we rejoiced in the most glorious "but God." We who have been saved were in the spiritual graveyard. We were without spiritual life and without hope. "But God," because of His abounding mercy, found us and gave us life.

The above verse presents us with another thrilling instance of "but God." The instance in the first reading can be called "the 'but God' of salvation or regeneration." The instance before us now can be called "the 'but God' of providence." Yes, we are dealing here with God's providence in the life of one of the Bible's most heroic men—Joseph.

You know about Joseph. Because he was the firstborn son of Jacob's beloved wife Rachel, his father loved him more than he did the sons of his other wives. (No, the Bible doesn't endorse polygamy, but sinful men have often endorsed it.) Jacob's partiality toward Joseph was so obvious that Joseph's brothers intensely hated him and wanted to be rid of him. One day their opportunity arrived, and they sold him into slavery in Egypt.

In Egypt, Joseph was falsely accused by his master's wife and wrongly imprisoned. Joseph's special ability to interpret dreams finally brought him before Pharaoh, and his skill in interpreting Pharaoh's dream both released him from prison and made him second to Pharaoh in the land of Egypt.

Through a fascinating series of events, Joseph was reconciled to his brothers. He then resettled them and their families, along with their father Jacob, in the land of Egypt. When Jacob died, Joseph's brothers began to vex themselves with the thought that Joseph would at long last get his revenge. But Joseph reassured them with the "but God" of Genesis 50:20. There was a sovereign hand at work in all that had happened. That hand was the hand of God. While God certainly didn't approve of the evil that Joseph's brothers had done to him, He was able to use that evil to further His purposes.

God's providence didn't come to an end with Joseph and his brothers. It lives on. What is God's providence? It is God governing every aspect of everything He has created so that He may achieve His purposes and bring glory to His name. God's providential ordering of things consists of three parts. *General* providence is God sustaining and preserving the created order. *Special* providence is God working in the lives of people. *Extraordinary* providence is God doing the miraculous.

There have been times in which God's people rejoiced in that area of special providence. It brought them tremendous consolation to believe that God was at work in the circumstances of their lives for His glory and for their good. This doesn't appear to me to be one of those times. We have become fixed on our own comfort and ease, and we seem to think God should be equally fixed on it. When something comes along to disturb us or disrupt us, we think God has failed us and we besiege heaven with our "Why?" questions.

Sour circumstances make it very difficult for us to believe that the same hand that so expertly governed the life of Joseph to a good end has lost none of its expertise. The devil is always ready to pronounce on our difficult circumstances as proofs that God doesn't love us and that our faith is vain. He will always make sure we read our difficulties in the most God-adverse manner possible. Meanwhile, God Himself urges us in His Word to trust Him and obey Him. He urges us to reason in this way: Can the God who put His Son on the cross to deliver us from eternal condemnation suddenly turn against us? Is the God who delighted to save us through His Son now finding His delight in making us miserable through hard circumstances? That can never be! The heart of love that sent Jesus has not changed. So when our circumstances are most trying, let's rest in that heart of love and say with Joseph: ". . .but God. . ."

July 6

A Deed to Win Your Heart

From God's Word, the Bible...

Then Jonathan and David made a covenant, because he loved him as his own soul. And Jonathan took off the robe that was on him and gave it to David, with his armor, even to his sword and his bow and his belt.

1 Samuel 18:3-4

I definitely have this event in my "Things I Would Like to Have Seen" category. Perhaps the Lord will replay it for me on His celestial video machine.

At first glance, it doesn't appear to be so much. Jonathan pledges his friendship to David. I'm sure many would place it in their "So What?" category.

But look again, and look closer. Here is Jonathan, the son of King Saul and the apparent heir to his throne, declaring himself to be the friend of the man who was perceived by many to be Israel's next king. They should have been rivals! Reason would seem to say that Jonathan should have placed the tip of his sword squarely under David's chin, pressed just hard enough for it to draw a bit of blood, and said: "If you know what's good for you, you will drop any notion of being king. That throne belongs to me!"

But, no, Jonathan doesn't do what reason would seem to dictate. He lays that very sword at David's feet, along with his robe, his armor, his bow, and his belt. This is Jonathan relinquishing his claim to the throne. This is Jonathan pledging his friendship to David. This is Jonathan declaring that he will never be David's enemy, that he will never employ his weapons against him.

Does this mean Jonathan had lost his senses? A royal heir might easily get only one shot at being king, so is Jonathan giving it up? How are we to explain this? It's obvious that David had won Jonathan's heart. What had David done to win his heart? He, David, had slain the giant Goliath, and in doing so had delivered the Israelites from being enslaved by the Philistines. And David had won this victory in the most unlikely way imaginable—with a shepherd's sling and a stone!

The biblical account of Jonathan laying his robe, armor and weapons before David isn't here to extol the virtue of friendship. It isn't here to urge us to try to be friendlier with those we consider to be rivals. It's rather here, as is the case with all biblical accounts, to drive us to Christ.

The Lord Jesus has won for His people a greater victory over a greater enemy than David did. When David came on the scene, the Israelites were facing the prospect of bondage. When Jesus came on the scene, we were already enslaved to Satan (Eph. 2:1-3). We were already part of his miserable dominion (Col. 1:13). The Lord Jesus defeated Satan, freed us from our bondage to him, and brought us into His own kingdom. And Jesus did all this by means of an instrument that would seem to be far more ineffective than David's sling and his stone. The instrument the Lord Jesus used? A Roman cross!

Our sin makes us part of Satan's dominion. It gives Satan the right to hold us in bondage. On the cross, Jesus paid the penalty for all who will believe in Him. He received in the place of sinners the wrath of God against their sins. With that penalty paid, Satan has no right to us any longer and has to let us go.

David became the champion of his people by defeating Goliath. In Christ we have a greater champion because he defeated a greater Goliath, that is, Satan himself.

David's heroic act had won Jonathan's heart. Has the greater act of the Lord Jesus won our hearts?

We can't truly appreciate Jonathan's attitude toward David if we don't compare it to that of his father Saul. Even though the Lord was clearly at work in David for the benefit of the entire kingdom, Saul never gave his heart to David. There was no room in Saul's heart for anything or anyone except himself.

The Bible calls each of us to lay before Christ our robe of self as well as our armor and weapons of sin. We can respond to Jesus as Jonathan did to David, or we can emulate Saul by wrapping ourselves more tightly in the robe of self and clutching more firmly the weapons of sin. Saul's opposition to David didn't turn out well, and neither will opposition to the Lord Jesus.

Gone to the Birds

From God's Word, the Bible...

He sends the springs into the valleys;
They flow among the hills.
They give drink to every beast of the field;
The wild donkeys quench their thirst.
By them the birds of the heavens have their home;
They sing among the branches.
He waters the hills from His upper chambers;
The earth is satisfied with the fruit of Your works.

Psalm 104:10-13.

Some time ago I was asked to preach in a Bible Conference for Laurel Creek Baptist Church in East Tennessee. Through the years it has been my privilege and pleasure to preach in many country churches. So I went with the expectation that this church would be like many others. I was in for a pleasant surprise. The services were very well attended. The building was very close to being full for four out of the five services. But the thing that really got my attention was the singing of those people. How they sang! I shall never forget their triumphant, glorious singing of these words:

My sin, oh, the bliss of this glorious thought –
My sin—not in part, but the whole –
Is nailed to the cross and I bear it no more,
Praise the Lord, praise the Lord, O my soul!

We've all heard it said that something or someone has "gone to the dogs." I would say those dear folks had "gone to the birds." They had, as it were, taken their places as pupils and let the birds teach them. Martin Luther once said: ". . .we have as many teachers and preachers as there are little birds in the air."[2]

In Matthew 6, Jesus used the birds to tell us that those who trust in God need not worry and fret. But the psalmist points to the bird to teach another lesson, that is, the importance of singing praises to God.

Psalm 104 is a psalm of praise. It is a psalm that celebrates the greatness of God. Notice how it begins:

2 Martin Luther (1521), *The Sermon on the Mount,* translated by Jaroslav Pelikan, Vol 21 of Luther's Works (Concordia 1956), pp197-8.

Bless the LORD, O my soul!
O LORD my God, You are very great:
You are clothed with honor and majesty. . .

From that initial burst of praise, the psalmist proceeds to celebrate the marvels of God's work of creation. As he works his way through creative wonder after creative wonder, he finally comes to the springs of water from which the animals drink. He says of these springs:

By them the birds of the heavens have their habitation;
They sing among the branches.

Perhaps the psalmist still had the singing of the birds on his mind as he began wrapping up the psalm, (v. 33):

I will sing to the LORD as long as I live;
I will sing praise to my God while I have my being.

Christians are to be God's singing people. Why? I can give you some God-oriented answers: because God commands it (Ps. 95:1-2; 96:1-2; 100:1-2; 146:1-2; 147:1,7; 148:1-4; 149:1,5; 150:1-6), enjoys, it and deserves it.

I can also give you a devil-oriented answer: we should sing because the devil hates to hear us offering praise to our God. It stands to reason. If he hates God, and he certainly does, he has to hate praise to God. So if you want to make the devil sick, sing!

I can also give you an unbeliever-oriented answer: our singing (if it is loud and triumphant and not muffled and mealy-mouthed) can arrest the attention of those who aren't Christians and convince them that they urgently need the Christ who makes us sing. Many people live without a reason to sing. Our singing can't help but make an impression on them.

Although these are very compelling reasons, the distressing fact is many of us don't sing as we should. We focus on our inability instead of our responsibility, that is, if we can't sing well, we think we shouldn't sing at all. We think of reasons we shouldn't sing instead of reasons we should. When that is the case, we need to go to Bird School. We should let the birds' singing remind us to sing.

I see myself now in Bird School. Mr. Bird asks: "Why are you here?" And I respond: "I'm hoping you can help me improve in my offering praise to God." And Mr. Bird says: "The best help I can give you is to send you to another school. It is called 'Cross School.'"

Mr. Bird has made his point. While it's okay for me to look at the birds and let them remind me to sing, my greatest need is always to look at the cross of Christ, where Jesus died for sinners like you and me. If that doesn't make me sing, nothing will.

July 8

A Good Meeting

FROM GOD'S WORD, THE BIBLE...

So the eunuch answered Philip and said, "I ask you, of whom does the prophet say this, of himself or of some other man?" Then Philip opened his mouth, and beginning at this Scripture, preached Jesus to him.

ACTS 8:34-35

It occurs to me that a good bit of my life has been taken up with meetings of various kinds. I've been involved in lots and lots of meetings—some good, some not so good. Some things are essential for a good meeting. There must be attendees. There's no meeting if no one shows up. There should be an agenda. And something should be achieved.

In Acts 8:26-39, Luke (the author of Acts) describes for us a good meeting. He tells us about *the attendees*. There were two men. One was a man who is not named. He is only identified as "a man of Ethiopia, a eunuch of great authority" (v. 27). The other was Philip, who is first mentioned in Acts 6:1-6 and earlier in this eighth chapter of Acts (vv. 4-8).

Two men were present? Yes. But another person was present as well—the Holy Spirit. It was He who arranged this meeting. He had been working on both sides to make this meeting occur—on the Ethiopian's side and on Philip's side.

The Ethiopian was returning to his homeland from Jerusalem. He had been there to worship God. Why would a man from Ethiopia go all the way to Jerusalem for that purpose? The Ethiopians surely had their own gods. Yes, but this particular man wasn't satisfied with those gods. So he went to Jerusalem, but he wasn't satisfied there either. Searching he came to Jerusalem, and still searching he headed for home.

How are we to explain the yearning and disillusionment of this man? The Spirit of God was behind it, preparing this Ethiopian for the most profound discovery of his life.

The Spirit also worked on Philip's side. After an angel instructed Philip to take the road that ran from Jerusalem to Gaza (v. 26), the Spirit took over and commanded Philip to overtake the chariot in which the Ethiopian was riding (v. 29). Through this process, we see Philip as a ready and obedient participant. Let's learn from him to desire and work toward being instruments of the Lord.

That brings us to *the agenda* for this meeting.

As he traveled along, the Ethiopian was reading from the fifty-third chapter of Isaiah's prophecy. When Philip asked if he understood what he was reading, the Ethiopian admitted his bewilderment. Was the prophet speaking of himself or of someone else? Philip knew the answer. It was Jesus of whom Isaiah was speaking. Isaiah 53 is a prophecy of the Messiah, and the Lord Jesus is the Messiah. More to the point, Isaiah 53 is a prophecy of the Messiah dying for sinners, and Jesus died for all sinners who will believe in Him and His redeeming work.

What happy words are these: "Then Philip opened his mouth, and beginning at this Scripture, preached Jesus to him" (v. 35).

So the Holy Spirit made sure that Jesus was the agenda for this meeting. If Jesus is on the agenda, and He is accurately presented, the meeting can't help but be good.

This account of Philip comes as a stirring reminder that the business of the church is to preach Jesus. When the Ethiopian asked Philip about whom the prophet was writing, Philip didn't say: "Never mind this prophecy. Let me ask you how you are doing as a family man." Nor did he say: "I will share with you some principles for managing your finances and give you some insights into developing a more forceful personality."

That is the type of thing the church today is often saying, but it is most emphatically not what Philip said.

The final component of this meeting is *the achievement*. There have been lots and lots of meetings that didn't accomplish anything, but the Holy Spirit made sure this meeting was productive. The Ethiopian was saved. Philip urged him to believe in Jesus with all of his heart, and he, the Ethiopian, responded: "I believe that Jesus Christ is the Son of God" (v. 37). And he gave evidence of his conversion to Christ by submitting to baptism (v. 38).

What a good meeting this was—an Ethiopian, Philip and the Holy Spirit! What a good agenda—Jesus! And what a good outcome—conversion!

Because this was such a good meeting, all of us who know Christ will enjoy another good meeting. We will get to meet the Ethiopian in heaven.

July 9

Bright Truths for Bleak Times

From God's Word, the Bible...

But the following night the Lord stood by him and said, "Be of good cheer, Paul; for as you have testified for Me in Jerusalem, so you must also bear witness at Rome." And when it was day, some of the Jews banded together and bound themselves under an oath, saying that they would neither eat nor drink till they had killed Paul.

Acts 23:11-12

It was a bleak time for Paul. Roman soldiers had taken him into custody to prevent his fellow-Jews from killing him. But that didn't put an end to it. Forty of the Jews took an oath they would neither eat nor drink until they had killed Paul (v.14). They went to their religious leaders with a plan, and those men, who professed to be great believers in God's law, put their stamp of approval on it.

Was this a difficult time for Paul? I would say so. But there is more here than the description of hard circumstances. Interwoven into this account are four bright, encouraging truths.

First, we see that *no place is too hard for the Lord to find.*

After arresting Paul, the Romans put him "into the barracks" (v. 10). Paul may have been alone there, hidden from human view. Ah, but, he wasn't hidden from the Lord's view because we read: "the Lord stood by him" (v. 11). The religious leaders in the temple and the Roman commander in the palace were surrounded by comfort while Paul was in prison surrounded by the Lord. I'd say Paul had the better of it. It's better to be in a prison with Christ than to be in a palace without Him.

Do you feel as if you are hidden away in harsh circumstances? The same Lord who knew where to find Paul knows where to find you. He is with His people in every difficulty and every trial. When the Jews were captives in Babylon, they thought their situation was hidden from the Lord, but it wasn't (Isa. 40:27). And neither is ours.

A second bright truth is this: *No thought is too deep for the Lord to know.*

The forty conspirators, and the religious leaders who were cheering them on, thought that they had thrown a cloak of secrecy over their plan. But the Lord knew all about it.

Hostility toward God and His people is so prevalent today that we may find ourselves worrying about the future. What plans are being hatched against us by evil men? We may not know. It is enough that the Lord knows.

There's tremendous comfort in the Lord's knowledge. He not only knew what the Paul-haters were planning but He also knew it even before those evil men themselves knew it. The knowledge of God is perfect knowledge. He knows the wicked plans of wicked men, and He knows the anxieties and fears, the heartaches and heartbreaks His people endure in evil times.

Here is the third bright truth: *No person is too small for God to use.*

The evil plan is in place. The evil planners are secure in their belief that Paul's life is as good as over. One small detail changes everything. Big doors turn on small hinges! That small detail is Paul's nephew. Somehow he learns about the conspiracy, and he informs Paul and the Roman commander (vv. 16-22).

Paul's nephew! What was his name? We don't know. He emerges from obscurity to play a pivotal role in this whole affair and then goes back into obscurity. We have never met him before in Scripture, and we never meet him again. He could very well have been a common, ordinary fellow. But on this occasion the Lord used him.

We may think that we are too small or too ordinary for God to use, but that's never the case. God has always delighted in using ordinary things (David and his sling, Samson and his jawbone, the lad and his lunch, for example) to achieve extraordinary things.

What is the final bright truth in this passage? It is a glorious one: *No enemy is too great for the Lord to defeat.*

The conspiracy was strong, but God was stronger. He got Paul out of Jerusalem and to Rome, just as He had promised (v. 11).

Let Paul represent the gospel of Christ, and the forty men opposition to that gospel. Hatred of the gospel has been so intense that it has often seemed that it could not survive. But it will never die. Let the devil and his minions rage and conspire, no plot formed against God and His gospel can prosper.

Are these bleak times? Yes. But no amount of bleakness in this world can override or nullify these bright truths. Thank God!

July 10

Today Thy Mercy Calls Us

From God's Word, the Bible...

But when the kindness and the love of God our Savior toward man appeared, not by works of righteousness which we have done, but according to His mercy He saved us, through the washing of regeneration and renewing of the Holy Spirit, whom He poured out on us abundantly through Jesus Christ our Savior, that having been justified by His grace we should become heirsaccording to the hope of eternal life.

Titus 3:4-5

In my circles, the hymn *Today Thy Mercy Calls Us* falls into one of two categories: never discovered or almost forgotten. That's regrettable because it is a truly splendid hymn.

I can't tell you much about its author, Oswald Allen. He was born in England in 1816. His father, John Allen, was a banker. Oswald himself would also make banking his career. But he was also a devoted Christian and a hymn writer. In addition to authoring several hymns, Oswald published *Hymns of the Christian Life* in 1861. He died on October 2, 1878.

I can tell you that each verse throbs with encouragement, comfort and hope. Read and savor verses one and two:

Today Thy mercy calls us to wash away our sin.
However great our trespass, whatever we have been,
However long from mercy our hearts have turned away,
Thy precious blood can cleanse us and make us white today.
Today Thy gate is open, and all who enter in
Shall find a Father's welcome and pardon for their sin.
The past shall be forgotten, a present joy be given,
A future grace be promised, a glorious crown in heaven.

Several words in those verses seem to wave their arms at me and say: "Look at me!" The first of those words is *mercy*. It is, as the hymn's title indicates, the dominant theme in the hymn. What is mercy? It is showing compassion and kindness to an enemy or offender over whom we have power.

Someone has deeply offended or injured me. I have every right to punish, but I choose to forego that and show compassion instead. That is mercy.

It is, of course, God's mercy that Allen's hymn is celebrating. Here is the truth of the matter—we have deeply offended God by our sins. He has the perfect right to punish us with that punishment that He has pronounced on sinners, that is, eternal separation from Himself. But instead of exercising that right, He shows mercy.

How can God show mercy to sinners? Doesn't His justice demand that the penalty be carried out to the utmost? Does God show mercy by setting aside His justice? If He does so, isn't justice itself deeply offended?

The answer to those questions lies in another word that calls urgently for attention. It is the word *blood*, and that refers to the Lord Jesus Christ shedding His blood on the cross. That blood satisfied the claims of God's justice. It meant that there on the cross Jesus was taking the penalty that sinners deserve. When justice was satisfied, the way was cleared for God to show mercy to sinners. Justice demands that the penalty for sin be paid only once—not twice. If Jesus paid it for the sinner, there is nothing left for that sinner to pay.

In regard to all sinners who believe in Jesus, God has said to His justice: "Hush, and put your sword away. Jesus has died."

With the voice of justice silenced by Jesus, mercy can call to sinners to believe in Jesus. And it does call. Have you heard its call?

Perhaps you are thinking that there can be no mercy for you because you have been too great a sinner. You can and should rejoice in more words that cry for attention: *However great our trespass, whatever we have been.*

There's no such thing as too great a sinner. No one is a greater sinner than Jesus is a Savior. The Lord Jesus never says: "I can save this person because he's not much of a sinner, but I can't save that person over there because he's too much of a sinner." What kind of Savior would Jesus be if He could only save some sinners?

Are you wondering if you are hearing mercy's call? If you can say you want your sins forgiven and to be right with God, you may be assured that God's mercy is calling you. Thank God that you are hearing that call, and throw yourself on Jesus.

One more word from Allen's first verse should get our attention. It is the word *Today*. Mercy is calling today. So receive it today, and be thankful that it is great enough to cover all your sins.

July 11

Drops and Showers

From God's Word, the Bible...

I will make them and the places all around My hill a blessing; and I will cause showers to come down in their season; there shall be showers of blessing.

Ezekiel 34:26

The small country church in which I spent my childhood years would often sing the hymn of Daniel Whittle (1840-1901), *There Shall Be Showers of Blessing*. I recall that some would invariably add an "s" to "blessing," but it is one blessing with which the song deals. What is that blessing? It is the revival of God's people.

God's people often find themselves lacking in vitality and vigor. They can and do decline in their spiritual health. Some would have us believe that a graph of the Christian's experience would show a straight line steadily angling upward, but most of us know that such a graph would have to consist of a wavy line. Christians are sometimes up and sometimes down in their spirituality, and it can be amazing how low they can sink in their down times. The sad truth is that spiritual lowness often becomes widespread. It's not just a Christian here and there who is declining. It's rather a matter of most declining. And their decline involves both what they believe, and how they behave—that is, they become shaky in their convictions and cozy with both sins of commission and omission—doing things God has told them not to do and failing to do those things that He has told them to do.

In such times, God's people need revival. What is revival? It is God's people being brought back to spiritual health and vitality. It's a season in which God's people experience substantial improvement in their spiritual condition. Apathy and indifference are replaced with interest and zeal. Sins are abandoned, relationships are restored, church services are packed, people are saved—all of these and more happen when God sends the glorious blessing of revival to His people.

Here is the chorus of Whittle's hymn:

Showers of blessing,
Showers of blessing we need:
Mercy drops round us are falling,
But for the showers we plead.

I remember wondering about those "mercy drops." I eventually came to understand those drops to mean that God sends blessings even when most of His people are in a very unhealthy state. We are never totally without expressions of His mercy. When the gospel of Christ is accurately and powerfully preached, that is a mercy drop. When someone is saved, that is a mercy drop. When an individual Christian sees his or her decline and draws near the Lord again, that is a mercy drop.

In times of widespread spiritual decline, we should always be thankful for mercy drops. How precious they are! But we should never be satisfied with them. My assessment is that today's church is so content with the mercy drops that she is not pleading for the showers. We are satisfied with the trickle when we need the torrent.

Whittle encourages us to plead for those showers. He tells us in the first verse that God has promised to send "seasons refreshing," and he urges us in the third verse to pray:

Send them upon us, O Lord;
Grant to us now a refreshing,
Come, and now honor Thy Word.

Are we praying for revival? Are we pleading with God for it? Can we identify with these lines from Whittle's fourth verse:

There shall be showers of blessing:
Oh, that today they might fall. . . .

We can't make revival happen, but we can more earnestly desire it, and a more earnest desire may very well mean that it is actually beginning. We can begin to plead, but we will not plead until we see our need.

In the days of Elijah, the people of Israel were suffering from the physical drought God had sent. That drought was the result of a spiritual drought that had been in place for a very long time. The physical drought was God's punishment for the people turning from Him to serve idols. God used Elijah to break the spiritual drought and the physical drought. In the breaking of the latter, Elijah said to King Ahab: ". . .there is the sound of the abundance of rain" (1 Kings 18:41).

Let's be thankful for mercy drops, but let's plead for the showers of revival and keep pleading for them until we can say: ". . .there is the sound of the abundance of rain."

Oh, that today they might fall. . . .

A Great Man

FROM GOD'S WORD, THE BIBLE...

Now Naaman, commander of the army of the king of Syria, was a great and honorable man in the eyes of his master, because by him the LORD had given victory to Syria. He was also a mighty man of valor, but a leper.

2 KINGS 5:1

If a survey had been conducted to name the cool characters in ancient Syria, Naaman might very well have been most frequently mentioned. He was the coolest of characters. Commander of the Syrian army, brave and strong, highly regarded by the king, respected and admired by his countrymen—this was Naaman.

Naaman seemed to have the world by the tail, and he loved that world. It had given him wealth, success, and standing. It had checked all his boxes. Naaman knew how to move around in his world. He knew how to make things happen. He knew how to get things done.

As we read this verse, we might find ourselves expecting it to end with the words "and he lived happily ever after." Instead it ends with these five heavy words: "but he was a leper" (KJV).

Now there was an ugly fly in Naaman's ointment, a monkey wrench in his gears, a dark cloud in his sky, a horrible clang in his melody, and an upset for his apple cart.

Leprosy was the most dreaded disease of Naaman's time. It consisted of the slow eating away of the flesh until death came. It also meant living apart from others. Every part of this disease had to be repulsive to Naaman, but being isolated from the Syria he loved so much might have been the part that repulsed him the most.

When we first meet Naaman, he had apparently not yet arrived at the stage that would require his isolation. He was still moving around, but he knew isolation must come.

Now Naaman was getting a new angle on things. He was proud of himself, and he was proud of Syria. But his horrible leprosy made it clear that he couldn't help himself and his beloved Syria couldn't help him either.

Sick and helpless! What a strange and unfamiliar set of circumstances for Naaman!

Have you ever wondered why the Holy Spirit wanted this account included in the Bible? Is it possible that it was to serve as a mirror? Is the Holy Spirit holding Naaman before us so we can see ourselves? Are we to see ourselves in his love for life in this world? Are we to see ourselves in the way he proudly went along as if this life is all that matters? Are we to see ourselves in his smug assurance that his views on culture, life and religion were superior? Yes, I think so. But there's a more basic and essential seeing of ourselves in this Naaman mirror. We're to see in his leprosy our own more dreadful and deadly disease. Naaman's disease would eventually eat his flesh down to his bones. Our disease eats into our minds, our affections and our wills, darkening the first, degrading the second, and deadening the third.

Our disease is sin, and it truly is "our" disease. No one is exempt from it (Rom. 3:23). We are born with a sinful nature, and it doesn't take long for that nature to manifest itself in sinful words and deeds.

What is sin? It's refusing to live in accordance with the laws of the God who made us. Why is it serious? The God who made us will eventually be our judge. The God whose laws we have spurned will finally call us to account (Rom. 14:12; Heb. 9:27). And our law breaking will finally lead to death—eternal death, that is, eternal separation from the very God against whom we have rebelled.

Yes, sin is serious!

Can anything be done about our sin disease? The Bible answers with a thundering "Yes!" There was, as we shall see, a cure for Naaman, and there is a cure for sinners. Naaman's cure didn't come from himself or from Syria. It came from God. It is the same with our sin disease. The cure comes from God, and it comes in the form of His Son, the Lord Jesus Christ.

To those who object to the Bible affirming that Jesus is the only cure for our sin disease, I ask: "How many cures do we need?" I didn't reject the only cure because there weren't a dozen cures. I was glad for the one and accepted it by repenting of my sins and trusting in the Lord Jesus Christ.

July 13

A Young Girl

FROM GOD'S WORD, THE BIBLE...

And the Syrians had gone out on raids, and had brought back captive a young girl from the land of Israel. She waited on Naaman's wife. Then she said to her mistress, "If only my master were with the prophet who is in Samaria! For he would heal him of his leprosy."

2 KINGS 5:2-3

Naaman, the great man, had a great problem—leprosy! His bright sky was now darkened with despair. All he had ahead of him was a slow, agonizing death—or so it would seem.

Suddenly and quite unexpectedly, there was a bright beam of hope that shot across his dark sky. It came from an enslaved girl. One of Naaman's raiding parties had made a foray into Israel. This young girl was one of the tokens of their success. Cruelly ripped away from her home, she was now a servant of Naaman's wife.

When she learned about the leprosy of Naaman, she pointed out that "the prophet who is in Samaria" could heal him. That prophet was Elisha.

This young girl was a marvel. She was a blend of contentment, concern, and confidence.

Her *contentment* must surely amaze us. She could have been filled with bitterness about her circumstances. She could have even been angry with God for allowing those circumstances to come her way. But here she was accepting her circumstances and speaking about God. Yes, in speaking of Elisha, the man of God, she was speaking about God.

Christians are called to speak for God, but many of us are tongue-tied. Two things that tie our tongues are difficult circumstances and disappointment with God. We can't recommend God to others if we are angry with Him.

We also see *concern* in this young woman. She was concerned about the condition of Naaman. What an amazing thing! She could have secretly rejoiced in Naaman's leprosy and kept Elisha's name to herself, but she genuinely desired the best for her master.

Concern for others is the lifeblood of witnessing for Christ. Are we who know Christ genuinely concerned for those who don't know Him? Have we lost sight of the fact that each person in this world is bound for another world—the eternal world—and that faith in Christ is the only way to enter safely into that world?

Finally, we see her *confidence*. This girl would never have said what she did were it not for her confidence that she really possessed the answer for Naaman's problem. Consider her words: "If only my master were with the prophet who is in Samaria! For he would heal him of his leprosy."

We find no hesitation or doubt in her words. She could have said: "There is a possibility that my master might be healed by the prophet." But she didn't hedge or equivocate. She didn't know any doubt because she knew the God of Israel and how He was working through the prophet Elisha.

Many today would call her bigoted and dogmatic and would condemn her for trying to impose her beliefs on others. They would point out that the Syrians had their own religion, and she had no right to suggest that her religion was superior.

I get the impression that this young girl wouldn't have been fazed in the least by such charges. I think she would have been glad to say with the apostles Peter and John: ". . .we cannot but speak the things which we have seen and heard" (Acts 4:20).

She saw a need, she knew the answer, and she didn't concern herself with what others might think or say.

One reason so many Christians are silent about their faith these days is they lack confidence in the very message that they should believe with all their hearts. There is a lack of triumphant certainty among us. The language of the early church featured the words "We know." We prefer to use these phrases: "We think," "We believe," "We suggest."

In his sermons, the evangelist Vance Havner used to diagnose our problem in this way: "We believe that there is some darkness in our light and some light in the world's darkness."

This young girl helped Naaman. She also helps us. She calls us to be content with our circumstances, concerned about others, and to be supremely confident in the gospel, saying with Paul: "For I am not ashamed of the gospel of Christ, for it is the power of God to salvation, for everyone who believes. . ." (Rom. 1:16).

July 14

Mr. False Assumptions

FROM GOD'S WORD, THE BIBLE...

...Then the king of Syria said, "Go now, and I will send a letter to the king of Israel." So he departed and took with him ten talents of silver, six thousand shekels of gold, and ten changes of clothing. Then he brought the letter to the king of Israel, which said,
Now be advised, when this letter comes to you, that I have sent Naaman my servant to you, that you may heal him of his leprosy.
And it happened, when the king of Israel read the letter, that he tore his clothes and said, "Am I God, to kill and make alive, that this man sends a man to me to heal him of his leprosy? Therefore please consider, and see how he seeks a quarrel with me." So it was, when Elisha the man of God heard that the king of Israel had torn his clothes, that he sent to the king, saying, "Why have you torn your clothes? Please let him come to me, and he shall know that there is a prophet in Israel."

FROM 2 KINGS 5:4-8

The message for Naaman from the servant girl in his house was clear and unmistakable—Go to Elisha the prophet in Israel and be healed of leprosy (v. 3).

So we might expect to read that Naaman headed to Samaria, found the prophet, and received the cure. It might have been very simple had Naaman's king, the King of Syria, stayed out of the matter. But he interjected himself in two ways. First, he loaded Naaman down with silver, gold and garments (as implied in verse 5). Then he sent a letter along with Naaman to the King of Israel in which he stated that he was expecting the King of Israel to cure Naaman (v. 6).

With Naaman outside his door, the King of Israel was reading and reeling, that is, reading the letter and reeling with distress. How could he, the King of Israel, cure a man of leprosy? Was the King of Syria trying to provoke a quarrel?

We might call these kings the movers and shakers of their day, with the Syrian king doing the moving and the Israelite king the shaking.

At this point, two questions press upon us. The first is why the king of Syria filled Naaman's chariots with goods. The second is why he sent along the letter demanding that the king of Israel heal Naaman.

In each case the Syrian king was falsely assuming something. He sent the treasures because he falsely assumed that the cure could not be free. He sent the letter because he falsely assumed that the prophet Elisha worked for the king of Israel. The Syrian king had his own prophets, and he assumed that it was the same in Israel. If a prophet in Israel had the cure, that prophet must work for the king of Israel! So if the prophet worked for the king, it was six of one and a half dozen of the other as to who would actually do the healing.

The Syrian king had no category for a man like Elisha. Yes, the prophet worked for a king—not the king of Israel—but the King of Kings, that is, the Lord God Himself.

The treasure the Syrian king sent was based on a false assumption, as was the letter he sent. Let's just call the Syrian king "Mr. False Assumptions."

Mr. False Assumptions died centuries ago, but his descendants are still among us. The earth is well populated with them.

The Bible talks about the reality of our sin and the severity of it, but Mr. False Assumptions rejects that teaching out of hand because he assumes that we are all basically good.

The Bible's great theme is forgiveness for our sins through faith in the Lord Jesus Christ and His redeeming work on the cross. But Mr. False Assumptions merely dismisses it. Why? He assumes that if we really do need forgiveness for our sins, it is ludicrous beyond measure to believe that such forgiveness could come through a man dying on a cross.

In addition to telling us that the Lord Jesus provided salvation for sinners, the Bible says that there is nothing we can do to earn or deserve that salvation. It is the gift of God's grace. And how does Mr. False Assumptions respond? He tells us that he believes if we try to live a good life we will go to heaven when we die. And old hymn says:

Nothing in my hand I bring; Simply to Thy cross I cling.

Mr. False Assumptions goes along singing:

Something in my hand I bring–My own goodness, and to that I cling.

The truth that looms large before us at this point is quite plain. As long as the Syrian king, Mr. False Assumptions, was occupying center stage, there was no cure for Naaman. There he sat outside the palace door of the King of Israel still in his leprosy. There was no cure for him until Elisha occupied center stage. And there is no cure for our sins until we rid ourselves of our false assumptions and let Jesus Christ occupy center stage. Our hope for salvation lies not in man and his wisdom. Rather, it lies in saying with Jeremiah:

Heal me, O Lord, and I shall be healed;
Save me, and I shall be saved. . .
(Jer. 17:14)

July 15

Clean

From God's Word, the Bible...

So he turned and went away in a rage. And his servants came near and spoke to him, and said, "My father, if the prophet had told you to do something great, would you not have done it? How much more then, when he says to you, 'Wash, and be clean'?" So he went down and dipped seven times in the Jordan, according to the saying of the man of God; and his flesh was restored like the flesh of a little child, and he was clean. And he returned to the man of God, he and all his aides, and came and stood before him; and he said, "Indeed, now I know that there is no God in all the earth, except in Israel; now therefore, please take a gift from your servant."

From 2 Kings 5:9-15

It must have been an impressive sight—Naaman in his splendor with his retinue of servants and his chariots laden with silver, gold and garments.

Elisha didn't even bother to come out and look. The chariots of earth held little appeal for the one who had been dazzled by the chariot of heaven (2 Kings 2:11-12).

Naaman came to Elisha with more than shimmering silver and glittering gold. He came with expectations. Like his boss, the King of Syria, Naaman had false assumptions. If his king was Mr. False Assumptions, Naaman was Mr. False Assumptions, Jr.

It's plain that Naaman wasn't content to merely receive the cure from Elisha. He wanted Elisha to cure him in a certain way. How eager we are to dictate to God the way that He should do things! Lots of us want to serve God—as advisers!

What did Naaman expect? He wanted Elisha to come out and meet him and, in so doing, show him great respect and deference. Perhaps Elisha would ask him for his autograph! Then Elisha would perform a religious ceremony. He would "wave his hand over the place, and heal the leprosy" (v. 11).

It was not to be. Elisha didn't come out at all. He wasn't interested in Naaman's greatness. He didn't want his autograph. He merely sent out the message that Naaman was to "wash in the Jordan seven times" (v. 10).

Naaman was furious! Elisha's "cure" offended him. It was too humbling. A man of his standing must bathe in the muddy waters of the Jordan? It was preposterous! Here is the truly preposterous thing—an unclean man objecting to bathing in an unclean river!

Now it was time for Naaman's servants to step in and reason with him. Are we beginning to understand that Naaman was not the central character in this drama? It was God. While He was scarcely mentioned at all, God was at work. It was God who prompted the servant girl's testimony (v. 2). It was God who caused Elisha to take control of the situation (v. 8). And it was God who now moved Naaman's servants to speak to him.

These men employed simple logic. Leprosy was such a serious disease that any possibility of a cure had to be embraced. If the prophet had asked Naaman to do a difficult thing, he would have attempted it. How much more should he be willing to embrace a simple cure (v. 13)!

So Naaman did as Elisha commanded. Six times he immersed himself in the muddy waters of the Jordan, and nothing happened. But in full compliance with Elisha's command, Naaman took a seventh dip and came up a healed man. What blessed words are these: "and he was clean" (v. 14)!

Naaman immediately made his way back to Elisha to offer the testimony that there is only one God, the God of Israel (v. 15).

At this point, we see the point. All of this happened, not so much to heal Naaman of his leprosy, but rather to bring him to true faith in God, and to give glory to God.

Just as Elisha directed Naaman to do something of a repulsive nature, so God directs us to do something repulsive for the healing of our sin. God tells us to kneel in repentance and faith before the cross of Christ.

That cross repels us. It doesn't live up to our standards. In His infinite wisdom, God has determined that His plan of salvation will not satisfy man's wisdom (1 Cor. 1:21). The world looks at the cross of Christ and cries, "Foolishness!" But even God's foolishness is much wiser than the greatest wisdom men can ever generate (1 Cor. 1:25).

It doesn't appear now that God's foolish cross will actually prove to be His wisdom, but eternity will eventually tell the tale. An innumerable multitude of saved sinners will gather around God's throne to offer praise for Christ's "foolish" death on the cross (Rev. 5:9). Then the whole universe will know that death was not so foolish after all.

The choice before us is either to reject the crucified Christ so we can be considered wise by this foolish world or to receive the crucified Christ so we can be considered wise by the "foolish" God. When we stop rebelling against the cross, what was said of Naaman will be said of us: "and he [or she] was clean."

July 16

Where is My Heart?

From God's Word, the Bible...

But Gehazi, the servant of Elisha the man of God, said, "Look, my master has spared Naaman this Syrian, while not receiving from his hands what he brought; but as the Lord lives, I will run after him and take something from him."

2 Kings 5:20

Gehazi was an unusually blessed man. Very few have enjoyed anything comparable to the privileges that came his way. He was chosen by Elisha the prophet to be his servant. Elisha was no ordinary prophet. He was a miracle-working prophet. The most notable of Elisha's many miracles consisted of him raising a young man from the dead. Gehazi had a front row seat on that occasion (2 Kings 4:8-37).

It was another of Elisha's miracles, the healing of Naaman, that led to Gehazi's downfall.

Naaman had come to Elisha's house with enormous wealth, thinking that he would make Elisha wealthy if Elisha would only make him healthy.

But Elisha, uninterested in Naaman's wealth, flatly refused to accept a single shekel (vv. 15-16). Elisha wanted one truth to stand out in solitary grandeur in Naaman's mind—the healing he received was the gift of God's marvelous grace. It was something that had no connection with human merit.

Gehazi was there to observe Naaman's offer and Elisha's refusal. How those Syrian coins must have gleamed and glittered before his eyes! How appealing must the garments have seemed! How he must have winced when Elisha sent Naaman away!

Not sharing his master's view of things, Gehazi caught up with Naaman. He pretended that Elisha had experienced a change of heart and would now be happy to take some of Naaman's goods (v. 22). But Gehazi wasn't expressing Elisha's heart. He was expressing his own. He was revealing that his heart was in Syria. Israel was the nation that God had chosen to put the truth of His saving grace on display, and at this time Elisha was the man God had chosen to be the foremost spokesman for that grace. But as he stood there looking at Naaman's silver, gold, and garments, Gehazi must have realized that his heart wasn't in Israel and with the prophet Elisha. It wasn't in what God's grace and power could do for a man. It was rather in what Syria could do for that man. Gehazi's body was in Israel, but his heart was in Syria.

Gehazi asks each of us to ask himself: Where is my heart? Is it in God and

His gracious plan of salvation for sinners? Or is it in the fleeting and fading things of this world? Many these days seem to be Israelites, but they are actually Syrians. They profess to know God, but their hearts are not in worshiping Him or obeying Him. Their hearts are in the things of this world. Yes, they will have religion as long as they can think, talk, and act like the world. But tell them that they cannot have both, and they will choose the world.

Gehazi also speaks to pastors and churches who exist to declare God's gospel of grace. He asks them to ask themselves: *Are our hearts really in the gospel?* Those who insist on presenting Christianity as nothing more than a successful living technique have given us their answer.

Gehazi should have known that his plan wouldn't work. He had been associated with Elisha long enough to know that the prophet was in touch with the God from whom nothing is hidden.

Sure enough, when Gehazi returned from his ill-conceived venture, Elisha was waiting for him with a devastating announcement. The leprosy of Naaman was to cling to Gehazi and his descendants (v. 27).

The severe temporal judgment that befell Gehazi serves as a miniature picture of the eternal judgment that will eventually befall all those who deny God's gospel of grace.

In chasing after Naaman, Gehazi experienced an awful and wonderful moment of self-knowledge. It was awful because it showed him that his heart was far from God and the truth of God's grace. But it was also wonderful for this reason: in seeing his heart was far from God, he, Gehazi, could turn to God in true repentance and faith.

We should hope that the temporal judgment that befell Gehazi was the means that God used to bring him to his senses and to keep him from experiencing far worse judgment in eternity. And we should also hope that his story will be used by the Lord to help us know where our hearts are. Gehazi saw more riches in Naaman's gold than in God's grace. Now he warns us to not do the same.

Is your heart where the gospel would have it to be? Are you trusting in Christ alone? The call of Proverbs 23:26 is to all believers: "My son, give me your heart."

July 17

Buying Bread

From God's Word, the Bible...

He who is faithful in what is least is faithful also in much; and he who is unjust in what is least is unjust also in much.

Luke 16:10

In his book *I Give You Glory, O God*, Jerry Bridges relates an experience that powerfully riveted an important truth in his mind. He and his wife had gone to a small, specialty bakery to buy bread. They had with them a two for the price of one coupon. When they presented it to the salesclerk along with their two loaves of bread, she explained that the coupon was only good at their new bakery that was opening that day. Although that wasn't indicated on the coupon itself, Jerry and his wife agreeably complied by returning their second loaf to the shelf.

Much to their surprise, the clerk thanked them for being so kind and understanding. They soon learned that several customers had berated her that morning when they learned that the special deal didn't apply in that store.

Jerry Bridges and his wife didn't treat her that way. They acted as Christians ought to act. As Jerry and his wife talked about the experience, it occurred to him that Christians are always on duty even in such simple matters as buying bread.

Always on duty! That's the Christian. He or she must not take time off from being a Christian. There is no holiday, no vacation or no sabbatical in our Christianity. We're on duty when we speak. We're on duty when we're alone with our thoughts. We're on duty when we're with people we know and when we're with people we don't know. We're on duty when we're with people who deserve to be treated kindly and when we're with people who don't. We're on duty when we open the doors of our houses to go out into the world, and we're on duty when we close those doors to be with our families.

Sometimes it easier to act like a Christian in the face of life's big things than it is in the face of life's little things. A family is suddenly stricken with tragedy, and we make sure we are there to offer comfort and assistance. That's good, very good. But what about the clerk in the bread store? How have we treated her or him?

The truth is that we can be faithful in large things and fail to be in little things. But if we are faithful in the little things, we can be sure that we will be faithful in the large things.

Jesus is, of course, our example in this matter of always being on duty. He never took a break from living for the honor of His Father and for the glory of His name. He never gave way to irritability and short-temperedness. When a large multitude intruded on a time that He had set aside for rest for Himself and His disciples, there was not a trace of anger or irritability in Jesus. To the contrary, when Jesus saw the "great multitude," He was "moved with compassion for them, because they were like sheep not having a shepherd" (Mark 6:34).

On another occasion, Jesus' disciples may have showed some irritability when people began bringing their children to Jesus. But Jesus said: "Let the little children come to Me, and do not forbid them. . ." (Matt. 19:13-14).

Even on the cross, Jesus refused to lash out with anger but rather prayed: "Father, forgive them, for they do not know what they do" (Luke 23:34).

In these instances and in every instance from the life of Jesus, He was "leaving us an example" so that we "should follow in His steps" (1 Peter 2:21).

I will add my own word of testimony. I can say that I have never regretted any time that I acted as a Christian. I have always regretted those times in which I didn't.

On March 6, 2016, Jerry Bridges finished his earthly journey and entered the presence of his Lord. I can imagine the Lord receiving him with these words: "Well done, good and faithful servant." I can also imagine Jerry asking: "Lord, are you referring to the books I wrote?" And it wouldn't surprise me if the Lord responded: "No. I'm referring to the time you were buying bread."

July 18

Come and Go

From God's Word, the Bible...

But Naomi said, "Turn back, my daughters; why will you go with me? Are there still sons in my womb, that they may be your husbands? Turn back, my daughters, go—for I am too old to have a husband. If I should say I have hope, if I should have a husband tonight and should also bear sons, would you wait for them till they were grown? Would you restrain yourselves from having husbands? No, my daughters; for it grieves me very much for your sakes that the hand of the Lord has gone out against me!"

Ruth 1:11-13

People often say odd things. One coach had this to say to his players: "Two words summarize this sport—you never know."

Yogi Berra offered this observation on baseball: "Ninety per cent of this game is half mental."

Odd words come from those who either don't think or can't think.

In Ruth 1, we have Naomi saying a very odd thing again and again. It must have been because she didn't really stop to think about what she was saying.

I'm talking about what she said to her daughters-in-law. As she was preparing to leave Moab and go back to her home in Bethlehem, Naomi told Ruth and Orpah to stay in Moab. This was not merely a suggestion from Naomi. This was urging. This was persuasion. In verse 8, she says to them: "Go, return each to her mother's house." In verse 11, she says to them: "Turn back, my daughters; why will you go with me?" In verse 12, she says: "Turn back, my daughters, go your way."

Orpah finally did as Naomi asked. She turned and walked away. Now alone with Ruth, Naomi said: "Look, your sister-in-law has gone back to her people and to her gods; return after your sister-in-law" (v.15).

This doesn't seem to be such a big deal. Naomi is going back to Israel, and she wants her daughters-in-law to stay in their homeland. Why make a fuss about it? Here's the answer: Orpah had decided to turn back "to her gods," and Naomi urges Ruth to do the same.

Naomi was from Israel, and Israel was the nation to whom God had revealed Himself and His gracious plan of salvation. When Orpah and Ruth express their desire to go to Israel, Naomi tells them to go back to their gods! What a shocking thing for an Israelite to say! She tells them to turn away from

Israel where they could find the true knowledge of God and stay with their false gods in Moab.

There's only one way to explain it. While Naomi herself believed in the God of Israel, she was a backslider, and backsliders say and do strange things.

The truth is that Naomi shouldn't have been in Moab at all. She, her husband Elimelech, and their two sons had left Israel when a famine set in. That wasn't the right thing for them to do. The people of Israel were in a special covenant relationship with God. The land itself was part of that covenant. If the Israelites lived in faithfulness to God, the land would be fruitful. If they didn't, the Lord might send a famine to correct them (Lev. 26:14-29; Deut. 28:15-24).

The proper response to such a famine was spiritual in nature. It lay in the people honestly confronting their sins and seeking God's forgiveness. It was not to leave the land (Deut. 30:8-11).

The choice of Elimelech and Naomi to leave the land was, therefore, a choice to not be part of the solution. It was an indication that their hearts had strayed from the Lord. They were backsliders, a fact that Naomi herself admitted when she spoke of the Lord's chastisement (Ruth 1:20-21).

I can't help but compare the words of Naomi to Ruth and Orpah to the words Moses spoke to his brother-in-law, Hobab. "Come with us," Moses said, "and we will treat you well; for the LORD has promised good things to Israel" (Num. 10:29).

"Go," said Naomi. "Come," said Moses. Naomi was wrong; Moses was right.

Ruth refused to be persuaded by Naomi. We might say the Lord's persuasion was more powerful than Naomi's, leading Ruth to say:

Entreat me not to leave you,
Or to turn back from following after you;
For wherever you go, I will go;
And wherever you lodge, I will lodge;
Your people shall be my people,
And your God, my God.
(RUTH 1:16)

We should also note that Jesus has a "come" and "go" of His own. Regarding the matter of knowing God in this life, the Lord Jesus, unlike Naomi, always says "come" and never "go." It doesn't matter how sinful we may have been, the Lord Jesus always says: "Come" (Matt. 11:28).

But if we go through this life rejecting His invitation to come to Him in repentance and faith, we will eventually hear Him say: "Go" (Matt. 7:23).

July 19

Prayer: Important and Difficult

FROM GOD'S WORD, THE BIBLE...

. . .praying always with all prayer and supplication in the Spirit, being watchful to this end with all perseverance and supplication for all the saints. . .

EPHESIANS 6:18

In my years of walking with the Lord, I've become convinced of two things regarding prayer:

- Nothing is more important;
- Nothing is harder.

We surely don't need to be persuaded about the importance of prayer. That truth is prominently displayed in the Bible. I've never attempted to count them, but it has been said that there are 650 prayers in the Bible. A total of 650—that's a lot!

The Bible also emphasizes the importance of prayer by telling us that the greatest heroes of the faith prayed: Abraham, Moses, Elijah, David, Paul—they were all men of prayer.

The Apostle Paul often stressed the importance of prayer. He writes to Timothy: "Therefore I exhort first of all that supplications, prayers, intercessions, and giving of thanks be made for all men. . ." (1 Tim. 2:1). The phrase "first of all" means "as a matter of first importance."

Paul also urged the church in Colosse to "continue earnestly in prayer" (Col. 4:2). And to the church in Thessalonica, he says: "Pray without ceasing" (1 Thess. 5:17).

While prayer is prominently displayed in the Bible, it is particularly displayed in the life of Jesus. If anyone would seem to have needed not to pray, it was Jesus, who was fully God and fully man. But pray Jesus did. Luke tells us that he prayed often (5:16) and, on at least one occasion, all night (6:12). He also makes note of Jesus praying on other occasions (9:28; 11:1; 22:41). Furthermore, Luke tells us that Jesus taught his disciples to pray (11:1-4). On another occasion, Jesus shared a parable to drive home the point that "men always ought to pray and not lose heart" (Luke 18:1).

What a lesson there is in this! If Jesus thought it necessary to pray, how much more should we!

In light of the emphasis the Bible puts on prayer we can't doubt its importance. We rather have to agree with these words from J.C. Ryle:

"Prayer is the very life-breath of true Christianity."[3]

But prayer—real prayer—isn't easy. True prayer isn't merely repeating without feeling the same few phrases we've used over the years. True prayer is coming to God the Father on the basis of the redeeming work of Jesus and in the power of the Holy Spirit to express worship, confession, and thanksgiving and to make our requests known.

Why do we find prayer to be so difficult? One answer is that the devil, knowing far better than we the importance and value of prayer, strives mightily to hinder us in our praying. Some of the Puritans used to say that the devil "fetches a mischief against us" when we pray.

We tend to think that the church must move forward through programs, promotions and personalities. The devil fears none of these. He knows that if the church is to move forward it will be on her knees. So he trembles when we get on our knees.

Another reason that prayer is difficult can be found in ourselves. As Pogo said: "We have met the enemy, and he is us."

I'm saying prayer is hard work, and we are naturally inclined to seek our own ease and comfort.

To these we can add yet another reason prayer is hard for us: it often seems to accomplish nothing at all.

It ought to be enough for us that the Lord wants us to pray! We may not be able to put a finger on anything that prayer is accomplishing. We may not be able to identify an answer. But let us keep on praying because the Lord Jesus desires that we do so.

And of this we may be assured: if we keep on praying, we will eventually find that prayer accomplished far more than we ever thought possible. Our problem is always thinking we see the whole picture and that we are, therefore, in a position to pronounce outcomes. But the truth is that we see only a tiny part of the picture, and the part we see is never sufficient for us to be pronouncing on prayer or any other part of God's working.

Prayer is both important and difficult. The question before each of us is whether we will let the importance outweigh the difficulty or the difficulty outweigh the importance.

3 J.C. Ryle *Expository Thoughts on Luke*, The Banner of Truth Trust, vol. ii, p.253.

July 20

Things That Help Me Pray: Loading up on the Privilege

From God's Word, the Bible...

O You who hear prayer,
To You all flesh will come.

Psalm 65:2

Where is your eye when you pray? I'm talking about your spiritual eye. In other words, what are you looking at when you pray? Are you looking at the duty of prayer—*I know I'm supposed to do this, so I might as well get it out of the way?*

Or are you looking at the privilege? Look at the duty, and prayer will be drudgery. Look at the privilege, and prayer will be a delight.

I see the privilege of prayer in terms of two poles—a north pole and a south pole, if you will. God is one pole and I the other.

Think about God. You and I have never in our best moments ever come anywhere near a true and adequate conception of the greatness, the grandeur, and the glory of God. He is the eternal God without beginning or end. He is the God who has made all things and who rules over all things. He is the object of the adoration and worship of countless numbers of angels. He is the God of the "omnis"—omniscient (all-knowing), omnipotent (all-powerful) and omnipresent (present everywhere). God is self-existent, self-sufficient, and sovereign. He is righteous, just and holy. He is gracious and good. He is kind and merciful. And God is immutable. That means He is unchanging. He is at this moment all the things that I have mentioned, and He will be all those things tomorrow and forever.

And with all that, we have only scratched the surface. God is greater than our greatest thought of Him. Theologians can't explain Him. Scientists can't observe Him. Poets, painters, and musicians can't capture or express Him. All of them together are like children playing on the shore of the surging ocean, totally unaware of the vast depths beyond.

So there is one of the poles of prayer. And I—and you—are the other pole. Did I liken the privilege of prayer to the North Pole and the South Pole? Those two poles are 12,430 miles apart. But the distance between God and us is immeasurable.

That distance is great if we speak of it only in terms of God the Creator and of man the creature. It is infinitely greater if we speak of it in terms of the Holy God and sinful man. How vast is that gap!

Here, then, is the privilege of prayer. It spans the gap between God and man, the gap between heaven and earth. I can talk to the God who is so far and so incomprehensibly beyond me. I can speak here on earth and be heard in heaven!

God hearing the prayers of His people would be privilege enough, but it goes beyond that. God also delights in those prayers. Just as doting parents delight in the babbling of their infants, so God delights in the prayers of His people. God's delight is such that He keeps those prayers. He stores them in bowls (Rev. 5:8). Those prayers are never lost. When we get home to heaven, we will find that our prayers are already there ahead of us.

Many suffer these days from the culture of the celebrity. They are fascinated by celebrities from the world of entertainment and/or the world of sports. They would consider it an immense honor if they could speak a few words to one of their celebrities, and if that celebrity would take a mere moment to really listen. The celebrities of this day are to God as a speck of dust is to a mountain, as a teaspoon of water is to an ocean, and as the light of a match is to the sun. If we were to regard it as a privilege to speak to a mere celebrity, how much more should we regard it as a privilege to speak to God?

If we're to pray as we ought, we must load up on the privilege of prayer, that is, think much about that privilege. The more we focus on it, the more we will delight in prayer and the more we will find ourselves singing with Fanny J. Crosby:

Blessed hour of prayer,
Blessed hour of prayer,
What a balm for the weary,
Oh, how sweet to be there!

July 21

Things That Help Me Pray: Loading up on the Purchase

FROM GOD'S WORD, THE BIBLE...

For you were bought at a price; therefore glorify God in your body and in your spirit, which are God's.

You were bought at a price; do not become slaves of men.

1 CORINTHIANS 6:20; 7:23

I have never found it easy to pray. Almost anything in the Christian life is easier for me than really laying hold of God in genuine prayer. I'm always in need of help when it comes to this most vital work.

I have tried to learn how to help myself in praying. One thing I've learned is to load up on the privilege of prayer, that is, to fill my mind with the fact that I, a weak, undeserving sinner, can actually be heard in heaven. I can have the ear of the sovereign, majestic God!

Another thing that helps me to pray as I ought is to load up on the purchase. Every Christian surely knows what I'm talking about. There is one great purchase as far as the Christian is concerned. That is Christ purchasing us by the shedding of His blood on the cross.

It comes down to this for me—the more I think about what the Lord Jesus Christ did for me on the cross, the more I feel like praying.

I sometimes think that we rob ourselves of real appreciation for what Jesus did on that cross by not personalizing what He did there. The floodgates of joy, gratitude and praise are opened in my mind and heart when I stop to ponder that Jesus died for me. Jerry Bridges puts it this way:

> There was a period in my early Christian life when my concept of God's love was little more than a logical deduction: God loves the world; I am a part of the world; therefore, God loves me. It was as if God's love were a big umbrella to protect us all from His judgment against sin, and I was under the umbrella along with thousands of other people. There was nothing particularly personal about it. Then one day I realized, "God loves me! Christ died for me.[4]

4 Jerry Bridges, *The Practice of Godliness*. NavPress: Colorado Springs, CO, 1983, p. 32.

I also think we rob ourselves of deep appreciation for what Jesus did on that cross by thinking of His death in physical terms only. Yes, Jesus died physically, and death by crucifixion was as horrible a death as there could be. But it was not the physical aspect of His death that saves us. It was not the mere fact that He was crucified that saves us. Lots of men were crucified in those days.

We will never appreciate Jesus' death to the degree that we should if we don't understand that it was a special death. Jesus, a special man (the God-man), died a special death because of a special arrangement with God the Father. That special arrangement was this: God the Father would pour out on His Son the wrath that I deserve for my sins. The thing that made the death of Jesus so special is that He actually took an eternity's worth of wrath for my sins.

Through my sin I had essentially sold myself out to the penalty for my sin, the wrath of God. But when Jesus took that wrath in my place, He paid that penalty. He paid my debt and purchased me from sin and God's wrath. Now I can happily take as my own the words of Philip Bliss:

I will sing of my Redeemer,
And His wondrous love to me;
On the cruel cross He suffered,
From the curse to set me free.
Sing, oh, sing of my Redeemer,
With His blood He purchased me,
On the cross He sealed my pardon,
Paid the debt, and made me free.

I will tell the wondrous story,
How my lost estate to save,
In His boundless love and mercy,
He the ransom freely gave.
I will praise my dear Redeemer,
His triumphant pow'r I'll tell,
How the victory He giveth
Over sin, and death, and hell.

I will sing of my Redeemer,
And His heav'nly love to me;
He from death to life hath brought me,
Son of God with Him to be.

Purchased by Christ on the cross? My debt paid? Redeemed from wrath? As I load my mind and heart with Christ on the cross in my place, prayer doesn't seem quite so difficult,

Things That Help Me Pray: Loading Up on Praise

From God's Word, the Bible...

Praise the Lord!
Praise, O servants of the Lord,
Praise the name of the Lord!
Blessed be the name of the Lord
From this time forth and forevermore!
From the rising of the sun to its going down
The Lord's name is to be praised.

Psalm 113:1-3

I have never met a Christian who thought prayer was unimportant. I have never met a Christian who thought he or she had mastered prayer. I have also never met a believer who disagreed with my assessment that nothing the Christian is asked to do is harder than praying.

I am far from having mastered prayer, but I have discovered over the years that I am helped in my praying if I load up on some things. It helps me to load up on the privilege of prayer and on the price the Lord Jesus paid for me on the cross.

Today, I'm adding a third thing that helps me pray, namely, praise. I try to load up on praise because praise helps me pray. The more I praise God in my praying, the more I feel like praying. Praise primes the pump of prayer. I have found it to be so, and I think you will find it to be so as well.

How does praise help us to pray? First, *it warms our hearts toward God* as we think about who God is and what He has done for us.

It's impossible to pray from a cold heart, that is, a heart that is cold toward God. Sadly enough, our hearts are constantly bent toward coldness. Just try to pray from a cold heart and see how far you get. But praising God causes the coldness to melt away and warmth to come in.

It's not mere coincidence that the Bible puts so much emphasis on praise. The Bible mentions praising God approximately 250 times, with 130 of those occurring in the book of Psalms.

How very much we have for which to praise God! We have past blessings, present blessings, and glorious promises of future blessings. We have temporal blessings (those that pertain to life in this world), and we have spiritual blessings. We have obvious and open blessings (those that are very apparent to us), and we have hidden or disguised blessings (those circumstances in which God is working for our good even when we can't see or discern it). We have daily blessings and special seasons of blessings.

We consider every blessing to be good, and every good thing comes from God (James 1:17).

Praise helps us pray in a second way. *It gives us perspective on our needs.* As we think about who God is and what He has done, we begin to realize that He is more than sufficient to meet our needs. Our needs begin to shrink to their proper size when we place them alongside the greatness of God. In praising God, we find help for our needs before we ever get to our needs.

An example of this is found in Acts 4. The early church was in deep trouble. Peter and John had been threatened and told not to preach in the name of Jesus (Acts 4:17-21). When they were released, they told their fellow believers about the threat, and the first response of those believers was to pray. But notice how they began their prayer: "Lord, you are God, who made heaven and earth and the sea, and all that is in them. . ." (Acts 4.24).

Their praying began with God rather than with the trouble, and in beginning with God they found help for their trouble.

So I lay it down as a fundamental rule of praying that we should always begin with praise to God and worship of God. This is what Jesus taught His disciples when He gave them what is known as The Lord's Prayer. My view is that it would be more correct to call it "The Model Prayer." No, Jesus didn't give them this prayer with the intent that they should only say those words every time they prayed and nothing else. This prayer set before them a pattern for prayer or principles for prayer.

As we look at this pattern, we see that it begins with praise:

Our Father in heaven,
Hallowed be Your name.
(Matt. 6:9b)

The prayer also ends with praise:

For Yours is the kingdom and the power and the glory forever. Amen.
(Matt. 6:13b)

If Jesus filled The Model Prayer with praise, we should fill our prayers with praise. The more we do, the more delight we shall find in prayer.

Things That Help Me Pray: Lightening the Load

From God's Word, the Bible...

Now this is the confidence that we have in Him, that if we ask anything according to His will, He hears us. And if we know that He hears us, whatever we ask, we know that we have the petitions that we have asked of Him.

1 John 5:14-15

Loading up on certain things helps me to pray. It helps me to fill my mind with the privilege of prayer, with the price Jesus paid for me on the cross, and with praise to God. It also helps me to pray if I lighten my load. It sounds like a contradiction, but it isn't. To pray well means we must load up on those things that help us, and unload those things that hinder us.

One thing we often load ourselves down with is unanswered prayer. We think of instances in which we specifically asked God to do some good thing for us or to keep some evil thing from us, and the good thing didn't happen but the evil thing did.

Because we didn't get what we asked for, we have soured on prayer. We think it does little or no good. We have loaded ourselves down with the problem of unanswered prayer. That is heavy baggage indeed, and we will pray very little or very poorly as long as we carry it.

So we need to think through this business of unanswered prayer. We correctly assume that prayer consists of equal parts of wisdom and power. Someone must know what needs to be done. That's the wisdom part. And someone must be able to do what needs to be done. That's the power part.

Our grand blunder is to think that we supply the wisdom part and God supplies the power part. We would never openly admit it, but we think we know what God ought to do in our lives. So we go to God in our wisdom to ask Him to supply the power, that is, to ask Him to do what we want done.

In doing this, we refuse to grant to God the prerogatives that we reserve for ourselves in parenting. No good parent will say: "My child supplies the wisdom part, and I supply the power part." In other words, no wise parent will do whatever his or her child wants him or her to do.

Every good parent has the best interests of the child at heart. With that being the case, the parent sometimes answers "Yes" to what the child asks. Sometimes, for reasons the child may not understand, the parent answers

"No." Does the parent only have the best interest of his child in view when he or she says "Yes"? Does a "No" mean the parent has suddenly lost his or her concern for the child? Not at all! The "No" comes from the same heart of love as the "Yes." And sometimes, the parent answers with a "Not now," and that answer also comes from the same heart of love. In each case, the parent is exercising wisdom in determining what is best for the child.

God is wiser than the wisest human parent. Sometimes God answers our prayers with "Yes." But sometimes He answers with "No" or "Not now." But with each answer, it is God who is supplying the wisdom. He knows what we need, what we don't need and when to give us what we need.

We need to mind our own business on this matter of prayer. Our business is not to fret over our prayers seeming to be unanswered. Our business is to pray. I sometimes think that this is the most important passage in the Bible on the matter of unanswered prayer:

Lord, my heart is not haughty,
Nor my eyes lofty.
Neither do I concern myself with great matters,
Nor with things too profound for me.
Surely I have calmed and quieted my soul. . .
(Ps. 131:1-2a)

Some imagine themselves storming into the presence of God to ask: "Why didn't you give me all the things that I asked for?"

They will certainly be surprised to hear God respond: "Why didn't you ask Me for all the things that I wanted to give?" (James 4:2).

We need to concern ourselves much more with the unasked prayer than with the unanswered prayer. And when we finally come into the glory of His presence, we will most surely discover that our unanswered prayers were not really unanswered after all. And we will further discover that those circumstances which we considered to be lapses in God's wisdom were, in fact, part of His wisdom.

July 24

Keep on Praying!

From God's Word, the Bible...

Then He spoke a parable to them, that men always ought to pray and not lose heart, saying: "There was in a certain city a judge who did not fear God nor regard man. Now there was a widow in that city; and she came to him, saying, 'Get justice for me from my adversary.' And he would not for a while; but afterward he said within himself, 'Though I do not fear God nor regard man, yet because this widow troubles me I will avenge her, lest by her continual coming she weary me.'" Then the Lord said, "Hear what the unjust judge said. And shall God not avenge His own elect who cry out day and night to Him, though He bears long with them? I tell you that He will avenge them speedily. Nevertheless, when the Son of Man comes, will He really find faith on the earth?"

Luke 18:1-8

Have you lost heart in prayer? To keep His disciples from losing heart in prayer, Jesus gave them a parable. Because we easily lose heart in praying, we need this parable as much or more than they.

Jesus' parable features a woman who was in dire need. Her husband had died. That was calamity enough in those days. But this woman had even more on her plate. She had "an adversary" (v. 3). Someone had done something to make her life very difficult. Perhaps this person had swindled her out of the little money she had. Or perhaps he had prevented her from receiving something to which she was entitled.

Whatever the nature of the misdeed, this woman quite obviously had a legitimate legal claim. She went to the judge in her city pleading: "Avenge me of my adversary." (v. 3).

She was asking for justice, but this judge had no concern for justice. He was "a judge who did not fear God nor regard man" (v. 2).

What was this poor woman to do? She had asked and nothing had happened. If anyone could be excused for losing heart, it was she.

But she refused to give up. She decided to make a pest of herself until this judge took action and gave her the ruling she needed. It wasn't because he suddenly took an interest in justice. No, he was exactly the same man that he had been before. It was just to get this woman out of his life.

Jesus made the application by raising this question: "And shall God not avenge His own elect who cry out day and night to Him, though He bears long with them?" (v. 7).

He then supplies the answer: "I tell you that He will avenge them speedily" (v. 7).

The point of the parable is very plain. If an unjust judge could be persuaded by persistence to do something for someone he did not care about, how much more can God be persuaded by the persistence of those whom He cares deeply about!

How do we know God cares for His people? There's a world of meaning in that word "elect" (v. 7). God's people are His people because he set His love on them even before the world began and chose to redeem them through His Son (Eph. 1:3-4).

Because God, unlike the judge in this parable, is kind and caring, prayer is not overcoming His reluctance but rather seizing on His willingness.

But if God cares so deeply and is so eager to answer, why do we have the problem of unanswered prayer?

Much of our problem stems from having a different view or understanding of prayer than God. We have a tendency to view it exclusively as a way to get things from God. Whatever we want and when we want!

But God has not appointed prayer as the means for only giving us things. It is also one of the ways in which He trains us.

Is it not true that parents do the same with their children? Do they not use the requests of their children as opportunities for training them? God, the wise Father, gives to us in much the same way as wise parents give to their children. We do not give our children everything for which they ask, because they sometimes ask for things that are not good for them. They sometimes ask in the wrong way. They sometimes ask after they have been particularly sullen, ungrateful, and disobedient. And we sometimes let them ask more than once so they will have greater appreciation for the gift when it comes. That which is too easily gained is not usually highly prized!

We are far too casual in prayer already. Think about how casual we would be if we were given everything for which we ask as soon as we ask!

Of this we may be assured: if we keep on praying, we will eventually find that prayer accomplished far more than we ever thought possible. Our problem is always thinking we see the whole picture and that we are, therefore, in a position to pronounce. But the truth is that we see only a tiny part of the picture, and the part we see is never sufficient for us to be pronouncing on prayer or any other part of God's working.

Let's ever be mindful in our praying that people all around us need the Lord. They need to see their sins and their coming judgment. They need to be pointed to the Lord Jesus Christ who came to this earth and went to the cross to provide forgiveness for sinners. And we need to pray that the Holy Spirit will enable people far and wide to lay hold of the gospel in true faith. If we've been doing such praying, let's keep on. If we haven't, let's start.

"Help, I Have Done Awful Things!"

From God's Word, the Bible...

Seek the Lord while He may be found,
Call upon Him while He is near.
Let the wicked forsake his way,
And the unrighteous man his thoughts;
Let him return to the Lord,
And He will have mercy on him;
And to our God,
For He will abundantly pardon.

Isaiah 55:6-7

The devil wants to keep unbelievers from coming to faith in Christ and believers from serving Christ. He often uses the same argument with each. To the unbeliever, he says: "You're too bad to be saved." To the believer, he says: "You're too bad to serve."

The answer is the same in each situation. God's grace is greater than our sins. God can save the most stained sinner. God can restore the most soiled saint.

Let's call the roll of some of the very worst sinners. King Manasseh of Judah sacrificed his own sons to idols. But Manasseh was forgiven. Saul of Tarsus was a ferocious persecutor of the church. But Saul was saved and became the Apostle Paul, the foremost preacher of the church. Augustine was deeply entrenched in sin, but he was saved. John Newton was one of the most disgusting and vile reprobates who ever came along, but Newton was saved and became the author of the hymn *Amazing Grace*.

And God hasn't used up His grace in saving such men. His grace constantly renews itself. There is as much of it today as there has ever been. There's enough for you. One of the most frequent responses I've received from people as I've presented the gospel is this: "If you only knew what I've done, you wouldn't say that I can be forgiven."

I do say it. You are not a greater sinner than Christ is the great Savior.

And what about soiled saints? Yes, every saint is soiled in some way. Christians aren't perfect in this life. Perfection comes later. Let's call the roll of a few of those soiled saints. Noah got drunk (Gen. 9:20-23), Abraham lied about his wife (Gen. 12:10-20; 20:1-18), Moses lost his temper (Num. 20:7-11), and David committed adultery and murder (2 Sam. 11:1-27).

Then we fast forward to the New Testament, and we immediately think of Simon Peter. Given the opportunity to stand up and speak up for the Lord Jesus, Peter failed. He denied the Lord—not once, not twice, but three times!

There was so much Peter could have said about the Lord. When he was accused of being one of Jesus' disciples, Peter could have said: "Yes, I'm one of His disciples and proudly so. I've seen Him open the eyes of the blind and the ears of the deaf. I've seen Him make the lame to walk and the mute to speak. I've seen Him cast out demons, still storms, and feed multitudes. I've even seen Him raise three people from the dead."

Yes, that and a thousand other things is what Peter could have said, but, alas, he did not. He denied Christ. Denial would have been bad enough in and of itself, but Peter denied in a very shocking and vehement way. He wasn't content to merely say: "You must have me confused with someone else." The Gospel of Matthew tells us that he even laced his denials with cursing (Matt. 26:74).

But there was forgiveness for Simon Peter. The very Lord that he had denied sought him out and asked him three times if he, Simon, loved Him. And each time Simon Peter answered: "Yes." How gracious of the Lord to give Simon the opportunity to reverse each one of those nasty denials (John 21:15-19)!

When we as Christians fall into sin, the devil always wants us to debate within ourselves whether God can forgive. While the devil calls us to debate whether forgiveness is available, the Lord calls us to delight in it and to avail ourselves of it. He assures us that He casts our sins behind His back, not to be seen again, and casts them as far from us as the east is from the west, never to be remembered again.

When the devil says to us: "You have sinned. You must stop serving the Lord," we need to hear the words of Samuel to the people of Israel: "Do not fear. You have done all this wickedness; yet do not turn aside from following the LORD, but serve the LORD with all your heart" (1 Sam. 12:20).

Stained sinners and soiled saints are all called to rejoice in God's forgiving grace.

Grace, grace, God's grace,
Grace that will pardon and cleanse within;
Grace, grace, God's grace,
Grace that is greater than all our sin!
(JULIA H. JOHNSTON)

July 26

"Help, I'm Disappointed with God!"

From God's Word, the Bible...

You are of purer eyes than to behold evil,
And cannot look on wickedness.
Why do You look on those who deal treacherously,
And hold Your tongue when the wicked devours
A person more righteous than he?
Though the fig tree may not blossom,
Nor fruit be on the vines;
Though the labor of the olive may fail,
And the fields yield no food;
Though the flock may be cut off from the fold,
And there be no herd in the stalls—
Yet I will rejoice in the Lord,
I will joy in the God of my salvation.

Habakkuk 1:13; 3:17-18

We know about disappointments. We expect something to turn out a certain way, and it doesn't. So we're disappointed.

A lot of people wouldn't hesitate to say that they are disappointed with God. They believe that He has failed them in some way. Perhaps He appeared to break a promise, seemed to not answer their prayers, didn't protect them from hardship or didn't appear to prosper the work that they did for Him. Or it may be that they simply have not experienced in the Christian life what they expected to experience, that is, they haven't felt God's presence, haven't experienced joy in serving Him, or haven't found strength for facing life's difficulties.

Disappointment with God isn't a new thing. It has been in existence for a very long time, and some of the greatest people in the Bible experienced it. Job was disappointed that God let him suffer although he had lived righteously. Jonah was disappointed that God didn't judge the Ninevites. Mary and Martha were disappointed that Jesus didn't come to heal their brother before he died. Paul must have been disappointed that God didn't remove his thorn in the flesh.

And here we have Habakkuk. He was disappointed that God was planning to use the Babylonians to bring judgment upon the Jews when they, the Babylonians, were the more sinful of the two.

What are we to do when we are disappointed with God? *We should begin by checking our expectations*. We often want to obligate God to do things that He has never obligated Himself to do. God has never promised that He will exempt His people from trials and difficulties. As a matter of fact, He has said the opposite (Acts 14:22; 2 Tim. 3:12; 1 Peter 4:12).

If we insist on believing that God's purpose is to make life easy for us, we are going to be constantly disappointed with Him. God has made us to know, love, serve, trust, and glorify Him. With those things as His purpose, we may be sure that He is going to do things quite differently than He would if our ease were His purpose.

After we get our expectations in order, *we must learn to delight ourselves in God*. That is the big lesson we learn from Habakkuk. He began with being disappointed with God, but he came out in a good place (Hab. 3:17-19).

How did Habakkuk get to this good place? It wasn't because his situation suddenly changed. His people were still sinful, and God was still planning to use the more sinful Babylonians as His instrument of judgment. It was because Habakkuk made the deliberate decision to draw his joy from God rather than from his circumstances.

We find the Apostle Paul doing the same. Even though he was imprisoned, Paul made the determination that he would rejoice in the Lord (Phil. 1:18; 4:4).

Habakkuk and Paul determined to draw their joy from God because they understood that they had nothing without God. We would do well to learn from them. In the midst of our disappointments and frustrations, we are to delight ourselves in God. We certainly don't have all the answers with Him, but we have no answers without Him. Think about it for a moment. Take God out of the equation, and we still have our disappointments and sorrows, but without God we have nothing else. It's better to have those disappointments and sorrows with God than to have them without Him.

What does it mean to delight ourselves in God? It means delighting in those things that God Himself delights in: His perfections (Jer. 9:23-24), His Son (Isa. 42:1; Matt. 3:17), His Son's redeeming death (Isa. 53:10), His Word (Ps. 138:2), His day (Isa. 58:13-14), public worship (Ps. 149:1,4), prayer (Prov. 15:8), and obedience (1 Sam. 15:22-23).

Another thing for us to do when we are disappointed with God is look to our future. Disappointments aren't permanent for God's people. If God doesn't ease them for us in this life, He most certainly will in the life to come. In heaven there will be no disappointments.

If we want to get to that land of no disappointments, we must repent of our sins and trust the Lord Jesus Christ and in His atoning work. Those who come to God through Christ will not be disappointed because God never fails to save the sinner who trusts in Christ.

July 27

"Help, I Find It Hard to Believe!"

From God's Word, the Bible...

Then He said to Thomas, "Reach your finger here, and look at My hands; and reach your hand here, and put it into My side. Do not be unbelieving, but believing."
And Thomas answered and said to Him, "My Lord and my God!"

John 20:27-28

Christianity offers the most indescribably glorious benefits imaginable. It tells us that we can have forgiveness for our sins and right standing with God on the basis of what the Lord Jesus Christ has done. It further tells us that all who repent of their sins and believe in Christ have eternal life awaiting them in a world that is free from pain, sorrow and death.

Many would like to believe this message, but they find it hard to do so for several reasons:

- these things sound to good to be true;
- an overwhelming majority appear to reject these things;
- many of those who claim to believe these things live as if they don't really believe them;
- many other religions make conflicting claims;
- many highly intelligent people reject Christianity.

Put Thomas, one of Jesus' original twelve disciples, into the category of those who find it hard to believe. He was asked to believe something that seemed impossible, namely, that Jesus had risen from the dead. This was such a staggering claim that it did indeed seem too good to be true.

But Thomas should have believed in the resurrection of Jesus. He had more than sufficient reasons for doing so. He was present on those occasions when Jesus predicted His resurrection (Matt. 16:21; 17:22-23; 20:17-19). He had seen Jesus raise three people from the dead (Mark 5:35-43; Luke 7:11-17; John 11:38-44). And the testimony he heard about Jesus' resurrection came from ten men whom he, Thomas, knew to be completely dependable and trustworthy.

Thomas was not asked, therefore, to believe for no reason, but rather to believe on the basis of sufficient reasons. He wasn't called to make a leap of faith into the dark with the unfounded hope that all would turn out well.

But with these sufficient reasons in hand, Thomas refused to believe. With sufficient evidence, he demanded total evidence: "Unless I see in His hands the nails, and put my finger into the print of the nails, and put my hand into His side, I will not believe" (v. 25).

Eight days after Thomas made his emphatic statement, the risen Lord suddenly appeared. After greeting all of His disciples (v. 26), the Lord directly addressed Thomas: "Reach you finger here, and look at My hands; and reach your hand here, and put it into My side. Do not be unbelieving but believing" (v. 27).

Isn't it amazing that Jesus was so kind and tender toward Thomas? His doubt deserved a severe reprimand, but Jesus' reprimand was more encouraging than severe.

Thomas wasn't rebuked because he had refused to believe without any reasons but rather because he refused to believe with more than enough reasons. He wasn't rebuked because he refused to take a blind leap of faith but rather because he refused to believe on the basis of inescapable reasons.

Thomas didn't carry out his plan to touch the nail prints and to place his hand in Jesus' wounded side. Hearing Jesus quote his own words was sufficient for him to abandon his doubt. When Thomas heard those words, he realized that the risen Christ had been silently and invisibly present when he, Thomas, had spoken them.

In an instant, Thomas realized that the resurrection of Jesus was a fact that couldn't be denied. He also realized the meaning of that resurrection. It proved that Jesus was both Lord and God (v. 28).

Thomas' experience has value for each of us. Every believer struggles to believe at one time or another. We are all, as Thomas was, secondhand believers. We are called to believe on the basis of witnesses. The fact that we struggle shouldn't drive us to despair. We aren't Christians because we have full or perfect faith but rather because we have faith. Even weak faith is true faith.

When we find it hard to believe, we need to learn to doubt our doubts and believe our beliefs. We need to let Thomas remind us that there is sufficient evidence on which to base our faith. And we need to remember that we don't believe in Christ because He has answered every question that has ever popped into our minds but rather because He has given us answers that we can't get around.

July 28

"Help, I Think God Isn't Fair!"

FROM GOD'S WORD, THE BIBLE...

If I had said, "I will speak thus,"
Behold, I would have been untrue to the generation of Your children.
When I thought how to understand this,
It was too painful for me—
Until I went into the sanctuary of God;
Then I understood their end.

PSALM 73:15-17

Do you sometimes think God hasn't been fair to you? Have you stumbled over that problem? You have tried to live for the Lord, and troubles and hardships seem to dog your steps. Meanwhile, you look around and see people who don't have the slightest interest in God, and they are getting along very well.

Asaph, the author of Psalm 73, ran smack dab into this problem. He was trying to honor God, and what did he have to show for it? Let him answer:

. . .all day long I have been plagued,
And chastened every morning (v. 14).

What a testimony! Asaph says he had difficulty all day and every day! Meanwhile, the wicked seemed to be living carefree lives (v. 5).

Asaph began looking at people who had no interest in God, and it appeared to him as if they were getting along splendidly. Then he began looking at himself. He was trying to honor God with his life and obey His commandments. But he didn't seem to be doing so well.

What did Asaph notice about those ungodly people? He writes:

They are not in trouble as other men;
Nor are they plagued like other men (v. 5).

For a moment Asaph let himself imagine that those wicked people living such easy lives must surely die hard. But as he thought about that, he realized it was not the case. He says:

There are no pangs in their death,
But their strength is firm (v. 4).

So far as Asaph could tell, the wicked pretty much had it made—they were living easy lives and dying easy deaths. On top of that was their attitude. One would expect such people to show a smidgen of gratitude and a dash of humility, but these people seemed to go about without either. They were brandishing pride as though it were a chain around their necks (v. 6). They didn't hesitate to speak "loftily" (v. 8). Instead of thanking God for the things they were enjoying, they "set their mouth against the heavens" (v. 9).

Asaph couldn't help but wonder. Shouldn't living for God count for something? It wasn't so much that he was wishing that the wicked would do worse than he. It was rather that he was wishing that he could do as well as they.

Prosperity for the wicked and adversity for the righteous—it wasn't fair! It seemed to Asaph as if God wasn't paying attention (v. 11) because it was obvious to him, Asaph, that God would certainly set matters right if only He were aware of them.

Life in this world is never a sufficient basis for determining who is doing well and who is not doing well. Asaph needed the long view, and that is exactly what he got when he went to the house of God. How thankful we should be for God's house where we are rescued from the short view of things and given the long view!

There in God's house Asaph saw how foolish it is to envy people who don't know God. They may appear to be doing all right, but they are standing on slippery ground (v. 18). Each day could be their last day, and each breath their last breath, and then eternity!

When I find myself walking in Asaph's footprints, it is very helpful for me to remember that the unbeliever on his best day is far worse off than the believer on his worst day.

Asaph came out in a good place. He realized that no matter how bad his circumstances were, he had God. God was with him in every situation of life, and God is the greatest of all treasures. So we find him saying:

Nevertheless I am continually with You;
You hold me by my right hand,
You will guide me with Your counsel,
And afterward receive me to glory (vv. 23-24).

When the devil suggests to those of us who know the Lord that He is being unfair to us, let's learn from Asaph to take the long view. And let's learn to ask ourselves this question: How it is possible for the One who through His Son is giving us eternal life in heaven to ever be unfair to us? If He never blessed us with anything else, we would still be immeasurably blessed.

"Help, I Think God Has Forgotten Me!"

From God's Word, the Bible...

But Zion said, "The Lord has forsaken me,
And my Lord has forgotten me."
"Can a woman forget her nursing child,
And not have compassion on the son of her womb?
Surely they may forget,
Yet I will not forget you.
See, I have inscribed you on the palms of My hands;
Your walls are continually before Me.

Isaiah 49:14-16

The last twenty-seven chapters of Isaiah are a marvel. The prophet was enabled by the Spirit of God to look down the corridor of time and see his people in captivity in Babylon. And the Spirit prompted Isaiah to write these chapters to provide comfort for those captives. The prophet was enabled to see so that he might soothe.

We can't begin to grasp all of the sorrows that the captivity brought to those people. Right at the top of the list of those sorrows was the feeling that God had abandoned them (v. 14).

As we read their melancholy words, we might be saying of ourselves: "Been there. Done that." It's common for God's people to go through such heart-wrenching problems that they think God has forsaken them and forgotten them.

But that is never the case. It may seem to be true, but it isn't true. Through Isaiah, the Lord let those people know that He hadn't forgotten them. He conveys His ongoing concern and care for them by using three figures. The first is *the devoted mother* (v. 15).

We can all think of instances in which mothers have indeed abandoned their children, but those instances are unusual and exceptional. When we hear the word "mother," the thing that immediately comes to mind is faithfulness and not faithlessness.

God assures His people that He is not like the rare mother who does forsake her children. What is generally true of mothers—refusing to forsake their children—is most certainly true of Him. He emphatically says: "I will not forget you."

The Lord proceeds to add *the figure of the inscribed hands* (v. 16a).

People in those days would often write the name of their god on their hands. Here God tells the captives that He had written their names on the palms of His hands. Written? No! It's much stronger than that. Writing can be erased. God had *inscribed* or engraved their names on His hands.

It's impossible for us to forget words that are indelibly etched on the psalms of our hands. Those words are ever before us, and God's people are ever before Him. Even when it seems that He has forgotten them? Yes, even when it seems that He has forgotten them! The God who has written us on His hands can never "write us off."

The final picture the Lord uses to assure His people is that of *the still standing walls* (v. 16b).

If someone had mentioned the walls of Jerusalem to those captives, they would have been quick to speak along these lines: "The walls of Jerusalem don't exist. The Babylonians knocked them down. And those destroyed walls prove that God doesn't care about us anymore."

But God said those destroyed walls were "continually" before Him. Here is a blessed thing! Where those captives saw ruins, God saw walls. This was His way of assuring them that the captivity was not the final word for them. He would in due time bring them out of captivity, restore them to the land of Judah, and the walls of Jerusalem would stand again. God's word of judgment is never His final word for His people.

The devil still points to our harsh circumstances (some of which, like the captives of old, we have brought upon ourselves) as proofs that God has forgotten us. We should respond by pointing him to those captives in Babylon and what God said to them. But we do even better if we point him to the cross of Christ. That is the supreme proof that God loves His people even more than a devoted mother loves her child.

As we gaze at that cross, we must surely see the proof that God has engraved the names of His people on His hands. God would never have allowed the hands of His Son to be nailed to that cross if He didn't have our names on His hands.

And God did it all so that He might replace the ruins of our sin with the walls of His salvation.

We can be confident that God will never forsake His people. But there was a time when He did forsake someone. That time was on the cross. There He actually forsook His Son so all who believe in Christ will never be God-forsaken in eternity (Matt. 27:46). Have you believed on Him?

Purchasing and Preserving

From God's Word, the Bible...

Buy the truth, and do not sell it,
Also wisdom and instruction and understanding.

Proverbs 23:23

This verse calls us to both make a purchase and to preserve what we purchase. We are to buy the truth and not sell it.

To make this purchase, we must first believe that there is such a thing as truth. We can't purchase something that doesn't exist. Many tell us that there is no such thing as absolute truth. They state as an absolute truth that there is no such thing as absolute truth! What an incredible irony!

I answer them with an absolute truth of my own—they are wrong, dead wrong!

There is such a thing as truth, and there is one truth that is more important than any other: it is the truth of the Bible. On the night before He was crucified, the Lord Jesus said to God the Father: "Your word is truth" (John 17:17; see also Ps. 119:142,151). Jesus, the God-man from heaven, would be the one to know.

The Bible does not contain all that is true, but all that is in the Bible is true! How blessed we are to have it!

We are to purchase the truth of the Bible. We can purchase a Bible without purchasing the truth of it. To purchase something is to pay the price for it. What is the price of the truth of the Bible? It is diligent study! We have not purchased the truth if we merely know the Bible is the Word of God. We must burrow into it by reading it, studying it, and listening to it proclaimed, remembering as we do these lines from Joseph Hart:

These hath God married, and no man shall part:
Dust on the Bible and drought in the heart.

If we're not studying the Bible as we should, it is accumulating dust; and no good comes from a dusty Bible. Dust on the Bible equals, Hart says, drought in the heart. We might say dust on the Bible creates dust in the heart. What kind of dust? Spiritual dust! The dust that robs us of spiritual vitality and productivity!

All that is in the Bible is true and all of its truth is important, but there is one truth in the Bible that is more important than all the others. That is the truth about the Lord Jesus Christ. As a matter of fact, He is the central theme of the Bible (Luke 24:27,44). Take Him out and you have no Bible left!

The Bible reveals both the truth of Jesus' person (who He was) and His work (what He did to provide salvation for sinners).

Who was He? God! What did He do? He added to His deity our humanity. So He was now fully God and fully man—the God-man! In our humanity, He lived in perfect obedience to God. Then He died on the cross to receive the wrath of God in the place of sinners. After that He arose from the grave and ascended to the Father in heaven. This is the gospel! This is the truth! And what precious truth it is! It is soul-saving truth for the sinner and soul-thrilling truth for the saint.

We must buy this truth. What is its price? Is it a thousand dollars? A million? Ten million? If eternal life could actually be purchased with dollars, many people would be willing to spend a great sum for it. But the purchase price isn't a matter of dollars. Salvation through Christ is free. To buy the truth about Christ simply means we must hear it and heed it.

The Bible says receiving Christ is a matter of believing in Him (John 3:16,36; Acts 16:31). Have we really heard this? Have we really heeded it?

After purchasing the truth, especially the truth of the gospel, we are to preserve it. That means we are to hold on to it at all costs. We are not to "sell out" to false teachers and their teachings, no matter how popular and appealing they may be.

When it comes to the truth, far too many of us are sellers rather than buyers! It's a brutal fact that many will fall for Bible-denying, Christ-denying teachings if those teachings are presented in a humorous and entertaining way. Let us not be counted in their number. Let us know the truth of the Bible, love that truth, and never sell out.

July 31

Wisdom from Annie Johnson Flint

FROM GOD'S WORD, THE BIBLE...

And He said to me, "My grace is sufficient for you, for My strength is made perfect in weakness." Therefore most gladly I will rather boast in my infirmities, that the power of Christ may rest upon me.

2 CORINTHIANS 12:9

Annie Johnson Flint (1866-1932) encountered much hardship in life. When she was only three, her mother died. Her father, stricken with serious disease, arranged for the Flint family to take custody of his children.

Annie had just begun her career of teaching when she was afflicted with arthritis. The disease worsened until it made her an invalid. Her foster parents also died only months apart, leaving Annie and her sister alone and facing financial hardship. These circumstances were such that they would seem to have knocked the faith right out of Annie. But they didn't. Annie had come to faith in Christ when she was only eight years of age, and that faith grew stronger as she traveled her difficult and challenging path. Her problems prompted her to write hymns in which she expressed confidence in God's loving grace and sufficient grace. These may very well be the best-known lines that she ever wrote:

He giveth more grace when the burdens grow greater;
He sendeth more strength when the labors increase.
To added affliction He addeth His mercy;
To multiplied trials, His multiplied peace.
His love has no limit; His grace has no measure.
His power has no boundary known unto men.
For out of His infinite riches in Jesus,
He giveth, and giveth, and giveth again.

The trials I have experienced in life haven't come near those that Annie Johnson Flint knew, but I have often sung my difficulties away with those wonderful words. I have also been immensely blessed by these lines from Annie:

God hath not promised skies always blue,
Flower-strewn pathways all our lives through;
God hath not promised sun without rain,
Joy without sorrow, peace without pain.

God hath not promised we shall not know
Toil and temptation, trouble and woe;
He hath not told us we shall not bear
Many a burden, many a care.

God hath not promised smooth roads and wide,
Swift, easy travel, needing no guide;
Never a mountain, rocky and steep,
Never a river, turbid and deep.

But God hath promised strength for the day,
Rest for the labor, light for the way,
Grace for the trials, help from above,
Unfailing sympathy, undying love.

We needlessly add to the weight of our burdens when we take them to mean that God has failed to keep His promises to us. It's the devil who wants us to think that God has promised to do things for us that He has not promised. And he keeps us from laying claim to what God has promised.

Annie Johnson Flint had a clear view of what God hasn't promised and what He has. God has never promised that our skies will always be cloudless and blue. He has never promised flower-strewn paths, sun without rain, smooth roads and easy travel. If we think that He has promised these things, we will be bitter toward Him when difficulties come our way, and that will keep us from drawing comfort from the things He has promised—strength for the day, rest for the labor, light for the way, grace for the trials, and help from above.

And the best of all that God has promised us is His unfailing sympathy and undying love. If we doubt that sympathy and love, we must look to the cross until this logic is drilled into our hearts: If God would go to that extent to save us, He will never fail to love us. And, hard as it is for us to believe, our trials are part of that love.

Chris Machen calls us to trust the Lord in these words:

Bow the knee; Trust the heart of your Father when the answer
Goes beyond what you can see. Bow the knee;
Lift your eyes toward heaven and believe the
One who holds eternity.
And when you don't understand the purpose of His plan,
In the presence of the King, Bow the knee

I think that Annie must smile approvingly from heaven's glory when she hears the singing of those words.

THE MONTH OF AUGUST

My Dog Knows It's Sunday

... And 30 Other Bible-Based Meditations

I don't know how my dog Molly knows, but she knows. She knows when Sunday arrives. I've tried to figure out how she knows, and I keep coming up empty. But from the very time she gets up on Sunday, she seems to act differently than on other days. Early on Sunday mornings, I place my Bible on the small table by the garage door. But Molly always senses its Sunday before I do that. I wonder what her clue is. Do we know as much as Molly? Do we know that Sunday is special? Do we love Sundays?

Contents

August 1

My Dog Knows It's Sunday

From God's Word, the Bible...

Now on the first day of the week, when the disciples came together to break bread, Paul, ready to depart the next day, spoke to them and continued his message until midnight.

Acts 20:7

I don't know how my dog Molly knows, but she knows. She knows when Sunday arrives. I've tried to figure out how she knows, and I keep coming up empty. But from the very time she gets up on Sunday, she seems to act differently than on other days. Early on Sunday mornings, I place my Bible on the small table by the garage door. But Molly always senses its Sunday before I do that. Before my wife and I start getting dressed for church, Molly knows its Sunday. Maybe it's the hymns. Sylvia and I always listen to hymns as we get ready for church. But Molly seems to know its Sunday before we crank up the hymns. I wonder what her clue is.

Whatever it is, Molly knows its Sunday, and she knows Sunday is different than the other days of the week. It's special. Do we know as much as Molly? Do we know that Sunday is special?

I've seen many changes among God's people over the years. One of the biggest is their attitude toward Sunday. When I was growing up it was commonly believed that God's people should treat Sunday as a day of rest from the things that occupy us the rest of the week. It was regarded as a day for public worship and a day to minister to others.

But many no longer believe that. They believe that there are only nine commandments, not ten. They insist that the Sabbath day commandment no longer applies. They look upon it as something that pertained only to the Jews in the Old Testament era.

It's true, of course, that we no longer observe the Sabbath on Saturday, as the Jews did. The resurrection of Christ was an event of such monumental significance that it changed the day of worship from the seventh day to the first. We can see that change in the life of the early church (Acts 20:7; 1 Cor. 16:2), which apparently made it because the Lord revealed that they should do so.

But the change from the seventh day to the first day doesn't mean that we should treat the day as if it were like all the other days.

Many no longer have a Lord's Day. They have a Lord's Hour, or maybe two hours. We've reached the point where it's acceptable to go to church for an hour on Sunday morning (if it's convenient and there's nothing else we want to do), and then go back to life as usual.

Churches used to encourage people to give the whole of the Lord's Day to the Lord by having both morning and evening worship services, but that practice is largely gone. Church leaders blame church members for the loss of Sunday evening services. They tell us that they had to stop them because the people wouldn't attend. And church members blame church leaders for not giving the Sunday evening services the effort that they deserved.

Several years ago, a lady confronted me in a rather blustery way: "Preacher, we don't have to go to church on Sunday evening. The Bible doesn't command it."

My response was this: "Why don't we want to?" Even if God hadn't commanded us to set apart one day to worship and praise Him, I should think that we would have thought of it ourselves.

What kind of Christianity is it that makes us want to do just as little as we can? What kind of Christianity is it that makes us want to minimize?

I'm happy that the Lord Jesus didn't take the minimal approach to saving us. I'm glad He didn't say to the Father: "Yes, I will go to Bethlehem, but I will not go to Calvary. I will go to earth to show them that You love them, to show them how to live and to teach them Your ways, but I will not die for them. I will not take the wrath that they deserve for their sins."

A minimal Christ doing the minimum for us would never have saved us. Why do we want to do so little for Him when He has done so much for us?

Molly doesn't know much about Sunday except that it's a special day. We who know so much more than she should go out of our way to make it, not just another day, but a special day.

August 2

"He Never Woke Anybody Up"

FROM GOD'S WORD, THE BIBLE...

And do this, knowing the time, that now it is high time to awake out of sleep; for now our salvation is nearer than when we first believed.

Therefore He says:
"Awake, you who sleep,
Arise from the dead,
And Christ will give you light."

ROMANS 13:11; EPHESIANS 5:14

A woman was speaking about her pastor who had recently left to serve another church. She had very kind and positive things to say. "He was a very nice man," she said. "We really loved him," she said. To those statements she added two or three more compliments. It was obvious that she held him in high esteem.

Then she said something rather startling: "But he never woke anybody up."

Those words prompted me to do some soul-searching about my own preaching. Am I waking anybody up?

Sinners need to be awakened. That's for sure. One of our old hymns describes those apart from Christ as "slumbering on the brink of woe."

Saints also need to be awakened. It's very easy for us to slip into a spiritual sleep. No, it's not the sleep of our unconverted days; it's the sleep of indifference or apathy.

I'm sure that the Spirit of God alone can actually awaken sleeping sinners and drowsy saints. But I'm equally sure that the Spirit of God is pleased to use human instruments to accomplish His purposes. He could work without us, but He has chosen to work through us. He can and does work through our words, our actions, our giving, and our prayers to do His awakening work.

Among the means the Spirit uses is the preaching of God's Word, the Bible. The Holy Spirit calls and equips preachers to be awakening agents.

What kind of preaching awakens people? It's not necessarily loud preaching, but an occasional break away from a chatty monotone would be welcome.

The need is rather for seriousness in preaching. Many preachers these days undercut any possibility of waking anybody up by presenting their messages in a very casual, lighthearted way. They seem to be saying: "I'm not very serious about this, and you shouldn't be, either." Listening to them never leaves the impression that they are preaching to eternity-bound people. Their primary concern appears to be getting their hearers to like them. They themselves are really the focus of their own sermons.

No preacher should set out to make his hearers dislike him. The need is rather for the preacher to step to one side so that the people can focus on God. The preacher who insists on showcasing his own cuteness and cleverness will find it hard to get the listeners to think about anything else.

I recall the story of a well-known man going to hear the great George Whitefield preach. When the service was over, someone asked him if Whitefield had convinced him to believe. The man replied: "No, but he convinced me that *he* believes."

The first task of the preacher may very well be to convince his hearers that he believes. He certainly can't expect to convince them to believe if he doesn't first convince them that he believes. Believes what? That God is the holy judge before whom we must all stand and give account! That we are all totally unprepared for that meeting because we have sinned against God time after time! That God has graciously provided through His Son, the Lord Jesus Christ, the way for our sins to be forgiven so that we can stand before Him without fear when He judges! That what the Lord Jesus Christ did for sinners applies to us when we repent of our sins and trust wholly in His redeeming work! That being freed from the condemnation of our sins through Christ is such a wonderful thing that we should gladly devote ourselves to loving the Lord and living for the glory of His name!

In short, preachers are to be great believers in great truths. They are to be men who feel the weight of eternity, but many preachers these days leave the distinct impression that they are either unfamiliar or ill at ease with the central Christian message. Eternity doesn't seem to weigh heavily upon them. They seem to be more in tune with the times than they are with the truth.

Ours is a time of deep sleep. Sinners sleep in one way and saints in another. This time cries for awakening. But what if those charged with awakening others are asleep? How, then, can they be used to awaken anyone else?

August 3

"The word of the LORD came"

From God's Word, the Bible...

Now the word of the Lord came to Jonah the son of Amittai, saying. . .

Jonah 1:1

"The word of the Lord came to Jonah, the son of Amittai. . . ." Now things are different for Jonah. His life is no longer the same. His nest of comfort has been torn up. Everything is now in disarray. Why? Because the word of the Lord that came to Jonah said something that he didn't want it to say. It told him to go to Nineveh, the capital city of Assyria, and "cry out against it" (v. 2). Nineveh, that "great city" was great in wickedness, and the Lord was fed up with both the city and its wickedness.

But that word from the Lord displeased Jonah. He didn't like it. You're thinking that Jonah had such a soft, easygoing spirit that he couldn't bear the thought of God threatening to judge people. But, no, that wasn't it. To the contrary, Jonah, the Jewish prophet, would have welcomed judgment for the Ninevites, who were the sworn enemies of his people. If they were told to repent, they might repent; and if they repented, the judgment Jonah wanted to come wouldn't come.

So Jonah was face to face with the unpleasant word of God.

We shouldn't think the story of Jonah has nothing to do with us. The word of God still comes to us today. I can't say for sure how the word of the Lord came to Jonah. Was it by God speaking out loud? Or was it by a deep, inner persuasion? I don't know. But I can tell you the principal way that the word of God comes today. It comes through Scripture. Yes, the Bible is God's book. He caused it to be written, and He speaks through it to us. He tells us what He wants us to do and what He wants us not to do.

What a marvel the Bible is! It consists of sixty-six books written by approximately forty men over a period of 1,600 years. And these forty men came from many walks of life and represented various levels of learning. David and Solomon were kings. Paul was a scholarly rabbi. Peter and John, on the other hand, were common, ordinary fishermen, and Matthew was a tax collector.

Those details wouldn't be so impressive if it weren't for the fact that all of these men over all those ages produced a book that has one glorious theme—God providing forgiveness for sinners through His Son, the Lord Jesus Christ.

Through the Bible, God speaks to us. He calls us to repent of our sins and trust in His Son. He calls us to see sin in all of its ugly reality and to hate it as He hates it. He calls us to see how helpless we are in dealing with our sin and to flee to the way of salvation that He has provided. He calls us to abandon our own wisdom and bow before His wisdom, the wisdom that He used to put together the plan of salvation.

God doesn't stop speaking to us in the Bible when we bow before Him in repentance and faith and receive His salvation. He tells us to live for His honor, praise, and glory after we're saved.

Some think they can avoid the word of the Lord. If they don't read or hear it, they're not responsible for it! That's their reasoning. So they spend their lives as if God hasn't spoken at all or as if His words don't apply to them. All who think along such lines would do well to check with Jonah. The little book that bears his name exists to show us the utter folly of trying to avoid the word of the Lord. God speaks in the Bible whether we read it or hear it, and He holds us responsible for it even if we ignore it.

The book of Revelation tells us that on the great day of final judgment, certain "books" will be opened (Rev. 20:12). I don't doubt for a moment that the Bible will be among those books. On that day, people will be confronted with how God expected them to live and will be made to see how their lives measured up or failed to measure up.

Awesome thought! The Bible itself will be on hand to greet us when we go out into eternity. Let us heed it now so we don't have to fear it then.

August 4

Why Believe the Bible?

From God's Word, the Bible...

And so we have the prophetic word confirmed, which you do well to heed as a light that shines in a dark place, until the day dawns and the morning star rises in your hearts; knowing this first, that no prophecy of Scripture is of any private interpretation, for prophecy never came by the will of man, but holy men of God spoke as they were moved by the Holy Spirit.

2 Peter 1:19-21

The word of the Lord came to Jonah, and the word of the Lord still comes to people today. The primary way that we receive God's Word is through Scripture.

But how can we be sure that the Bible is really God's Word? I wasn't a Christian very long until I discovered that the Bible was widely rejected as the inspired Word of God. The impression that the skeptics created was that those who believed the Bible did so because they were ignorant know-nothings and not because there was any compelling evidence.

I soon learned that I had several substantial reasons for accepting the inspiration and authority of the Bible:

- its many, many fulfilled prophecies (Jesus Himself is estimated to have fulfilled 325 Old Testament prophecies. The mathematical probability of one man doing this is off the charts!);
- its survival even though it has been fiercely attacked;
- the changed lives of those who believe the Bible and seek to obey it;
- the correspondence of the Bible to what we observe all around us;
- the astounding discoveries of archaeologists.

These are very persuasive evidences. But the truly decisive thing for me was that Jesus obviously accepted the authority of the Scriptures, and Jesus was not just another man. The miracles that He performed and the way He spoke made it plain that He was the God-man, that is, God in human flesh. But the supreme proof of His identity was His own resurrection from the dead. Ordinary men don't come out of their graves, but Jesus came out of His grave, proving, as Paul says, that He was and is "the Son of God with power" (Rom. 1:4).

How can we be sure that Jesus actually arose from the dead? The tomb was empty. Many people saw Him, and many of them were changed by Him.

Presented with such evidence, any unbiased jury could hand down only one verdict—Jesus arose!

With such evidence for such a person, doesn't it make sense to accept His testimony regarding the Bible? Even if it means I must set aside the conclusions of thousands of scholars, I will accept the testimony of Jesus. His credentials put Him in a class by Himself.

This is the Jesus who put His stamp of approval on Holy Scripture, and the question each believer must face is quite simple: how can we call Him our Lord if we reject what He taught about the Bible? We would also do well to ask this: if Jesus was wrong about the Bible, what else was He wrong about?

It's clear that Jesus endorsed the Old Testament during His public ministry. He explicitly affirmed its authority (Matt. 5:17-18; John 10:35). In His controversies with the religious leaders, He appealed to it as His authority (e.g., Matt. 22:23-33). He also seems to have gone out of His way to certify those parts of it that are most often dismissed as myths. Adam and Eve (Matt. 19:4-5), Noah and the ark (Matt. 24:37-39), the fiery judgment on Sodom and the terrible fate of Lot's wife (Luke 17:28-32), the miraculous ministries of Elijah and Elisha (Luke 4:25-27), Jonah and the great fish (Matt. 12:39-41)—all were treated by Jesus as historical facts.

But what about the New Testament? It wasn't in existence during Jesus' ministry. Are we supposed to believe that He accepted something that didn't exist?

This brings us to the concept of pre-endorsement. This means that Jesus assured in advance that the New Testament would indeed be the infallible Word of God. He did so by promising His disciples that the Holy Spirit would call things to their remembrance, thus providing for the Gospel accounts (John 14:26); would guide them into all truth, thus providing for the epistles (John 16:13); and would show them things to come, thus providing for the book of Revelation (John 16:13).

So no matter where we turn in Scripture, we may rest assured that the Lord Jesus Himself has, as it were, initialed every page!

And the same Holy Spirit who caused the Bible to be written works within us to convince us that it is God's Word. We don't believe the Bible simply because the Bible tells us to believe the Bible but rather because the Spirit of God tells us to believe it as we read it.

August 5

How the Word of God Comes to Us (1)

From God's Word, the Bible…

All Scripture is given by inspiration of God, and is profitable for doctrine, for reproof, for correction, for instruction in righteousness, that the man of God may be complete, thoroughly equipped for every good work.

2 Timothy 3:16-17

"The word of the Lord came to Jonah, the son of Amittai. . . ." And, as we've noticed, God's Word comes to us primarily through the Bible.

The Bible speaks to us in various ways. One is the way that a doctor speaks to his or her patients. That manner of speaking generally consists of two parts—diagnosis and prescription.

The Bible speaks to us in those same ways. First, there is *the diagnostic way*. As a doctor diagnoses the physical condition of his or her patient, so the Bible diagnoses our spiritual condition.

With our physical condition, the main thing we want from our doctor is the truth. We don't want him or her to sweep the truth under the rug because we might find that truth to be unpleasant. If a doctor did that, we would soon offer a two-word diagnosis of our own: bad doctor!

The Bible is a good doctor. It tells us the truth about ourselves—very unpleasant truth! It tells us that we are all sinners (Rom. 3:23), and that our sins merit the judgment of God (Rom. 6:23). We were made by God to live for the glory and the honor of His name. We were to do that by worshiping and obeying Him. But sin pulls us away from that grand purpose. It causes us to worship ourselves and to rebel against God's commandments.

In the previous reading, I mentioned that one reason to believe the Bible is that it corresponds to what we see around us. When I take a long look at the world and at myself, I see the sinfulness that the Bible tells me about.

The Bible also comes to us in *a prescriptive way*. Doctors diagnose diseases, and they prescribe treatments for those diseases.

The Bible very emphatically declares that we are sinners, but it also prescribes a cure. That cure is the Lord Jesus Christ. He came to this earth for the specific purpose of healing or saving sinners (Matt. 1:21; Luke 19:10).

What exactly did Jesus do? He first took our humanity. As one of us, He could do something for us or on our behalf. In our humanity, He lived without sin. Since He had no sin of His own to pay for, He could pay for the sins of others. And pay He did! On the cross He received the penalty for sinners so all who believe in Him don't have to pay that same penalty themselves. But that's not all. After He died on the cross, He arose from the grave. In so doing, He proved that He was indeed God in human flesh, and that His death on the cross did indeed provide the salvation that sinners need.

What Jesus did in His living, dying, and rising is the way of salvation. Please notice that it is "the way," not "a way" (John 14:6; Acts 4:12; 1 Tim. 2:5-6). This teaching disturbs lots of people. In their opinion, to say that there is only one way of salvation is to be narrow-minded, bigoted, and intolerant.

But if these same people were to be told by their doctors that they have a very serious disease for which there is only one cure, they would be glad for that cure! They wouldn't fuss and fume about it, and they wouldn't refuse to accept it because there weren't a dozen other cures.

For the horrible disease of sin, I don't need a dozen cures. I only need one. And if Jesus is the cure, I say: "Let me have Jesus." And I can have Him by repenting of my sins and trusting in what He did for sinners. You can have Him too!

So the Bible comes to us in a diagnostic way, telling us about our sins. And it comes to us in a prescriptive way, telling us about what the Lord Jesus did and urging us to believe in Him. It's not surprising, then, that John Burton could write these words:

Holy Bible, Book divine,
Precious treasure, thou art mine;
Mine to tell me whence I came;
Mine to teach me what I am;
Mine to chide me when I rove;
Mine to show a Savior's love. . . .

August 6

How the Word of God Comes to Us (2)

FROM GOD'S WORD, THE BIBLE...

The LORD is my shepherd;
I shall not want.
He makes me to lie down in green pastures;
He leads me beside the still waters.
He restores my soul;
He leads me in the paths of righteousness
For His name's sake.
Yea, though I walk through the valley of the shadow of death,
I will fear no evil;
For You are with me;
Your rod and Your staff, they comfort me.

PSALM 23:1-4

We have noticed that the Word of God comes to us as a doctor to diagnose and prescribe. We can also say that it comes to us as a shepherd. The Lord Jesus, who is the Good Shepherd, uses the Word of God to shepherd us.

The Bible refers to God's people as sheep (Ps. 95:7; 100:3; John 10:26-30). We probably shouldn't take this as a compliment. Sheep are rather dumb and helpless. They are easy prey for predators, and they easily stray.

Sheep need a shepherd. They can't survive and thrive without one. The shepherd does four main things for his sheep. He feeds them, protects them, guides them, and finds them when they stray.

The Lord Jesus, who is the Good Shepherd, uses the Word of God to shepherd us. He *feeds* us with it. It is the food that God has developed and designed for our spiritual growth and health (1 Peter 2:2).

Psalm 23:1 refers to the shepherd making his sheep lie down in green pastures. The Word of God is our green pasture. If we don't feed on it as we should, we make ourselves scrawny sheep.

The Lord also *protects* us through God's Word. Just as there are predators who are eager to dine on sheep, so God's people are constantly surrounded with spiritual predators who are happy to dine on them.

The Bible protects us from these spiritual predators by first telling us that they exist. The Bible often warns us about false teachers. It also informs us about the nature of their teachings (2 Cor. 11:1-4, 13-15; Gal. 1:6-9; Phil. 3:1-2, 17-19; 2 Peter 2:1-22; 1 John 4:1-3; Jude 3-19).

False teachers are very subtle. They don't blatantly announce that they are false teachers who are out to undermine and destroy our faith. They may very well profess to love the Bible. The key thing to keep in mind is what they do with the Bible. Do they accurately proclaim its message? The Bible's main subject is the redeeming work of Christ. When we are listening to preachers and teachers, we should always ask ourselves if they are exalting Christ in the same way that the Bible does. Are they proclaiming His supernatural birth, His sinless life, His substitutionary and sacrificial death, His stunning resurrection and ascension, and His soon-coming return?

The Lord also *guides* us with the Word of God. Psalm 23 refers to the Lord leading His sheep "beside still waters" (v. 2). Because sheep won't drink from turbulent water, the shepherd must use large stones to stop the current and create quiet waters so the sheep can drink and be refreshed. The Lord uses His Word to calm and refresh our spirits. Psalm 23 also mentions the shepherd leading his sheep in "the paths of righteousness" (v. 3). The Bible tells us what righteous living is, namely, conforming our lives to its teachings. It shows us the blessings that come our ay when we engage in righteous living, and the heartaches that come our way when we don't.

The Bible guides us to righteous living by giving us both negative and positive commands, that is, it tells us not to do certain things, and it tells us to do certain things. It also gives us examples of people who lived righteously and of those who didn't.

Finally, the Lord also *finds* His straying sheep by using His Word. In Psalm 23:3, David mentions the Lord restoring his soul.

Sheep are always prone to stray, as Jonah did. But the Lord doesn't give up on us when we stray. We don't cease to be His sheep when we stray. Once a sheep, always a sheep! That's how it is with us when we belong to Him. When we stray, He doesn't re-save us, but He does restore us. And He often uses the Word of God to do so. He may cause one of its warnings to suddenly spring to mind. Or He may remind us of one of His promises. He may even prompt us to think of the experience of Jonah and to determine that we are going to follow Jesus and not Jonah.

As the word of the Lord came to Jonah, so it comes to God's people today in a shepherdly way. How very blessed we are to have it! May God help us to heed it!

August 7

Races and Runners

From God's Word, the Bible...

Now the word of the Lord came to Jonah the son of Amittai, saying, "Arise, go to Nineveh, that great city, and cry out against it; for their wickedness has come up before Me." But Jonah arose to flee to Tarshish from the presence of the Lord. He went down to Joppa, and found a ship going to Tarshish; so he paid the fare, and went down into it, to go with them to Tarshish from the presence of the Lord.

Jonah 1:1-3

The word of the Lord came, and Jonah went—in exactly the opposite direction! He found a ship going to Tarshish. Many commentators think this Tarshish was located in Spain.

Take a glance at a map, and you easily get the picture. Jonah was in Israel. Nineveh was east of there in Assyria, and Tarshish was west of Israel in Spain. And Spain was not just a little west of Israel. It was *really* west.

So Jonah's decision to go to Spain was disobedience with an exclamation point. Jonah wasn't merely refusing to go to Nineveh. He was going to get as far away from it as possible. Jonah's answer to serving God in the far East was to go to the far West!

There was a time when Jonah ran for God and ran well. God would say, "Go there," and he would go. God would say, "Go over yonder," and Jonah would go (2 Kings 14:25).

But God has now commanded him to go to Nineveh, and he is running away. Was he running from his responsibility? Yes, he certainly was. But verse 3 tells us two times that he was running "from the presence of the Lord."

This, then, is the connection we must make: when we run from obedience, we run from God.

Some seem to have the idea that they can live close to God and disobey His commands. It isn't so. To run from God's commands is to run from God Himself. Those who think that they can throw down their spiritual responsibilities at the drop of a hat and still be close to God are fooling themselves. We have a tendency to assume that we are close to God if we have warm, fuzzy feelings about Him. But the Lord doesn't leave us to define for ourselves what constitutes closeness to Him. He defines it for us, and His definition includes obedience to His commands (Luke 6:46).

The first part of Jonah's story, then, is the story of God setting a race before Jonah, and Jonah refusing to run that race.

Jonah always makes me think of another runner in another race. Before this world saw its first day, God the Father said to His Son: "I have a race for You to run. It is the race of saving sinners. This race will require You to take their humanity and to live without sin in that humanity. It will cause You to be hated and despised by many, and to die on a Roman cross a special kind of death, one in which You will actually endure My wrath against sinners."

The Lord Jesus looked at the race set before Him by the Father and said: "I will run it." And run it He did! Without faltering or stumbling, He ran redemption's race until He burst across the finish line on the cross as He cried out: "It is finished!" (John 19:30). Had Jesus stopped short in His race, there would have been no salvation for any of us. But He didn't stop short. Thank God for Jesus, the faithful runner! He is the greatest runner who has run the greatest race.

All of us who have taken Jesus as our Lord and Savior now have our own race to run. It is the race of loving Him, worshipping Him, serving Him, trusting Him, and, yes, obeying Him. Our choice is ever to run the Jonah race or the Jesus race. The author of Hebrews urges us to run the latter: ". . . let us lay aside every weight, and the sin which so easily ensnares us, and let us run with endurance the race that is set before us, looking unto Jesus, the author and finisher of our faith, who for the joy that was set before Him, endured the cross, despising the shame, and has sat down at the right hand of the throne of God" (Heb. 12:1b-2).

Jonah refused to run the Jesus race. He ran the Jonah race, and he ran into trouble. We can be assured that he would now tell each of us to not do as he did. He would tell us to run the Jesus race, no matter what the cost.

August 8

Why Jonah Ran

From God's Word, the Bible...

You ran well. Who hindered you from obeying the truth?

Galatians 5:7

Why did Jonah run from God? On *the surface level*, we must say Jonah didn't love those whom God loved. God loved the Ninevites (Jonah 4:2). Jonah didn't. Jonah wanted the Ninevites to be None-evites. As far as he was concerned, it was a good thing for God to be planning to bring judgment upon them. If there were no Ninevites, they could never be a threat to the people of Israel.

It's never a good thing when we try to do God's thinking for Him, and that's exactly what we like to do. When it comes to the governing of the affairs of this world, we want to come alongside God and say: "Let me help You with that."

We need to realize that God does His own thinking, and His thinking is never mistaken. Elihu was certainly right to ask of God:

Who has assigned Him His way,
Or who has said, "You have done wrong"?
(Job 36:23)

Centuries later, the prophet Isaiah similarly asked:

Who has directed the Spirit of the Lord,
Or as His counselor has taught Him?
(Isa. 40:13)

The Apostle Paul may have been thinking of the questions of both Elihu and Isaiah when he wrote:

For who has known the mind of the Lord:
Or who has become His counselor?
(Rom. 11:34)

God told Jonah to go to Nineveh, and Jonah essentially said to God: "You can't mean that!" In regard to the things of God, those words can easily pop into our minds and burst from our lips. They may very well do so more frequently in connection with the cross of Christ than with any other matter. When God points to His Son dying on the cross and declares that as our only hope for salvation, many want to say to Him: "You can't mean that!"

That cross makes no sense at all to us if the Spirit of God doesn't enlighten us (1 Cor. 2:14). A man dying on a cross is the way for us to have our sins forgiven and to go to heaven? How ridiculous! And we are supposed to come humbly to that cross repenting of our sins, trusting in what Jesus did there, and renouncing every other hope for salvation? Absurd! We are intelligent, sophisticated human beings, and we refuse to accept such ludicrous teaching!

After all of our posturing and pontificating and our ranting and raging, God still points to that cross and says: "That's My way of salvation!" To everyone who says to Him: "You can't mean that," God simply says: "I most certainly do!" And those of us who have been rescued from our sins by that cross gladly chime in with the Apostle Paul: "For the message of the cross is foolishness to those who are perishing, but to us who are being saved it is the power of God" (1 Cor. 1:18).

Psalm 2 powerfully pictures this for us. The great people of the earth "take counsel together" against God and His Son and arrogantly assert that they are not going to bow in submission. How does the Lord respond? Does He fly into a panic? Hardly. He rather laughs at them and says:

Yet I have set My King
On the holy hill of Zion.
(Ps. 2:6)

We don't have to be among the great people of this earth to make their great mistake. Whether great or small, the person who thinks he or she knows better than God had better think again.

We must also go to *a deeper level* to explain Jonah's running. I will put it bluntly: he was a backslider.

Backsliding used to be a commonly used word. It's not so common any more. But the fact that the word has become rare doesn't mean that backsliding itself has become rare.

What is backsliding? It is the Christian losing ground. It's not him or her losing salvation. That can never be! (John 10:27-30; Phil. 1:6). It's rather the Christian sliding back or slipping back from where he or she once was and ought still to be. It's the Christian slipping in love, that is, loving the highest thing (God) less and loving lower things more.

By including the account of Jonah in the Bible, God put backsliding in all of its ugliness on display so we can see it, be repulsed by it, and not do it.

August 9

Backsliding

From God's Word, the Bible...

Yet they did not obey or incline their ear, but followed the counsels and the dictates of their evil hearts, and went backward and not forward.

And they have turned to Me the back, and not the face; though I taught them, rising up early and teaching them, yet they have not listened to receive instruction.

Jeremiah 7:24; Jeremiah 32:33

Since Jonah has brought up the subject of backsliding, we need to consider it. Why consider something so unpleasant and distasteful? One reason is its prominence in Scripture. Verses that use some form of the word "backslide" appear seventeen times in the Bible. Then there are the other words that the Bible uses for backsliding such as "forsake" (appearing approximately fifty times) and "depart" (Isa. 59:13; Heb. 3:12). Then we have the sad accounts of saints who backslid at some point. Noah, Lot, Jacob, Samson, David, Solomon, and Simon Peter all come readily to mind.

Another reason is that the subject is of practical importance. The wellbeing of our families, our churches, our nation, and ourselves all hinge to a large degree on God's people staying close to Him.

In the previous reading, we defined backsliding as the Christian slipping back or sliding back from where he or she once was and ought still to be.

Let's take a stroll down memory lane to that time when we were converted. Conversion means change, and there is no more radical change than becoming a Christian. The Apostle Paul likens it to becoming a new creature (2 Cor. 5:17).

Conversion radically changed our thinking. We came to see ourselves as guilty sinners before a holy God. We saw ourselves facing eternal destruction, and we came to understand that Christ's atoning death on the cross was the only way that we could be freed from God's wrath. How exceedingly precious the gospel was to us in those days!

Conversion also profoundly changed our desires. Sinful things lost their luster as we began to enjoy God's Word, prayer, and church services. We had a zeal for God and a desire and determination to do His work. We also had a love for God's people and a desire for others to know Him.

Conversion also changed our behavior. We began to order our lives in keeping with God's commandments. Old habits melted away as we began giving priority to pleasing God.

Backsliding affects each of those areas. Our thinking is not as much in tune with God's Word as it was. The gospel doesn't seem quite as precious to us as it once did. Our desires are also affected. We discover that we don't have our hearts in serving the Lord. Coldness has set in. Zeal has been replaced with a lack of interest. Our behavior is also affected as we go back to some of the sinful behavior that we had laid aside.

Conversion to Christ consists of a forsaking, on the one hand, and an embracing on the other. In conversion we radically broke with our sins, our false gods, and our worldly thinking and doing to embrace God as the only true God and our rightful sovereign. We took His ways as our ways, His laws as our laws, His cause as our cause, His people as our people and His Word as our authority.

Backsliding is going back to embrace those things we forsook for God. It is a forsaking of God for those things that we once forsook for Him.

What causes us to backslide? We know that we have a very powerful and clever enemy, the devil. If he can't prevent us from coming to Christ, the next best thing for him is to prevent us from living as a Christian ought to live. The Apostle Peter portrays him as a prowling lion who is seeking to devour Christians (1 Peter 5:8).

We also know that the world is very strong and alluring. It is always exerting pressure on us to conform to its thinking and doing (Rom. 12:2). It's a sad fact that many individual Christians, many pastors, and many churches seem to fear being out of step with the world. The latest opinion poll seems to be more important to them than the Bible.

We also know that our flesh is very weak, causing us to crave those things that "war against the soul" (1 Peter 2:11).

The Lord Jesus was "in all points tempted as we are," yet He did not sin (Heb. 4:15). Jesus knew all about the devil, the world, and the flesh. He was confronted by the strength of each, but He didn't waver. He forged ahead to complete the work of redemption. The more we look to Him, the less inclined we will be to backslide.

August 10

Watch!

FROM GOD'S WORD, THE BIBLE...

Watch, stand fast in the faith, be brave, be strong.

Be sober, be vigilant; because your adversary the devil walks about like a roaring lion, seeking whom he may devour. Resist him, steadfast in the faith, knowing that the same sufferings are experienced by your brotherhood in the world.

1 CORINTHIANS 16:13; 1 PETER 5:8-9

Jonah's experience of backsliding warns all us who know the Lord to be watching ourselves. All of us are watching certain things. I don't mean to say that we never take our eyes off these things, but rather we are continually aware of them and prepared to take appropriate action to preserve and protect them. We watch our appearance, our manners, our children, our reputations, our possessions, our health, our driving, and so on. People used to watch their language, but that particular watching seems to be less and less common.

Think about all of these watchings. What do they have in common? When we say we're watching something, what are we really saying? Aren't we affirming in each case that something we value could very well be threatened in such a way that we would be deprived of our enjoyment of it? We value our health, but we're always aware that there are threats to it that we must guard against, so we can continue to enjoy it. The Bible teaches us that a close walk with God is something of real value that is constantly being threatened. It is something that we can be deprived of if we aren't awake and alert.

How valuable is it to walk close to God? If we fail to do so, we:

- cause Him to be displeased with us (Eph. 4:30; 1 Thess. 5:19);
- bring a hardness into our own hearts (Ps. 95:7-8);
- bring harm to others (2 Sam. 12:14);
- rob ourselves of spiritual comfort and assurance (Ps. 32:3-4);
- invite God to visit us with chastisement (Heb. 12:7; 1 Cor. 11:31-32).

It's plain, isn't it? A close walk with God is worth watching. So let's watch. Let's watch our prayer life. How easy it is to be careless here! It's easy to say: "I know that I should pray, but I just don't feel like doing it." The key is to pray until we do feel like doing it. When Simon Peter, James, and John didn't feel like praying in the Garden of Gethsemane, Jesus said to them: "Watch and pray, lest you enter into temptation. The spirit truly is ready, but the flesh is weak" (Mark 14:38).

Let's watch our church attendance. If we've been cutting back, we must devote ourselves afresh to being faithful. I'm always astonished when I hear someone say that there aren't any commands in the Bible for us to attend church. Every time I hear that I call to mind these words: "And let us consider one another in order to stir up love and good works, not forsaking the assembling of ourselves together, as is the manner of some. . . ." (Heb. 10:24-25a).

Let's watch how we respond while we are in the services of the church. Do we allow ourselves to be distracted by other things and preoccupied with other things? We all know that it is very easy to be present in church without really being present. Over the years, I have frequently noticed among those who attend services what I call "the donut effect." While they are present, they are "glazed over." They don't know or appreciate what is going on in the service because they are not really there.

All too often we let duty swallow up delight. We attend services because we regard this as our duty to do so, but we take no delight in the services. We listen to the preaching because it is our duty to do so, but we don't delight in the truth of God.

Let's make sure we dwell much on the cost of walking afar off from God. It is, as noted above, a costly thing.

Let's make sure that we dwell much on what the Lord Jesus Christ did for us when He died on the cross. And when it comes time to observe the Lord's Supper, let's be sure that we are present—really present—to think deeply with profound gratitude about the Lord Jesus going to the cross to shed His blood for us. The cross of Christ, rightly perceived, always warms our hearts and wards off coldness. It is always our greatest protection against backsliding.

Jesus, keep me near the cross,
There a precious fountain
Free to all—a healing stream,
Flows from Calvary's mountain.

In the cross, in the cross,
Be my glory ever;
Till my raptured soul shall find
Rest beyond the river.
(Fanny J. Crosby)

If we want to watch against backsliding, we must watch the cross.

Storms and Sleepers

From God's Word, the Bible...

But the Lord sent out a great wind on the sea, and there was a mighty tempest on the sea, so that the ship was about to be broken up.

Jonah 1:4

If we take one step down the wrong road, it may be very hard for us to find an exit ramp. Jonah took one step on the wrong road when he thought that he knew better than God on the matter of the Ninevites. He took another step on that same road when he actually thought he could escape from God.

For a while, Jonah must have thought that he had succeeded. Everything seemed to fall into place. He apparently journeyed from Gath-Hepher to Joppa without incident. He found a ship that was sailing far from Israel. He had enough money to pay the fare. The ship soon got underway. Jonah was able to go to sleep in the hold of the ship. And there was no sign of God anywhere! Perhaps God had changed His plan to send a prophet to Nineveh. Or perhaps He had found Himself another prophet. Whatever the case, Jonah was off the hook—or so it seemed!

Many years ago, a popular song featured this line: "I fought the law, and the law won." Jonah was about to learn in very dramatic and powerful ways that the one who fights God ends up singing: "I fought the Lord, and the Lord won."

Jonah's experience on the ship gives us insight into the nature of God. For one thing, God is all-knowing. He never needs information. He didn't need anyone to tell Him about Jonah's slipping and sleeping, that is, his slipping down to Joppa and sleeping in the ship.

And God is all-powerful. When He wants to do something, He never lacks the resources to get it done. In Jonah's case, God had a storm, the ship's captain and crew, and a fish all lined up and waiting.

If we could only keep in our minds the all-seeing, powerful God, it would surely keep us from many foolish thoughts, words, and deeds, and from the many heartaches produced by those things.

First came the storm. A frightful one it was! The wind was so "great" and the tempest so "mighty" that "the ship was about to be broken up."

That storm came directly from God! It was "sent out" by Him. The words "sent out" translate a Hebrew word that means "hurled." Get this picture: Jonah is blissfully sleeping in a ship, and God takes dead aim at that ship and hurls this storm toward it as a man would hurl a javelin.

Wasn't God being rather vindictive and vengeful toward Jonah? Will you be surprised if I say God hurled that storm toward His disobedient prophet with a heart of love? It was love that refused to let Jonah go. It was love that was determined to bring him back. How thankful we should be for divine love that refuses to give up on us!

O Love that wilt not let me go,
I rest my weary soul in Thee;
I give Thee back the life I owe,
That in Thine ocean depths its flow
May richer, fuller be.
(George Matheson)

The storm raging and Jonah sleeping! That calls to mind another boat, another storm, and another sleeper. Jesus was in a boat with His disciples when "a great tempest arose on the sea" (Matt. 8:24). While the storm raged, Jesus slept. But with those details we come to the end of the similarities with the prophet. Jonah was sleeping to escape a demanding ministry. The Lord Jesus slept as a result of meeting the many demands of ministry (Matt 8:1-22). And the storm in which Jonah slept came to correct him. The storm in which Jesus slept came as an opportunity for Him to correct His disciples for their little faith and for them to see more of His glory (Matt. 8:26-27). Also, the storm in which Jonah found himself stopped when he was thrown overboard (Jonah 1:15). The storm that came upon Jesus stopped as a result of His command and while He was still in the boat.

What a difference between Jonah and Jesus! Having had crucial work set before him, Jonah played the part of an escapee. But Jesus never tried to escape from the work the Father set before Him. Instead of turning from it, He set His face toward it. Because He didn't try to escape God's commands, all who turn to Him in repentance and faith can escape their sins and condemnation.

August 12

The Captain and the Crew

From God's Word, the Bible...

So the captain came to him, and said to him, "What do you mean, sleeper? Arise, call on your God; perhaps your God will consider us, so that we may not perish." And they said to one another, "Come, let us cast lots, that we may know for whose cause this trouble has come upon us." So they cast lots, and the lot fell on Jonah. Then they said to him, "Please tell us! For whose cause is this trouble upon us? What is your occupation? And where do you come from? What is your country? And of what people are you?" o he said to them, "I am a Hebrew; and I fear the Lord, the God of heaven, who made the sea and the dry land."

Jonah 1:6-9
(Read the whole passage in Jonah 1:4-16.)

It's one thing to run. It's quite another to escape. Jonah had run from God, but he hadn't escaped Him. God was in pursuit, and God always pursues faster than we can flee.

As noted in the previous reading, God had His instruments all lined up for bringing Jonah back to where he needed to be. First in line was the storm. Then came the captain of the ship, his crew, and the casting of lots.

God used the captain to rebuke Jonah for sleeping when he should have been praying. Ouch! A pagan rebuking a child of God for not praying!

I wonder when Jonah last prayed—really prayed! Backsliding and praying don't go hand in hand. If we pray, we don't backslide. If we backslide, we don't pray. Jonah had been backsliding

God also used the crew to wring from Jonah the truth about himself. Sad, isn't it, when a child of God conceals his faith from unbelievers!

The crewmembers somehow sensed that there was something unusual about this storm. They weren't willing to chalk it up to mere chance. They were convinced that this storm was someone's fault, and they were determined to discover the guilty party by casting lots.

Jonah knew he didn't have a chance when those lots were cast. He knew why the storm had come. It was the Lord who had sent it because of his disobedience, and he also knew whose hand would direct the hand that cast those lots. It was God's hand, and, just as Jonah expected, the lot fell on him, and the sailors demanded an explanation from Jonah. Then the truth came out. Jonah identified himself as a Hebrew and as a servant of the Lord and told them that he had "fled from the presence of the Lord" (v. 10).

So the sailors now knew the reason for the storm. It was Jonah. But what were they to do with him? Jonah solved the problem for them. The only way for them to calm the tempest was to throw him overboard (v. 12). Those sailors tried to spare him, but the storm only increased in its ferocity. The only thing left to do was what Jonah asked them to do.

So the prophet who was unwilling to save the pagans of Nineveh now saves the lives of these pagan sailors by laying down his life. As we know, it didn't actually cost Jonah his life, but he surely thought it would. This must surely make us think of the One greater than Jonah who was never for one moment unwilling to save the godless. This One knew for sure that He would have to lay down His life to save sinners, and lay it down He did. His name is Jesus (John 15:13).

Jonah correctly thought that he would save the lives of those sailors by laying down his life. What he didn't know until later was that he was also saving their souls. He was no sooner overboard than the storm ceased, and those men turned to the God of Jonah in true faith (v. 16).

We read no more of these men in Scripture, but it could very well be that they went on to Spain and there planted the seeds of the gospel.

What a joy it will be to meet these men in heaven and hear each one give his own account of a dreadful storm, a disobedient prophet, and God's saving grace!

This part of Jonah's story is dripping with irony. Jonah, who should have been a man of prayer, has to be told by a pagan captain to pray. Jonah, a man of God who should have always been eager to confess his identity and his God, has to have that confession wrung from him. And Jonah, unwilling to be part of saving the pagans in Nineveh, is used by God to save pagans on a ship.

Have we learned from Jonah? Have we learned to constantly guard against backsliding? Have we learned to ever nurture the life of prayer? Have we learned to always be ready to confess our faith? Have we learned to desire the salvation of all sinners? Most importantly, have we learned to look beyond Jonah, the unwilling prophet, to the One who is greater than Jonah, that is, the Lord Jesus Christ, who earnestly desires the salvation of sinners?

August 13

One Big Gulp

From God's Word, the Bible...

Now the Lord had prepared a great fish to swallow Jonah. And Jonah was in the belly of the fish three days and three nights.

Jonah 1:17

If Jonah thought he would perish in the sea, he was in for a huge surprise. That huge surprise came in the form of a huge fish. That fish was the last in the string of instruments that God had lined up to bring His backsliding prophet to obedience.

When Jonah hit the water, the fish was waiting. That fish gulped Jonah down without so much as a spoonful of tartar sauce! One big gulp was all that it took. One big gulp and Jonah was down. Farther down than he had ever been before. Farther down than he ever thought he could go. Down into the belly of a fish, and into the depths of the sea!

Are we really supposed to believe this happened? I respond to that by asking this question: Do we own Jesus as our Lord? If we do, we must not deny that Jonah was swallowed by that great fish because Jesus Himself used this account to affirm His own resurrection (Matt. 12:39-40). To deny the fish, we must deny the teaching of the Lord.

Let's say for a moment that Jonah was not actually swallowed by the fish. We can agree that Jesus either didn't know this or that He did. Now *if Jesus didn't know* that Jonah wasn't swallowed, Jesus was mistaken because He obviously thought something occurred that didn't.

But what *if Jesus knew* that Jonah wasn't swallowed by the fish? That would make Jesus devious in that He used something He knew didn't happen to convince His followers that His resurrection would happen.

So if we say Jonah wasn't actually swallowed by the fish, we must choose between a mistaken Jesus (who thought Jonah was swallowed) or a devious Jesus (who knew Jonah wasn't swallowed but acted as if he were).

The Lord Jesus was not mistaken or devious. He knew the truth about Jonah, and the truth was that Jonah was swallowed by the great fish and was, therefore, a most appropriate and fitting picture of Jesus' soon-coming resurrection.

Did Jonah actually die while he was in the fish? It could be that he did. If so, God resurrected him, and that would certainly make him an even more perfect picture of the resurrection of Jesus. We can ask Jonah in heaven.

One thing we know for sure is that Jonah prayed while he was in the fish.

We may be surprised that Jonah was swallowed by a fish. We surely aren't surprised that Jonah prayed from that fish. How he prayed! It would help us to pray if we would keep in mind that God always has ways to bring us to prayer. Let's discipline ourselves to pray so the Lord won't have to discipline us to pray.

There is tremendous encouragement from Jonah praying while he was in the belly of the fish. He shows us that we can pray from any place or from any set of circumstances, and still be heard by God. When we feel as if we are in the belly of a whale all on our own, we can pray. What a consolation!

The way to read the book of Jonah is to keep one eye on Jonah and the other eye on Jesus. As we read about the prophet plummeting into the depths of the sea because of his disobedience to God, our minds should be drawn to Jesus on the cross. It was there that Jesus plummeted into the immeasurable depths of God's wrath. But Jesus plummeted into those depths, not because of His disobedience to God, but rather because of ours (Rom. 5:6,8; 2 Cor. 5:21; 1 Peter 2:24). Jonah went unwillingly into the abyss for God to accomplish a great purpose. The Lord Jesus went down to far greater depths for God to accomplish a far greater purpose.

There is, as we noted above, another link between Jonah and Jesus. The fish wasn't the final resting place for Jonah, and the grave wasn't the final resting place for Jesus. He burst from His grave in glorious resurrection life, and He lives today.

Up from the grave He arose,
With a mighty triumph over His foes;
He arose a victor from the dark domain,
And He lives forever with His saint to reign.
He arose! He arose!
Hallelujah! Christ arose!
(Robert Lowry)

August 14

Jonah's Revival

FROM GOD'S WORD, THE BIBLE...

Then Jonah prayed to the LORD his God from the fish's belly. And he said: "I cried out to the LORD because of my affliction,
And He answered me.
"Out of the belly of Sheol I cried,
And You heard my voice.
For You cast me into the deep,
Into the heart of the seas,
And the floods surrounded me;
All Your billows and Your waves passed over me."

JONAH 2:1-3
(Read the whole passage in Jonah 2:1-9.)

Some have described the events recorded in Jonah 3 as the greatest revival in history. What occurred in Nineveh, wonderful as it was, cannot accurately be called revival. It can certainly be called a spiritual awakening or even the result of revival, but not revival. The word "revival" means being restored to life, vitality, zeal or vigor. Revival is something that can only be experienced by God's people, and the Ninevites were pagans. Revival presupposes God's people being in a state of spiritual coldness and then being reinvigorated.

So the real revival in the book of Jonah is that which the prophet himself experienced while he was in the fish's belly. Before the fish swallowed him, Jonah was in a state of spiritual coldness and disobedience. While he was in that fish, he was spiritually renewed or restored.

Jonah 2 relates the prayer that Jonah prayed from the fish. Prayer is, of course, the primary means that God uses to revive His people (2 Chron. 7:14).

Let's notice three things about Jonah's prayer. First, there is *the time of it*. We shouldn't rush past these words: "Then Jonah prayed to the LORD his God from the fish's belly" (v. 1).

These words tell us that God's chastisement of His prophet had achieved its purpose. The chastisement was severe. Jonah says he was in the belly of hell (v. 2), tucked away out of God's sight (v. 4), at the very bottom of the mountains (v. 6), where he felt locked up by the bars of the earth (v. 6).

Jonah describes the breadth of his chastisement by saying he was in the midst of waters on every side (v. 5). No matter where he looked, no end was in sight. He described the outward dimension of it by saying that weeds were wrapped around his head (v. 5), and he described the inward dimension of it by saying his soul fainted within (v. 7). His affliction touched both his body and his spirit.

We should also notice *the tone of the prayer*. Jonah twice says that he "cried." This is a word of energy, urgency, and fervency. It doesn't allow for half-heartedness. This is prayer with sweat on it.

One very large challenge these days is getting God's people to pray. Another large challenge is getting them to pray as they pray, that is, getting them to pray with fervency. We can be sure that revival hasn't yet come if we are content to mumble lazily in our prayers. When revival comes, the tone of prayer always changes.

The final thing for us to notice about Jonah's prayer is *the type that it was*.

It was very much a prayer of confession. First, Jonah confessed his idolatry. He says: "They that observe lying vanities forsake their own mercy" (v. 8). The phrase "lying vanities" is the Bible's frequent way of depicting idols as vain, empty delusions (Deut. 32:21; Jer. 10:14-15; 14:22).

But we don't read anywhere that Jonah had fallen down before a god of wood or stone to worship. So why did he confess idolatry? We must keep in mind that idolatry is putting anything in the place of God and giving it the honor and allegiance that belong to God. When Jonah disobeyed God, he was essentially placing his desires above God's commands. That's idolatry. Jonah's idol was himself.

Jonah also confessed the truth of God's sovereignty by saying: "Salvation is of the LORD" (v. 9).

Jonah has finally come to recognize what he should have understood at the outset and would have understood, had he not been so busy playing God himself. He sees that God, as the sovereign ruler of this universe, has the right to extend His mercy to whomever He wishes. Jonah had thought that the Ninevites were unworthy of salvation. He now sees from his own desperate situation that he is wholly dependent on God's mercy for deliverance while being, like the Ninevites, unworthy of that deliverance. If God were to deliver him, unworthy as *he* was, how could he dispute God's right to grant an even greater deliverance to the unworthy Ninevites?

Jonah was spiritually revived as he prayed. We should be thankful for his revival. We should be even more thankful for Jesus, who never needed revival because He never faltered in the work of redemption that the Father had given Him to do.

Experiencing Revival

From God's Word, the Bible...

O Israel, return to the Lord your God,
For you have stumbled because of your iniquity;
Take words with you, And return to the Lord.
Say to Him, "Take away all iniquity;
Receive us graciously,
For we will offer the sacrifices of our lips.
Assyria shall not save us, We will not ride on horses,
Nor will we say anymore to the work of our hands,
'You are our gods.'
For in You the fatherless finds mercy."
"I will heal their backsliding,
I will love them freely,
For My anger has turned away from him."

Hosea 14:1-4

The account of Jonah's revival in the belly of the fish summons us to consider the subject of revival more fully. Today we answer that summons by looking to another of the Old Testament prophets—Hosea. Hosea ministered to the nation of Israel from 754 to 714 B.C.

Throughout his prophecy, Hosea sounds the somber notes of sin and judgment. In this passage, he sounds the joyful note of hope. His message of hope is built around the word "return" (v. 1), a word he uses fifteen times in this prophecy. What a comforting word! We can come back to God! No matter how far we have strayed and how miserably we have failed, we can come back to God!

The people of Israel had turned their backs on God and had turned their faces toward sin. They had spurned God and embraced sin. The Lord here calls them to reverse what they had previously done. He calls them to turn their backs on their sins and turn their faces toward Him.

What He said to those backslidden Israelites speaks with equal force to us when we backslide.

First, He shows us *why we need to return to Him* (v. 1).

The people of Israel needed to return to God because they had "stumbled" because of their "iniquity."

Sin always makes us stumble. We cannot walk uprightly before God and walk in sin. We cannot walk close to God and walk in sin.

The New International Version translates the phrase "stumbled because of your iniquity" in this way: "Your sins have been your downfall!"

The devil would have us believe that sin is the way to happiness, satisfaction, and fulfillment. The truth is just the opposite. Sin is the way to heartache, misery, and ruin. Cain, Lot, Esau, Saul, and Judas Iscariot are some examples of men who painfully learned the truth about sin.

Hosea was not content to urge the people to return to God. He also declares *how we can return to Him* (vv. 2-3).

He says we are to "take words" with us. We must honestly talk to God about our sins.

This is what the prodigal son did when he returned to his father (Luke 15:21). This is what David did when he returned to the Lord after sinning so grievously (Ps. 51).

The Apostle John writes: "If we confess our sins, He is faithful and just to forgive us our sins and to cleanse us from all unrighteousness" (1 John 1 9).

It isn't enough, of course, to merely mouth empty words without sincerity of heart. Our words of repentance must come from hearts that are broken with the enormity of the sin. They must be words that ask God to take away the iniquity and to graciously forgive. They must include words of renunciation. As the nation of Israel was to renounce an alliance with Assyria as the means for achieving future security (v. 3), so our own return to God must feature a true renunciation of our dependence on every other resource as well as our idols.

Finally, the Lord tells us *what to expect when we return to Him* (v. 4).

The Lord assures us that He will "heal" our backsliding. What a wonderful thing healing is! Imagine someone who has suffered long from a painful, debilitating disease. He has had surgery and taken various treatments. Then one day his doctor says: "You can consider yourself to be healed."

That's essentially what God said to those people. Their backsliding was like a terrible disease. But God offered complete healing for it. He still heals backsliding today.

The Lord also assures us that He will love us "freely" when we return to Him (v. 4). We all know what it is to have people be cool and reserved toward us. God was promising to love His people warmly and without reserve. God receives backsliders spontaneously and warmly. He never makes returning difficult! Once again, we can look at the parable of the prodigal son for a picture of how God receives backsliders.

Let's remember that the God who loved us enough to put His Son on the cross for us doesn't stop loving us when we backslide. And when we backslide, let's seek true revival. Jonah's experience pictures it for us, and Hosea proclaims it to us. If we need revival, let's look to Jonah and listen to Hosea.

The Resurrection of Jesus

From God's Word, the Bible...

He is not here; for He is risen, as He said.
Come, see the place where the Lord lay.

Matthew 28:6

"After Jonah experienced true spiritual renewal in the belly of the fish, he was "vomited . . . onto dry land" (Jonah 2:10).

We have been noting at various points that there is a link between Jonah's experience in the fish and the resurrection of Jesus. The former portrays the latter. This is not mere fanciful conjecture. The Lord Jesus Himself made the link in response to the Pharisees' request that He give them a sign. The only sign He gave them was "the sign of the prophet Jonah" (Matt. 12:38-39). Jesus then proceeded to say: "For as Jonah was three days and three nights in the belly of the great fish, so will the Son of Man be three days and three nights in the heart of the earth" (Matt. 12:40).

Someone may want to point out that Jesus didn't actually mention His resurrection in those words. True. But it is unquestionably implied. The Pharisees knew that Jonah didn't stay in the belly of the fish. So they had to know that Jesus was affirming that He would not stay in "the heart of the earth." By appealing to Jonah, Jesus was proclaiming His upcoming resurrection.

Let's first consider *what proves Jesus' resurrection*.

We need not be in doubt whether Jesus arose. The evidences for it are too many and too substantial. The stone of His tomb was rolled away. The tomb was empty. Those appointed to guard the tomb were in a stupor. Angels were present. The grave clothes of Jesus were left behind in a particularly convincing configuration. Many saw the risen Lord (500 on one occasion—see 1 Cor. 15:6)! And the disciples were changed from cowering wimps into bold evangelists.

If these evidences aren't enough for us, the problem is with us. If convincing evidence doesn't convince us, we just don't want to be convinced.

Why do some not want to be convinced? The answer is in our second consideration—*what Jesus' resurrection proves*.

The first thing is this: if Jesus arose from the dead, there can be no doubt that He was the person He claimed to be, namely, the God-man. Yes, Jesus emphatically claimed to be God in human flesh (John 14:9), and the resurrection proves it (Rom. 1:4). Ordinary men don't spring from their graves!

Why do people reject Jesus' resurrection? It means Jesus is God. That means He has authority over us. He can tell us how we ought to live and how we ought not to live. And we all want to live as we see fit. One man, when confronted with the powerful evidences for the Christian faith, was asked if he was willing to accept those evidences and receive Christ. His response was most telling: "No, I won't become a Christian, because I don't want the world to be like that."

Christianity says the world should bow before the authority of Jesus. That would make it quite different than what it is. And this man liked the sinful world the way it is. It wasn't the lack of evidence that drove him from Christianity. It was the implications of the evidence.

The fact that we deny Jesus' resurrection doesn't destroy it. We can deny it and Jesus' lordship, but a day is coming in which the folly of such denial will be plain for all to see. On that day every knee will bow before Jesus, and every tongue will confess that He is Lord (Phil. 2:9-11).

A second thing that the resurrection proves is this: God was entirely satisfied with the death of Christ in the place of sinners. God is the One whom we have offended through our sins, and it is God who must be satisfied. The fact that God is the One who raised Jesus from the dead proves that God was satisfied with His redeeming death.

In one sense, the cross was the verdict of sinful men on Jesus. By nailing Him there, they were pronouncing Him to be a fraud. The resurrection was the verdict of God on Jesus, and what a radically different verdict it was! God was reversing or setting aside the verdict of sinful men on His Son, and pronouncing His own verdict on Him. By raising Jesus from the dead, God was setting the record straight regarding His Son.

Jonah points us to Jesus' resurrection, and Jesus' resurrection points us to what we should do with Jesus. We should bow humbly before Him as God and receive the gift of salvation that He achieved for us on the cross.

August 17

Re-sending, Repenting, and Relenting

FROM GOD'S WORD, THE BIBLE...

Then God saw their works, that they turned from their evil way; and God relented from the disaster that He had said He would bring upon them, and He did not do it.

JONAH 3:10
(Read the whole passage in Jonah 3:1-10.)

The third chapter of Jonah seems to fall quite naturally into three parts: re-sending, repenting, and relenting. Jonah was re-sent, the Ninevites repented and God relented.

The fact that God re-issued his original call to Jonah is most encouraging. Our God is the God of the second chance, and the third and the fourth and. . . . God doesn't hold our sins and failures against us. When we repent, He forgives and forgets. The Apostle John wonderfully consoles us with these words about the Lord: "If we confess our sins, He is faithful and just to forgive us our sins and to cleanse us from all unrighteousness" (1 John 1:9).

There were once two men who became reconciled after being at odds with each other. When asked if it was true that they had buried the hatchet, one of these two men replied: "Yes, but I left the handle sticking up in case I need the hatchet again."

God never leaves the handle sticking up. How very thankful we should be! The Lord could have left Jonah to perish in the sea or in the fish, but He didn't. Our failures are not final with God if we will repent.

Jonah's task was an unpleasant one. He had to walk through the city crying: "Yet forty days, and Nineveh shall be overthrown!" (v. 4).

It was the message of God's judgment. That has never been a pleasant message! It is regarded today as the height of arrogance and insensibility. It's not politically correct.

The fact that we so despise the message of God's judgment only means that we don't know God or ourselves. We don't realize how holy God is and how sinful we are. If we could get a true understanding of these things, we would not find the message of His judgment surprising; rather, we would find the message of His mercy surprising!

Jonah's preaching in Nineveh met with huge success. The people "believed God, proclaimed a fast, and put on sackcloth, from the greatest to the least of them" (v. 5).

A whole city turning to God! That would have been something to behold.

Oh, that we could see the same today in city after city in our society!

The repenting led to relenting. The Ninevites repented and God relented—that is, God turned away from the judgment that He was planning to send against Nineveh.

This creates a problem for us. The Bible plainly affirms that the Lord never changes (Ps. 102:27; Mal. 3:6). But here we find Him changing His mind about the Ninevites. The solution to this dilemma is to keep in mind the distinction between God's character and His dealings with us. God's essential character is one of intense hatred for sin. That can't change. But it's because He can't change in that way that He does change in His dealings with us. In other words, when we turn wholeheartedly from sin, it is because of His unchangeable hatred toward sin that causes Him to turn from His judgment.

We should let the re-sending, the repenting and the relenting of this chapter speak to us about the Lord Jesus Christ.

Unlike Jonah, Jesus didn't have to receive a second call from God the Father to undertake the work of redemption. One call was enough. The Father set the work before the Son, and He gladly and willingly took it up.

In another respect, the Lord Jesus was like Jonah. Jonah came to Nineveh preaching the forthcoming judgment of God, and Jesus also declared God's judgment. This comes as a shock to those who dreamily entertain the notion that Jesus came to this earth to only proclaim God's love. Is the problem that these folks haven't read the Gospels or rather that they have refused to believe what they read? It was Jesus who told people that they would most certainly perish if they refused to repent (Luke 13:3). It was Jesus who told His hearers to fear God because He has the power to cast into hell (Luke 12:5).

It was also Jesus who happily assured all those who repent of their sins that God will turn from His judgment. Consider His words: "Most assuredly, I say to you, he who hears My word and believes in Him who sent Me has everlasting life, and shall not come into judgment, but has passed from death into life" (John 5:24).

Have you passed from death into life?

August 18

Jonah's Message and Ours

From God's Word, the Bible...

For the wages of sin is death, but the gift of God is eternal life in Christ Jesus our Lord.

Romans 6:23

In Jonah 3 we see Jonah finally arriving in the city of Nineveh and beginning to preach. His was a bare-bones message: "Yet forty days and Nineveh shall be overthrown" (Jonah 3:1).

But folded into that message were certain brawny, muscular truths—the fact of their sin, the fact that God is holy and detests sin (Why would He judge it if that weren't the case?), and the willingness of God to forgive sin (Why would He send a prophet if that weren't the case?).

The Ninevites didn't need for Jonah to elaborate. They understood quite well that he was warning them about judgment to come because of their sins. And they understood sincere, thorough repentance was the only way for them to deal with their sin (Jonah 3:8).

The church as a whole as well as individual Christians are called today to bear witness to these truths just as Jonah was called centuries ago. We are called to proclaim the gospel. The gospel is the good news of what God has done in and through His Son, Jesus, to forgive sinners of their sins, to give them right standing with God now, and eternal glory in the future.

The gospel message assumes human sinfulness and divine judgment. It is only good news because sin and judgment are bad news. No one wants to hear bad news, but it's oftentimes necessary. A doctor doesn't withhold from a patient the unpleasant truth about his or her physical condition. The doctor's concern isn't what will make the patient happy; it's rather what is true about the patient.

Because so many in the church today seem to find Christianity's true message to be more unpleasant than unbelievers do, they make this their message: "You're okay. Now let us tell you how to live a better life."

Much of modern-day evangelism is based on the premise that people are living perfectly miserable lives, and they need to come to Christ so their lives can be improved.

The truth is that, on the one hand, there are many non-Christians who are living perfectly happy lives. What about them? Do they need Christ?

On the other hand, there are lots of Christians who have very difficult lives. I've known believers who battled illness for a good part of their lives.

I've known others who constantly endured financial hardship, so much so that it was always hard for them to make ends meet.

We must be very careful about presenting the Christian message in such a way that we end up telling people that they don't need it.

The Bible's approach to evangelizing unbelievers is radically different from what has become so very common in our time. The Bible begins with our sins. The Apostle Paul writes: "For all have sinned and come short of the glory of God" (Rom. 3:23).

The Bible puts us all on equal footing. Some will always be better off in this life than others. Some will invariably have better health, more money, and more happiness than others. Some will always live in finer houses, drive nicer cars, and take more extravagant vacations.

But there's one way in which we are all alike: we're all sinners. Many object to this assertion. They often say something like this: "I know I'm not perfect, but I don't really consider myself a sinner." They use a subjective test—how they feel about themselves—to determine if they are sinners.

God, on the other hand, uses an objective test. He tells us to lay our lives alongside the Ten Commandments, keeping in mind as we do so that it's not enough to keep those commandments in a mere external fashion. For example, it's not enough to refrain from murdering someone, as the Sixth Commandment requires (Ex. 20:13). We must also refrain from hating that person (Matt. 5:21-22). Each of God's commandments testifies against us. Each one hands down the guilty verdict on us.

It's because we are all sinners that we all need Christ. Why? Because He alone has provided the way for our sins to be forgiven! He came to this earth to live without sin so He could bear our sins when He died on the cross (1 Peter 2:24).

So God's message to each of us is that we will eventually be "overthrown" if we don't turn to Christ in repentance and faith. Let's heed God's message to us as the Ninevites heeded His message to them.

August 19

The Pitiful Prophet Who Couldn't Pity

FROM GOD'S WORD, THE BIBLE...

Then God said to Jonah, "Is it right for you to be angry about the plant?" And he said, "It is right for me to be angry, even to death!" But the LORD said, "You have had pity on the plant for which you have not labored, nor made it grow, which came up in a night and perished in a night. And should I not pity Nineveh, that great city, in which are more than one hundred and twenty thousand persons who cannot discern between their right hand and their left—and much livestock?"

JONAH 4:9-11
(Read the whole passage in Jonah 4:1-11.)

It's a pity that the book of Jonah didn't end with chapter 3. If it had only ended there we would have been left with a whole city turning to God in true repentance. We would have come away from this book with rejoicing. And we would have been spared the sight of the pitiful prophet who couldn't pity. Yes, Jonah is pitiful in chapter 4. He is a sad and pathetic figure. If the book had concluded with chapter 3, we would regard Jonah as a hero. But chapter 4 forces us to take another view of him. It causes us to shake our heads in dismay. It causes us to pity him, the pitiful prophet.

Most preachers would rejoice to see just a few converts. Jonah had a whole city of them, but he didn't rejoice. Those converts made him "exceedingly" displeased and "angry" (v. 1). They caused him to pray to the Lord, and a pitiful prayer it was! Jonah angrily accused God of being too kind, too loving, and too forgiving (v. 2). And he asked God to end his life then and there (v. 3).

So Jonah set up his little camp outside Nineveh to see what would happen to the city. He may have thought that his complaining would cause God to go back to His original plan to judge Nineveh. While Jonah waited to see (v. 5), he surely had to know what he would see. Nineveh would be spared, and it would be spared because God takes special delight in sparing repentant people.

But Jonah still had to see. So he set up a camp outside the city and waited for the forty-day period to end (Jonah 3:4).

God was already at the site Jonah picked for his camp. God had certain things prepared for His petty prophet. God always has His plans and preparations. First, there would be a "plant" to shelter Jonah from the oppressive heat (v. 6). No, there's no need to get into the business of how a plant could grow so quickly. We're talking about God, here, and God can always make special things happen.

Jonah was grateful for that plant, but, alas, it didn't last. God sent a worm to so damage the plant that it withered (v. 7). And then God sent "a vehement east wind" (v. 8). That wind, along with the brutal heat from the sun, caused Jonah to once again express the desire to die (v. 8).

I think if I had been making the decisions at this point, I would have granted Jonah's wish. But what a sight we get of God here! He continues to be kind to His exasperating prophet. He tenderly asks Jonah: "Is it right for you to be angry about the plant?" (v. 9). And, of course, Jonah blusteringly declares that he has a perfect right to be angry.

Then God dropped the hammer. Jonah pitied a mere plant, but he was angry with God for pitying people and livestock (vv. 10-11).

The book abruptly ends with a question, a question that is left hanging without Jonah's answer. It's such an abrupt ending that some might be inclined to think that we don't have the whole book of Jonah, that the last part of it got lost somewhere along the way.

I'm convinced that the question is left unanswered for another reason. God wants us to answer it for ourselves. It's as if He says to us: "It's not important for you to know how Jonah answered this question. What is important is how you answer it."

And how do we answer it? Do we have more concern for things than we do for the souls of men, women, and children?

Jonah is the pitiful prophet because he couldn't pity needy souls. Let's now look away from the sad sight of Jonah to the wonderful sight of Jesus. The Lord Jesus could never look upon people without being moved with compassion and pity (e.g., Mark 6:34). It was that heart of compassion that brought Him to this earth all the way from heaven's glory. And it was that same heart of compassion that drove Him to the cross where He died that we might live.

What was wrong with Jonah? He didn't pity Ninevites. Thank God, there's nothing wrong with Jesus. He pities sinners.

Come, ye sinners, poor and needy,
Weak and wounded, sick and sore;
Jesus ready stands to save you,
Full of pity, love and pow'r.
(Joseph Hart)

The Compassion of Jesus

From God's Word, the Bible...

"O Jerusalem, Jerusalem, the one who kills the prophets and stones those who are sent to her! How often I wanted to gather your children together, as a hen gathers her chicks under her wings, but you were not willing! See! Your house is left to you desolate; for I say to you, you shall see Me no more till you say, 'Blessed is He who comes in the name of the Lord!'"

Matthew 23:37-39

Two men sit outside two cities. But there the similarity ends. One man sits with a heart of stone, knowing that the destruction he yearned to see would not come. Centuries later, the other man would sit outside another city with a broken heart, knowing that destruction would most certainly come.

The first man, of course, was Jonah, and the city was Nineveh. The second man was Jesus, and the city was Jerusalem.

With perfect, unerring foreknowledge, the Lord Jesus could see destruction coming upon Jerusalem. And come it did in A.D. 70 at the hands of the Romans. But Jesus took no delight in the thought of judgment, which is ever God's "strange" work (Isa. 28:21, KJV). God ever delights in people turning from their sins in true repentance.

In the sorrowful words of the above passage, Jesus mentioned His desire to "gather" Jerusalem's people to Himself "as a hen gathers her chicks under her wings." But those people would have none of it. They refused to be gathered, and their refusal stirred and moved the compassionate heart of the Savior.

Matthew doesn't specifically say that Jesus wept over the city on this occasion, but, since He had done it before (Luke 19:41), it wouldn't be surprising if He wept again as He spoke these words.

The compassionate heart of Jesus—what a treasure! It was that compassionate heart that brought Him to this earth in the first place. The Apostle Paul wonderfully states: "For you know the grace of our Lord Jesus Christ, that though He was rich, yet for your sakes He became poor, that you through His poverty might become rich" (2 Cor. 8:9).

The Lord Jesus didn't have to come to this earth. He could have refused to do so, but His heart wouldn't allow Him to refuse.

Throughout His public ministry, the compassion of His heart was on display. On one occasion, the mere sight of "a great multitude" caused Him to be "moved with compassion for them because they were like sheep not having a shepherd" (Mark 6:34).

When Jesus encountered two blind men, He "had compassion and touched their eyes." And they immediately received their sight (Matt. 20:30-34).

As the Lord was entering into the city of Nain, He encountered a large group of people leaving the city to go to the cemetery. A widow had lost her son. When Jesus saw this woman, He "had compassion on her." That compassion compelled Him to raise her son from the dead (Luke 7:11-17).

It was the compassion of Jesus that later caused Him to weep outside the tomb of Lazarus before He raised him from the dead (John 11:34-44).

Jesus' ministry featured many miracles—healing the sick, feeding multitudes, stilling storms, casting out demons, and, yes, raising the dead—and all of them were works of compassion.

It was Jesus' compassion that put Him on the cross. His death there was the supreme manifestation of His compassion. How great is His compassion? On the cross, He bore the wrath of God in the place of sinners.

The end of Jesus' public ministry didn't mean the end of His compassion. He ascended to the right hand of the Father in heaven, and there, as our High Priest, He sympathizes "with our weaknesses" (Heb. 4:14-15).

We must never forget that when Jesus ascended to the Father in heaven, it was in His resurrected humanity. Since He is in heaven in our humanity, it is not just that Jesus can sympathize with us in our humanity. It is rather that He cannot help but sympathize with us.

By the way, the fact that Jesus has gone into heaven in resurrected humanity is the guarantee that all who trust Him as their Lord and Savior will eventually follow Him into heaven in resurrected humanity. He is in heaven as our "forerunner" (Heb. 6:20).

When the devil suggests to us that the Lord Jesus doesn't feel sympathy and pity for us, we need to remind him that Jesus is our compassionate High Priest in heaven.

Callous Jonah and compassionate Jesus! May God help us to both appreciate the compassion of the Lord Jesus and to emulate it!

Chastisement

From God's Word, the Bible...

If you endure chastening, God deals with you as with sons; for what son is there whom a father does not chasten?
Now no chastening seems to be joyful for the present, but painful; nevertheless, afterward it yields the peaceable fruit of righteousness to those who have been trained by it.

Hebrews 12:7,11

The prophecy of Jonah confronts us with the reality of God's chastisement. To say God chastised Jonah is to say that He punished and disciplined His prophet.

Some reject out of hand the idea that God chastises. To them it is unworthy of God. It makes Him a mean, vindictive ogre who enjoys making people miserable.

But the Bible teaches otherwise. The go-to passage on the matter of God's chastisement is Hebrews 12:3-11. It first affirms that God chastises all of His children. The author indicates that we must be careful about denying the reality of God's chastisement. Such denial may mean that we don't truly have God as our Father (vv. 7-8).

The passage also shows us the reason for God's chastisement. It's not because He enjoys being unkind and harsh. It's rather due to the love that He has for all of His children. The one the Lord loves is the one that He chastens (v. 6). Yes, God has a general love for all people. We refer to that as "common grace." But God has a special love for His children, those who have come to Him in repentance of their sins and with faith in His Son, the Lord Jesus Christ. Those who enjoy that special love are those whom He chastens.

Still further, this passage reveals the intent of the chastening. It is to bring forth in us "the peaceable fruit of righteousness" (v. 11). God's chastening makes us more righteous, that is, it makes us conform more and more to the commandments of the Lord. And the more we conform to those commandments, the more peace we have!

The devil would always have us to believe that sin brings us happiness and peace, but that's a lie. Disobedience to God brings nothing but misery and woe.

As one who has had to minister to many people in their dying moments, I can tell you that I have never heard one of them express regret that he or she didn't sin more. But I've heard several express regret about not being more obedient to the Lord.

How did the Lord chastise Jonah? Let's count the ways. First, there was the tossing ship. Then there was the gulping fish. Let's not forget the gnawing worm. Finally, there was the oppressing wind.

In those four acts of chastisement, we can see the two major forms that chastisement takes. One form is the sending of adversity (the storm, the fish, and the wind). The other form is the withholding of blessing (the destruction of the vine by the worm).

We usually associate God's chastisement with adversity. If we start drifting into sinful living, and no adversity comes, we are inclined to think that God isn't chastising us. However, we need to keep the other side of the equation in mind, that is, the withholding of blessings. How much are we missing because of our disobedience? What blessings could we be enjoying if we weren't being disobedient to God?

Many churches these days are trying to cope with shriveling attendance and declining interest. We often look at these sad realities and ask what can be done to change them. And we usually answer in terms of having more appealing programs and finding ways to "relate" to the modern generation.

Where are those who dare point out that it is possible for churches to grieve God and to experience His discipline? Where are those who suggest that the condition of the churches may very well be due to God withholding His blessings from us because we haven't been faithful in our doctrine and in our conduct? Where are those who call the church, not to better programs and promotions, but to repentance and revival?

Repentance is always the antidote for chastisement. It was when Jonah repented that the fish vomited him on to dry land. When we sin, God chastises to bring us to repentance.

The ever-active devil wages war on the teaching of chastisement. When the Lord sends it our way, the devil never hesitates to suggest that it is proof that the Lord doesn't love us. "If God loved you as much as you think, you wouldn't be going through this," the devil suggests. The proper response is to say: "Devil, I regard God's chastisement not as evidence that God doesn't love me but rather as proof that He does."

And don't forget to point the devil to the cross of Christ. That is always the greatest proof of God's love for us.

August 22

Where's the Mumbo? Where's the Jumbo?

From God's Word, the Bible...

Your word is a lamp to my feet
And a light to my path.

Psalm 119:105

Many years ago, a prominent British politician was asked if he was a Christian. He replied in this way: "I believe in the ethics of Christianity but not in the mumbo-jumbo."

How do we happen to have the term mumbo-jumbo in our vocabulary? Some think it came from a strange ritual that African husbands used to frighten disobedient, rebellious wives into submission. Others suggest that it refers to a grotesque idol that was worshiped by certain African tribes.

This much is clear: at its root, mumbo-jumbo refers to superstitious, meaningless rituals that obscure and create confusion.

If mumbo-jumbo is designed to obscure or create confusion, we must surely say that politicians specialize in it. And here is a politician criticizing Christianity for it! What an amazing and rich irony!

So what about Christianity? Is it mumbo-jumbo, as the politician suggested? Is it based on superstition or on fact? Does it consist of meaningless rituals? Is it confusing?

Here is the central tenet of Christianity—God sent His Son into this world to save sinners (Matt. 1:21; Luke 19:10; 1 Tim. 1:15).

That certainly seems clear enough to me. Where is the mumbo? Where is the jumbo?

It certainly isn't mere superstition to believe that we are sinners. The fact of sin is written large before our eyes every single day of our lives. We see it all around us, and, if we care to admit it, we see it in ourselves. The very fact that the politician to whom I've been referring would applaud Christian ethics tells us that he was indirectly admitting the fact of sin. There would be no need for ethics if it weren't for sin. By the way, this politician lived through the two world wars that put the reality of sin in graphic display and focus.

Is it mere superstition to believe that Jesus actually lived? The mumbo-jumbo politician wasn't denying the existence of Jesus. He knew better than that! Only a handful of people are silly enough to believe that Jesus never lived.

Is it mere superstition to say Jesus came from heaven? The prophecies He fulfilled, the miracles He performed, the words that He spoke, the lives that

He changed—and, most of all, the grave that He conquered—unite to say Jesus was from heaven.

And what about Jesus' death on the cross? Is that mumbo-jumbo? The Bible says otherwise. It isn't silly superstition to believe that Jesus was crucified, and it isn't baseless superstition to believe that His was a special death, a death designed to accomplish something special, namely, forgiveness for sinners. How are we to respond to those who think the cross of Christ is mere superstition? Let's point them to the countless millions who have found, in that cross, relief from the guilt of their sins, and release from the fear of judgment to come.

And what about baptism and the Lord's Supper? Are they nothing more than confusing, superstitious rituals? The former, baptism, is the way we publicly profess our faith in Christ and identify ourselves with Him. And the Lord's Supper is the public celebration and commemoration of the saving work of Jesus on our behalf. Superstitious and confusing rituals? They make perfect sense to me!

I'm inclined to think that many who reject Christianity do so not because there is no evidence for it but because they don't like where the evidence leads. And I'm inclined to think that those who think Christianity is confusing may, in fact, find it to be too plain about their sins and about judgment to come. They reject it because they fancy themselves to be very intelligent, and salvation provided by a man dying on a cross seems absurd to them.

If Christianity is mumbo-jumbo, I have this to say: Blessed mumbo-jumbo! It gives me the assurance that my sins are forgiven and that I have a home in heaven through Christ. So I want my cup filled with it. Let me drink it dry, and then please fill it again and again!

And what about the politician who dismissed Christianity as mumbo-jumbo? He died many years ago. So now he knows the truth of the matter. If we don't know the truth of Christianity now, death will finally make it clear to us.

The Man Who Got His Bible Back

From God's Word, the Bible...

But you must continue in the things which you have learned and been assured of, knowing from whom you have learned them, and that from childhood you have known the Holy Scriptures, which are able to make you wise for salvation through faith which is in Christ Jesus.

2 Timothy 3:14-15

A young medical student was strapped for cash. So he sold his Bible for a small amount. It was the Bible that his mother had given him. She had written his name on its flyleaf. Let that soak in! A young man sold his Bible for a small amount! Yes, he was in need of money, but the small amount he received for his Bible wouldn't have made any real difference in his financial situation. It's apparent that he didn't really value the Bible. I'm not talking about a dollars-and-cents value but rather about the value of its message, which is the Lord Jesus Christ and the saving mission that brought Him to this earth. The person who understands the treasure that the Bible is might give it away to someone who needs it, but it's unlikely that he will sell it. If he does, he will quickly replace it with another.

But let's get back to the young medical student. He went on to complete his training and began his career. One day a seriously injured man was brought to the hospital. His injuries were so severe that nothing could be done to save him. He told the doctor that he had no relatives but that he would like for his landlady to come and bring him "the book."

"What book?" the doctor asked.

"She will know," was the reply.

The man only lived a few days, but the doctor noticed on his daily visits that he was always calm, peaceful, and smiling.

When it came time to dispose of his few possessions, a nurse held up a book and asked: "What shall we do with this?" What kind of book is it?" asked the doctor.

"It's the Bible," the nurse replied.

The doctor looked at the Bible, and, to his utter astonishment, it was the very Bible that he had sold so many years before. His name, in his dear mother's handwriting, was still there.

As he stood gazing upon his old Bible, the doctor thought about the peace that the dying man had enjoyed in his last days. He was sure that peace came from the very Bible that he had sold long ago for what he would call "a ridiculous price."

So the doctor kept the Bible. He got it back, but he also got something that he had never possessed before. He read the Bible's message of salvation and received the Lord Jesus Christ as his Savior.

That doctor was W.P. Mackay of Scotland. He is probably best known to us as the author of these words:

We praise Thee, O God, For the Son of Thy love;
For Jesus, who died, And is now gone above.

We praise Thee, O God, For Thy Spirit of light,
Who has shown us our Savior, And scattered our night.

All glory and praise, To the Lamb that was slain,
Who has borne all our sins, And hath cleansed every stain.

This is a hymn about the salvation that Mackay came to understand and to receive. It is the salvation provided by Christ "who died and is now gone above." It is the salvation that came to us as a result of the Spirit of God enlightening us. He is the "Spirit of light" who showed us the Savior and "scattered our night." It is the salvation that was purchased for us when Jesus died on the cross a sin-bearing death. He bore "all our sins" and "hath cleansed every stain."

But Mackay's hymn is also about something else. It's about God's people losing sight of the wonder and glory of their salvation and allowing themselves to become cold and indifferent. So Mackay's fourth verse and chorus read:

Revive us again; Fill each heart with Thy love;
May each soul be rekindled, With fire from above.

Hallelujah! Thine the glory! Hallelujah! Amen!
Hallelujah! Thine the glory! Revive us again.

Mackay's hymn, *Revive Us Again*, has a mystery running through it. On one hand, it celebrates the glory of salvation. On the other hand, it recognizes the need for revival. With such a glorious salvation, how is it that we ever need revival? But we often do. How can we continue to feel awe about salvation and continue to be warmly devoted to the Lord? Perhaps we need to get our Bibles back.

A Hymn's Question Answered

FROM GOD'S WORD, THE BIBLE...

For to me, to live is Christ, and to die is gain. But if I live on in the flesh, this will mean fruit from my labor; yet what I shall choose I cannot tell. For I am hard-pressed between the two, having a desire to depart and be with Christ, which is far better.

PHILIPPIANS 1:21-23

It was late on the evening of September 21, 1921, and hymn-writer William J. Kirkpatrick was still working at his desk. After she had been sleeping for a while, his wife noticed that the light in his study was still on. "Don't you think you had better come to bed?" she called. He responded: "I'm all right, dear, I have a little work I want to finish. Go back to sleep, everything is all right."

She went back to sleep and once again awoke to see his light still on. This time he didn't answer her call. She went to the study to find his lifeless body still sitting in his chair and slumped over his desk.

The poem on which he had been working read:

Just as Thou wilt, Lord, this is my cry,
Just as Thou wilt, to live or die.
I am Thy servant, Thou knowest best,
Just as Thou wilt, Lord, labor or rest.
Just as Thou wilt, Lord, which shall it be?
Life everlasting waiting for me –
Or shall I tarry, here at Thy feet?
Just as Thou wilt, Lord, whatever is meet.

Kirkpatrick had asked: "Lord, which shall it be?" And the Lord had answered. It was not to be more life on this earth. It was to be death. But in answering with death for Kirkpatrick, the Lord was not shortchanging him or mistreating him. He was doing the best possible thing for His servant, receiving him into His presence where he would know nothing but perfect peace and joy.

We who believe Christ can allow ourselves to love life in this world so much that we give the impression that death is the ultimate disaster. We can begin to regard life in heaven as second best to life in this world. But heaven is always best, and death is never a disaster for the child of God.

Many centuries before Kirkpatrick entered this world, the Apostle Paul essentially asked the Lord the same question: "Which shall it be, Lord, life or death?" The apostle felt torn. On one hand, he had a desire to remain on this earth for a while so he could continue to labor for the Lord. On the other hand, he had an intense desire "to depart and be with Christ," which he described as being "far better."

It was always Christ with the Apostle Paul. To live was to serve Christ. To die was to be with Christ. With those two possibilities, there was no way that Paul could lose.

The most important question anyone can ask is this: "Am I sure that I'm going to heaven?"

I'm convinced that the major thing that keeps people from asking themselves that question is the belief that nothing has to be done to enter heaven. But there is something that has to be done. We have to repent of our sins and trust in the Lord Jesus Christ. He is the way to heaven, and there is no other way (John 14:6; Acts 4:12). He came from heaven to make the way for sinners to go to heaven.

I'm certainly not in the category of the Apostle Paul, or, for that matter, William J. Kirkpatrick. But I can say that I am looking forward to heaven. This world has given me my fill of tears and heartaches. What a blessed thing it will be to live in a land where there is no crying, no pain, no sorrow, and no death!

All of God's people will eventually receive the Lord's call to enter heaven, even as William Kirkpatrick did. But now we wait, and while we wait, we sing:

There's a land that is fairer than day,
And by faith we can see it afar;
For the Father waits over the way
To prepare us a dwelling place there.

In the sweet by and by,
We shall meet on that beautiful shore;
In the sweet by and by,
We shall meet on that beautiful shore.

We shall sing on that beautiful shore
The melodious songs of the blessed;
And our spirits shall sorrow no more,
Not a sigh for the blessing of rest.
(Sanford Fillmore Bennett)

It will be a joy to land on "that beautiful shore" and to see the Apostle Paul and William J. Kirkpatrick. But the best sight of heaven will be the Lord Jesus Christ, and the best sight of Christ will be His nail-pierced hands.

August 25

The Message of Heaven in the Mockery of Hell

FROM GOD'S WORD, THE BIBLE...

Then they spat in His face and beat Him; and others struck Him with the palms of their hands, saying, "Prophesy to us, Christ! Who is the one who struck You?"

Likewise the chief priests also, mocking with the scribes and elders, said, "He saved others; Himself He cannot save. If He is the King of Israel, let Him now come down from the cross, and we will believe Him. He trusted in God; let Him deliver Him now if He will have Him; for He said, 'I am the Son of God.'"

MATTHEW 26:67-68; MATTHEW 27:41-43

Mockery was a major part of what Jesus had to endure the last hours of His life. Matthew records five distinct episodes of the mockery heaped upon Him. Two of those episodes occurred before Jesus was nailed to the cross. They were that of the religious leaders after they sentenced Him (Matt. 26:67-68) and that of the soldiers as they prepared Him for crucifixion (27:27-31). The other three episodes occurred while Jesus was on the cross. These instances of mockery came from some who passed by (27:39-40), the religious leaders (27:41-43), and from the two thieves crucified alongside Jesus (27:44).

So two of the five instances of men mocking Jesus came from the religious leaders. I want us to think about those two instances. More specifically, I want us to look for the message of heaven in their mockery.

I'm calling the mockery of the religious leaders the mockery of hell because it was driven and inspired by the devil himself. How do we know this? First, it was the mockery of hardness, and hardness comes from hell.

The hardness of their mockery is easy to see. They had just sentenced a man to die. In his splendid little book, *The Cross He Bore,* Frederick Leahy writes:

> To sentence someone to death is an awesome responsibility. One does not expect that judges who have passed such a sentence will almost immediately turn to revelry or frivolity. They should be burdened men. A solemn silence should pervade the courtroom. There should be a profound awareness of the majesty of the law.[5]

5 Frederick S. Leahy, *The Cross He Bore,* The Banner of Truth Trust, Edinburgh, Scotland, 1996, p.43

But these men were so hardened in their sinfulness that they couldn't feel the awesome weight of the sentence they had just pronounced.

Theirs was also the mockery of hell because of its blindness. These leaders were blinded in regard to the true identity of the man before them. Little did they know that they were mocking, not just a king, but the King of kings and the Lord of lords. They were mocking the very One who had given them life and the very One who at that moment was giving them the breath they needed to express their vicious insults and the strength they needed to deliver their crushing blows.

How were they supposed to know who Jesus was? He had stacked proof on top of proof in the many miracles that He had performed. But these men couldn't see the truth about Jesus. They were blind to it, and blindness to the truth about Him comes right out of hell (2 Cor. 4:4).

Theirs was also the mockery of hatred. These men didn't merely disagree with Jesus. They hated Him with a fierce hatred. Why did they hate Him so intensely? He had claimed to be their Messiah, but He wasn't the kind of Messiah that they wanted. They wanted a temporal Messiah who would break their bondage to the Roman government and lead Israel to great glory.

They thought their hatred for Jesus was well founded and justified, but hatred for Christ is always hell-fueled and hell-driven.

As we've noticed, there were two instances of the religious leaders mocking Jesus. One was immediately after they sentenced Him. The other was while He was on the cross. As they stood at the foot of the cross, they cried: "He saved others; Himself He cannot save" (Matt. 27:42).

In their hardness and their blindness, these men didn't realize that they were actually telling the truth about Jesus. They were, in fact, declaring the very message of heaven. There at the foot of the cross, these men became preachers of the gospel of Christ. No, they didn't realize it then, and most of them probably never realized it. But their lack of understanding doesn't change the fact that it was the message of heaven they declared.

Jesus came to this earth to provide redemption for all who will believe in Him. To do that, He had to die a special death on the cross. It was special because He actually received the wrath of God in the place of sinners. If Jesus had come down from the cross to save Himself, the plan of redemption would have failed. He could not simultaneously save Himself from the cross and save sinners.

So in the mockery of hell heaped on Jesus, we hear the message of heaven. And the joke is on the devil.

August 26

Easter: Amazing, but Not Surprising

From God's Word, the Bible...

Then, as they were afraid and bowed their faces to the earth, they said to them, "Why do you seek the living among the dead? He is not here, but is risen! Remember how He spoke to you when He was still in Galilee. . ."

Luke 24:5-6

Easter is, as one hymn writer put it, "Our triumphant, holy day." Every Christian loves Easter. Easter thrills Christians.

But I have to say that while Easter thrills me, it doesn't surprise me. To the contrary, I would be surprised if there had been no Easter.

Now, Christmas and Good Friday surprise me. Immensely so! Christmas was born in the heart of God centuries before Jesus was born. Before the world began, God looked down the long corridor of time and saw that the man He intended to create would fall into sin and bring disastrous consequences upon the entire human race. So Christmas was born. God looked at the forthcoming human sin in all of its nastiness and filthiness and decided that He would send His Son into the midst of it all. He would send His Son into this world as one of us. His Son would take our humanity even to the point of actually being born of a woman and coming into this world as a tiny baby.

The Father set this plan before the Son there in eternity past. And the Son agreed! He didn't have to agree. The Son of God could have said: "I am not going to humiliate Myself for sinners who have trampled My Father's commands and spit in His face." And the Son wouldn't have done wrong if He had refused to come. He could have left us to ourselves in the sin and misery that we brought upon ourselves, and He Himself would still have been pure and holy.

But what is this? He agrees to come! He agrees there when the Father first set the plan before Him, and as human history begins and the centuries begin to come and go, He, the Son, still agrees.

Finally, the time arrives. The date that God the Father circled on the calendar back there in eternity past finally comes. And God the Son does just as He agreed to do. He steps into human history as a baby. Now we have a marvel that can't be measured or described. The infinite God is in a tiny package. God is in that baby born in Bethlehem. It would have been amazing to me had the Lord agreed to come to this earth as a full-grown man, but He comes as a baby! Charles Wesley attempts to describe this marvel in these words:

Our God contracted to a span,
Incomprehensibly made man.

We will never appreciate the fact that Jesus came until we appreciate the fact that He didn't have to come.

Christmas is stunning to me. And so is Good Friday. It tells me that this One who didn't have to come went to a cross and died.

Just as He didn't have to come, so He didn't have to die. He could have spoken a mere word and instantly slaughtered those who wanted to nail Him to the cross. Or after they nailed Him there, He could have stepped down in a blaze of glory. He didn't need the angels of heaven to assist Him, but He could have called them (Matt. 26:53). And one wonders if those very angels didn't surround Calvary with bated breath as they expected His command.

But He didn't step down from the cross, and He didn't call for the angels. He stayed on the cross to die, and die He did, crying in His last moments: "It is finished!" (John 19:30).

A man dying! What's so unusual about that? In this case, it was a man dying a death that He didn't have to die to achieve something for people who didn't deserve it. On the cross, Jesus received the wrath of God that we deserve so we don't have to experience that wrath if we will receive for ourselves what He did there. Once again, we look to Charles Wesley:

'Tis myst'ry all: th' Immortal dies:
Who can explore His strange design?
In vain the firstborn seraph tries
To sound the depths of love divine.
'Tis mercy all! Let earth adore,
Let angel minds inquire no more.

God takes our humanity and dies! Christmas? Amazing! Good Friday? Absolutely astonishing!

And now Easter comes to tell us that this One who came at Christmas and died on Good Friday has risen from the grave. And I have to say: "Of course, He did. How could it be otherwise?"

August 27

A Psalm for Cave Dwellers

From God's Word, the Bible...

Be merciful to me, O God, be merciful to me!
For my soul trusts in You;
And in the shadow of Your wings I will make my refuge,
Until these calamities have passed by.
I will cry out to God Most High,
To God who performs all things for me.

Psalm 57:1-2

David wrote this psalm from a cave. Why was he, the hero who had slain Goliath, dwelling in a cave? He was hiding from King Saul, who hated him and wanted to kill him.

David wouldn't have been in this cave if he hadn't been in trouble. We can call it "the cave of David's trouble."

If David's cave represents trouble, we have to say we're all cave dwellers from time to time. It's possible to live in a comfortable house and still be a cave dweller.

What does David the cave dweller have to say to all the rest of us cave dwellers?

First, he shows us that *the cave of our trouble can and should be the cave of our refuge.* From the cave of his trouble, David cries to God:

And in the shadow of Your wings I will make my refuge
Until these calamities have passed by (v. 1).

The picture here is of the little chick that runs to its mother to take refuge under her wings. David's circumstances were such that he felt as helpless and frightened as that chick. As the chick was confident that his mother would protect him, so David was confident that God would protect him. We know, of course, that the hen can't protect her chicks from every conceivable danger. But God is sufficient for us in every trial and every circumstance.

David also shows us that *the cave of our trouble can and should be the cave of our prayer.*

Prayer is the way in which David took refuge in God. This whole 57th Psalm is a prayer. It shows us that:

- we should pray when we are in trouble;
- we can and should speak honestly to God;
- we must pray sincerely from our hearts;
- we must pray with a consciousness of the greatness of God.

David also encourages us to believe that *the cave of our trouble is the cave of God's purpose for us*. He tells us that God "performs all things" for him (v. 2).

So David wasn't in this cave by accident. His presence there didn't catch God off guard or take Him by surprise. That cave was part of God's purpose for him. It was necessary to make him into the man that God wanted him to be, the man who could serve as king over Israel and write psalms such as this one.

We're inclined to take our difficult circumstances to mean that God has forsaken us or that He doesn't care for us. We must learn to look at those circumstances as proofs that He hasn't forsaken us, and He does care for us.

A marvelous day of explanation is coming for every one of God's people. God will finally explain what His purpose was in sending various hardships our way. When He explains, we will see the whole picture, and we will be amazed at what He accomplished with us through our trials.

Yet another lesson that David offers us is this: *the cave of our trouble can and should be the cave of our opportunity.*

Every trial that comes our way gives us the opportunity to examine our hearts and to say with David:

> *My heart is steadfast, O God, my heart is steadfast (v. 7).*

And every trial gives us the opportunity to confess our faith in God and to offer praise to Him, as David did (vv. 9-11).

Finally, David shows us that *the cave of our trouble will not always be the cave of our trouble.* David knew that his own "calamities" would pass by (v. 1).

Our calamities will pass by as well. We see many of them pass by in this life. Things come and trouble us for a while, and then they are gone. When this happens, we must not forget to thank God for His goodness to us. How quick we are to complain when trouble comes! How slow we can be to thank God when the trouble passes!

The fact that some calamities don't pass by in this life doesn't mean that they will never pass. Our troubles aren't eternal. A day is coming when every single trouble will pass by for the children of God. And that will all be due to the saving work of Jesus Christ.

The only calamity that never passes is the one that applies to those who don't receive Christ (John 3:36). Have you turned away from sin and are you trusting in Him?

August 28

Mistaken Assumptions

From God's Word, the Bible...

. . . but supposing Him to have been in the company, they went a day's journey, and sought Him among their relatives and acquaintances.

Jesus said to her, "Woman, why are you weeping? Whom are you seeking?" She, supposing Him to be the gardener, said to Him, "Sir, if You have carried Him away, tell me where You have laid Him, and I will take Him away."

Luke 2:44; John 20:15

Two occasions, two assumptions, two mistakes—that's the story of these two verses of Scripture.

On the first occasion, we have the mistake of assuming Jesus to be present when He was actually absent.

On the second occasion, we have the mistake of assuming Jesus to be absent when He was actually present.

The first mistaken assumption was that of Joseph and Mary. Having gone to Jerusalem to attend the Feast of the Passover, they were on their way back to Nazareth. It was common in those days for pilgrims to Jerusalem to travel in companies or caravans. Joseph and Mary were in their caravan and a day's journey from Jerusalem. They assumed that Jesus was "in the company," but He wasn't. He had "lingered behind in Jerusalem" (Luke 2:43).

It was back to Jerusalem for Joseph and Mary when they realized their error. There they found Jesus in the temple engaged in dialogue with "the teachers" (v. 46), who were "astonished at His understanding and answers" (v. 47).

Joseph and Mary had wrongly assumed that Jesus was present when He was absent. I wonder how often their error has been repeated through the centuries. I wonder how frequently it is being repeated in our time.

It's so very easy for us to assume that the Lord is present in our church services when He has actually withdrawn. The church can be very much like Samson of old "who did not know that the Lord had departed from him" (Judg. 16:20).

But isn't the Lord always with His people? Yes, there is a sense in which He is. But we might say He can be present and absent at the same time. He can be present but withdrawn. He can be present, but not present to bless. His can be a grieved presence. We can think of it in terms of a husband and wife being present in their home but so alienated from each other that they are in fact absent from each other.

What causes the Lord to be so grieved with His churches that He withdraws from them? He's surely grieved when we distort and misrepresent His truth to make it fit modern beliefs and assumptions. He must surely be driven away by irreverent and silly shenanigans that make the church seem more like a carnival than a church. He's offended when we go through the motions of worship while our hearts are far from Him. He's most certainly vexed when His people live without regard to His commandments. Nothing is sadder than for God's people to assure themselves that the Lord is with them when He's not even on the premises.

The urgent need of this hour is for God's people to cry to Him to "come down," or, should we say, "come back?" (Isa. 64:1).

Now we come to the mistaken assumption of Mary Magdalene on the day of Jesus' resurrection. With the risen Christ standing right there before her, Mary Magdalene supposed Him "to be the gardener."

Jesus was present, but she assumed that He was absent. Even though Jesus had promised that He would rise from the grave, Mary Magdalene was not expecting it. She was lacking in faith.

We can do the same as she. We can look at the increasing evil of the world and the steadily growing hatred for Christianity as proofs that the Lord has completely withdrawn from us and left us to fend for ourselves. The Lord calls us to believe that while He doesn't approve of the evil all around us, He is working through it to bring all things to this end: every knee bowing before King Jesus, and every tongue confessing that He is Lord! (Phil. 2:9-11).

Satan would also have us look at our trials and hardships as indications that God is absent from us. But Scripture affirms that the very hardships that seem to indicate God's absence prove His presence. God is always at work in the lives of His people to conform them to the image of Christ. To achieve that end, He employs different methods. When He chooses to send difficulties our way, it doesn't mean that He has abandoned His purpose for us. It rather means that He is advancing that purpose through those very difficulties.

Assuming Christ to be present when He is absent will keep us from truly seeking Him. Assuming Christ to be absent when He is present will keep us from enjoying Him. So let's check our assumptions.

August 29

My Heavenly Father Watches Over Me

FROM GOD'S WORD, THE BIBLE...

"Therefore do not worry, saying, 'What shall we eat?' or 'What shall we drink?' or 'What shall we wear?' For after all these things the Gentiles seek. For your heavenly Father knows that you need all these things."

MATTHEW 6:31-32

To say William Clark Martin was a hymn writer is a gigantic understatement. He wrote hundreds and hundreds of hymns. We know little about William Martin. He was born on Christmas Day in 1864, and he died on August 30, 1914. He served as a pastor of Baptist churches in Connecticut, Massachusetts, Indiana, and Florida.

Some of his hymns have unusual titles: *Although Satan is Busy, I Get Along Quite Easy, Be a Sunny, Sunny Christian, Do Not Draw the Curtains over the Windows of the Soul,* and *I Cannot Explain It for Grace is So Strange.*

The best known of Martin's hymns is *My Heav'nly Father Watches Over Me.*

I trust in God wherever I may be,
Upon the land, or on the rolling sea,
For come what may, from day to day,
My heav'nly Father watches over me.

Refrain
I trust in God, I know He cares for me;
On mountain bleak or on the stormy sea;
Though billows roll, He keeps my soul;
My heav'nly Father watches over me.

He makes the rose an object of His care,
He guides the eagle through the pathless air,
And surely He remembers me;
My heav'nly Father watches over me.

I trust in God, for, in the lions' den,
On battlefield, or in the prison pen,
Through praise or blame, through flood or flame,
My heav'nly Father watches over me.

The valley may be dark, the shadows deep,
But, oh, the Shepherd guards His lonely sheep;
And through the gloom He'll lead me home,
My heav'nly Father watches over me.

It's easy to see why this hymn has been a favorite of God's people through the years. It calls us away from that thing which is easy for us to do—worrying—to embrace that thing which we often find so hard to do—trusting God.

This is a hymn of many extremes. It takes us from the land to the sea and from the lions' den to the battlefield and the prison pen. It takes us from the "mountain bleak" to the valley, which is "dark" with "shadows deep."

The common denominator in these various figures is hardship or difficulty. As he journeys through this world, the Christian often finds the mountain to be "bleak," the sea to be "stormy," and the valley to be "dark."

We can be thankful that while difficulty is often the case, it's not always the case. Every Christian has his share of bright days and calm seas. But there is something that is always the case—and that is the care of our heavenly Father. He knows each of us, just as He knows each rose and makes each one "an object of His care." He knows each eagle that soars through the air, and He guides each one through "the pathless air."

Any Christian who thinks that he or she is too small or insignificant to be noticed and known by God is simply wrong.

I like Martin's hymn very much. I need it. I need to be reminded that I'm always the object of my heavenly Father's care. I need to be reminded that I can trust Him in all of the variables of life.

But I have to say that I would like Martin's hymn even better if he had written a verse about why we must believe that our heavenly Father cares for us. So I hope he won't mind if I add this verse to his splendid hymn:

I trust in God, I know He cares for me;
He proved it beyond dispute on Calvary.
His Son took sin's blow, so I can know;
My heavn'ly Father watches over me.

August 30

Blessed Assurance

From God's Word, the Bible...

These things I have written to you who believe in the name of the Son of God, that you may know that you have eternal life, and that you may continue to believe in the name of the Son of God.

1 John 5:13

Christians love to sing Fanny Crosby's hymn *Blessed Assurance*, but many would probably admit that they lack the very assurance that they sing about. In my years as a pastor, people often came to me with this lament: "I'm not sure that I've been saved."

There are three possibilities on this matter of assurance—assured and not saved, saved and not assured, and both saved and assured.

In the above verse, the Apostle John expressed the desire for his readers to be in the third category. He wanted them to be saved and assured that they were saved. To that end, John counseled them to ask themselves these questions:

- Are they keeping the Lord's commandments?
- Are they confessing the truth about the Lord Jesus?
- Are they demonstrating love toward their brothers and sisters in Christ?

It's interesting that John mentioned each of these three tests three times in his short epistle. We find the commandment test in 2:3-6; 2:8-3:10; 4:13-21, the confession test in 2:18-27; 4:1-6, 13-21, and the love test in 2:7-11; 3:11-18; 4:7-12.

The commandment test can be particularly challenging for us. The reason is that we know how frequently we fail to live as we should. The commandment test seems to suggest that we should be free from sin, and we know that we aren't.

The love test can also prove to be very challenging. We sometimes find it hard to love some of our Christian family. Someone put it in these memorable words:

To live above with the saints we love,
That will be glory;
But to live below with the saints we know,
That's a different story.

We will always be in trouble if we think John is requiring perfection of us. That is, in fact, what many unbelievers seem to require. They think Christians claim to be perfect, and they can be very eager to dismiss Christianity as meaningless when they see any sin in a Christian.

But Christians aren't perfect in this world, and the apostle himself admits that in no uncertain terms: "If we say that we have no sin, we deceive ourselves, and the truth is not in us" (1:8).

Do Christians fail? Yes. But these things are also true of believers:

- They agree that the commandments of God are good and right.
- They know that they should obey them, and they strive to do so.
- They are grieved when they fail, and they repent.

Christians don't enjoy sin. It makes them miserable. Unbelievers are comfortable in sin, but Christians aren't. While hogs enjoy wallowing in the mud, sheep don't.

Some Christians say that they never lack assurance of their salvation because they have the witness of the Spirit. They remind us of these words from the Apostle Paul: "The Spirit Himself bears witness with our spirit that we are children of God. . . ." (Rom. 8:16).

We certainly don't want to deny that there is such a thing as the witness of the Spirit! But we must also not use that precious witness to exempt ourselves from the evidences given by the Apostle John. In other words, we must never say that we don't need to keep the commandments of the Lord or love our brothers and sisters in Christ because we have the witness of the Spirit. The witness of the Spirit is in tandem with these evidences and not in isolation from them.

The most helpful thing to me on this matter of assurance comes by looking to the Lord Jesus Christ. He is not only my Savior. He is my assurance. The devil wants to shift our focus from the Savior to our experience of salvation. He will tell us that we should have felt this and we should have said that when we received the Lord. The fact that we didn't feel as we should have and didn't say what we should have mean we're not saved. So argues Satan. But our assurance doesn't rest on us having a certain kind of salvation experience. It rests rather on Christ. We may not have had a perfect experience, but He died on the cross. When Satan seeks to shift our focus from Christ to ourselves, we must always shift it back to Christ, saying with Fanny Crosby:

Blessed assurance, Jesus is mine!
Oh, what a foretaste of glory divine!

August 31

Liar and Truth-Teller

From God's Word, the Bible...

Finally, my brethren, be strong in the Lord and in the power of His might. Put on the whole armor of God, that you may be able to stand against the wiles of the devil.

Ephesians 6:10-11

The acronym is LIAR. It is the *Lexicon of Intentionally Ambiguous Recommendations*. For someone who has proven himself to be a lazy employee, one might recommend him to another business by saying: "You would be very fortunate to get this person to work for you." For an employee who has been habitually in trouble with the law, one could say: "He is a man of many convictions." For an employee who is lacking in qualifications, one could write: "I most enthusiastically recommend this candidate with no qualifications whatsoever." Or one might say: "All in all, I cannot say enough good things about this candidate or recommend him too highly."

What about the employee who is so poor that the company would be better off to leave the position vacant? Here's the "recommendation" for that: "I can assure you that no person would be better for the job."

For a former employee who couldn't get along with his fellow-employees, one might say: "I am pleased to say that this candidate is a former colleague of mine."

And here is the "recommendation" for the person who deserves no consideration at all: "I would urge you to waste no time in making this person an offer of employment."

In this lexicon, the term "intentionally ambiguous" is the delicate, sanitary name for deception, and while we might find these "recommendations" to be clever and funny, we wouldn't enjoy being on the receiving end of them.

Deception has been going on for a very long time. It is almost as old as the human race itself. Satan was the original practitioner of it in the Garden of Eden, and he continues to use it with great success. He is the master deceiver.

One of Satan's favorite ways to practice deception is by putting ministers into pulpits who distort the message of Christianity. The Apostle Paul put it in these words: ". . . Satan himself transforms himself into an angel of light. Therefore it is no great thing if his ministers also transform themselves into ministers of righteousness, whose end will be according to their works" (2 Cor. 11:14b-15).

Satan uses his false ministers to lull people to sleep in regard to spiritual matters. He uses them to say that we are basically good and that we need not worry about the matter of sin. He uses them to persuade us that if there is such a thing as sin, it isn't serious because there is no judgment to come. He uses them to convince us that all are headed for heaven and, therefore, don't need the Lord Jesus as our Savior.

The thing the Bible always stresses about the devil is his subtlety. He doesn't come to us in a frightful way. Paul says he "transforms himself into an angel of light." His ministers don't come across as uncouth, crude clodhoppers. They are smooth, suave, sophisticated, clever, and funny. They are so personally appealing that naïve listeners assume that they couldn't possibly be wrong. But wrong they are, as those who heed them will eventually learn.

On the other hand, the Lord Jesus is the supreme truth-teller. He told the truth about the devil when He said: ". . .he does not stand in the truth, because there is no truth in him. When he speaks a lie, he speaks from his own resources, for he is a liar and the father of it" (John 8:44).

He also plainly warned about the devil's ministers: "Beware of false prophets, who come to you in sheep's clothing, but inwardly they are ravenous wolves" (Matt. 7:15).

He also tells us the truth about ourselves. He confronts us with the reality of our sinfulness (John 3:19-20) and with the certainty of divine judgment (Matt. 25:31-46).

Still further, He tells us the truth about Himself, affirming for us that He came from God (John 8:42) to provide salvation for sinners, and that we will have that salvation if we repent of our sins (Luke 13:5) and trust in Him (John 3:16,18).

The Bible is not "intentionally ambiguous" about Satan or the Lord Jesus. It is intentionally unambiguous about both, and it calls us to be intentionally unambiguous about them as well by rejecting the devil and his schemes and by receiving Christ and His salvation.

THE MONTH OF SEPTEMBER

Rover and the Cows

… And 30 Other Bible-Based Meditations

I used to marvel at Rover. Milking time would come, and Dad would say: "Rover, get the cows!" But Rover wouldn't immediately dash off as one might expect. He would listen until he heard the bell that Dad had put around the neck of one of the cows. Then he would dash off, find the cows and slowly herd them home. It was obvious that he relished doing his job. It was something that made him feel proud.

Contents

September 1

Rover and the Cows

From God's Word, the Bible...

Whatever your hand finds to do, do it with your might; for there is no work or device or knowledge or wisdom in the grave where you are going.

Ecclesiastes 9:10

We finally decided it would be best to let Rover retire. Rover was our dog through my childhood years. When he was just a pup, Dad trained him to "get the cows." That meant Rover was supposed to find the cows in the pasture and herd them to the barn.

I used to marvel at Rover. Milking time would come, and Dad would say: "Rover, get the cows!" But Rover wouldn't immediately dash off as one might expect. He would listen until he heard the bell that Dad had put around the neck of one of the cows. Then he would dash off, find the cows, and slowly herd them home. It was obvious that he relished doing his job. It was something that made him feel proud.

Rover did a good job for a long time. But as he began to age, his interest in getting the cows began to wane. It was no longer something that he wanted to do. It may have been the accumulating aches and pains of old age that caused him to hate the job that he used to love. But the change was evident for all to see. We would tell him to get the cows, and he would look away. He might even growl. When we insisted, he would finally and reluctantly go. The most obvious change was in the way he brought the cows home. Instead of slowly herding them, he began to drive them as fast as he could. When the cows got to the barn, they would be winded and sweaty.

So there was nothing to do except let Rover retire and drop his monthly social security check in the mail. Rover seemed to enjoy his retirement, most of which he spent sleeping in the warm sunshine and perhaps nostalgically recalling the glory days when he happily went to the get the cows.

Finally, the end came for Rover. I arrived home one day from my college commute to hear my Dad say: "I've got a job for you to do. I want you to bury Rover." It was one sad job. The tears flowed as I shoveled the dirt over my true and faithful friend.

As the years slide by and the aches and pains accumulate, I understand more and more Rover's desire to retire. Having retired from the pastorate a few years ago, I can say that retirement is more than okay. If I had known I was going to enjoy it so much, I would have done it long before I did! But there are dangers associated with it. We must never allow ourselves to think that we can retire from living for the glory of the Lord. We may find it necessary to step aside from "getting the cows," that is, from those ministries that call for the physical and mental strength of youth. But that doesn't mean we stop serving the Lord altogether. We older saints can strive to excel in prayer to the Lord and encouragement to others. I have benefited much from senior saints who have given themselves to these things. I now hope I can follow their good example.

The text above tells us to do with all our might whatever our "hand finds to do." My hand doesn't find as much to do as it did several years ago, but the things it does find to do are to be done heartily as unto the Lord.

When we find our interest in the work of the Lord faltering, we need to look to the Lord for more strength and motivation. Let our motto always be "looking unto Jesus" (Heb. 12:2). Looking to Him as He died in our stead on the cross will always increase our interest in the things of God and our strength for serving Him.

I've often been asked over the years if animals will be in heaven. I never hesitate to say that they will. The salvation of human beings is only one part of God's plan of redemption. The other part is God putting this physical order back to where it was before sin entered (Rom. 8:18-22). Since animals were part of the original creation, I expect them to be present in the new creation.

I hope my good friend Rover will be there. Perhaps there will even be occasion for me to say to him: "Come on Rover. Let's go get the cows."

September 2

The Greatest of All Miracles

From God's Word, the Bible...

And the Word became flesh and dwelt among us, and we beheld His glory, the glory as of the only begotten of the Father, full of grace and truth.

For He made Him who knew no sin to be sin for us, that we might become the righteousness of God in Him.

For Christ also suffered once for sins, the just for the unjust, that He might bring us to God, being put to death in the flesh but made alive by the Spirit.

John 1:14; 2 Corinthians 5:21; 1 Peter 3:18

The Bible tells us about many miracles. Which is the greatest? I don't hesitate to say it's Jesus Himself.

The miracle of Jesus is threefold—His incarnation, His death, and His resurrection. The above texts set forth the threefold miracle of Jesus as Him being made flesh, made sin, and made alive.

First, there is *the miracle of Jesus' incarnation*, which C.S. Lewis calls "The Grand Miracle." He writes: "Every other miracle prepares for this, exhibits this, or results from this."

Think about it! The Second Person of the Trinity took our humanity without divesting Himself of His deity! So now we have the God-man—fully God and fully man!

The Apostle John saw proof of this as he was with Jesus for more than three years. During this time, he and the other disciples closely observed Jesus. They "beheld" Him.

There were times in which Jesus appeared to be nothing more than mere flesh, that is, as another human being! But every time John and the others thought they were seeing another man in Jesus, He would, as it were, pull back the robe of His humanity so they could see the underlying deity.

Then there is *the miracle of Jesus' death*. Some look at Jesus dying on the cross and say: "There surely is no miracle in a man dying! Nothing is more commonplace than that!"

We may very well be inclined to say that if we think of Jesus' death in physical terms only. But this wasn't just another man dying another death. It was much more than that. The Apostle Paul reveals the much more when he says Christ was "made sin" for us.

Yes, Jesus died physically in the most horrible way imaginable. But the real suffering was enduring the penalty for sin, which is eternal separation from God! While Jesus was on the cross, He actually suffered an eternity's worth of separation from God so all who believe in Him don't have to experience that same separation themselves. That's why Jesus cried: "My God, My God, why have You forsaken Me?" (Matt. 27:46).

How could Jesus in the space of the six hours He was on the cross experience an eternity's worthy of God's wrath? We've noticed that He was God in human flesh. As God, He was an infinite person, and as an infinite person He could receive in a finite length of time an infinite amount of wrath. Jesus, as an infinite person, could receive in a finite length of time what we as finite people would have to receive in an infinite amount of time.

The miracle of Jesus' death is that He bore the weight of all our sins.

The miracle of the incarnation led to the miracle of the cross, and the miracle of the cross led to *the miracle of Jesus' resurrection.*

It was essential that Jesus die the special kind of death upon which He and the Father had agreed. It was essential for Him to receive the penalty for those sinners who would believe on Him so that there would be no penalty left for them.

But as vital as the cross was, it would have been to no avail if Jesus' body had rotted away in the tomb. His resurrection was also vital. It proved Him to be God in human flesh, and, in doing so, proved that His death on the cross was of infinite value. It also proved that God was entirely satisfied with the death of Christ in the place of sinners. God is the One whom we have offended through our sins, and it is God who must be satisfied. The fact that God is the One who raised Jesus from the dead proves that God was satisfied with His redeeming death.

In one sense, the cross was the verdict of sinful men on Jesus. By nailing Him there, they were pronouncing Him to be a fraud. The resurrection was the verdict of God on Jesus, and what a radically different verdict it was! God was reversing or setting aside the verdict of sinful men on His Son, and pronouncing His own verdict on Him. By raising Jesus from the dead, God was setting the record straight regarding His Son.

The incarnation, death, and resurrection join their voices to point us to the miracle of Jesus. Have you heeded their voices?

September 3

Father, Whate'er of Earthly Bliss

From God's Word, the Bible...

And we know that all things work together for good to those who love God, to those who are the called according to His purpose.

Romans 8:28

An old Welsh hymn uses the memorable phrase "life's cruel pounding." I would say Anne Steele could easily relate to that phrase. One blow came when her mother died when Anne was only three. Another blow came when at age nineteen she suffered a serious injury to her hip after being thrown from a horse. Yet another blow came when her fiancée drowned the day before their wedding. Further difficulties came her way when her stepmother and her sister died. Added to these were the burdens of caring for her sick father for many years as well as her own ongoing health problems.

In the midst of it all, Anne found comfort in writing hymns and poems (well over three hundred in number).

When her fiancé died, Anne took up her pen to write a long poem entitled *When I Survey Life's Varied Scene.* The last three verses of that poem made their way into many hymnals under the title *Father, Whate'er of Earthly Bliss.*

These three verses (and the long poem from which they were taken) are a prayer. Isn't it interesting that Anne chose to let the pounding of life drive her to God instead of away from Him? Life pounded, and she prayed! Prayer is always a strong and sure refuge in our hours of great need. We're bound to regret not availing ourselves of that refuge more often. Many have looked back over their lives with the wish that they would have prayed more. I've never heard of anyone wishing that he or she had prayed less.

Anne's prayer is bulging with trust. She says:

Father, whate'er of earthly bliss,
Thy sovereign will denies;
Accepted at Thy throne of grace,
Let this petition rise:

Yes, life had severely wounded her, but she rested in the knowledge that the sovereign God of the universe was her Father, and His throne was one of grace. The fact God is sovereign means that He rules the lives of His people to the glory of His name. Nothing comes our way apart from His knowledge and purpose. Nothing that happens to us gets around God. Everything springs from His heart and passes through His hands.

Our flesh screams out in protest: "You mean this hardship has come from God? Why would He do such a thing?"

We want answers, and we want them now! But we must wait for our answers, and we must believe as we wait that, when the answers come, they will reveal God's loving heart. When the book of explanation is finally read, we will not see any flaws in God's governance but only in our faith.

With confidence that God's throne is one of grace, Anne offered some petitions to the Lord. Verses two and three of her hymn relate them:

Give me a calm, thankful heart,
From every murmur free;
The blessings of Thy grace impart,
And let me live to Thee.

Let the sweet hope that Thou art mine,
My path of life attend;
Thy presence through my journey shine,
And bless its happy end.

In the midst of her trials, she wanted to have "a calm, thankful heart" and to be free from "every murmur." She didn't want to go through life complaining about what the Lord had sent her way. She understood that whether life be happy or sad, the Christian's business is always the same, that is, to live for the Lord.

Anne didn't ask for an easier life. She had the calm assurance that she belonged to the Lord. This was the "sweet hope" that she wanted to "attend" her as she walked the "path of life." She wanted the Lord to make His presence known to her as she journeyed along, and she wanted to know His blessing as she reached life's happy end. Life itself may be difficult for the Christian, but the ending is happy because it sweeps us into that realm where we will see our Lord and know difficulties no more.

By the way, Anne did indeed have a "happy end." When she died at age sixty-two in 1778, she was very peaceful. And her last words were: "I know that my Redeemer liveth."

How thankful we should be for that word "Redeemer"! It refers, of course, to the Lord Jesus Christ. He came from heaven to bring us back from sin and to God. Knowing Christ as our Redeemer outweighs the heaviest hardship, or, for that matter, all of our hardships.

September 4

What's Your Strategy?

From God's Word, the Bible...

But the righteousness of faith speaks in this way, "Do not say in your heart, 'Who will ascend into heaven?'" (that is, to bring Christ down from above) or, "'Who will descend into the abyss?'" (that is, to bring Christ up from the dead).

Romans 10:6-7

Many these days admit that the United States is more divided than at any time since the Civil War. At the mere mention of any issue, conservatives take one side and liberals the other.

There is still one issue on which we must all agree. We are going to die (Heb. 9:27). Yes, Christians who are living when Jesus comes will be exempt from death (1 Thess. 5:16-17), but the vast majority of us will die.

So here's my question: What's your strategy for facing the sobering reality of death?

Many will deny it, but most of us intuitively know that death is not the end. It isn't the cessation of existence. God has put eternity into our hearts (Eccl. 3:11).

So in asking for your strategy for facing death, I'm asking for your strategy for entering eternity. A strategy is a plan of action that is designed to achieve a desirable end. Do you have a plan of action for dying and going into eternity? What we really need is for someone who is an expert on such matters to come and help us. If we could only reach up to heaven and bring someone down! He could explain these things to us! And we would be very happy to hear and to heed!

If we could only find someone who has actually conquered death, someone who arose from the grave! He could give us the strategy we need for facing death! We would be more than ready to listen if such a person could be found!

The Bible tells us to stop our search for someone to come down from heaven or to come up from the grave. It's not that such a person can't be found. It's rather that such a person has been found. There's no need to search further. The need now is for people to listen to Him.

This person is Jesus Christ. He is the One who came down from heaven. Here's what He said to Nicodemus: "No one has ascended to heaven but He who came down from heaven, that is, the Son of Man. . . ." (John 3:13).

Jesus is also the One who came up from the grave. Here are His words about that: "I am He who lives, and was dead, and behold, I am alive forevermore. Amen. And I have the keys of Hades and of Death" (Rev. 1:18).

Jesus is the One, and the only One, who can speak with authority about dying and going to heaven. He came from heaven, He died, and He rose again.

How can we be sure that Jesus came from heaven? He did things that could only be done by someone from heaven. Benjamin Warfield explained His miracles in this way:

> When our Lord came down to earth He drew heaven with Him. The signs which accompanied His ministry were but the trailing clouds of glory which He brought from heaven which is His home.[6]

And how can we be sure that Jesus arose from the grave? The Apostle Paul gives us the answer in these words: ". . . this thing was not done in a corner" (Acts 26:26).

Jesus' resurrection wasn't hidden away from public view. Many saw the empty tomb and the risen Christ.

But there's a problem. Multitudes who think they would be willing to listen to such a person aren't willing to listen to Christ at all. It's just like Jesus said to Nicodemus: "Most assuredly, I say to you, We speak what We know and testify what We have seen, and you do not receive Our witness" (John 3:11).

Jesus came from heaven to speak to us about heaven, but we must be willing to receive His words. He came from heaven to receive on the cross the penalty for sinners so those sinners may go to heaven. But we must be willing to repent of our sins and trust in Him in His saving work on the cross.

Jesus arose from the grave to prove that He was indeed from heaven and that what He did on the cross is sufficient for our sins. And now Paul says to us: ". . . if you confess with your mouth the Lord Jesus and believe in your heart that God has raised Him from the dead, you will be saved" (Rom. 10:9).

Jesus is the strategy we all need for facing death and going to heaven. Have you made Him your strategy?

6 Benjamin B. Warfield, *Counterfeit Miracles* (Edinburgh: The Banner of Truth Trust, 1972), p.3.

September 5

Yokes of Wood and Iron

From God's Word, the Bible...

"Go and tell Hananiah, saying, 'Thus says the Lord: "You have broken the yokes of wood, but you have made in their place yokes of iron."

Jeremiah 28:13

A yoke was a wooden device placed over the neck of an ox to enable it to pull a wagon or a plow. Sometimes oxen were "yoked" together as a team. The yoke represented servitude.

As he declared the word of the Lord to the people of Judah, Jeremiah also wore a yoke. No joke—this prophet wore a yoke!

Jeremiah's yoke was intended to convey this solemn truth: God had put Babylon's yoke of servitude on Judah (Jer. 27:2,11). The Babylonians had already taken some of Judah's citizens into captivity, and another invasion would soon come. Resistance from the people of Judah would only lead to greater disaster (27:8,11). The need, then, was for the Jewish people to submit to the yoke of Babylon as an ox submits to the yoke of its master.

We must not think Jeremiah's message consisted only of gloom and doom. He also stressed the grace of God, which would produce the release of the Jews from Babylon after seventy years.

Even with this note of grace, Jeremiah's message wasn't a popular one. A lot of people didn't like it. Hananiah was one of them. Believing that God had already broken the yoke of Babylon and that those who had been taken captive would soon return (vv. 2-4), Hananiah decided to take bold action. He confronted Jeremiah at the temple in the presence of the priests and other worshipers, took the yoke from his neck, and smashed it (v. 10). He then declared: "Thus says the Lord: 'Even so I will break the yoke of Nebuchadnezzar king of Babylon from the neck of all nations within the space of two full years'" (v. 11).

Wonderful, but wrong! That was Hananiah's message.

After this incident, the Lord told Jeremiah to go to Hananiah with this message: "Thus says the Lord: 'You have broken the yokes of wood, but you have made in their place yokes of iron'" (v. 13).

The forthcoming captivity to the Babylonians was a yoke of iron. It couldn't be broken. It would definitely happen (v. 14).

But there was more. A yoke of iron is heavier than one of wood. By his false message, Hananiah had made things worse. He had caused the people to "trust in a lie" (v. 15). The captivity would be hard for those who knew it was coming. It would be even harder for those who believed it wasn't coming.

It was the Lord who was bringing captivity to the people of Judah. In telling them that it wouldn't happen, Hananiah was preaching "rebellion against the LORD" (v. 16). Part of the price for his false message was his own death, which came within two months of his encounter with Jeremiah (vv.1, 17).

That long-ago day may seem to have no value in this day when most people know little or nothing about prophets, Babylonians or yokes. But the truth is that old day is this day. Hananiah and Jeremiah are still with us. Hananiah wants to make people feel good. He doesn't want them to be weighed down with talk about sin and judgment, and the need for repentance.

But then there is Jeremiah. He talks about those very things that Hananiah spurns. He talks about the reality of our sins, and he tells us about judgment to come. He calls us to repent of our sins, and he assures us that God will graciously forgive us if we do repent.

Hananiah's message sounds good and makes us feel good, but it is Jeremiah's message that will actually do us good.

The passing of time proved Jeremiah's message to be correct. The Babylonians did come once again to Judah and took most of the people into captivity, and after seventy years the Jews were released from their captivity and restored to their homeland.

Hananiah's smashing of Jeremiah's yoke makes me think of another object of wood—the cross of Christ. As Hananiah hated Jeremiah's yoke, so there are modern Hananiahs who hate that cross of wood. They want to smash that cross, that is, destroy its message. They are "enemies of the cross of Christ" (Phil. 3:18).

Those who hate the message of the cross can never destroy it. The cross lives on! In hating that cross they only succeed in making for themselves a yoke of iron—a much heavier burden—the burden of eternal separation from God.

September 6

A Soldier of the Cross

FROM GOD'S WORD, THE BIBLE...

You therefore must endure hardship as
a good soldier of Jesus Christ.

2 TIMOTHY 2:3

Isaac Watts didn't look much like a soldier. He was stumpy and homely. Stumpy? Yes, he was five feet tall. Homely? Yes, that too. He had a large head, small eyes, and a hooked nose. Some of his unappealing appearance may have resulted from a serious bout with smallpox when he was very young. Whatever the cause, it proved to be very costly to him. A beautiful young woman declined his proposal of marriage with these words: "Mr. Watts, I only wish I could say that I admire the casket as much as I admire the jewel."

We understand that the term "casket" in those days often referred to a jewel box. As a person, Watts was a jewel, but, alas, his body made a very poor jewel box.

When he was very young, Watts began to write poetry. And it wasn't long until he began to notice the singing in his church. After a service in which it was notably poor, Watts said to his father: "The singing of God's praise is the part of worship nearest heaven and its performance among us is the worst on earth."

His father responded by urging him to do something about the situation. Young Isaac did exactly that. He spent that afternoon writing the hymn *Behold the Glories of the Lamb*, which his church sang that very night. They loved it and urged him to write more. Write he did, producing 750 hymns and earning for himself the title "The Father of English Hymnody." Some of his best-known hymns are *When I Survey the Wondrous Cross*; *At the Cross*; *Jesus Shall Reign*; *O God, Our Help in Ages Past,* and *Joy to the World*.

Watts was also a pastor. In 1701 at age twenty-six, he became the pastor of the Mark Lane Independent Church in London. Although often plagued by ill health, he continued to serve there until his death on November 25, 1748.

So Watts' life often brought him hardship and disappointment, but nothing deterred him from serving the Lord. Those who use the slightest inconvenience as an excuse to step aside from service would do well to learn from him. In the hymn *Am I a Soldier of the Cross?* Watts asks:

Must I be carried to the skies
On flowery beds of ease. . . ?

Watts answered that question for himself with an emphatic "No!" He didn't think his difficulties entitled him to "flowery beds of ease." He was a soldier of the cross.

The author of Hebrews urged his readers to be "looking unto Jesus" (Heb. 12:2). We should do so every day and in every way. When we look to Him on this matter of difficulties, what do we see? The first thing is this: no one ever had to endure more hardship than He. The next thing is this: Jesus didn't let the adversities He encountered drive Him away from the work that He came to this earth to perform—the glorious work of redemption. If He had done so, there would have been no salvation from sin and no eternal life for any of us.

We may have allowed ourselves to think from time to time that the work of redemption was, as the saying goes, "a piece of cake" for Jesus. After all, He was God! How hard could it have been for Him? We won't have the complete answer to that question until we finally get to heaven. When we get that answer, we will be astounded. We do know that His saving work:

- caused Him to cross the incredible chasm between being the Prince of heaven and being a helpless baby in a manger;
- caused Him to leave the courts of heaven where the triune God was perfectly loved, worshiped, and obeyed, and come into this realm in which there was much of sin and little of love, worship, and obedience toward God. How it must have grieved Him to live every day with sin and shame all around!
- caused Him to go to the cross where He actually endured the wrath of God in the place of unworthy, undeserving sinners.

When we feel as if our problems exempt us from serving the Lord, we do well to recall Isaac Watts, who didn't opt out from serving God. We do even better to think of Jesus: "For consider Him who endured such hostility from sinners against Himself, lest you become weary and discouraged in your souls" (Heb. 12:3).

September 7

Surveying the Cross

From God's Word, the Bible...

But God forbid that I should boast except in the cross of our Lord Jesus Christ, by whom the world has been crucified to me, and I to the world.

Galatians 6:14

Isaac Watts, a soldier of the cross, wrote some marvelous hymns about the Lord Jesus dying on the cross. Two of my favorites are *When I Survey the Wondrous Cross* and *At the Cross* (or *Alas, and Did My Savior Bleed*?).

In the first of these he calls us to "survey" the cross. To "survey" something is to do far more than casually glance at it. It is to thoroughly inspect something until we can form a proper appraisal of it. How many of us can say that we have surveyed the cross of Christ? How many of us have formed a true and accurate appraisal of it?

Watts wants us to look steadily at the cross until we see the "wondrous" nature of it. A wondrous thing is something that causes us to marvel with amazement. Part of the sadness of this age is that we marvel at things that aren't really all that marvelous and we fail to marvel at those things that are.

The marvel of the cross lies in the One who was there and in what He was doing there.

Who was on that cross? Watts tells us it was "the Prince of glory." It was the One who came from the glories of heaven to this earth. It was the glorious Son of God who left behind all the glorious trappings of heaven and the praises of the angels so that He could take our humanity. No, He didn't lay aside His deity to do this. God can't quit being God. It's rather that He added to His deity our humanity.

The person who was on that cross is part of what makes it wondrous. The other part of what makes it wondrous is what He was doing there. Watts makes this explicit in *At the Cross*:

Was it for crimes that I have done,
He groaned upon the tree?

Jesus was not on the cross for Himself. He was not there because He deserved to be. He was there because we deserve to be. It was our "crimes" that put Him there. Our crimes are our sins. Sins are crimes. Our sins are lawbreaking. God has given us laws by which we are to live, and we choose to break them rather than keep them.

The Lord Jesus was on the cross as if He were a lawbreaker even though He Himself had never broken any of God's laws. He was there to receive the penalty for our lawbreaking.

Isn't the penalty for our sins far greater than physical death? Yes! Now we're getting to the very heart of the cross. It was far more than Jesus dying physically. How many of us have surveyed the cross enough to realize this? It was Jesus receiving the wrath of God on our lawbreaking. It was Jesus enduring an eternity's worth of separation from God so that all who repent of their sins and trust in Him don't have to endure that same penalty.

The Prince of Glory on the cross to receive my hell—that's the wonder of the cross! Watts saw it and marveled. Have we seen it?

Once we see what Watts saw, we can easily understand these words from *When I Survey*:

Forbid it, Lord, that I should boast,
Save in the death of Christ my God!
All the vain things that charm me most,
I sacrifice them to His blood.

Were the whole realm of nature mine,
That were a present far too small;
Love so amazing, so divine,
Demands my life, my soul, my all.

This is the response of adoring praise and firm resolve. Has the Prince of Glory received the wrath of God for me? I will give up "the vain things" of this world to live for Him. I will give Him "my life, my soul, my all."

We find a similar response in *At the Cross*:

But drops of grief can ne'er repay
The debt of love I owe:
Here, Lord, I give myself away,
'Tis all that I can do!

Our choice is never between a cross-centered Christianity and another kind of Christianity for this simple reason: there is no Christianity apart from the cross. The choice is rather this: Will we intently study the cross until we see the wonder of it, or will we only lightly ponder it?

September 8

We're Marching to Zion

From God's Word, the Bible...

So the ransomed of the Lord shall return,
And come to Zion with singing,
With everlasting joy on their heads.
They shall obtain joy and gladness;
Sorrow and sighing shall flee away.

Isaiah 51:11

The year 1707 saw the release of Isaac Watts' stirring, happy hymn, *We're Marching to Zion*. I well remember the small church in which I grew up triumphantly singing these words (the refrain was added later by Robert Lowry):

Come, we that love the Lord,
And let our joys be known;
Join in a song with sweet accord,
And thus surround the throne.
We're marching to Zion, Beautiful, beautiful Zion;
We're marching upward to Zion, The beautiful city of God.

The word "Zion" sometimes appears in Scripture as a reference to the city of Jerusalem. In other places, it refers to the heavenly city, the New Jerusalem, which is the destiny of all of God's people. It's the heavenly Zion that Watts' hymn puts before us. The message of the hymn is quite plain. The thought of going to heaven ought to so fill our hearts with joy that we can't help but sing.

Watts took a dim view of those who claim to have their sins forgiven and to be on their way to heaven but refuse to sing:

Let those refuse to sing,
Who never knew our God;
But children of the heav'nly King,
May speak their joys abroad.

Someone might excuse himself for not singing by saying: "I will wait until I get to heaven." Watts' response to such thinking is found here:

The men of grace have found
Glory begun below;
Celestial fruits on earthly ground
From faith and hope may grow.

The hill of Zion yields
A thousand sacred sweets,
Before we reach the heav'nly fields,
Or walk the golden streets.

Heaven is the future possession of God's people, but it's also our present possession. Glory has already begun here "below." "Celestial fruits" can grow here on "earthly ground" as God's people exercise "faith and hope." Faith is the confidence, the calm assurance, of what we as Christians possess through Christ. Hope is stronger. It is eagerly looking forward to possessing that which we are sure of. Faith makes us sure. Hope makes us eager.

Watts also affirms that heaven is even now yielding for us "a thousand sacred sweets." These are to be enjoyed now before we reach "the heavenly fields or walk the golden streets."

What are these "sweets"? They are the blessings—the spiritual privileges—that are ours to enjoy as we journey to our heavenly home. These may not be exactly one thousand in number, but they are numerous—far more than most of us realize. When we get to heaven and look back over our earthly pilgrimage, we will be amazed at the number of ways God blessed us.

This is a world of tears, but all our tears aren't enough to destroy the joy of knowing that heaven will be our home. So Watts urges us to put things in their proper perspective:

Then let our songs abound,
And every tear be dry:
We're marching through Immanuel's ground
To fairer worlds on high.

The Bible doesn't tell us to never cry. It rather tells us to use our hope of heaven to dry our tears.

In pointing us to heaven and urging us to rejoice in it, Watts doesn't fail to remind us of the way to get there. We walk to heaven on "Immanuel's ground."

The name "Immanuel" means "God with us" (Matt. 1:23), and it refers to the Lord Jesus who left the glories of heaven to come to this earth in our humanity. He came in flesh to be with us (John 1:14), but He also came to do something for us, that is, to die on the cross so that we might be saved.

There has to be ground on which we walk if we are to journey to heaven, and we walk on it by repenting of our sins and trusting in Him.

September 9

Rags and Old Clothes Never Looked So Good

From God's Word, the Bible...

Then Ebed-Melech the Ethiopian said to Jeremiah, "Please put these old clothes and rags under your armpits, under the ropes." And Jeremiah did so.

Jeremiah 38:12

One of the many joys of heaven will be meeting people of faith who appear only briefly in the Bible. I'm referring to people who emerged from obscurity to boldly act for the Lord before going into obscurity again. One of these is Ebed-Melech, the man of rags and old clothes.

We must, however, start with the prophet Jeremiah. He was God's truth-teller in a truth-hating time. The truth Jeremiah told the people of Judah was quite simple. Because of their continued disobedience to God and their refusal to repent, God was bringing calamity upon them in the form of the Babylonian Empire (Jer. 38:1-3).

Lots of people hated that message, and they hated Jeremiah for preaching it. The Jeremiah-haters thought his message must be false because it was unpleasant and made them uncomfortable. Multitudes hold the same view in our era!

Four men—Shephatiah, Gedaliah, Jucal, and Pashhur—decided to take action. They went to their king, the lily-livered Zedekiah, and asked permission to do away with the prophet. The king lamely responded to their request with these reprehensible words: "Look, he is in your hand. For the king can do nothing against you" (v. 5).

So these men, in one of the foulest of all deeds, seized Jeremiah and lowered him into the mud of a waterless cistern (v. 6). They wanted him dead, but they didn't want to actually shed his blood. So they would let him die from having no food or water and being in the cold and the damp. Heartless men, these four!

That brings us to Ebed-Melech, an Ethiopian eunuch who served in the king's palace. He could have excused himself from taking any action by telling himself that it was none of his business or that any action he took would only bring him trouble. If such thoughts entered his mind, he quickly dismissed them. He went boldly to the king who was sitting in a public place and spoke about Jeremiah in the cistern (vv. 7-9). Now the king was on the spot. While Jeremiah wasn't popular, few of Judah's citizens would have approved of him being tortured.

The king told Ebed-Melech to take thirty men with him to get Jeremiah out of the cistern. Why take thirty men? The king may have thought that Ebed-Melech would need them to protect him as he raised Jeremiah from the cistern. Those who put Jeremiah in the cistern would surely have been happy for Ebed-Melech to join him there.

Thoughtful man that he was, Ebed-Melech took some "old clothes and old rags" (v.12) for Jeremiah to have some cushioning. Lifting him from the mire of that cistern would require no small amount of tugging!

Because Ebed-Melech so kindly delivered the prophet from the cistern, the Lord promised to deliver him from the Babylonians (39:15-18).

How are we to explain Ebed-Melech? We surely have to trace his action back to God. We have to say that God's grace had so worked in his heart that he felt compassion for the prophet. We should learn from Ebed-Melech to show tender regard for those whom God has called to preach His Word (Matt. 10:41).

I see in Jeremiah's plight a picture of my own. As he was mired in the mud of that cistern, so I was once mired in the pit of sin and condemnation. And I see in Ebed-Melech a picture of the Lord Jesus Christ with a large difference. While Ebed-Melech used ropes, old clothes, and rags to raise Jeremiah from the cistern, the Lord Jesus Christ actually came into my cistern. He, who knew no sin, was made sin for me on the cross so that I could be delivered from it (2 Cor. 5:21).

Because of the saving grace of the Lord Jesus, I can now take as my own the words of David:

He also brought me up out of a horrible pit,
Out of the miry clay,
And set my feet upon a rock,
And established my steps.
He has put a new song in my mouth –
Praise to our God. . .
(Ps. 40:2-3a)

When I meet Ebed-Melech in heaven's glory, I will want to hear his account of pulling Jeremiah from the cistern. But I won't be surprised if he says: "Let me tell you, instead, about my cistern of sin that was far deeper than Jeremiah's and of the Savior who is far greater than I."

September 10

"Behold Your God"

From God's Word, the Bible...

O Zion, You who bring good tidings,
Get up into the high mountain;
O Jerusalem, You who bring good tidings,
Lift up your voice with strength,
Lift it up, be not afraid;
Say to the cities of Judah, "Behold your God!"

Isaiah 40:9

We often find the word "behold" in Scripture. It's a strong word. It calls us not to merely look at something, but to actually see it. How often we look without really seeing! We can go further. The word "behold" calls us to look intently at something until we feel a sense of wonder and admiration.

The church of the Lord Jesus Christ needs to recover the art of beholding. She often seems to be like a factory with machines droning and people moving about with dull familiarity. We seem to think Christianity is a product that has to be properly packaged and marketed if we are to get people to "buy" it. More specifically, Christianity is often presented as a product that insures success and happiness in this life. If certain levers are pulled and certain buttons pushed, the product will be purchased, and the customer will be happy. So the factory drones on.

The Christian faith ought to thrill our souls. But there's little thrill in five principles for this, six keys to that, or four secrets for the other.

The prophet Isaiah was enabled by the Spirit of God to look into the future. He saw a sobering thing. Most of his people, the people of Judah, would be in captivity in faraway Babylon. Life there would become humdrum and monotonous without anything to inspire or thrill.

So prompted by the Spirit, Isaiah wrote words that would bring comfort and wonder to those poor captives. While they were there in Babylon, they would be inclined to see nothing but Babylonians, difficulties, and sorrows. The need would be for them to lift up their eyes to see something greater than their situation.

Isaiah was the man God had selected to be the bearer of good news to Zion and Jerusalem (each a name for the people of God) in their captivity. What was Isaiah to say to them? The first thing was this: "Behold your God!"

The prophet was calling those captives to think about their God until their hearts were saturated with His glory and wonder. God couldn't be seen with physical eyes, but He could be seen with the eyes of faith.

With that initial "behold" in place, Isaiah quickly added two more. They were to behold the Lord God coming "with a strong hand" to "reward" them and to care for them as a shepherd (vv. 10-11). And they were to behold Him as the One who counts all the nations, including Babylon, as "a drop in a bucket" (v. 15). The promise was that their great God would, in due time, deliver them from Babylon and bring them back to their homeland. What a deliverance that would be! But it was at best only a faint picture of a far greater deliverance, namely, that of sinful people through the redeeming work of Christ.

Each "behold" caused Isaiah to launch into a breathtaking description of the greatness of God.

One of our newer songs, *Behold Our God*, marvelously gathers up Isaiah's description of God in these words:

Who has held the oceans in His hands?
Who has numbered every grain of sand?
Kings and nations tremble at His voice
All creation rises to rejoice.

Who has given counsel to the Lord?
Who can question any of His words?
Who can teach the One Who knows all things?
Who can fathom all His wondrous deeds?

Who has felt the nails upon His hands
Bearing all the guilt of sinful man?
God eternal humbled to the grave
Jesus, Savior, risen now to reign!

Chorus:
Behold our God seated on His throne, Come, let us adore Him!
Behold our King! Nothing can compare, Come, let us adore Him![7]

The reach of this song is truly thrilling, dropping, as it does, from the throne of the One who hold oceans and numbers grains of sand to the cross of Calvary where the Lord "felt the nails upon His hands" as He bore "the guilt of sinful man."

From his distant day, Isaiah calls to the church today. He calls us to stop focusing on the mundane and trivial and to behold our God, never forgetting as we do that the most glorious sight of Him is in His Son on the cross.

7 *Behold Our God*, sovereigngracemusic.org/music/songs/behold-our-god-who-has-held-the-oceans/ Words and music by Ryan Baird, Jonathan Baird, Meghan Baird, and Stephen Altrogge. © 2011

"Behold! the Lamb of God"

From God's Word, the Bible...

The next day John saw Jesus coming toward him, and said, "Behold! The Lamb of God who takes away the sin of the world!"

John 1:29

Any sensible list of the most astounding words ever spoken would have to include those of this verse. When John the Baptist saw Jesus approaching, he cried out: "Behold! The Lamb of God who takes away the sin of the world!"

John's was a Jewish audience. Those who heard this cry needed no explanation. Knowing what the lamb symbolized, they immediately knew what John the Baptist was saying about Jesus, and, yes, it was truly astounding.

Every year the Jews celebrated the Passover. That celebration commemorated the event of the release of their forefathers from slavery in Egypt many centuries in the past. How did that release come about? God sent His death angel over the land of Egypt to slay "the firstborn of man and the firstborn of animal" (Ex. 13:15). But He made a special provision for the Jews. They were to slay lambs and place their blood at the tops and at the sides of their doors. God promised that His angel would "pass over" every house marked with that blood (Ex. 12:3-7,13).

And those who heard John the Baptist's cry were also very familiar with Isaiah 53. A prophecy of the Messiah, it includes these words:

He was led as a lamb to the slaughter. . . (v. 7).

So John the Baptist was affirming in a powerful and unmistakable way that Jesus was the long-awaited Messiah. That was astounding.

Sadly enough, many of those who heard John's announcement on that day had lost their grip on the work of their Messiah. Even though a dying Messiah was definitely in their Scriptures, many were looking for a political leader.

But Jesus came to be what the Old Testament pictured and prophesied. He came to be the Lamb of God, which is to say He came to be God's way to forgive sinners of their sins, so they wouldn't have to experience the condemnation that those sins deserve. And that way—let us be forever clear on this—was by Jesus being the substitute for those sinners. The slain lambs in the first Passover were essentially substitutes. Their blood was shed so the blood of the Jews' firstborn wouldn't have to be shed. To say Jesus is God's

Lamb is to say that He, Jesus, was set forth by God to be the substitute for sinners. When He died on the cross, He received the wrath of God in the place of all who will trust in Him.

God's justice demands that the penalty for sin be paid. There's no way around that. But God's justice only demands that the penalty for sin be paid once, not twice. It would be unjust for God to demand payment twice. Here is the glory of the gospel—since Jesus made the payment for sinners on the cross, those who trust in Him don't have to make the payment again. They can rather sing with Elvina Hall:

Jesus paid it all,
All to Him I owe;
Sin had left a crimson stain,
He washed it white as snow.

And they can triumphantly and joyously take as their own these words from the Apostle Paul: "There is therefore now no condemnation to those who are in Christ Jesus. . ." (Rom. 8:1). And how do we get into Christ? We do so by renouncing every other hope for salvation and trusting wholly in His substitutionary work on the cross.

The Bible calls to us now to behold the Lamb, to look with wonder and amazement at Him dying on that cross. It calls us to marvel that on the cross Jesus received the wrath that we deserve.

We can only do this beholding now with the eyes of faith. But an indescribably glorious day is coming in which we will see Jesus, our Lamb, face to face. On that day, we will join in this glad anthem:

Worthy is the Lamb who was slain
To receive power and riches and wisdom,
And strength and honor and glory and blessing!
(Rev. 5:13)

Let's rejoice in Jesus, the wrath-bearing Lamb of God, but let's also remember that those who don't receive Him will one day cry to be hidden "from the wrath of the Lamb" (Rev. 6:16).

"Behold, Your King"

From God's Word, the Bible...

"Rejoice greatly, O daughter of Zion!
Shout, O daughter of Jerusalem!
Behold, your King is coming to you;
He is just and having salvation,
Lowly and riding on a donkey,
A colt, the foal of a donkey."

"Tell the daughter of Zion,
'Behold, your King is coming to you,
Lowly, and sitting on a donkey,
A colt, the foal of a donkey.'"

Zechariah 9:9; Matthew 21:5

It is the Passover season, and Jerusalem, filled with pilgrims, is abuzz. The buzz is about Jesus. Much of it is due to Him having raised Lazarus from the dead a few days back. That occurred in nearby Bethany.

On this particular Sunday, the Lord Jesus is in Bethany. Many people are there to watch His every move. Things begin to unfold quickly. Jesus gives two of His disciples kinglike commands about securing a donkey for Him to ride into Jerusalem. Some of the observers in Bethany begin to piece things together. Jesus is finally going to make His move. He is going to declare Himself to be the King of Israel. They run to Jerusalem to announce the news. Many there pour out of the city toward Bethany. Meanwhile, a large number is accompanying Jesus from Bethany. Somewhere between Bethany and Jerusalem the two crowds merge. Euphoria reigns as people spread their outer garments on the road along with palm branches that they had cut down. They suddenly join their voices in loudly crying:

"Hosanna to the Son of David!
'Blessed is He who comes
In the name of the Lord!'
Hosanna in the highest!"

None of this happens by accident. It is all a fulfillment of Zechariah's prophecy:

"Tell the daughter of Zion,
'Behold, your King is coming to you,
Lowly, and sitting on a donkey,
A colt, the foal of a donkey.'"

People welcoming their king! That's what we have here. It seems to be a wonderful thing. But something isn't right. Jesus is weeping as He approaches the city of Jerusalem (Luke 19:41-44).

What's wrong? While the people are beholding Jesus as their king and acclaiming Him as their king, they are in the grip of grievous error. They are beholding Jesus as the king they want Him to be instead of as the king He actually came to be. They are hailing Him as a mere temporal king, one who will free their nation from bondage to the Romans and usher in a golden age.

It's all right there in that word "Hosanna," which means "save now." They want a king who will save them politically, and will do it right now. But that's not the kind of king Jesus came to be.

And when they learn that Jesus isn't going to be the kind of king they want, they turn on Him. In one of the greatest ironies in all of history, many of those who are crying "Hosanna" on this Sunday will cry "Crucify" later that same week.

The Bible urges us to behold Jesus as our king, but it also warns us to not repeat the error of those who swarm around Jesus as He enters Jerusalem. We are to behold Jesus as the king that He is, and not as the king that we want.

It's very easy for us to forget the words that Jesus would speak to Pilate later in this week: "My kingdom is not of this world" (John 18:36).

So the question before us is this: Are we properly beholding Jesus as our king? We can ask it in this way: Are we standing in awe before Jesus as the king that He came to be?

What kind of king did Jesus come to be? The multitude was correct to think of Jesus as a king bringing salvation. But they were wrong in their understanding of that salvation. It wasn't salvation from the Romans that Jesus was offering. It was rather salvation from another kind of bondage—one that was far worse—the bondage to sin and Satan.

This is the bondage Jesus came to break, and He broke it on the cross for all who will repent of their sins and trust in Him.

Jesus, our bondage-breaker, now rules in the hearts of all His people. And He rules over the bewildering events and circumstances of this world for the good of His people and the glory of His name. The day is coming in which the kingship of Jesus will be apparent to all. On that day, He will be universally acknowledged as King of kings and Lord of lords (Rev. 19:16). The choice before us is to either gladly bow before His kingship now in wondering admiration or to bow before it later when He comes to judge those who spurn His salvation.

September 13

"Behold, the Man!"

FROM GOD'S WORD, THE BIBLE...

Then Jesus came out, wearing the crown of thorns and the purple robe. And Pilate said to them, "Behold the Man!"

JOHN 19:5

Pontius Pilate, the Roman procurator of Judea, was a man with a dilemma on his hands. He knew that the religious leaders of the Jews wanted Jesus to be crucified. To maintain peace, Pilate thought it necessary to do with Jesus as they wished. But he also knew that Jesus was innocent. Here, then, was his dilemma—was he to satisfy the demands of the Jews by crucifying Jesus or satisfy the demands of justice by not crucifying Him?

Shrewd fellow that he was, Pilate thought he could extricate himself from the dilemma by appealing to the Jews to feel pity toward Jesus. So he handed Jesus over to a contingent of Roman soldiers to be scourged. The soldiers did as Pilate requested, but they also added a couple of touches of their own by crowning Him with thorns and by clothing Him in a purple robe.

When the process was complete, Pilate brought the bloody and battered Jesus out to the Jewish leaders and exclaimed: "Behold the Man!"

It was Pilate's way of saying: "Look at this poor fellow. Can't you see that He has suffered enough and that there is no need to go further?"

But these leaders were in no mood for Pilate's scheme. They felt no pity for Jesus at all, but only contempt. And they expressed that contempt by crying: "Crucify Him, crucify Him" (v. 6).

In urging those heartless men to behold Jesus, Pilate wasn't making a theological statement. As far as he was concerned, Jesus was a man and nothing more. Pilate didn't realize that the One beside him was the most extraordinary person who ever lived. Jesus was a man, but He was much more than that. He was also God. He was the God-man.

If Pilate had realized that, he wouldn't have been asking people to pity Jesus. He would have been asking Jesus to pity him, guilty sinner that he was. If he had known the truth about Jesus, he would have fallen on his knees in wondering awe. Because he thought Jesus was an ordinary man, Pilate used the word "behold" to ask those religious leaders to merely look at Jesus. Had he recognized the uniqueness of Jesus, he would have used the word "behold" to call those men to stand in awe before the Lord of Glory. He would have called those men not to merely look at Jesus but rather to see Him. How often we look without seeing when it comes to the truth about Jesus!

Pilate wasn't aware that he was in the arena of the greatest marvel that has ever occurred, the marvel of God taking on our humanity. Do we see the marvel of it, or are we as blind to it as Pilate was?

It was a wonder that the Lord was in our humanity. He didn't have to be. He didn't have to take our humanity at all. He could have stayed in the glory of His heaven. But He took our humanity, and, let's make sure we never miss this: that humanity was real in every respect. It wasn't a pretend humanity.

It's also a wonder what the Lord Jesus did in our humanity. He did something that we haven't done in our humanity. He lived without sin. He refused to break any of God's laws. He never thought an evil thought, never spoke a wrong word, and never did a sinful deed. Having lived that perfect life, He went to the cross to die in our humanity. Death is the penalty for sin. Since Jesus had no sin, He didn't have to die. He died, not for Himself, but for us.

It's also a wonder that Jesus brought our humanity out of the grave, arising from it on the third day just as He promised that He would do.

It's a further wonder that He ascended to heaven in our humanity. He is not in heaven today in exactly the same way that He was before He came. He is there in resurrected, glorified humanity, and that is the guarantee that all who believe in Him will eventually be there with Him in resurrected, glorified humanity.

Pilate was oblivious to the truth of Jesus when he said: "Behold the Man!" He was a politician acting politically. But when I read his words, I say: "Yes, Pilate, let me do exactly that. Let me truly behold the man Jesus."

Behold His Sorrow

From God's Word, the Bible...

"Is it nothing to you, all you who pass by?
Behold and see
If there is any sorrow like my sorrow,
Which has been brought on me,
Which the Lord has inflicted
In the day of His fierce anger.

Lamentations 1:12

The book of Lamentations, as its title indicates, is a book of grief and mourning. The people of Judah had come under God's judgment, just as the prophets of the Lord had predicted. The Babylonians had invaded their land, destroyed Jerusalem, and carried off a large number of people into captivity. Faith was shaken, families were fragmented, and hopes were dashed.

Jeremiah, one of a small remnant left in the land, bemoans the plight of his people. In this book, he becomes the mouthpiece of the whole nation and reflects their pain and anguish.

In the verse before us, he pictures the nation sitting in desolation beside a road. As people pass by, she calls to them to take note of her condition and to have pity on her.

These words have spurred Christians through the years to think of the Lord Jesus crying these words as He was dying on the cross.

I now try to imagine myself at the foot of His cross. I hear Him asking me to behold His sorrow. And the first thing that comes to my mind is this: *it is a wonder that Christ had any sorrow at all.*

The Lord Jesus didn't begin to exist when He came to this earth. He existed with the Father and the Holy Spirit before the world began. And the triune God was perfectly happy before creation. Each person was happy in Himself, and each was happy with the other.

There wasn't any sorrow in God until sin entered the human race. Even then, God didn't have to feel sorrow. He could have acted in His justice and eternally destroyed Adam and Eve. He could have chosen to be happy with His justice.

Because of His grace, God sorrowed over the sin of His creatures and desired to redeem them. What a marvel it is that God should desire to save us!

Here is the second thing that comes to my mind as I hear the Lord calling me to behold His sorrow: *it is a wonder that Christ could be as sorrowful as He was.*

When He stepped into this world, the Lord Jesus must have found many reasons to rejoice. He must have rejoiced in hearing the birds sing, knowing that He had made them and given them their song. He must have rejoiced in the flowers, knowing that He had given them their delicacy and beauty. He must have rejoiced in the mountains, knowing that He given them their majesty.

But while the Lord Jesus was happy in His world, He became increasingly sorrowful toward the end of His life. When He entered the Garden of Gethsemane, He "began to be sorrowful and deeply distressed." He spoke these words to Peter, James, and John: "My soul is exceedingly sorrowful even to death" (Matt. 26:37-38).

The incredible agony He experienced in Gethsemane was the terrible prelude to a night and day of unspeakable suffering and sorrow. There was the sorrow of His arrest, which denied Jesus passage in the very world that He had created. There was the sorrow of the trials and the mockery. There was the sorrow of being led outside the city as if He was nothing more than garbage to be destroyed.

While these were all causes of indescribable suffering and sorrow, the greatest of all Jesus' sorrows was on the cross itself. There He endured the sorrow of separation from God the Father. The penalty for sin is eternal separation from God. Because Jesus took the place of sinners on the cross to pay the penalty for their sins, He actually had to endure there an eternity of separation from God.

The crux of the cross is this: God put on Christ the very sorrows of hell so all those who believe in Him don't have to experience those sorrows.

Christ would have known no sorrow at all if it hadn't been for us. He took our place. He carried our sorrows (Isa. 53:4-6).

In light of these things, I must also add this: *it is a wonder that we believers don't appreciate more the sorrows that Jesus endured on our behalf.* How often we take His sorrows for granted! How we need to pray:

Near the cross! O Lamb of God,
Bring its scenes before me;
Help me walk from day to day,
With its shadows o'er me.

September 15

Behold His Hands and Feet

From God's Word, the Bible...

"Behold My hands and My feet, that it is I Myself. Handle Me and see, for a spirit does not have flesh and bones as you see I have." When He had said this, He showed them His hands and His feet.

Luke 24:39-40

It was the evening of the day Jesus arose from the dead. The eleven disciples of Jesus were in Jerusalem listening to a couple of men who had seen the risen Christ. Suddenly the Lord Himself appeared and said, "Peace to you" (Luke 24:36). We might expect to read that those disciples were overjoyed to see the Lord, but they were terrified because "they supposed they had seen a spirit" (v. 37).

At that point Jesus told them to behold His hands and feet. There was something about those hands and feet to cause those men to wonder and admire. We can look at those same hands and feet through the lens of Scripture and join those disciples in wonder.

The pierced hands and feet of Jesus proved His resurrection. One glance at those hands and feet would have been enough for those disciples to realize that it was their crucified Jesus who was standing before them. One glance? Yes! The wounds created by the nails that held Him on the cross were still visible.

In calling for these men to behold His hands and feet, Jesus was calling for them to behold the truth of His resurrection. And in calling them to behold the truth of His resurrection, He was calling them to be amazed.

The resurrection of Jesus is indeed cause for amazement. Dead people don't just rise from their graves! What does Jesus' resurrection tell us about Him? It tells us that He was not an ordinary man but rather was the person He claimed to be, that is, God in human flesh. It tells us that His death on the cross was satisfying to God the Father. And it tells us that we can trust what Jesus had to say about the reality of sin, the coming of judgment, and the salvation that He came to provide.

The pierced hands and feet of Jesus also proved His resurrection was physical in nature.

This is important. Some people deny that Jesus' body actually came out of the grave. They allege that the disciples felt His presence even though He was dead, and they invented the resurrection stories.

But those pierced hands and feet made it plain that it was Jesus' body that was raised. The body that went into the grave came out of the grave.

Yes, the resurrected body was superior to the body that went into the grave, but it was the same body.

Still further, *the pierced hands and feet of Jesus show what lies ahead of those who die with faith in Christ*. The grave isn't the final destination for our bodies. On the night before He was crucified, Jesus, speaking of His resurrection as if it had already occurred, said to His disciples: "Because I live, you shall live also" (John 14:19).

Believers in Christ are destined to have bodies that are "conformed to His glorious body" (Phil. 3:21).

Finally, *the pierced hands and feet of Jesus reveal the greatness of what He did for His people*.

The Lord took a human body at Bethlehem. He lived and died in that body. He came out of the grave in that body, a vastly superior body to be sure, but still a body. He ascended to the Father in heaven in that body, and He still possesses that body to this very moment.

Here is the extent to which Jesus went to save us—He took our humanity forever. If we were in heaven right now, we could see in the risen body of our Lord Jesus Christ the same pierced hands and feet that His disciples saw when He appeared to them in Jerusalem. Matthew Bridges conveys this truth to us in these wonderful words:

Crown Him the Lord of love!
Behold His hands and side,
Those wounds, yet visible above,
In beauty glorified. . . .

The fact that Jesus is now in heaven in our humanity is the guarantee that all His people will eventually be in heaven with Him in their resurrected, glorified bodies. He is in heaven as our forerunner (Heb. 6:20). He has gone there ahead of us, and His presence there guarantees that we will follow.

As far as I'm concerned, there can be no doubt about it. The most glorious sight in heaven will be the pierced hands and feet of Jesus. What a joy it will be to behold them, realizing as we do that we are in heaven because those hands and feet were pierced on Calvary!

"Behold, He is Coming"

From God's Word, the Bible...

Behold, He is coming with clouds, and every eye will see Him, even they who pierced Him. And all the tribes of the earth will mourn because of Him. Even so, Amen.

Revelation 1:7

We've been spending some time with the word "behold." It is a blessed word because it calls us to look so intently that we see the marvel or wonder of the thing that we're seeing.

Some of the things the Bible tells us to behold can't be seen with the eye. We can't see God, but we are to behold Him (Isa. 40:9).

In the verse before us, John urges us to behold something that hasn't yet occurred. He writes of the Lord Jesus: "Behold, He is coming with clouds. . . ."

How do we behold something that is yet to come? We must use the eye of faith. Having faith means we hold with certainty to that which God has revealed to us in His Word. God has revealed that the Lord Jesus will come again. Faith lays hold of that and hangs on to it even though that teaching is often scorned.

The Apostle John was exiled on the Isle of Patmos when he received from the Lord the revelation that we know as the Book of Revelation (v. 9). This book was addressed to seven of the Lord's churches in Asia Minor. These churches were facing daunting challenges. The need was for them to use the eye of faith to look beyond those challenges to the coming of the Lord.

Our verse consists of thirty-three words, but there are worlds of meaning in those few words. These are some of the most comforting and terrifying words in all of the Bible, and, for that matter, in all of human history. They are comforting to the believer in Christ, and terrifying to the unbeliever. They deal with the revelation of Jesus at the end of human history, just before the Great White Throne Judgment described in Revelation 20.

What does this verse tell us about Christ's coming? First, *it will be a majestic and glorious event*.

The fact that the One who will come is the Lord of Glory (vv. 8,12-18) guarantees that the event itself will be glorious. And the fact that Jesus will come "with clouds" tells us that this will be a grand and magnificent event.

The second thing this verse tells us about the coming of Christ is that *it will be witnessed by all without exception.*

As we noted above, we can't now see with physical eyes the coming of

Christ, but that will change when He actually appears. John says: "every eye will see Him."

People throughout history have often been unaware of great events. It is true of people today. But no one will be unaware of this event. "Every eye will see Him."

Does that mean every single eye of every single person who has ever lived? Yes, it most certainly does! What about those who have died? Yes, even those who have died because by this time all of them will have been raised from the dead.

John especially emphasizes that those who "pierced," that is, crucified the Lord Jesus, will see Him. Who does he have in mind? The religious leaders of the Jews? Yes. The Roman soldiers? Yes. Pontius Pilate? Yes.

But in a larger sense, we have all pierced Christ. It was our sins that caused him to be crucified. I was there when He was crucified. I yanked the hammer from the hand of the Roman soldier and drove the nails into Jesus' hands and feet. I joined those soldiers in hoisting the cross into the air. I stood at the foot of the cross with Jesus' haters and added my own words of mockery. Yes, I was there because my sin was there.

The third thing this verse tells us about the coming of Christ is that *it will strike terror into the hearts of "all the tribes of the earth."*

We must take the phrase "all the tribes of the earth" to refer to unbelievers throughout the world. We know it doesn't refer to believers in Christ because John adds: "Even so, Amen." It's obvious that John won't be mourning when Jesus comes. Neither will any believer.

If we don't want to mourn on that day, we must mourn now in repentance and take Christ as our Savior. We must behold Him now as our Savior so we can behold Him without fear when He comes.

September 17

Behold! Alive Forevermore

From God's Word, the Bible...

I am He who lives, and was dead, and behold, I am alive forevermore. Amen. And I have the keys of Hades and of Death.

Revelation 1:18

It was the Lord's Day. The Apostle John was in exile on the Isle of Patmos. The Lord Jesus suddenly appeared to John in dazzling glory (Rev. 1:12-17). John "fell at His feet as dead" (v. 17). Interesting, isn't it? During Jesus' earthly ministry, John had walked with Him as one of His closest disciples, but there is no chummy familiarity here—only awestruck reverence.

Jesus appeared to John to deliver messages of encouragement to seven churches (v. 20). He begins by saying to all of them: "Do not be afraid; I am the First and the Last" (v. 17). He then makes four astounding assertions.

- I am He who lives;
- I was dead;
- I am alive forevermore;
- I have the keys of Hades and of Death.

If truth could be likened to real estate, we would have to say that there are vast chunks of ground that Jesus traverses here. In the midst of these assertions, Jesus urges John to "behold." John had beheld so much of Jesus, but he was still called to marvel at what the Lord was saying.

These four assertions can be grouped under two headings. *The first is that the living One died.*

Jesus is the living One. He says: "I am He who lives." This is more than Jesus claiming to be alive at that moment. It is essentially Jesus revealing Himself to be God. God enjoys life that is un-derived and independent. It isn't given to Him or sustained by anyone or anything outside God.

But Jesus also says that He "was dead." How could the Living One die? There was only one way, and that was by taking our humanity. God can't die, but, as we know all too well, humanity can and does.

Jesus took our humanity so that He could die! Why was it necessary? Death is the penalty for our sins—not just physical death, but eternal death. In dying, Jesus took that penalty so all who believe in Him don't have to receive it. Yes, on the cross Jesus received an eternity's worth of God's wrath in the place of sinners.

Our second heading is this: *the dead One is alive forevermore.*

Jesus died, but He didn't stay dead. He arose from the grave, and He lives today to never die again. Jesus then adds this spectacular statement: "I have the keys of Hades and of Death."

These happy words must be understood in more than one way because death has more than one form.

There is spiritual death. This is the alienation from God that we all have by nature because of our sins. Jesus has the keys to this kind of death. He can and does grant spiritual life to dead sinners. If we were to be locked in a room with no way out, we would be thrilled to hear someone say: "Don't worry, I have the key!" What a happy sound it would be to hear that key turning in the lock! What a delightful sight it would be to see that door swing open! I was once in the gloomy old fortress of spiritual death, but I heard the Lord Jesus say: "Don't worry, I have the key." And the creaky, old door of that fortress swung open. Now I'm free!

Jesus also has the key to physical death. During His earthly ministry, He met a woman on the way to the cemetery to bury her son. But Jesus essentially said to her: "Don't worry. I have the key right here in My pocket." And he raised that young man (Luke 7:11-17).

Jesus used those same keys with Jairus' daughter (Mark 5:22-43), with Lazarus (John 11:38-44), and once again in His own tomb.

The souls of all those who die in faith in Christ go to be with the Lord at the time of their death. But what about their bodies? Does death have the final victory over them? No, Jesus has the keys. When He comes again, He will unlock the graves of all those who know Him. Their bodies will be raised and reunited with their souls. What a day that will be! (1 Thess. 4:13-18).

We who know the Lord know these things, but are we truly beholding them? Are we rejoicing in the glory of them? Do we know anything of stunned wonder as we contemplate them? Our salvation doesn't need to be made more glorious. The need is for us to see the glory that is already there.

One Fine Stack

From God's Word, the Bible...

. . . giving thanks to the Father who has qualified us to be partakers of the inheritance of the saints in the light. He has delivered us from the power of darkness and conveyed us into the kingdom of the Son of His love, in whom we have redemption through His blood, the forgiveness of sins.

Colossians 1:12-14

Just call the Apostle Paul a "stacker." In this passage, he stacks one phrase on another to give us a magnificent view of salvation through Christ:

- God has qualified us (v. 12);
- God has delivered us (v. 13);
- God has translated us (v. 13);
- God has redeemed us (v. 14);
- God has forgiven us (v. 14).

That's one fine stack! Let's be sure we understand that these things apply only to Christians. Paul was writing to "brethren in Christ" (Col. 1:2) who had "faith in Christ Jesus" (v. 4). And these things all come from God. Salvation is all due to His grace. There is nothing for which any Christian can take credit. The seventeenth-century French theologian Jean Daillé quaintly says of salvation: "This wholly appertaineth unto God."

First, *God has qualified us* to partake of "the inheritance of the saints in the light." That inheritance begins in this life and culminates in heaven. God fits us to share the lot or portion of the saints in this life. This portion is "in the light." Believers, like everyone else, came into this world in a state of spiritual darkness, but God in grace has called them out of that darkness "into His marvellous light" (Eph. 5:8; 1 Peter 2:9). The children of light will finally enter the kingdom of light (Rev. 21:23-25). They will do so only because they have been qualified by the Lord.

We are sinners by nature. We have the darkness of sin in us and with us and, therefore, cannot enjoy the light that God has prepared in eternity. To partake of that, we have to be perfectly righteous. God Himself qualifies sinners to be partakers of the light of glory. In Christ, God provided the righteousness that He demands of us and He applies that righteousness to each believer.

Secondly, *God has delivered us* "from the power of darkness."

We all come into this world as part of Satan's very dark kingdom. The citizens of this kingdom have their minds blinded so they cannot see their true condition (2 Cor. 4:3-4). Those who stay in this kingdom will eventually be enveloped by eternal death (2 Peter 2:17; Jude 12-13).

Believers have been taken out of this kingdom by the Lord Jesus Christ. Through His redeeming death on the cross, He decisively defeated Satan and delivered all believers from his kingdom of darkness.

Thirdly, *God has translated us* "into the kingdom of the Son of His love."

This refers to the practice of removing people from one country and settling them in another. It would have been unspeakably glorious for God to deliver His people from Satan's kingdom, but He also makes them citizens of His own. His kingdom is as light as Satan's is dark.

It is "the kingdom of the Son of His love." How certain believers can be of their new citizenship! God loves His Son with an immeasurable and indestructible love. That same love is extended to all who are in Christ.

Thinking of Christ prompts Paul to add this phrase: "in whom we have redemption through His blood." So *God has redeemed us*.

The word "redeemed" means "bought back." Although believers belonged to God by virtue of creation, they were all taken prisoner by sin and held by the chain of God's law. That law demands that the sinner be punished with eternal separation from God.

But believers have been redeemed by Jesus shedding His blood on the cross. He received there the eternal separation His people deserve. God's law was, therefore, satisfied and they were freed. God paid the ransom for them through the death of His Son.

Finally, Paul tells us that we have in Christ "the forgiveness of sins." In other words, *God has forgiven us*.

To forgive is "to send away" or "to cancel a debt." Satan would have us believe that our sins constitute an insurmountable barrier to entering heaven. He points to those sins and says: "Look at them! You are not fit to enter heaven!"

But we do not fear a creditor pointing to a statement if it has these words stamped on it: Paid in Full. Christians don't fear Satan pointing to their sin debt because Jesus paid it in full.

What a stack this is! It reaches all the way from earth to heaven! How should we respond to it? By "giving thanks to the Father" (v. 12).

Trusting the Lord

From God's Word, the Bible...

Though He slay me, yet will I trust Him.
Even so, I will defend my own ways before Him.

Job 13:15

Do God's people serve Him only because they enjoy trouble-free lives? Do they stop serving Him when trouble comes?

Many would answer both questions with an emphatic "Yes!" Those who would do so probably haven't heard of Louisa M. Stead.

Louisa, her husband, and their daughter were enjoying a picnic on the coast of Long Island when tragedy occurred. Her husband drowned. There's a good bit of uncertainty about the details. Some accounts say Mr. Stead, in an attempt to save a boy, drowned with the boy. Another account says he saved the boy. Yet another says it was the Steads' daughter, Lily, who was saved by her father. This much we know—Mr. Stead drowned. This occurred in 1879 or 1880.

Trouble had now entered Louisa's life in a major way. How did she respond? Did she stop serving the Lord? She would seem to have had good reason to do so. Instead she and her daughter went to South Africa, where she served as a missionary for fifteen years. After that she married a pastor and served alongside him. The two of them became missionaries in Rhodesia in 1901 and ministered there until their retirement in 1911.

While in South Africa and only two or three years after her first husband's death, Louisa wrote these familiar words:

'Tis so sweet to trust in Jesus, Just to take Him at His Word;
Just to rest upon His promise, Just to know, "Thus saith the Lord!"
Jesus, Jesus, how I trust Him! How I've proved Him o'er and o'er'
Jesus, Jesus, precious Jesus! Oh, for grace to trust Him more!

It's apparent that Louisa had learned the meaning of trusting God. It isn't trusting that God will only do those things that we want done and not do those things that we don't want done. It's rather trusting that God will do what He has revealed in His Word. As we read the Bible, we discover that God has never promised that our lives will be trouble-free. Quite the opposite!

Which of God's many promises did Louisa have in mind when she wrote the first verse of her poem? We find the answer in this verse:

Yes, 'tis sweet to trust in Jesus,
Just from sin and self to cease;
Just from Jesus simply taking
Life and rest, and joy and peace.

The Lord hasn't promised that we will have no trials in life. He has promised to give "life and rest, and joy and peace" if we will trust Him. The "life" must surely mean the abundant life that Jesus promises in John 10:10. The "rest," "joy," and "peace" could refer to several promises, one of which—recorded in Isaiah 26:3—reads:

You will keep him in perfect peace,
Whose mind is stayed on You,
Because he trusts in You.

We see another promise Louisa had in mind here:

I'm so glad I learned to trust Thee, Precious Jesus, Savior, Friend;
And I know that Thou art with me, Wilt be with me to the end.

It's evident that Louisa treasured these words: "For He Himself has said, *'I will never leave you nor forsake you'*" (Heb. 13:5; see also Matt. 28:20).

The Bible offers many marvelous promises. Which one is the greatest? It is God's promise that He will cleanse us from all sin if we will trust in His Son, the Lord Jesus Christ. Louisa M. Stead conveys this in these words:

Oh, how sweet to trust in Jesus,
Just to trust His cleansing blood;
And in simple faith to plunge me
'Neath the healing, cleansing flood!

Much of our success as Christians comes from keeping things in perspective. Do hardships and sorrows come our way in this life? Yes. Do they severely hurt and wound us? Yes. Is it okay to grieve over them? Yes. But our true treasure doesn't lie in the absence of hardship. It rather lies in having our sins forgiven through Christ. Then no trial or difficulty, be it ever so severe, can touch that or change it. So we rejoice in these words from Paul: "For I am persuaded that neither death nor life, nor angels nor principalities nor powers, nor things present nor things to come, nor height nor depth, nor any other created thing, shall be able to separate us from the love of God which is in Christ Jesus our Lord" (Rom. 8:38-39).

September 20

Three Nots and One Is (1)

From God's Word, the Bible...

I marvel that you are turning away so soon from Him who called you in the grace of Christ, to a different gospel, which is not another. . .

Galatians 1:6,7

The Apostle Paul usually begins his letters with expressions of appreciation for his readers and with prayer for them but he does not do so in his letter to the Galatians. After wishing his readers grace and peace (v. 3), he plunges right in. There is no time for preliminaries. The issue is far too important for that.

And what is the issue? It is the gospel of Jesus Christ. The Galatians have professed faith in the gospel, but now they are moving away from it.

Paul's love for the gospel won't allow him to take this lightly. So he writes to rebuke them and to call them back to faith in the gospel.

I wonder what Paul would say if he were to write our churches today. Would he accuse us of abandoning the gospel?

On October 31, 1517, Martin Luther stepped to the door of the church in Wittenburg, Germany, and nailed there his nineth-five theses. The sixty-second read: "The treasure of the church is the most holy gospel of the glory and grace of God."

How many churches and pastors today can honestly say the gospel is the treasure of the church? It certainly does not seem so. Pastors load their sermons with tips for living this life, making sure that they add generous doses of humor as they go along. There can't be much talk about sin and judgment because such topics would make their hearers feel bad. If there is no sin and no judgment, there can be no gospel, which is, of course, God's answer to sin and judgment. And if the gospel is not preached, it cannot be called the treasure of the church.

The truth is that we need Paul's words in the above passage as much as the Galatians of old needed them. We can divide those words into four headings, the first of which will receive our attention in today's reading, and the other three in tomorrow's reading. In these four headings, we have the Apostle Paul talking about three things that would seem to be the case, but are not, and one thing that would not seem to be the case but really is.

Paul first mentions *a gospel that is not really a gospel.* He says he is astonished that the Galatians are turning from the gospel of Christ to "a different gospel, which is not another" (v. 6).

The gospel of Jesus Christ is the good news of God's grace. It is the good news of what God has done in and through His Son, the Lord Jesus Christ, to forgive sinners of their sins (v. 4).

But the Galatians are now showing themselves to be soldiers who have deserted the army. They are spiritual deserters! They are now setting aside the gospel of grace to embrace a Christ-plus teaching. John R.W. Stott writes of the Galatians that:

> They did not deny that you must believe in Jesus for salvation, but they stressed that you must be circumcised and keep the law as well. In other words, you must let Moses finish what Christ has begun. Or rather, you yourself must finish, by your obedience to the law, what Christ has begun. You must add your works to the work of Christ. You must finish Christ's unfinished work.[8]

Recent surveys indicate that many people today essentially hold the same notion—that salvation is a matter of believing in Jesus and doing good works.

What such people do not understand is that the gospel has to be completely grace or completely works. One negates or cancels out the other. If it is grace, it can't be works. If it is works, it can't be grace (Rom. 4:4; 11:6). Yes, salvation produces good works (Eph. 2:8-10; Titus 2:11-14), but good works do not produce salvation.

If the gospel is a matter of our works, it is not really a gospel at all. The gospel is good news, but there is no good news in salvation by works. It is bad news. God demands perfect righteousness of us, and no matter how many good works we do, we can never do enough.

Let us always be clear on this: we cannot modify or amend the gospel and still have the gospel. After our tampering, we have something, but it is no longer the gospel.

8 John R.W. Stott, *Only One Way: The Message of Galatians*, Inter-Varsity Press, 1968, p. 22.

September 21

Three Nots and One Is (2)

FROM GOD'S WORD, THE BIBLE...

. . . but there are some who trouble you and want to pervert the gospel of Christ. But even if we, or an angel from heaven, preach any other gospel to you than what we have preached to you, let him be accursed. As we have said before, so now I say again, if anyone preaches any other gospel to you than what you have received, let him be accursed. For do I now persuade men, or God? Or do I seek to please men? For if I still pleased men, I would not be a bondservant of Christ.

GALATIANS 1:7-10

In yesterday's reading, we found Paul stressing a gospel that is not really a gospel. Today we look at two additional things that are not true and one thing that is true.

Paul's second emphasis is *teachers who are not really teachers.*

Why had the Galatians gotten into such a mess? It was because of men who "trouble you and want to pervert the gospel" (v. 7), "Judaizers," whose position is stated so clearly by Luke, the author of Acts: "Unless you are circumcised according to the custom of Moses, you cannot be saved" (Acts 15:1).

These men professed to be teachers, but they were actually troublers (the word for "trouble" in verse 7 means to "shake" or "agitate"). Do we understand this? To tamper with the gospel is to trouble the church!

We are living in very difficult and threatening days. Christianity is under attack on every hand. But the greatest danger to Christianity is never the hatred and opposition of those without. It is always those within who pervert the gospel.

Paul's third emphasis is *a choice that should not really be a choice. He* could anticipate some of his readers defending the false teachers: "But, Paul, these men are so brilliant and so interesting. How could they possibly be mistaken?" He answers in the strongest possible way. On one hand, he says, they, the Galatians, have the gospel that "we have preached to you" (v. 8). This is the apostolic message. On the other hand, here comes now "an angel from heaven" (v. 8) to preach another gospel. So they have before them the apostolic message of God's grace and the angelic message of man's works. What should they do? Keep in mind, that the angel is very dazzling and impressive! Many would say that this is a hard choice. But Paul says it should not be a choice at all!

We are not to accept any message on the basis of how impressive the messenger is. We are to judge the messenger by the gospel and not judge the gospel by the messenger!

Having noticed Paul's "nots," we now turn our attention to an "is," namely, *a curse that really is a curse.*

Paul closes this passage by pronouncing a curse, an "anathema" (devoted to destruction) on all those who preach "any other gospel" other than the gospel of the grace of God (v. 9).

Some profess to be upset by Paul's language. They consider it to be an ill-advised, intemperate outburst that is out of keeping with the spirit of Christianity. They think that Paul, if given the opportunity to do so, would take this back or delete these words. But Paul meant every word of this curse, and he meant every word for two reasons: the glory of Christ and the good of men and women.

Paul knew the truth about the person of Jesus. He was not just another man but God in human flesh. Paul also knew why Jesus came to this earth. It was to provide salvation for sinners. If what Jesus did was not sufficient for the salvation of sinners, as the Judaizers insisted, Jesus had failed. And if Jesus failed, there was certainly no point in glorifying His name. So the Judaizers' teaching robbed Jesus, the God-man, of His glory.

It also robbed people of the hope of salvation. If God in human flesh could not achieve salvation for sinners, what hope was there for those sinners to achieve it for themselves?

With the glory of Christ and the good of sinners in mind, Paul could do no other than pronounce a curse on those who detracted from Christ and the salvation he came to provide. James Denney was right on target when he wrote these words:

> If God has really done something in Christ on which the salvation of the world depends, and if He has made it known, then it is a Christian duty to be intolerant of everything which ignores, denies, or explains it away. The man who perverts it is the worst enemy of God and men.[9]

If we find Paul's words upsetting, we have all the proof we need that we are not as zealous for the gospel as we should be.

9 James Denney, *The Death of Christ*, Tyndale Publishing House, 1964, p. 66.

The Wonder of Ordinary Days

FROM GOD'S WORD, THE BIBLE...

Then He who sat on the throne said, "Behold, I make all things new." And He said to me, "Write, for these words are true and faithful."

REVELATION 21:5

Ordinary days usually have to pass before we appreciate how very wonderful they were. As I was growing up on my family's farm, the days seemed to be, well, so ordinary. Get up, eat breakfast, milk the cows, feed the chickens, go to school, come home, milk the cows—you get the idea.

The people seemed ordinary, too. Dad always wore bib overalls with a faded shirt, and Mom her apron. My brother and I usually wore jeans and shirts that were patched and oftentimes unpatched. I decided when I started my college education in the 1960s that I should get some new clothes. Imagine my surprise when I got there and saw all the students wearing patched and torn clothes! I had been in style for years without realizing it.

Mom's meals were always very good, but also very ordinary. The menu didn't vary much. Even Sunday dinner had an ordinariness about it—consisting always of fried chicken, mashed potatoes, gravy, and a vegetable or two.

Church was ordinary, too. The Sunday School hour was straightforward teaching of the Bible with no bells and whistles. The worship hour always featured the singing of the same old, gnarled hymns. The preaching was always delivered straight from the Bible with no attempts to be chatty and humorous. It was plain and fervent.

Sometimes the ordinariness would make me sigh. It would often seem to be more than I could bear, and I would yearn for something new and exciting. But now I look back on those ordinary days and wish that I could go back and experience again some of what I knew then. I have come to realize over the years that our blessing is in what we have and not in what we don't have. In other words, we can so fret over what we don't have that we fail to appreciate what we do have.

It's good for Christians to look back with nostalgia to the good times of long ago, but our primary look must always be forward. No matter how good the past has been, we Christians can always truthfully say: "The best is yet to come."

What about heaven? Will it be ordinary or extraordinary? The answer, I think, is that it will be both. Heaven ordinary? Yes. When we finally enter our final state—a new earth with a heavenly city (Rev. 21 and 22), lots of things will never change. The streets of gold and gates of pearl will always be in place, as will the twelve foundations. The tree of life will never be barren, and the river of life will never run dry.

But heaven will also be extraordinary. How could it be anything else? We will never get tired of it. The extraordinariness of it will always make the ordinariness of it extraordinary.

And the extraordinariness of heaven won't be just a matter of the beauty of it, but the constant awareness of what we've been saved from. One glance at hell is all we will need to appreciate the glory of heaven. And the extraordinariness of heaven will flow from the constant awareness of how we came to be there, that is, through the redeeming work of Christ. As I've said so often before, the most glorious sight of heaven will be the sight of Christ, and the most glorious sight of Christ will be His nail-pierced hands and feet. Those nail prints will constantly serve as reminders of the tremendous price that He paid on the cross for our redemption.

Heaven will always be the same, but the sameness will never seem same. There will always be greater glories to discover. When we think we have exhausted heaven, we will discover that heaven is inexhaustible.

These well-worn lines catch the blend of both the ordinariness and the extraordinariness of heaven, as expressed by John P. Rees in John Newton's hymn, *Amazing Grace*:

When we've been there ten thousand years,
Bright, shining as the sun;
We've no less days to sing God's praise
Than when we first begun.

Something that can be experienced for ten thousand years must surely have an ordinariness about it. But the fact that all through those years we will be singing God's praise tells us that we will always find heaven to be extraordinary. The challenge before us in ordinary days here is to look beyond them to the ordinary, extraordinary days of heaven.

Brother Lester's Testimony

From God's Word, the Bible...

Do not marvel that I said to you, "You must be born again."

John 3:7

Brother Lester was a deacon in the first church that I served as pastor. He was a common, ordinary man—just a simple farmer. But he loved the Lord with all of his heart, and he loved to serve the Lord. Brother Lester was one of the most faithful supporters of the church that it has been my privilege to know over the many years of my ministry.

In our evening worship services at Panama Baptist Church, Panama, Illinois, we would occasionally take time for testimonies. Brother Lester would always testify. And he would always begin in exactly the same way, by saying: "I've been a Christian all my life."

Those words must have come as a shock to those who didn't know Brother Lester. We're not born into this world as Christians. But all would become clear when Brother Lester would quickly add his last name. It was Christian. So he was born a Christian—Lester Christian.

Brother Lester would then, in his plain and simple way, tell us that even though he was born with the name Christian, that didn't really make him a Christian. He had the name from birth, but he didn't really become a Christian until he was saved by the grace of God.

I've heard lots of testimonies over the years, most of which were quite easily forgotten. But I've never forgotten Brother Lester's powerful testimony.

It sounded a warning that many need to hear. I've met some who assumed that they were Christians because they were born and reared in Christian families. I've even met some who assumed that they were Christians because, in their words, "America is a Christian country." I suppose if these people had been born in garages, they would think themselves to be automobiles, or if they had been born in barns, they would think themselves to be cows!

Nicodemus was all tangled up on this issue. It's not enough to merely say he was a Jew. He was eminent among the Jews, having earned for himself the title "the teacher of Israel" (John 3:10).

But with all his learning, Nicodemus didn't understand what is necessary to enable a person to go to heaven. He obviously thought that being born a Jew was synonymous with going to heaven. He equated the two. Jesus pressed home the point that being born physically as a Jew didn't qualify him for heaven. Entering heaven required another kind of birth—a spiritual birth.

Jesus put it in these words: "That which is born of the flesh is flesh, and that which born of the Spirit is spirit" (v. 6).

It has become common over the last several years to hear the phrase "born-again Christian." That is repetitive. We might as well say "Christian Christian" for this reason: to be born again is to be a Christian, and to be a Christian is to be born again. There's no entering heaven without being a Christian, and there's no being a Christian without being born again. Jesus said to Nicodemus: "Most assuredly, I say to you, unless one is born again he cannot see the kingdom of God" (v. 3).

This new birth isn't something that we can produce any more than we could produce our physical birth. It is something that takes place as the Spirit of God visits us in regenerating grace. When the Spirit visits us in this way, we come to see how sinful we are and what a dreadful thing it will be to stand before a holy God in our sins. When we come to this point of despair, the Holy Spirit points us to Christ who came from heaven (v. 13) to die on the cross (v. 14) so that we can have salvation from our sins and everlasting life (vv. 15-17). When the Spirit of God enables us to see the enormity of our sins, the horror of coming judgment, and the saving work of Christ, we flee from our sins in repentance and we flee to Christ in faith.

Lester Christian's testimony always served us well. It reminded us that physical birth alone isn't sufficient to enter heaven. We must, by the power of God's Spirit, look to Christ and to Him alone.

September 24

When We Are Cast Down

From God's Word, the Bible...

As the deer pants for the water brooks,
So pants my soul for You, O God.
My soul thirsts for God, for the living God.
When shall I come and appear before God?
My tears have been my food day and night,
While they continually say to me,
"Where is your God?"

Psalm 42:1-3

Even David didn't live constantly in the warmth of the sunshine of God's presence. Even David knew what it was for the sun to hide behind the clouds and for the cold chill of doubt and uncertainty to creep over him. In this psalm, we find him confessing that his soul was "cast down" (Psalm 42:5,6,11), even to the point that he wept day and night (v. 3). He had gotten so low that he felt completely forsaken by God (v. 9).

How did David get into such a state? Part of it was due to the trouble he was experiencing. He may have written this psalm when his son Absalom tried to replace him as king over Israel. It's clear that David had no access to the Lord's house when he penned this psalm (vv. 2, 4). That was certainly the case when Absalom rebelled against him.

David's trouble was made worse by the taunting of his enemies, who were quick to construe his situation as evidence that he had been wrong to trust in God. If his faith were valid, God would be helping him! Since God wasn't helping him, his faith was false.

Troubles abound and taunters surround! That's David's sad lament in this psalm.

So what did David do? For one thing, he talked to God. There's a good bit of prayer in this psalm. The fact that God didn't feel near didn't keep David from praying. If we put off praying until God feels near, we won't pray. The trick is to pray until God feels near. We must be careful about making our feelings the engine that pulls the train of prayer. They should be the caboose that follows.

David was very candid in his praying. He didn't try to hide what he was feeling. He honestly admitted this soul was "cast down" (v. 6) and that he felt as if God had forgotten him (v. 9).

One of the great things about God is that He allows us to come to Him to honestly express our doubts, frustrations, and anxieties. God isn't fragile. He won't break.

If we feel that God has forgotten us, let's cry out to Him. Let's seek Him earnestly. It could be that He withdraws from us so He can kindle within us a burning desire for greater evidences of His presence. God's purpose in withdrawing from us may be to make us cry with David:

As the deer pants for the water brooks,
So pants my soul for You, O God.
My soul thirsts for God, for the living God.
(vv. 1-2a)

If God withdraws from us, we may rest assured that it is so He may come back to us in a larger way.

Yes, David talked to God in the midst of his troubles and his taunters. But he also talked to himself. He reproved or reproached himself. Twice he says:

Why are you cast down, O my soul?
And why are you disquieted within me?
(vv. 5, 11)

Having reproved himself, David begins to reason with himself. He recalls evidences of God's faithfulness in the past (v. 6) and he assures himself that God will be lovingly kind to him in the present (v 8).

Reproving himself and reasoning with himself! That's what David did. In doing so, he shows us the art of dealing with ourselves. He urges us when we are in trouble to stop listening to ourselves and to start talking to ourselves. That sounds like nonsense, but it is really a vital principle. We are listening to ourselves when we allow ourselves to think of all the things that are against us, saying: "Just look. I have all these troubles and all these people who are opposed to me. Why can't it be the way it was a few years ago?" And on and on we go.

We stop listening to ourselves when we begin to call to mind what we know about God. Although He seems to withdraw from us, He will never completely abandon or forsake us. Although our problems may seem to indicate otherwise, He loves us with an undying love. Although our problems can be great, our God is always greater. How do we know these things? They are all in the Bible, the book of God's love. That same book also tells us about the greatest evidence of God's love for us—the unspeakably wonderful gift of His Son who provided a full salvation to all who would call upon Him.

September 25

What Simeon Says

FROM GOD'S WORD, THE BIBLE...

"Lord, now You are letting Your servant depart in peace,
According to Your word;
For my eyes have seen Your salvation."

LUKE 2:29-30

We're familiar with the children's game *Simon Says*. The game starts with someone being designated as Simon. The role of Simon is to give commands to the other children. Every command that begins with "Simon says" must be obeyed. But if any obey a command that doesn't begin with those words, they are out of the game. The game continues until everyone is out except one. That person wins and becomes the next Simon.

To win the game, players must listen very carefully to "Simon." In Luke 2:25-35, we meet, not a Simon, but a Simeon. He has such important things to say to us that we must carefully listen.

He is speaking now from the pages of Scripture. Can you hear him? He first speaks to us *about fulfillment*.

Mary and Joseph had brought the baby Jesus to the temple "to present Him to the Lord" (v. 22). Simeon was there. He is described to us as "just and devout" (v. 25). He was also a waiting man. He was waiting "for the Consolation of Israel" (v. 25). That means that he was waiting for the Messiah to come.

God first promised the coming of the Messiah to Adam and Eve in Genesis 3:15. That was many centuries before Simeon ever made his appearance on the human stage. Many may have begun to doubt whether the Messiah would ever come. Not Simeon! And when he saw Mary and Joseph there at the temple with Jesus, he realized that the one for whom he had been waiting had arrived. A flash of revelation from God let Simeon know that Jesus was the Messiah. So Simeon took Jesus "up in his arms and blessed God" (v. 28).

Imagine holding your eternal salvation in your own arms and looking at it with your own eyes! That's what Simeon did. It's even better to hold that salvation in our hearts, and that we can all do by trusting in Christ as our Savior.

Let's listen to Simeon again. Now he is speaking to us *about being Spirit-filled*. Luke mentions the Holy Spirit three times in verses 26 and 27. The Holy Spirit was "upon" Simeon (v. 25). The Holy Spirit had revealed truth to Simeon (v. 26). The Holy Spirit had led Simeon to the temple (v. 27). I would summarize all of that by saying Simeon was Spirit-filled.

What is it to be filled with the Spirit? It's not a matter of being highly emotional, as some imagine. It's rather a matter of being focused on the Lord Jesus. The more Christ-centered we are, the more Spirit-filled we are. We must always remember that the Holy Spirit's primary task is to exalt Christ (John 16:14).

Let's listen to Simeon yet again. Now he is speaking to us *about a matter of immense importance—dying.*

Simeon had received a promise from the Lord that he wouldn't die until he had seen the Messiah (v. 25). That promise was now fulfilled as he held Jesus in his arms. Having seen Jesus, Simeon was ready to die. He says:

Lord, now you are letting
Your servant depart in peace,
According to Your word. . .
(V. 29)

If we were reading Simeon's words in Latin, we would find the first two words to be "nunc" (now) "dimittis" (dismiss). "Now dismiss," is what he says to the Lord.

We're all facing dismissal from this life. We all have an appointment with death (Heb. 9:27). Death is not only coming most surely upon us but also most rapidly upon us. A few years ago, I went to visit a man in the hospital. He held his forefinger about a half-inch away from his thumb and said: "Life lasts about that long."

Yes, life speeds by, and then our dismissal comes.

But we can face our dismissal with peace. J.C. Ryle writes of Simeon:

> He speaks like one for whom the grave has lost its terrors, and the world its charms. He desires to be released from the miseries of this pilgrim-state of existence, and to be allowed to go home. . . .He speaks as one who knows where he is going when he departs this life, and cares not how soon he goes.[10]

What gave Simeon peace in the face of dismissal? His faith in the Lord Jesus! If we are to enjoy Simeon's peace, we must share his faith.

10 J.C. Ryle, *Expository Thoughts on Luke*, The Banner of Truth Trust, 1986, Vol. i, p. 67

September 26

The Devil in the Dates

From God's Word, the Bible...

"But of that day and hour no one knows, not even the angels of heaven, but My Father only."

Matthew 24:36

It has happened again. This time it was "a Christian numerologist" who set the date for Christ's return. The date was April 23, 2018. I'm writing this chapter on April 26, 2018. What does that tell you? It tells you that once again a prediction of the Lord's return didn't come true.

I say "once again" because this has happened several times over the years. One such prediction that the Lord would come on May 21, 2011, was widely reported in the news.

I have never been able to understand why so-called "Christian leaders" feel the need to set a date for Christ's coming when the Lord Jesus Himself so plainly said no one will know the day or the hour when it will occur. The thing we most need to know about the date of His coming is that we don't know it. And we can't know it. Preachers don't know it. Scholars don't know it. Even the angels of heaven don't know it. Only God the Father knows when the Lord Jesus will come again, and I think if someone should guess the date by accident, the Lord would change it.

So someone set a date for the Lord's return, and it didn't happen. Does it really matter? Why make a big deal out of it? It does matter, and it is a big deal. The problem, you see, is the devil gets into this date-setting business. He uses the failures of the date setters to discredit Christianity. He claps his hands in glee when we make Christianity look foolish in the eyes of the world.

On the matter of the Lord's return, the Bible doesn't put the emphasis on the time of it. To the contrary, the Lord Jesus said to His disciples: "It not for you to know times or seasons which the Father has put in His own authority" (Acts 1:7).

Here's where the Bible puts the emphasis: "Therefore, since all these things will be dissolved, what manner of persons ought you to be in holy conduct and godliness. . .?" (2 Peter 3:11).

The Lord's coming is not a date to be circled on the calendar. It's a trumpet call to godliness!

It should be enough for us to know that the Lord is coming. The Bible testifies to the certainty of this with very emphatic statements from Jesus (John 14:3), the angels (Acts 1:11), the Apostle Paul (1 Thess. 4:16), the author of Hebrews (Heb. 10:37), and the Apostle John (1 John 3:2).

When He comes, He will bring with Him the souls of all those believers who have died, will raise their bodies from their graves, and will reunite those souls and bodies. He will also catch up or snatch away those believers who are still living on the earth. Without having to pass through death, these people will see their limited, frail, mortal bodies transformed into bodies such as the Lord Jesus now has (Phil. 3:20-21). All of this will happen in the blink of an eye (1 Cor. 15:51-52).

With such glorious things of which we can be certain, why should we focus our attention on something that is uncertain, that is, the date at which it will all occur?

It's okay for Christians to appear foolish in the eyes of the world if our foolishness is where God wants it to be. The cross of Christ is the point at which God wants us to appear foolish. Paul writes: "For the message of the cross is foolishness to those who are perishing, but to us who are being saved it is the power of God" (1 Cor. 1:18).

A man dying on a cross to provide salvation for sinners? It seems so utterly absurd. But that cross brings glory to God, and in His own time, He will show it to be the greatest wisdom. God uses that cross to humble sinners so He can bring them to Himself in repentance and faith.

Setting the date for the Lord's coming is different. It brings no glory to God because He has told us to not do it. It's rather an attempt of men to bring glory to themselves. The devil always applauds every one of our sad attempts to exalt ourselves.

September 27

God at Work in His World

From God's Word, the Bible...

Moreover the Lord said to me, "Take a large scroll, and write on it with a man's pen concerning Maher-Shalal-Hash-Baz. And I will take for Myself faithful witnesses to record, Uriah the priest and Zechariah the son of Jeberechiah." Then I went to the prophetess, and she conceived and bore a son. Then the Lord said to me, "Call his name Maher-Shalal-Hash-Baz; for before the child shall have knowledge to cry 'My father' and 'My mother,' the riches of Damascus and the spoil of Samaria will be taken away before the king of Assyria."

Isaiah 8:1-4
(Read the whole passage in Isaiah 8:1-8.)

Isaiah chapter 8 is part of what is sometimes called "The Book of Immanuel." This section, reaching from Isaiah 7:1 to 12:6, is rich with promises about the coming Messiah (e.g., 7:14; 9:6-7; 11:1-5,10).

This portion of Isaiah was written at a particularly tense time. Armies were marching, kings were plotting, and people were grumbling. All were trembling.

We can't understand these times if we fail to distinguish between four kingdoms: Judah, Israel, Syria, and Assyria.

Assyria, the power of the day, was gobbling up smaller nations. The kings of Judah, Israel, and Syria were very alarmed. What were they to do?

The obvious way for a weak country to make itself stronger is by forming an alliance with another nation. Israel and Syria did this, and they were pressuring Judah to join them.

But Ahaz, king of Judah, had what he considered to be a better idea. He decided to form an alliance with Assyria, that gobbler of other nations.

No sooner had Ahaz done this than he realized he now had another problem. The kings of Israel and Syria were so enraged by his alliance with Assyria that they decided to invade Judah.

In trying to save himself from one enemy (Assyria), Ahaz had created for himself a new enemy (the allied Israel and Syria), and this new enemy was much closer to home.

Ahaz was so scared that ". . . his heart and the heart of his people were moved as the trees of the woods are moved with the wind" (Isa. 7:2).

Into this troubled situation, God sent Isaiah to deliver a message to Ahaz. It was a message about quick and easy pickings (vv. 1-4), surging waters (vv. 5-8), and Immanuel (v. 8).

The quick and easy pickings part amounted to God assuring Ahaz that he didn't need to worry about Israel and Syria because God was going to make those nations quick and easy pickings for Assyria.

God conveyed this message to Isaiah by announcing that he and his wife were to have a son whom they were to name Maher-Shalal–Hash-Baz, which means "quick and easy pickings." Before this baby could say "Momma" or "Dada," Israel and Syria would be destroyed by Assyria.

The *surging waters part* of the prophecy dealt with the future of Judah. The fact that Israel and Syria would be destroyed didn't mean that Judah was home free. God was displeased with the alliance Ahaz had made with Assyria. He had made it clear that the nation of Judah was to depend on Him for its security—not on alliances with godless nations.

The Lord chose to picture this in terms of rivers. He says the people of Judah had essentially refused the softly flowing water of one river to launch out on the extremely turbulent and treacherous water of another.

The softly flowing river was God's government. The turbulent and treacherous river was Assyria with whom the people of Judah were now allied. They, the people of Judah, would find that the waters they had chosen would be too much for them, coming up to their necks and threatening to completely overflow them! We can see the fulfillment of this prophecy by reading 2 Kings 18 and 19.

The Immanuel part of the prophecy amounts to God allowing Ahaz to listen to what God the Father had to say to His Son, the Messiah, who would be called Immanuel (God with us). In verse 8, God assures the Messiah that the land of Judah wouldn't be destroyed, and that there would still be a land into which He would come.

Nations, kings, alliances from centuries ago! It's enough to make the head swim! Can these things have any meaning for us? They do indeed! They remind us that God isn't shut out of His world. He knows every detail, and He is involved in all the events. These things also remind us that God is often at work in this world in judgment. Many of the things we interpret as results of political decisions are really evidences of God judging human disobedience. These things also show us that nothing that is going on in the world will keep God from fulfilling His promises. The turbulence of that era didn't keep Christ from coming, and the turbulence of our era won't keep Him from coming again. So let's trust God in the turbulence.

In all these things, whether in times of turmoil or times of relative peace, the ageless gospel of God's reconciling work through His Messiah—Jesus—is offered to sinners. Even if you live in troubled times, you may still know peace with God through our Lord Jesus Christ, God's Immanuel.

September 28

Mr. Encourager

From God's Word, the Bible...

Then news of these things came to the ears of the church in Jerusalem, and they sent out Barnabas to go as far as Antioch. When he came and had seen the grace of God, he was glad, and encouraged them all that with purpose of heart they should continue with the Lord. For he was a good man, full of the Holy Spirit and of faith. And a great many people were added to the Lord.

Acts 11:22-24

Barnabas didn't start out as Barnabas. His name when he became a Christian was Joses. There was nothing wrong with that name. It meant "increaser." His parents may have given it to him to express their hope that he would become a prosperous man.

But while Joses was a good name, it just didn't seem to fit. As the early disciples spent time with Barnabas, they felt strange calling him "increaser." They couldn't be around him very long without him encouraging them in some way. It didn't matter what their circumstances were, Barnabas encouraged them. If they lost a loved one, he encouraged them. If they became weary in the Lord's work, he encouraged them. If they felt inadequate for their tasks, he encouraged them. If they felt guilty over a sin, he encouraged them. If they were fearful of what the future might bring, he encouraged them.

Because Barnabas unfailingly encouraged all those around him, it became as natural as breathing for his fellow-Christians to call him "encourager." That's what the name Barnabas means (Acts 4:36).

One example of Barnabas' encouraging ministry is seen in the case of the Apostle Paul. After he was converted to Christ on the road to Damascus, Paul, then known as Saul of Tarsus, found difficulty in aligning himself with the disciples of the Lord Jesus. They were all afraid of this man who had been the most vigorous and unrelenting persecutor of the church. Perhaps his "conversion" was nothing more than a clever ruse to carry out further persecution!

Barnabas stepped into that situation. He brought Saul before the disciples and explained to them how he had found the Lord, or, we should say how the Lord found him (Acts 9:26-27). In doing so, Barnabas broke down he barrier between Saul and the other Christians and brought peace. That is the type of thing an encourager does!

When we encounter Barnabas again, this time at Antioch, we find him still encouraging. Seeing many new converts, Barnabas took a personal interest in them and encouraged them to remain true to the Lord (Acts 11:23).

Barnabas, it seems, never missed an opportunity to do whatever was necessary. He spoke encouraging words, and he did encouraging things.

We need the example of Barnabas. These are very discouraging days, and God's people seem to be a very discouraged lot. Sometimes the discouragement comes to us because of the times in which we live—times of increasing hostility toward Christians. We're seeing more and more of this hostility expressed in outright persecution. Sometimes the discouragement is personal in nature. We have committed a grievous sin or we have labored hard for the Lord without success. Or it may be that we are facing a very taxing problem such as sickness, conflict with someone, or the loss of a loved one.

There are many reasons for discouragement, and there are many discouraged Christians. It is vital, therefore, for us to become encouragers as Barnabas was.

We certainly can't leave Barnabas without asking how he came to be the way that he was. What made him such an encourager? We must attribute it to the grace of God that worked in him. Barnabas was saved by grace and equipped by grace. But we must go further. The grace of God worked in all those early saints, but Barnabas stood out among them.

Perhaps the clue to Barnabas is found in these words: ". . . he was a good man, full of the Holy Spirit and of faith" (Acts 11:24).

Barnabas was a full man! Full of the Holy Spirit! Full of faith! Our days cry for Christians to be full men and women—not filled with money, career, pleasure, and sports—but filled, as Barnabas was, with the Holy Spirit and faith. If we would be like Barnabas, we must be filled with those things that filled him.

How do we become filled with the Holy Spirit and with faith? There is only one way, and that is by being filled with the Word of God. Do we want more of the Spirit? The Word of God is "the sword of the Spirit" (Eph. 6:17). Do we want more of faith? Faith comes by hearing, and hearing by the Word of God (Rom. 10:17).

Barnabas will never make the list of the best-known men in the Bible. But he certainly deserves our admiration and emulation.

Coming up from the Wilderness

From God's Word, the Bible...

Who is this coming up from the wilderness,
Leaning upon her beloved?
I awakened you under the apple tree.
There your mother brought you forth;
There she who bore you brought you forth.

Song of Solomon 8:5

The Song of Solomon is the love song of the Bible. It relates in poetic form how King Solomon of Israel fell in love with a country girl, a Shulamite, and took her to be his wife.

In this verse, the happy couple is seen walking back toward the city after taking a stroll through a barren, wilderness area. Someone, perhaps a relative of the Shulamite, sees them approaching and exclaims:

Who is this coming up from the wilderness,
Leaning upon her beloved?

These aren't the words of one who was ignorant of the bride's identity, but rather the words of one who is happily taking note of what has taken place. The Shulamite girl is now the wife of the king! Who would have ever thought such a thing could happen? Here, then, is what this person was saying: "Can this be the simple country girl that I know who is now walking with the king?"

The one who uttered these words was filled with wonder over what he was seeing.

The Song of Solomon pictures for us a love that is even more wonderful—that which Christ has for His church and which His church has for Him.

Now here is something to marvel about: the church of Christ is coming up out of the wilderness, leaning all the while on her Beloved!

This world is very much like a wilderness for God's people—filled with difficulties and taxing our resources. Why is it this way? The Bible gives us the answer. This world didn't start out this way. The world has gone from being a garden to a wilderness, and sin is the reason. Sin is the great wrecker. It never improves or upgrades anything. It only ruins.

While Christians often sigh as they walk through this wilderness, they have a reason to rejoice. The church of which they are a part is coming out of the wilderness. The reason the church is on her way out of the wilderness is that she has a Beloved. She has One who loves her more than words can express, and One whom she loves.

The church's Beloved is the Lord Jesus Christ. He is the One who set His love on the church even before time began. He saw her there in the wilderness of the world, and, because of His love for her, He Himself decided to go into the wilderness to bring her out. This brought Him all the way from heaven to the cross where He endured the wrath of God in the place of His church.

Someday the church's walk through this wilderness will be over. The Lord Jesus who now walks with her through His Spirit will lead her out. What a glorious day that will be! He will escort her to join Him in heaven. Heaven won't be a wilderness. Wilderness living will be forever gone when Jesus comes for His people.

So we wait for that splendid day, but we wait in the wilderness. How do we go about this business of waiting? How do we handle the hardships, disappointments, and sorrows of wilderness living while we wait? Our text gives us the answer. We must lean on our Beloved One, the Lord Jesus.

That word "leaning" is rich in implications. It means that the church is conscious of her own weakness. She realizes that the wilderness is too much for her if she is left to her own strength.

But it also means that the church is keenly aware that her Beloved does have the resources that wilderness living demands. Isn't it encouraging to know that the Lord cares enough for us to allow us to lean on Him? He sympathizes with us (Heb. 4:15-16), and He urges us to trust Him. So let us lean on Christ.

As we lean on him, let's trust Him in every circumstance of life. Let's trust Him to care. Let's trust Him to strengthen us. Let's trust Him to have a purpose for us in the midst of our difficulties. Let's trust Him to finally bring us out of the wilderness. Let's trust every promise He has given in His Word. Let's lean on our Beloved, singing as go:

Leaning, leaning,
Safe and secure from all alarms;
Leaning, leaning,
Leaning on the everlasting arms.
(Elisha A. Hoffman)

September 30

The Happiness in the Hatred

From God's Word, the Bible...

Yes, and all who desire to live godly in Christ Jesus will suffer persecution.

2 Timothy 3:12

I hate to be hated. I want to be liked. But I am hated, increasingly so, it seems, by people who don't even know me. The reason is that I'm a Christian.

Hostility toward Christians is growing by leaps and bounds all around the world, even in countries founded on Judeo-Christian principles. Large numbers of people seem to be oblivious to this problem. That's not surprising. Many in the news media find it convenient to ignore it because they harbor hostility toward Christians themselves.

How are we to explain this hatred? Christians just seem to be so out of step! They insist on believing that God created the world, that humans are fundamentally flawed by sin, and are in need of forgiveness. They continue to insist that there's a judgment to come, and, very annoyingly, they maintain that there's only one way for people's sins to be forgiven and that way is Christ. Such beliefs fly in the face of the accepted dogmas of the day.

And there's an increasing tendency these days to link Christianity with all that has been wrong with the world in the past. As far as many are concerned, Christianity is the religion of white people who enjoy oppressing people with other skin colors! Have Christians failed in many ways through the centuries? Yes. But Christians have also been in the forefront of correcting many of the ills of society. By the way, not all are Christians who claim to be such. It's good to keep that in mind when attributing failures to "Christians" down through the centuries.

At the root of much of the hatred toward Christianity is the belief that it is an impediment to creating the kind of world that the haters want and, therefore, it must be destroyed.

One example of hatred for Christians surfaced on Facebook when a photo was posted of Christian teenagers at a restaurant giving thanks for their food. The reaction was swift, and, in many cases, severe. One person wrote: "I'm so tired of the arrogance many religious people display and their disdain for non-believers." Another person responded: "So tired of Christians pushing their beliefs onto everyone else."

Simply giving thanks for a meal is showing "disdain" for unbelievers? Who knew? It's a way of "pushing" their beliefs on others? If these Christian teenagers had stood up in the restaurant and said: "We are going to pray over our food, and we want you all to be quiet," that would constitute "pushing their beliefs" on others. But that's not what happened. And why is it that the critics of Christianity don't apply the same standard to themselves? Do they worry about pushing their beliefs on to others? Ask Christian bakers and florists about that!

Yet another response read: "If you are confidant (*sic*), in your beliefs then you don't feel the need to 'save' everyone else."

That's hilarious! Nothing is more common these days than those on the left of the political spectrum trying to "save" the rest of us from bias, climate change, economic injustice, guns, knives, sodas, micro-aggressions, and sexual hang-ups. It's not that those on the left are wrong on every issue. It's rather that they tend to think no one is entitled to an opinion except themselves.

While I don't enjoy being hated for my beliefs, I have to say that I find some happiness in the hatred. One reason is that it confirms the teaching of the Lord Jesus, who said: "If you were of the world, the world would love its own. Yet because you are not of the world, but I chose you out of the world, therefore the world hates you" (John 15:19).

Another part of my happiness in the midst of the world's hatred comes from knowing that the Lord will be with His people to strengthen and help them. The Apostle Paul, who knew very well what it was to be hated for Christ, was able to say in the midst of it: "But the Lord stood with me and strengthened me. . ." (2 Tim. 4:17a).

There's also happiness in knowing that the faith I hold dear will eventually prove to be triumphant. The Apostle John says: "And this is the victory that has overcome the world—our faith" (1 John 5:4b).

While the Christian-haters can destroy Christian buildings, businesses, and bodies, they can't destroy Christianity. The only way for that to occur is for the Christ on whom it is built to be destroyed. That can't happen.

Bonus Reading

The Bottle

From God's Word, the Bible...

You number my wanderings;
Put my tears into Your bottle;
Are they not in Your book?

Psalm 56:8

Psalm 56 is a prayer. The New King James Version supplies this heading for the psalm: *Prayer for Relief from Tormentors*. Under that title is the note that David wrote it when he was captured by the Philistines in Gath (1 Sam. 21:10-15).

I've never had much trouble with the first seven verses. David cries to God for mercy because he feels that his enemies are about to "swallow" him. No problem understanding that. He says his enemies "hound" him "all day." Yep, got that. He says he will trust in God when he is afraid. Copy that.

But I always found verse 8 to be a bit befuddling, especially that "bottle" business. I took David's phrase about God "numbering" his "wanderings" or "flutterings" to mean that he would not have one more difficulty than the number God had allotted to him. It's comforting to know that our trials, no matter how numerous, have an end. For believers in Christ, they don't last forever.

And I took David's phrase about his flutterings already being in God's "book" to mean that there is a purpose behind all of them. That purpose is recorded in God's book of explanation, the book which will be read to God's people when they get home to heaven. All of our trials will then make perfect sense.

But what about that bottle? What did David mean when he asked God to put his tears into His bottle? Some suggest that he was asking God to always remember his trials, as if God could forget.

It finally occurred to me that for someone to catch our tears in a bottle that person would have to be very near to us. No one can catch tears in a bottle if he or she is standing ten or twenty feet away.

So I think David was asking God to be very near him as he was facing trouble. Nothing helps us more when we are in horrible circumstances than knowing that our God is near, near to sympathize, to strengthen, to encourage, to uphold. When problems mount up around us, we not only want God to be near; we want Him to make us know that He is near.

In August of 1932, Thomas A. Dorsey was leading the singing in a church service in St. Louis, Missouri. Someone handed him a telegram that contained these brutal words: "Your wife just died." He called home, but the person who answered could only frantically repeat these words: "Nettie is dead! Nettie is dead!"

Dorsey immediately enlisted a friend to drive him home. When he arrived, he received another jolt of devastating news. His baby boy had also died.

After going through the first few days of horrible grief, Dorsey said: "I began to feel that God had done me an injustice. I didn't want to serve Him anymore or write any more gospel songs."

But something happened a few days later to change his mind. Feeling a calmness coming over his spirit, he went to the piano and began to play. Here's how he described it: "As my fingers began to manipulate over the keys, words began to fall in place on the melody like drops of water falling from the crevice of the rock." Those words are well known among Christians:

Precious Lord, take my hand,
Lead me on, help me stand;
I am tired, I am weak, I am worn;
Thru the storm, thru the night,
Lead me on to the light,
Take my hand, precious Lord,
Lead me home.

When my way grows drear,
Precious Lord, linger near;
When my life is almost gone,
Hear my cry, hear my call,
Hold my hand, lest I fall;
Take my hand, precious Lord,
Lead me home.

The Lord has to be very near us to take us by the hand or to catch our tears in a bottle.

"I wish," someone says, "that I could be sure that the Lord is near enough to take me by the hand or to catch my tears."

Look to Jesus. His name is Immanuel, which means "God with us." Because Jesus took our humanity, it's true to say that He sympathizes with us in our humanity, but, true as that is, it's not quite strong enough. It's rather that because Jesus took our humanity, He can't help but sympathize with us. And, sympathizing with us, He holds our hands and His bottle.

That same Jesus also experienced tears. He is a sympathetic high priest to all who come to God through Him and He promises mercy and grace to help in time of need (Heb. 4:14-16); have you come to Him? Are you on your way to heaven?

Books Included in this Series

My Coffee-Cup Meditations includes the following

A Dog and A Clock (Series#1)

The "Thumbs-Up" Man (Series#2)

When God Blocks Our Path (Series#3)

Fading Lines, Unfading Hope Series#4)

The Day the Milk Spilled (Series#5)

"Where Are the Donuts?" (Series#6)

Sure Signs of Heavenly Hope (Series#7)

My Dog Knows It's Sunday (Series#8)

Rover and the Cows (Series#9)

Apples of Gold in Silver Settings (Series#10)

Old Houses, New Houses (Series#11)

Golden Key and Silver Chain (Series#12)

The Last Words of Moses

מגיד
MAGGID

Micah Goodman

The Last Words of Moses

TRANSLATED BY

Ilana Kurshan

Maggid Books

The Last Words of Moses

First English Edition, 2023

Maggid Books
An imprint of Koren Publishers Jerusalem Ltd.

POB 8531, New Milford, CT 06776-8531, USA
& POB 4044, Jerusalem 9104001, Israel
www.maggidbooks.com

The publication of this book was made possible through the generous support of *The Jewish Book Trust.*

ISBN 978-1-59264-558-9, *hardcover*

Printed and bound in the United States

In loving memory of Irving and Beatrice Stone,
who dedicated their lives to the
advancement of Jewish education.
We are proud and honored to continue in their legacy.

Their Children, Grandchildren, Great-Grandchildren
and Great-Great-Grandchildren
Jerusalem, Israel
Cleveland, Ohio USA

Author's Dedication

This book is dedicated to
my beloved Mom and Dad
Maggie and Jerry Goodman

Contents

Preface

THE DISAPPEARANCE OF MOSES

The ancient Egyptian pharaohs did not die. Their sons continued their dynastic line. Their bodies were mummified and preserved in pyramids, burial tombs of enormous proportions and magnificent appointments. These were not places where the dead lay, but where they lived on. Death was defeated by the cult of death.[1]

Moses was raised as an Egyptian prince, but his death could not have been less Egyptian.[2] His body was not preserved, and the site of his grave remains a mystery to this day.[3] Moses's death is a rejection of the

1. Edward F. Wente, "Egyptian Religion: Afterlife," *ABD* 2: 410–411. Also see the documentation from the tomb of Sety I in Bojana Mojsov, "The Ancient Egyptian Underworld in the Tomb of Sety I: Sacred Books of Eternal Life," *The Massachusetts Review* 42, no. 4, Egypt (Winter 2001–2002): 490–493.
2. A. H. Gardiner, *The Attitude of the Ancient Egyptians to Death and the Dead* (Cambridge, 1935); A. J. Spencer, "Ancestor Worship," *Death in Ancient Egypt* (Harmondsworth, UK: Penguin Books, 1982), *ABD* 1: 240.
3. "So Moses the servant of the Lord died there, in the land of Moab, at the command of the Lord. He buried him in the valley of the land of Moab, near Beth-Peor, and no one knows his burial place to this day" (Deut. 34:5–6). The ancient Jewish Sages cite these verses in discussing why the burial place of Moses is not disclosed. There are various original answers proposed, including the following: "'And no one knows' – R. Ḥama bar Ḥanina said: Why was Moses's burial place kept a secret from human beings? Because it was known to the Holy One, blessed be He that the Temple would one day be destroyed and Israel would be exiled from its land; lest people flock to Moses's grave and cry and plead with Moses, and lest he stand up then and there and avert the decree, because the righteous are more beloved unto God when they are

Egyptian cult of death. There was no mummified corpse, no pyramid, no heirs. His death was his disappearance. Even in his last moments, the man who took the Jews out of Egypt sought to eradicate all traces of Egypt from the Jews.

But Moses did not really vanish. Just before he died, he delivered his life's greatest oration, full of ideas that were new, even revolutionary. He wrote down this parting address and it became a book, Deuteronomy, the fifth book of the Bible. It was the last words of Moses that immortalized him.[4]

The Bible famously relates that God commanded Moses to speak to a rock and ask for water, but instead of using words he struck it with a stick, and on account of this disobedience he was denied entry into the Land of Israel. Moses's downfall is prefigured at the very beginning of his leadership career, in his encounter with God at the burning bush. There he was initially reluctant to accept the mantle of leadership on the grounds that he had a speech impediment. Moses said that he had "uncircumcised lips" and a "heavy mouth," insisting that he was "not a man of words." In the end, though, he overcame his fears and accepted the position of leader. The Egyptians were defeated and the children of Israel were redeemed from bondage. However, Moses's mission was not completed. He had always expected to bring the nation through the desert and into the Promised Land, but he was fated to remain outside its borders. Moses's "heavy mouth" did not prevent him from embarking on his mission, but it did prevent him from completing it.

This irony is even more striking in light of the content of Moses's final address, in which he expresses his dying wish not to remain on the eastern side of the Jordan but rather to be present among the people of

---

dead than when they are alive" (Sota 13a). For more on the rabbinic understanding of Moses's death, see Bezalel Landro, "The Death of Moses Our Teacher" [Hebrew], *Maḥanaim* 116 (5727). Also see Y. Blidstein, *The Sadness of Nevo: The Death of Moses in Rabbinic Midrashim* [Hebrew], 5768. George Coats argues that these verses serve to make Moses even more heroic. See G. W. Coats, *Moses: Heroic Man, Man of God,* JSOT 57 (Sheffield, 1988): 152, n. 12. See introduction below, note 12, where he quotes Wildavsky.

4. As discussed below, Deuteronomy is Moses's book, a claim the text itself attests. For more detail, see the appendix at the end of this book.

Israel once they cross into the land. The measure of the success of his address lies in the enduring nature of his words. Again and again, Moses enjoins the people to continue to invoke his address. They are commanded to write parts of it down on one of the stones on Mount Ebal when they enter the land. And when they appoint a king, it is incumbent upon that king to write down this speech and consult it throughout his reign. Furthermore, every seven years the nation is required to come together and listen to a public reading of Moses's final address. In the end, Moses did not enter the land. His speech entered in his stead.

The entry into the land is also an entry into the dynamics of power. After entering the land, conquering it, and establishing a secure foothold, the weak nation of slaves that left Egypt is transformed into a ruling power in the land of Canaan. Moses seeks to prepare the people for this reality – to teach them how to defend themselves from the moral and spiritual danger inherent in the transition from weakness to strength.

Success can inflate the ego and cripple the conscience. This was Moses's concern, and it remains relevant in our own day as well: Can we attain power and also maintain our sensitivity? The book of Deuteronomy envisions a society that has material abundance but is not materialistic, a powerful society that is not drunk on power. Moses does not lead the people into the land, but the message he instills in their consciousness is intended to guide them on the challenging journey from weakness to strength.

RELIGION AND POWER

Religion is as ancient and universal as humanity itself. Religious scholars refer to humankind as "homo religiosus." Spinoza saw religion's enduring hold as a manifestation of humanity's deepest fears. The future, uncertain and largely uncontrollable, is frightening and threatening.[5] Religion is a response to fear. In ancient Egypt, religion promised control not only over life, but over death as well. By contrast, what was revealed to Moses not only offered no such sense of control but shattered the illusion of

5. Baruch Spinoza, *A Theologico-Political Treatise*, trans. C. Warshavsky (Jerusalem: Magnes, 5722), 1–3.

control altogether. The book of Deuteronomy heralded a new religious and spiritual consciousness.

Moses offers a new approach to religion, and to politics as well. Religion and politics are intimately connected. Some thinkers maintain that religion was created by political forces in order to enable the few to govern the many. According to this view, religion offers nearly limitless power to those who know how to manipulate it.[6] Is the purpose of religion to provide people with a sense of control, as Spinoza held, or to control them? Perhaps both are true.

In the book of Deuteronomy, however, Moses divorces religion from power. The religion that Moses proposes to the people is not about control. And the politics he proposes are disassociated from religion. But what kind of religion does not promise a person control over his life? And what kind of politics limits the power of those who rule? Deuteronomy is about the power of limited power. It is about a new kind of religion and a new kind of politics. These are Moses's two revolutions.

THE STRUCTURE OF THIS BOOK

Moses's two revolutions are the subject of the first part of this book, in which I will present the central ideas of the new religious-spiritual consciousness that Moses describes in his final address. These ideas have their roots in the first four books of the Bible, but they achieve their full flowering in Deuteronomy. We will then consider how these two revolutions both stem from an even larger and more fundamental idea about the nature of God.

In the second half of this book, we will turn from the philosophical to the practical. We will discuss Moses's painful realization of how difficult, if not impossible, it would be to achieve what he proposed in his address. As a prophet, Moses was able to foresee that success would become the occasion for failure. The conquest of the land would confound the consciousness of the people. While in part one we will discuss a religion that does not offer the promise of control, in part two we will

---

6. See, for instance, Paul Radin, *Primitive Religion* (New York: The Viking Press, 1937), 52. For a clear articulation of the cynical interpretation of religion, see Robert Wright, *The Evolution of God* (New York: 2010), 39–45.

discuss how having control undermines the religious mindset. Part one is theological, focusing on a new idea about the nature of God. Part two is psychological and deals with the nature of humankind and its way of coping with the challenge of success.

Part three traces the impact of Moses's final address in the days and years after it was delivered. Were the significant and sophisticated ideas he put forth accepted and realized in biblical times? We will examine the legacy of the address by closely studying two of Moses's successors: Joshua, who fulfilled its dictates, and King Solomon, who abrogated them. In the end, we will ask: Can these two revolutions be realized in modern Israel?

This book regards the book of Deuteronomy as a human document authored by Moses whose inclusion in the Bible lends it divine authority. But most rabbinic commentators challenge the assumption that the book has a human rather than a divine author, and most academic scholars challenge the assumption that the book was authored by Moses, attributing it instead to one of the sages of the First Temple period. And so both the rabbis and the academics reject the notion that Deuteronomy is Moses's book, a claim that Deuteronomy itself asserts. My goal is to understand the book as it seeks to be understood. For a more detailed explanation of this exegetical choice in light of the rabbinic and academic alternatives, and further discussion of whether Moses did indeed write the book of Deuteronomy, see the appendix. Until then, we will accept what the book itself asserts – that Deuteronomy is Moses's actual words.

My approach is not academic, but it is not the approach of classical rabbinic commentators either. I am not focusing on the historical sources of the book of Deuteronomy or its later midrashic interpretations. The questions that drew me to Deuteronomy are primarily philosophical. I was interested in the religious, psychological, and political ideas it contains – ideas which I have spent the better part of a decade attempting to hone and articulate. Like my previous two books, *Maimonides and the Book That Changed Judaism* and *The Dream of the Kuzari,* this is a book about a book – an attempt to demystify some aspects of Deuteronomy's profound but also cryptic message.

My curiosity about the book of Deuteronomy began with reading Moshe Weinfeld's *Deuteronomy and the Deuteronomic School,* which considers Deuteronomy's religious outlook.[7] I experienced Deuteronomy as a sort of introduction to biblical philosophy, and a window through which to survey the biblical worldview more generally.

I realized that Deuteronomy is also a window to Israeli society, particularly its religiosity and politics. But in the book of Deuteronomy, I found something for myself as well. The great sixteenth-century mystic known as the Ari, Rabbi Isaac Luria, said that every Jew has his own letter in the Torah. In various sections of Deuteronomy, I found my letter, and perhaps my book as well.

The Last Words of Moses is dedicated to all those who seek to peer through the window that Moses opened to biblical philosophy. It is also dedicated to anyone who wishes to understand, through Deuteronomy, the challenges of modern Israel.

This book may be read on two levels. There is the text that you are reading now, which includes the primary discussion, namely the philosophical story I seek to tell. And then there are the footnotes, which I employed in order to keep the book's main argument free of digressions and interruptions. Some of the ideas I will present in this book are original, and some were put forth by others before me. Some are controversial; others are authoritative. Anyone who is interested in these details is welcome to delve into the footnotes. My writing here is intended to allow for a smooth reading experience, and it includes, by its nature, some generalizations. Qualifications and clarifications may be found in the notes.

I am grateful to the many individuals who helped in the course of my work on this book. First, thank you to my dedicated research assistant, Dror Yaakov, whose fingerprints are visible both in the footnotes and appendix. Friends and scholars read various drafts of the manuscript and eliminated errors, added clarity, and bolstered my claims. Professor Uriel Simon, Professor Alexander Rofé, Dr. Dror Bondi Dr. Roni Megidov, Dr. Shraga Bar-On, Efrat Shapira Rosenberg, Noam Zion, Rav Avia HaCohen, Dr. Yoshi Fargeon, Dr. Hillel Mali, and Yivniya Kaploun – I am

7. Moshe Weinfeld, *Deuteronomy and the Deuteronomic School* (Oxford: Clarendon Press, 1972).

grateful to all of you for the loving and tough critique which challenged me to hone my arguments and drew me further into the philosophical depths of the book of Deuteronomy. This book was also blessed by the wisdom of friends and experts in various fields. My thanks to Boaz Lifshitz, Milka Elimelech, Dr. Ran Baratz, Dr. Danny Tenne, Rabbi Professor Daniel Sperber, Rani Elon, and Eliran Zered.

I am grateful to Tirza Eisenberg, Yael Yannai, Yuval Elezri, Sarit Rosenberg, and Ormi Zartel, as well as the dedicated staff at Kinneret Zmora-Bitan Dvir publishing house, for all the professional attention they devoted to my original Hebrew manuscript.

I am grateful to Koren Publishers and Maggid Books, especially publisher Matthew Miller and editorial director Rabbi Reuven Ziegler, as well as Aryeh Grossman, Shira Finson, Debbie Ismailoff, Caryn Meltz, Ita Olesker, and Tali Simon.

I am grateful, too, to Rabbi Dr. Donniel Hartman for the intellectual climate at the Shalom Hartman Institute in Jerusalem, where I wrote this book. Shmuel Rosner was more than just an editor; he was also a friend and partner. I feel privileged to work with you, Shmuel. Thank you.

From the bottom of my heart, I am grateful to Rav Dani Segal, Rosh Midrasha Beit Prat; Anat Silverstone, Executive Director of Beit Prat; Ayelet Kahane, and the entire Beit Prat staff for their support of my writing and for their unwavering belief – even in hard times – in our ability to fulfill Moses's vision within Israel society.

Above all, I am grateful to my life partner and my closest friend, Tzippi.

This book is dedicated to my parents, with great love.

Introduction

Moses on Moses

THE HUMAN IN THE DIVINE

The book of Deuteronomy is the fifth and final book of the Torah, and the Torah – according to Jewish tradition – is divine. The book of Deuteronomy, however, presents itself as a human document. Most of the book is comprised of three addresses which complement one another, all delivered by Moses.

Moses speaks in first person. He tells the nation its story through the lens of his own personal perspective. Up until the book of Deuteronomy, Moses is a hero of the Torah. In the final book, he becomes a narrator. This is one of the great enigmas in the Bible. How is it possible that the last book of the divine Bible is a humanly created document?[1]

One answer was proposed by the Portuguese Jewish philosopher Don Isaac Abrabanel, who lived during the Renaissance. According to Abrabanel, Moses wrote the book of Deuteronomy, but then God included it in the Bible.

---

1. The halakhic tradition reflects an internal hierarchy within the Tanakh, with the Torah (*Ḥumash*) at the pinnacle. According to the rabbinic Sages, this hierarchy is reflected in the laws about which books may be placed on top of others. *Ḥumashim* may be placed on top of volumes of the Prophets or the Writings. But volumes of the Prophets or the Writings may not be placed on *Ḥumashim*. See *Mishneh Torah, Sefer Ahava, Hilkhot Tefillin UMezuza VeSefer Torah* 10:5.

> Because Moses himself spoke these words, and the Divine Wisdom, may it be blessed, saw fit to command that it be written as a book along with the other parts of the Torah.[2]

The book of Deuteronomy was included in the Torah, and thus it became the human section of the divine Torah.

Deuteronomy repeats much of what was already said in the biblical books that precede it. It reviews the laws that were previously promulgated and the stories that were previously told. But it is not an exact repetition. The stories that are retold in Moses's final address are not identical to the original versions. There are fundamental differences – some quite significant – between the versions that appear in the book of Deuteronomy and the versions that appear in the previous books. The human reconstruction of the divine Torah refashions this text and interprets it anew. The last book of the Torah is also the first commentary on it.

In Akira Kurosawa's film *Rashomon,* a single event is narrated from different, conflicting perspectives. When the perspective shifts, the story changes as well. The first four books of the Torah are narrated from God's perspective, but in the book of Deuteronomy, the same story is narrated from the perspective of a human being, namely Moses. The Torah was complete only once these two perspectives were both included.

This is how Rabbi Abraham Joshua Heschel articulated this notion:

> The Pentateuch consists of five books. The *Shulḥan Arukh* consists of only four books. Where is the missing part of the law? Answered Rabbi Israel of Rushin: The missing part is the person. Without the living participation of the person, the law is incomplete.[3]

2. Abrabanel attributes the narrative of Deuteronomy to Moses, but he attributes the laws directly to God. See Abrabanel's commentary on Deuteronomy 1:1.
3. Abraham Joshua Heschel, *God in Search of Man* (New York: Farrar, Straus & Cudahy, 1955), 311.

MOSES ON THE STORY OF MOSES

Moses narrates the nation's history in his address. He tells of the Exodus from Egypt, the challenges of the wilderness, and the Revelation at Sinai, and he details the nation's sins and chronicles its wars. How does Moses tell the story of Moses? By barely mentioning himself at all. Here is one example:

> Remember the long way that the Lord your God has made you travel in the wilderness these past forty years, that He might test you with hardships to learn what was in your hearts – whether you would keep His commandments or not. He subjected you to the hardship of hunger and then gave you manna to eat, which neither you nor your fathers had ever known, in order to teach you that man does not live on bread alone, but that man may live on anything that the Lord decrees. The clothes upon you did not wear out, nor did your feet swell these forty years. Bear in mind that the Lord your God disciplines you just as a man disciplines his son. Therefore, keep the commandments of the Lord your God. Walk in His ways and revere Him. (Deut. 8:2–6)

In Moses's narrative, it is God who takes the Jews out of Egypt and leads them through the desert. Where is Moses? Moses, the hero of the story, avoids any mention of his role.[4]

Moses emphasizes two central events when retelling the nation's history: the enslavement in Egypt and the journey through the wilderness. Each consists of a challenge. In Egypt there is the challenge of

---

4. The story of the waters of Meriva appears three times in the Torah: Exodus 17:1–7, Numbers 20:1–13, and Deuteronomy 8:15. In the first two accounts, it is Moses who extracts water from the rock: "Then the Lord said to Moses...'I will be standing there before you on the rock at Horeb. Strike the rock and water will issue from it, and the people will drink.' And Moses did so in the sight of the elders of Israel" (Ex. 17:5–6); "And Moses raised his hand and struck the rock twice with his rod. Out came copious water, and the community and their beasts drank" (Num. 20:11). But in the book of Deuteronomy, Moses says: "Who led you through the great and terrible wilderness with its seraph serpents and scorpions, a parched land with no water in it? Who brought forth water for you from the flinty rock?" (8:15).

dealing with an enslaving civilization, and in the wilderness there is the challenge of an absence of civilization. The Jewish people must confront both. After escaping Egypt, they must survive in the barren expanse of the wilderness.

Moses does not just narrate the people's story; he also teaches them how to tell their story to future generations. And in this version, too, he excises himself from the narrative.

> You shall say to your children, "We were slaves to Pharaoh in Egypt and the Lord freed us from Egypt with a mighty hand. The Lord wrought before our eyes marvelous and destructive signs and portents in Egypt, against Pharaoh and all his household, and us He freed from there, that He might take us and give us the land that He had promised on oath to our fathers. (Deut. 6:21–23)

Anyone who has read the Passover Haggada closely has surely noticed that Moses is hardly ever mentioned. But the sages who removed Moses from the Haggada were not the first to do so. The first person to excise Moses from the Exodus narrative was Moses himself.[5]

This is an interesting and important paradox: The book of Deuteronomy is the sole human book in an otherwise divine Torah. And it is specifically the human book that does not glorify man, but exalts God instead.

And it is not just God's role that is emphasized. Moses shifts the focus from himself so that the people assume a more significant role. This is evident, for instance, when Moses retells the story of appointing chiefs for each of the tribes:

> Thereupon I said to you, "I cannot bear the burden of you by myself. The Lord your God has multiplied you until you are today as numerous as the stars in the sky. May the Lord, the God of your fathers, increase your numbers a thousandfold,

5. At all of the points in the story when Moses recounts the Exodus from Egypt, he never makes any reference to himself. Only God takes the Israelites out of Egypt. See Deuteronomy 4:20, 37; 5:14; 6:21–23; 8:14; 9:26; 11:3–4; 15:15; 20:1; 24:18; 26:8.

> and bless you as He promised you. How can I bear unaided the trouble of you and the burden and the bickering? Pick from each of your tribes men who are wise, discerning, and experienced, and I will appoint them as your heads." You answered me and said, "What you propose to do is good." So I took your tribal leaders, wise and experienced men, and appointed them heads over you: chiefs of thousands, chiefs of hundreds, chiefs of fifties, and chiefs of tens, and officials for your tribes. (Deut. 1:9–15)

The appointment of the chiefs is first described in the book of Exodus (18:13–26), in *Parashat Yitro*. But there the story is very different. In the book of Exodus, the sage advice to decentralize the judicial system is offered by Yitro, Moses's father-in-law, after he witnesses Moses's struggle to manage on his own. Moses accepts his advice and imposes a new system of government on the people. But the book of Deuteronomy describes a very different reality. Moses recognizes his limitations on his own. Only then does he seek out advice, not from Yitro, but from the people. He institutes a system of chiefs after consulting with the people and receiving their consent: "You answered me and said, 'What you propose to do is good'" (Deut. 1:14).

This is the case, too, when Moses retells the story of the spies sent to scout out the land of Canaan:

> Then all of you came to me and said, "Let us send men ahead to reconnoiter the land for us and bring back word on the route we shall follow and the cities to which we shall come." I approved of the plan, and so I selected twelve of your men, one from each tribe. (Deut. 1:22–23)

According to the account in the book of Numbers (chapters 13–14), where we first encounter the spies, they are sent to scout out the land in accordance with God's explicit instructions. But when Moses revisits the story in the book of Deuteronomy, it seems that it was the people's idea to scout out the land. As in the account of the appointment of chiefs of the tribes, here too, in the story of the spies, the decision is made by

Moses in consultation with the people. And here too, Moses accepts the people's advice: "I approved of the plan" (Deut. 1:23).

That is, Moses recasts the events of the past. He depicts a period in which the children of Israel did not have a dominant leader imposing his decisions upon them, but rather someone who consulted with them – not a distant leader who received instructions from God and then told the people what to do, but a figure attentive to their wishes and needs. It was not a true democracy, but the major decisions were all made in unison.

What emerges from the Torah is reminiscent of the Rashomon effect, with God's perspective on the human story and then the human perspective on God's Torah. Removing himself from the center of the story of the miraculous journey through the wilderness, Moses makes more room for God. By diminishing his role in the political story about the appointment of chiefs, he makes more room for the people.

As we will now see, Moses tries even further to narrow the gap between him and the people when he presents the people as also having prophetic powers.

MOSES'S PROPHECY AND THE PEOPLE'S PROPHECY

The prophet has often been regarded as someone with a unique spiritual constitution.[6] But Moses believed that all people are equal. As he saw it, prophecy is not a reflection of any fundamental difference between the prophet and the rest of humanity. There is no metaphysical gulf between the prophet and his audience.

At least, this is the conclusion that emerges from the way Moses tells the people the story of how he became the nation's prophet. It all began at Sinai, where God revealed Himself to the entire people. Everything that we might expect would have happened to the prophet alone, and everything that would otherwise distinguish him, happened to the entire nation at Sinai. God spoke to the people and passed on His laws directly, without mediation. The nation's response was dramatic:

> The Lord spoke those words – those and no more – to your whole congregation at the mountain, with a mighty voice out of

6. See Goodman, *The Dream of the Kuzari* [Hebrew] (Dvir: 2012), part 2.

> the fire and the dense clouds. He inscribed them on two tablets of stone, which He gave to me. When you heard the voice out of the darkness, while the mountain was ablaze with fire, you came up to me, all your tribal heads and elders, and said, "The Lord our God has just shown us His majestic presence, and we have heard His voice out of the fire. We have seen this day that man may live though God has spoken to him." (Deut. 5:19–21)

This collective and egalitarian Revelation seems to suggest that there is no fundamental distinction between the prophet and the nation. Everyone can be a prophet. Moreover, the collective Revelation is not supposed to be a onetime event, but rather to continuously unfold. However, as the Torah goes on to relate, the people feel that they cannot bear the force of God's direct Revelation, and they ask for relief. They request that Moses put an end to this egalitarian arrangement and switch to a different model:

> You go closer and hear all that the Lord our God says, and then you tell us everything that the Lord our God tells you, and we will willingly do it. (Deut. 5:24)

It is the people who ask not to hear the voice of God directly any longer. Instead, they ask Moses to convey God's words to them, and God obliges:

> The Lord heard the plea that you made to me, and the Lord said to me, "I have heard the plea that this people made to you; they did well to speak thus." (Deut. 5:25)

This is an interpretation of the idea that first appears in the book of Exodus regarding the nature of Moses's prophecy:

> "You speak to us," they said to Moses, "and we will obey, but let not God speak to us, lest we die." (Ex. 20:16)[7]

7. Compare Deuteronomy 5:19–6:3. Scholar Jeffrey Tigay contends that according to the account in the book of Deuteronomy, the revelation at Horeb was a parallel event to the Revelation at Sinai. In other words, the Torah contains two parallel stories of

Moses in Deuteronomy is not God's messenger to the people, but the people's messenger to God.

At the beginning of Deuteronomy, Moses reports to the people on a revelation that was not described previously in the Torah. Moses relates that after a long wait at the foothills of Mount Sinai, God revealed Himself to the people once again: "The Lord our God spoke to us at Horeb, saying, 'You have stayed long enough at this mountain. Start out and make your way to the hill country of the Amorites'" (Deut. 1:6–7). According to the plain meaning of the text, God revealed Himself to the entire nation: "The Lord our God spoke to us at Horeb." But there is a problem with this understanding, because this revelation took place after the Revelation at Sinai, that is, after the collective revelation had already been replaced by a private revelation to Moses alone, per the people's request. To whom exactly did God reveal Himself this time – to the entire people, or just to Moses? The book of Deuteronomy does not seem to distinguish between Moses's prophecy and the people's prophecy. Deuteronomy does not attend to the specifics of just *who* heard God's word. Revelation to Moses was revelation to the entire people.

When it comes to his own prophetic career, Moses's address omits salient autobiographical details. He does not tell of his childhood, his Egyptian period, or his personal revelation at the burning bush, which was arguably the most formative moment of his life. According to the account that the people hear during Moses's last days, Moses took on the role of prophet at Sinai. From Sinai on, all the roles are reversed: Exodus relates that God revealed Himself at the burning bush and sent Moses to the people in order to convey His will. But according to the revised account in Deuteronomy, the nation sent Moses as an intermediary to convey God's will to them. Moreover, according to the theology that Moses presents in Deuteronomy, all the men and women of Israel can prophesy. Moses is no different from the rest of the nation. The fact

---

revelation: one at Sinai (Exodus), and one at Horeb (Deuteronomy). According to Tigay, Moses waited forty years until his parting address, and only then passed on to the people the laws he had heard at Horeb. See the introduction to the JPS edition of Deuteronomy, p. xiv. Also see Baruch Y. Schwartz, "The Torah: Its Five Books and Its Four Accounts" [Hebrew], in *Biblical Literature: Introductions and Studies*, ed. Tzipora Talshir (Jerusalem: Yad Ben Zvi, 5771), 209–210.

that he is a go-between is not an indication of any qualitative difference between him and the nation. It simply reflects the fact that he was chosen by the people to act as their representative.

This is how Moses describes the way prophecy worked in the past, and this is how he shapes the way it will work in the future. After his death, there will be other prophets who will also speak to God in the name of the people. Moses describes these future prophets in clear, simple terms: "The Lord your God will raise up for you a prophet from among your own people, like myself; him you shall heed" (Deut. 18:15). Every prophet will be comparable to Moses. Just as, according to Moses, at Sinai there was no difference between him and the rest of the nation, in the future every prophet who arises will be like him.[8]

What then is the source of the traditional belief in the fundamental superiority of Moses's prophecy to all others? Why is there such a widespread belief that Moses's prophecy was one of a kind, both unprecedented and unmatched? The source of this notion is also in the book of Deuteronomy, but not in Moses's words. The final verses of the book are spoken about Moses, but not by Moses. They tell us something about Moses that he never said himself: "Never again did there arise in Israel a prophet like Moses."[9]

That is, there is a stark disparity between what Moses says in the book of Deuteronomy and what the final verses have to say about him.[10] According to Moses, the humblest of all men, every prophet will be like

8. Moses already intimated in Numbers that he wished that there were no distinction between himself as prophet and the rest of the nation: "Would that all the Lord's people were prophets, that the Lord put His spirit upon them!" (Num. 11:29).
9. Deuteronomy 34:10.
10. According to the tannaitic midrash on this verse, the author of the final verses of Deuteronomy was Joshua: "'So Moses the servant of the Lord died there' – Moses wrote until this point, and Joshua wrote the rest." Also see Bava Batra 15a, where this idea is cited in the name of R. Yehuda or R. Neḥemya. This gave rise to medieval halakhic debates about the permissibility of reading these final verses without a minyan, i.e., a quorum of ten. For more on the history of this debate, see Abraham Joshua Heschel, *Heavenly Torah: As Refracted Through the Generations*, trans. Gordon Tucker (Bloomsbury, 1996).

him. But according to the final verses of the Torah, there will never be a prophet of his equal.[11]

SHAPING THE PAST FOR THE FUTURE KING

Why does Moses excise himself from the story of the Exodus from Egypt and the journey through the wilderness? Why does he downplay the differences between himself and the nation? Why does he blur the distinction between his prophecy and theirs? We can suggest two possible explanations, one political and one psychological.

Very often, the rewriting of the past is not about the past but about the future. Perhaps Moses wants to diminish the role of future leaders. When Moses describes the future king to the people of Israel, he does not depict an autocratic ruler but rather a leader who is subordinate and faithful to the law:

> Let it [the Torah] remain with him [the king] and let him read it all his life, so that he may learn to revere the Lord his God, to observe faithfully every word of this Torah as well as these laws. Thus he will not act haughtily toward his fellows or deviate from the commandment to the right or to the left, to the end that he and his descendants may reign long in the midst of Israel. (Deut. 17:19–20)

Submission serves to temper the arrogance of a king. The ruler will not feel exalted above everyone else if he himself is ruled by the law: "Thus he will not act haughtily toward his fellows."

I will consider Deuteronomy's idea of monarchy as part of the discussion of the book's political outlook. For the time being, I will just point out that Moses seeks to cultivate leadership that is not separate

---

11. In contrast to Joshua's response, Moses believes in the possibility of other prophets like himself arising. This is the impression that emerges from Moses's words to Eldad and Medad: "A youth ran out and told Moses, saying, 'Eldad and Medad are prophesying in the camp!' And Joshua son of Nun, Moses's attendant from his youth, spoke up and said, 'My lord Moses, restrain them!' But Moses said to him, 'Are you wrought up on my account? Would that all the Lord's people were prophets, that the Lord put His spirit upon them!'" (Num. 11:27–29).

and distant from the people. A king who is subject to the law will be less apt to elevate himself above his subjects. Instead, he will remain at their side, as one of them.

Moses needed to rewrite his own role, too, as the political leader of the people during their journey through the wilderness. Because he wanted to shape the image of the future leader as someone who is not exalted above the nation, he depicts himself in the same way. In order to shape a certain political future, he depicts a past in which society was not hierarchical, a past whose leader was modest.[12]

This is a political explanation. By contrast, the psychological explanation for the alternative history that Moses writes has to do with an open wound: the sin of the Golden Calf.

THE TRAUMA OF THE GOLDEN CALF

The rabbinic Sages described the sin of the Golden Calf in pained and pointed imagery. They likened the behavior of the nation to "a bride who committed adultery beneath her wedding canopy" (Gittin 36b). The nation had just received the Torah, sealed a covenant with God – and then violated that covenant. The sin of the Golden Calf is a collective betrayal of God, and in response to that betrayal, God threatens to destroy the people. Only Moses's urgent and persuasive intervention saves the people from annihilation.

Why are the people unfaithful so soon after receiving the Torah? The answer appears in the biblical text itself. Moses has disappeared up the mountain: "For that man Moses, who brought us up from the land of Egypt – we do not know what has happened to him" (Ex. 32:1). The Israelites become convinced that Moses will not return, and they

12. These conclusions may be compared to those of Aaron Wildavsky in his book *Moses as Political Leader* (Jerusalem: Shalem Press, 2005), 2nd ed., which deals with the question of why Moses did not enter the Land of Israel. According to Wildavsky, one of the reasons was to forge a people that can learn and teach words of Torah on its own, and that can build a society based on Torah without depending on a leader to tell them how to act and what to do. Another reason is in order to preclude or uproot the belief in the divinity of Moses or any future leaders. This discussion extends through the fifth chapter of his book. See especially pp. 182–189.

promptly fill the void with a golden calf. As Maimonides put it, "They were seeking another Moses."[13]

Forty years later, Moses stands before the people and informs them of his imminent departure. He will disappear again, never to return; he will not enter into the land with them. Informed by past experience, he becomes fearful that after he is gone, the people will soon abandon their faith in God:

> For I must die in this land; I shall not cross the Jordan. But you will cross and take possession of that good land. Take care, then, not to forget the covenant that the Lord your God concluded with you, and not to make for yourselves a sculptured image in any likeness, against which the Lord your God has enjoined you. (Deut. 4:22–23)

When the people were merely anxious about the possibility that Moses had left them, they violated the covenant. What would happen when Moses truly left forever? The verse suggests that Moses fears that the sin of the Golden Calf will be repeated. In that story, the children of Israel are described as having been "quick to turn aside from the path.... They have made themselves a molten calf."[14] Moses warns about what must be avoided, what will bring not blessing but curse:

> If you do not obey the commandments of the Lord your God, but turn away from the path that I enjoin upon you this day and follow other gods, whom you have not experienced. (Deut. 11:28)

Moses does not just caution the people about what *may* transpire. At the end of the book – both the end of his speech, and the end of his life – he also foretells that the terrible scenario *will* happen:

> For I know that, when I am dead, you will act wickedly and turn away from the path that I enjoined upon you. (Deut. 31:29)

13. Maimonides, *Commentary on the Torah* 32:1.
14. Exodus 32:8.

The trauma is real and the fear is palpable.

And so, in his final words, Moses tells a story whose purpose is to enable the people to survive their separation from him. He refashions national memory in a way that puts him on the sidelines, as if he had never been the dominant figure in the life of the nation. Moses minimizes his own role in the drama of the Exodus from Egypt and the wilderness journey, perhaps out of a sense that in order to become independent of him, the people need to be convinced that they were never really dependent on him in the first place.

The story of the Golden Calf suggests that the real sin was not the worship of the calf, but the worship of Moses. The people say, "For that man Moses, who brought us from the land of Egypt – we do not know what has happened to him" (Ex. 32:1). Perhaps this is the root cause of their sin:[15] not the absence of the man who had taken them out of Egypt, but the belief that Moses and not God had liberated them. Moses needs to move the people out from the shadow of his commanding presence. In order to do so, he tells a new story. And he reinforces that story by creating a new ritual for the period after he has died.

A RITUAL WITHOUT MOSES

The relationship between the nation of Israel and God is based on a covenant: First Noah made a covenant with God,[16] and then Abraham

---

15. Rabbeinu Bahya (Spain, 1255–1340) alludes to this idea in his commentary on Exodus 10:7. "'How long shall this be a snare to us' – they said this for the sake of Moses, and similarly it is written, 'For that man Moses' (Ex. 32:1), because it was his hands that brought the plagues that were ensnaring them.... And the text has revealed to us, through the use of this language, that the people had turned to total heresy." Elsewhere, Rabbeinu Bahya tempers his view and explains that the children of Israel mistook Moses for an angel, not a god: "They held that Moses was an angel of the Holy One, blessed be He, not concerned with physical matters or human affairs. As proof, see what they say in his absence: 'For that man Moses, who brought us out of the land of Egypt.'" See Rabbeinu Bahya's commentary on Numbers 20:16, *Vayishlaḥ malakh*.
16. Genesis 9:8–17. In this episode, God makes a covenant with humanity and with "every living thing" (v. 10). The rainbow is a sign of this covenant, ensuring that God will not forget His promise. A similar motif appears in the story of the Mesopotamian flood. Following the flood, Ishtar held up her necklace of lapis lazuli and declared

did,[17] and then the entire nation of Israel did the same. "Covenant" is a political term that is familiar from the literature of the ancient Near East. It is most commonly used to express the system of relationships between strong empires and weak vassal states, whereby the leader of an empire commits to protect the vassal state, and the vassal state in turn pledges complete loyalty to the leader of the empire. Scholars of the Bible and the ancient Near East have argued that the biblical covenant was a refashioning of the ancient vassal treaty.[18] This insight hones our understanding of

---

that just as she would not forget her necklace, nor would she forget the calamity of the flood. See *The Epic of Gilgamesh*, tablet 11, lines 162–165; *The Epic of Atrahasis*, tablet 3, column 6, lines 2–4.

17. The first covenant between Abraham and God is known as the Covenant between the Pieces (Gen. 15), in which God first promised to give the land of Canaan to Abraham's descendants and Abraham was instructed to cut up various animals. Until this point, the promise was stated in the future tense, but at the Covenant between the Pieces it was expressed in the past perfect tense: "I have given this land to your descendants" (Gen. 15:18). That is, by means of the covenant, God has given the land. There were other ancient Near Eastern covenants, too, that involved the promise of a region of land as well as the segmentation of animals. In the covenant at Mari, a goat and calf were used, alongside other young animals. The way in which the rite was carried out was also similar. The one who received the gift was the one responsible for laying out the animals, the symbol of the covenantal promise; if one side did not fulfill its promise, it would end up like the animals. This is also what we find in Jeremiah 34:18–19, where the people who promise to free their slaves must pass between the pieces. See Abraham Melamet, "The Ritual of Making Covenants in Mari and in the Bible" [Hebrew], *Beit Mikra*, vol. 40, booklet 2 (Tevet–Adar 2) (Bialik Institute, 5755): 153–155. The second covenant that Abraham made with God was the covenant of circumcision described in Genesis 17:1–14, in which God pledged to be the God of Abraham and his descendants.

18. In the first half of the twentieth century, scholars of the Bible and the ancient Near East first discerned that the biblical covenant, especially the covenant in the book of Deuteronomy, is based on Hittite and Assyrian covenants. In 1954, American scholar George Mendenhall found that the fundamental elements of ancient Hittite covenants are the same as those of the biblical covenant. See George E. Mendenhall, "Covenant Forms in Israelite Tradition," *The Biblical Archaeologist*, vol. 17, no. 3 (September 1954): 49–76. Two years later, scholars discovered the treaty of Esarhaddon the son of Sennacherib, from the seventh century BCE, which also bore striking resemblance to the covenant in Deuteronomy. See Erica Reiner, "The Vassal Treaties of Esarhaddon," *Ancient Near Eastern Texts Relating to the Old Testament*, 3rd ed., ed. J. B. Pritchard (Princeton University Press, 1969), 534–541. For an English translation of the covenant from Sefire, which contains a list of curses strikingly

the Bible's innovation – it was not the idea of a covenant that was novel, but rather the way it was used. For the first time, a covenant was sealed to systematize the relationship not between two nations, but between a nation and God. And so the covenant that had political significance in Assyria takes on theological significance in the Torah.[19]

A covenant rests fundamentally on the agreement of two sides. The covenantal process at Sinai was not complete when God presented His demands to the people. It was complete only after Moses read the

---

similar to that in Deuteronomy 28:23–35, see Joseph A. Fitzmyer SJ, "The Inscriptions of Bar-Ga'yah and Mati'el from Sefire," *The Context of Scripture: Monumental Inscriptions from the Biblical World*, vol. 2, ed. William W. Hallow and K. Lawson Younger, Jr. (Leiden, Netherlands: Brill, 2003). For a comprehensive explanation and a full bibliography on the concept of covenant and on notions of loyalty in the ancient Near East, see Haim Tadmore, *Assyria, Babylonia, and Judea: Studies in the History of the Ancient Near East* [Hebrew], ed. Mordechai Kogan (Bialik Institute, 5766), 183–213. For a comparison of ancient Near Eastern and biblical covenants, see Weinfeld, *Deuteronomic School*, 59–157, especially 116–128. On the concept of covenant in the book of Deuteronomy, see Jeffrey Tigay, *The JPS Torah Commentary: Deuteronomy* (Philadelphia: The Jewish Publication Society, 1996), xiii–xv. Scholars have concluded that the covenant in the book of Deuteronomy is essentially an oath of loyalty that God imposes upon Israel, which includes elements of other covenants from other parts of the ancient world. I am grateful to Dror Yaakov for teaching me about this fascinating scholarly discussion.

19. The use of "covenant" to refer to an agreement with God rather than with a king is pertinent to the idea that the ancient Israelite faith related to God as a king. This was the case even before the Israelite kingdom had a human king. See Judges 8:23; I Samuel 8:7, 10:17. And perhaps for this reason, even when the Israelites did have a king, he was regarded as God's subject. Other ancient Near Eastern faiths also had divine kingdoms, but there were multiple gods and therefore multiple loyalties. By contrast, the Israelite faith was unique in demanding exclusive faith in the God of Israel. The monotheism that emerges in the book of Deuteronomy, along with the notion of God's kingdom, gave rise to a unique phenomenon in the ancient Near East – a vassal treaty between God and His people.

Biblical scholarship has established that the concept of a divine kingdom originated with Israel and was the basis for the book of Deuteronomy. See part 1 of this book's appendix. Also see Rofé, "Historiography at the End of the Monarchic Period: The Efrati Composition vs. the Mishneh Torah Composition" [Hebrew], *Beit Mikra* 38 (5753): 14–28. For a comparison between the notion of divine kingdom in Israel and this notion in other ancient Near Eastern peoples, see Y. Kaufmann, *The Religion of Israel* [Hebrew], vol. 2, book 1, 178–181.

people the "book of the covenant" and the nation responded, "We will do and we will listen" (Ex. 24:7). The people's consent is what ultimately rendered the covenant with God legally binding.

This is the understanding that emerges from the book of Exodus, but not from the book of Deuteronomy. In Deuteronomy, Moses reads the law to the people and speaks in terms of a covenant with God,[20] but the book makes no mention of the nation's consent.[21] What happened? The book of Deuteronomy does not document the people's consent. It instead charges the people to conduct a ceremony in the future to ratify the covenant and grant it legal force. This event is supposed to take place between Mount Gerizim and Mount Ebal, only after the people enter the land.

> See, this day I set before you blessing and curse: blessing, if you obey the commandments of the Lord your God that I enjoin upon you this day, and curse, if you do not obey the commandments of the Lord your God, but turn away from the way I command you this day and follow other gods, whom you have not experienced. When the Lord your God brings you into the land that you are about to enter and possess, you shall pronounce the blessing at Mount Gerizim and the curse at Mount Ebal. (Deut. 11:26–29)

---

20. See the verses quoted below, as well as Deuteronomy 26:17–19, 29:11. The book of Deuteronomy, as we will see below and as we see in Deuteronomy 17:18, is referred to as a *mishneh Torah*, a repetition of the Torah. Biblical philologist Naftali Tur-Sinai explained that the word *mishneh*, which has an Arabic root, can also mean "contract." See N. H. Tur-Sinai, *The Language and the Book: Fundamental Problems in the Knowledge of Language and Its Sources in Literature* [Hebrew], vol. 2 (Jerusalem: Bialik Institute), 224–226.
21. In this chapter, Moses refers to a covenant, but the text does not describe that covenant. "You have affirmed this day that the Lord is your God" (Deut. 26:17) – this verse sounds like a covenantal formula. It echoes Hosea's articulation of the covenant (chapter 2). Perhaps the verse is suggesting that one aspect of the covenant dates to Moses's time – "These are the terms of the covenant which the Lord commanded Moses to conclude with the Israelites in the land of Moab" (Deut. 28:69) – but sealing the covenant dates considerably later, to the ceremony at Mount Gerizim and Mount Ebal.

These verses, which allude to a major ceremony, are vague and incomplete. They are clarified only sixteen chapters later, when Moses explains what exactly is supposed to happen on Mount Gerizim and Mount Ebal:

> As soon as you have crossed the Jordan into the land that the Lord your God is giving you, you shall set up large stones. Coat them with plaster and inscribe upon them all the words of this Torah.... Upon crossing the Jordan, you shall set up these stones, about which I charge you this day, on Mount Ebal, and coat them with plaster. (Deut. 27:2–4)

The text describes a dramatic ceremony that must be orchestrated when the Israelites enter the land. As part of this ceremony, the words of the covenant will be inscribed on a stone, and the priests will read the fundamental tenets of the covenant, concluding with the line "Cursed be he who will not uphold the terms of this Torah and observe them" (Deut. 27:26). Then the people must respond "amen," marking the moment of consensus. There, between the mountains of Gerizim and Ebal, the people will ratify the covenant presented to them on the steppes of Moab. This ceremony at Gerizim and Ebal is the element missing from Moses's address to the people in Moab. The book of Deuteronomy describes an event that will continue to unfold: The covenant is heard in Moab, but it will be ratified only in Canaan. The covenant is thus divided in two parts. The first part takes place on the eastern side of the Jordan, and the second half takes place on the western side. The Torah is given in Moab but it is accepted in Canaan, giving rise to a new narrative. The ceremony of accepting the covenant must be performed in the land to which Moses will not be granted entry. The division of the covenant in two thus means that the children of Israel will have to accept the covenant in the absence of Moses, who transmitted it to them originally.

This is an ingenious inversion of the story at Sinai. In the Golden Calf episode, the people abrogated the covenant when Moses disappeared. But at Gerizim and Ebal, the people will *accept* the covenant when Moses disappears. This is the challenge that Moses sets out before them: they have to postpone the ratification of the covenant until they reach the other side of the Jordan without him.

It is hard not to be awed by the theological and political drama of Moses's final words. The great prophet and leader does not just remove himself from the story, he also removes himself from the covenant, which will be ratified in his absence. In so doing, he excludes himself both from the past and from the future.

We began this chapter with the double premise that the book of Deuteronomy is a human book, and it was composed by Moses. Now we close the chapter with the double conclusion: Moses's book removes Moses from the story, and the human book of the Bible serves not to celebrate man but to exalt God.

GOD HAS SPOKEN ONCE, TWICE HAVE I HEARD

Anyone who is accustomed to reading the Torah in light of rabbinic midrash finds it difficult to consider the biblical text in its own right. For instance, many readers are convinced that the book of Genesis states that Abraham shattered his father's idols – a story that appears only in the Midrash. Almost without noticing, we read rabbinic midrashim into the text of the Torah. And just as it is difficult to read the Torah without hearing the Sages' Midrash, it is even harder to read any verse from the Torah without considering the preceding chapters and verses. But this is what we will try to do in this book. We will try to read the book of Deuteronomy without reading into it everything we know from Exodus, Leviticus, and Numbers, so as to relate to Moses's final words as a separate literary unit. We will listen to Deuteronomy as it seeks to be understood, as an independent address that Moses conveys to the people before his death.

We will do so because this kind of reading leads to a surprising discovery. The ideas that appear in Moses's final address are very different from those presented in previous books of the Torah. The concept of God is different, the role of religion is different, and the understanding of human beings is different. The ideas contained in Moses's address are more challenging than those that precede it in the Torah. Inevitably, this will be a more disturbing and even off-putting reading experience. After all, while there are many traditional readers who have made their peace with the fact that there are conflicting interpretations of the Torah, it is much harder to accept that there are contradictions within the Torah itself.[22]

Rabbi Amnon Bazak proposes that we regard the differences between Deuteronomy and other books of the Bible as stemming from the different perspectives of their respective authors – Moses and God.[23] But the disparities between the religious ideas in Moses's final address and those in the rest of the Torah are vast, a veritable ideological chasm. Some of the contradictions between the books touch upon the essence of Jewish life. Moreover, the book of Deuteronomy comprises part of the divine Torah, and so Jewish tradition accords it divine status. At the same time, though, it contains first-person statements by Moses that seem to be spoken in the name of God. Moses's address includes verses such as, "I will grant the rain for your land in season.... I will also provide grass in the fields for your cattle" (Deut. 11:14–15). Who is the speaker in these verses, Moses or God?

Deuteronomy is a human book included in a divine work, and the divine voice bursts forth in a human address. When we consider the ideological tension between what is expressed in Moses's last words and what is in the rest of the Torah, we will have to confront the possibility that there are contradictions in the divine Torah. We may have to accept that our tradition is not just one of conflicting interpretations of the Torah, but of conflicting ideas within the Torah itself.

But can there be contradictions within the Torah? Rabbi Abraham Isaac HaCohen Kook, one of the great Jewish thinkers of the modern age, addressed this theological question:

> We as yet do not know the specific nature of prophecy and divine inspiration, nor do we even know if it can be that there are no contradictions in prophetic and divinely inspired sayings, as is the case in well-reasoned lectures, for perhaps the phenomenon which is beyond our comprehension is also beyond our

22. For a discussion of the consensus that has emerged in the academy regarding the contradictions between the book of Deuteronomy and other books in the Bible, see the appendix.
23. Rabbi Amnon Bazak, *To This Very Day* (Jerusalem: Maggid, 2020), 108–121.

> conditions for perfection, and all its contradictions are in harmony on some level, in no need of reasoned solutions. Nature does not fear contradictions, as does science, since it is incalculably greater than science.[24]

Many Jews believe that the Torah must be an internally consistent text, that it cannot possibly contain contradictions. This view is the basis for the exegetical enterprise of generations of sages, who were motivated by the need to reconcile any apparent contradictions. Rabbi Kook challenges this belief, arguing that faith in the Torah is not the same thing as faith in the internal consistency of the Torah. While absence of internal contradictions is a hallmark of a well-reasoned lecture, the divine Torah need not be evaluated by human criteria. God's Torah extends above and beyond the bounds of human logic, and it may be that God's voice can be best heard as several different and conflicting voices.

Tractate Nedarim of the Jerusalem Talmud (3:2) contains a list of all the internal contradictions in the Torah. At the end of the list there is no attempt to resolve these contradictions; there is simply an acceptance of them. In the words of Psalms, "God has spoken once; twice have I heard" (Ps. 62:12). God's voice is indeed one voice, but it must be heard as a multiplicity.

The assumption that the Torah does not and cannot contain any contradictions or paradoxes does not serve to strengthen God's word, but rather to attenuate it. According to Rabbi Kook, such an assumption reduces the divine word to the equivalent of a human lecture, albeit a superb one. But God's word is too exalted to be subjected to the same criteria by which we evaluate the lectures of human beings. When it comes to the study of God's word, there is a rich exegetical tradition that resolves contradictions and distills from them a single voice. But this fear of contradiction would bias our understanding of Deuteronomy, which

24. *Rav A. Y. Kook: Selected Letters*, trans. Tzvi Feldman (Maale Adumim, Israel: Ma'aliot, 1986), 19. For the original Hebrew, see *The Letters of Rabbi Abraham Isaac HaCohen Kook*, 2 (Jerusalem: 5722), letter 478, p. 108.

must be read independent of the preceding books of the Torah in order for us to hear its very different message.

Let us try to listen to the unique voice of Moses's parting address, not to gloss over its uniqueness but to highlight its significance. In the next part of this book we will discover that the book of Deuteronomy presents its own version of the ancient Israelite faith, one that will strongly influence the later development of Judaism. This version offers a different approach to religion and a different approach to politics, one that we will seek to understand in the pages that follow.

Part One

Moses's Two Revolutions

Chapter 1
A Temple Without God

MISHNEH TORAH

The book of Deuteronomy consists of a series of addresses. Some of its messages recur several times.[1] In large part, though, Deuteronomy can be considered as one single, continuous address.[2]

The book is also sometimes called *Mishneh Torah,* i.e., a repetition of the Torah.[3] According to rabbinic tradition, the term *mishneh Torah*

1. The first address, which serves as a preface to the book, spans Deuteronomy 1:6–3:20, and chapter 4 can be included as well. The second address spans Deuteronomy 5:1–28:68. The third spans Deuteronomy 29:1–30:20. For more on the academic scholarship about the composition of the book and the relationship between its parts, see Martin Noth, "Studies in the History of the Tradition" [Hebrew], *Uberlieferungsgeschichtliche Studien,* 28–31; Weinfeld, *Deuteronomic School,* 9–10; Cross, "The Themes of the Books of Kings and the Structure of the Deuteronomistic History," in *Canaanite Myth and Hebrew Epic: Essays in the History of the Religion of Israel,* 275; R. D. Nelson, *The Double Redaction of the Deuteronomistic History* (Sheffield, UK: Sheffield Academic Press, 2009), 18; Nelson, *Deuteronomy: A Commentary* (London: The Old Testament Library, 2002), 1–6; and Alexander Rofé, *Introduction to the Book of Deuteronomy* (Jerusalem: 5748).
2. In addition to the addresses, the book of Deuteronomy contains a poem (*Parashat Haazinu*) and a blessing (*Parashat Vezot Haberakha*). The address, poem, and blessing constitute Moses's three farewells.
3. See, for instance, Deuteronomy 17:18: "He shall have a copy of this *mishneh Torah* written for him on a scroll by the Levitical priests." For a sampling of the rabbinic understandings of this term, see *Pesikta Zutrata* (*Midrash Lekaḥ Tov*), Deuteronomy, *Parashat Shofetim,* 29b; Abrabanel's commentary on verse 14; and Sanhedrin 21b.

is used because Deuteronomy retells the story that appears in the first four books, without introducing any new material.[4] Similarly, the Septuagint refers to the book as *Deuteronomion*,[5] which means "second law," referring to the divine law that was transmitted to Moses at Sinai and then repeated at the steppes of Moab. And so, ostensibly, Deuteronomy is just a repetition of all that came before.

According to the talmudic intellectual tradition, knowledge is furthered and deepened by means of constant repetition and review: "A person who learns his lesson one hundred times does not resemble one who learns it 101 times" (Ḥagiga 9b). There is no comparison between a student who merely plows ahead and one who takes time to review. This is somewhat at variance with the Western intellectual tradition, in which the student is expected to advance to new material. In the talmudic tradition, greater emphasis is placed on the repetition and mastery of material already learned. The Talmud's name for the book of Deuteronomy, *Mishneh Torah*, projects the rabbinic model of study on the structure of the Torah itself, as if the Torah cannot come to an end until it is reviewed. Put another way, Torah is divine, but reviewing Torah is a human endeavor.

But there is a problem with this formulation, because Deuteronomy is not merely a straightforward repetition of previous material. There are major differences between Deuteronomy and the books that precede it. Not only is the history that Deuteronomy relates different – often very different – but the laws, too, are not always the same as the laws stipulated earlier.[6] Does the book of Deuteronomy repeat the Torah, or does it rewrite the Torah?[7] And does it repeat the Torah

4. See the first *Tosafot* on Tractate Gittin.
5. "Δευτερονόμιον," literally, "the repeated law."
6. Rabbi Samson Raphael Hirsch, in his commentary on Deuteronomy 1:3, provides a detailed list of those laws which are repeated by Moses and those which are omitted. He shows that the book of Deuteronomy contains more than one hundred commandments, more than seventy of which are new laws not mentioned in previous books of the Torah. Hirsch contends that the commandments that are repeated from the first four books are those that were important enough that the leaders of the people needed to be reminded of them before they entered the land.
7. On the relationship between Deuteronomy and the other books of the Bible in the academic literature, see this book's appendix, as well as Tigay, *JPS: Deut.*, xxiv–xxvi, 422–430. For a detailed discussion of the relationship between Deuteronomy,

entirely, or only selectively? In the coming pages, we will see that when Moses reviews the Torah's laws, he does not include them all.

THE LAWS THAT ARE OMITTED

Many laws are missing from the book of Deuteronomy,[8] including a significant portion of the ritual laws.[9] Moses makes no mention of the sin and guilt offerings brought in the Temple, and he refers only marginally to the burnt offering that is sacrificed three times a day.[10] There is not a word about the incense, the arrangement of the candles in the Menora, or the baking of the showbread. Deuteronomy is clearly aware of these laws,[11] but very little of what comprises the book of Leviticus is mentioned in Deuteronomy.[12] And so we might say that rather than repeating the Torah, Deuteronomy abridges it.[13]

Leviticus, and Numbers, see Weinfeld, *Deuteronomic School*, 190–243, and especially the introduction on 179–189.

8. See Weinfeld, *The Book of Deuteronomy and Its Editors* [Hebrew] (Continuing Education School for Teachers, 5721), 3–7.
9. As Nahmanides noted in his introduction to Deuteronomy, "This book is known to constitute a review of the Torah, in which Moses our teacher explains to the generation entering the land most of the commandments of the Torah that pertain to Israelites. He does not mention anything relative to the laws of the priests, neither about their performance of the offerings nor the ritual purity of the priests and their functions, having already explained these matters to them. The priests, being diligent in their duties, do not require repeated admonitions." See *Ramban: Commentary on the Torah*, trans. Charles B. Chavel (New York: Shilo, 1976), vol. 5, p. 3. In the pages that follow, I will offer an alternative explanation as to why the majority of the sacrificial laws are omitted.
10. Deuteronomy 12:6, 13–14, 27.
11. As an example of an allusion to the priestly material (Lev. 13–14), consider Deuteronomy 24:8: "In cases of a skin affliction, be most careful to do exactly as the levitcal priests instruct you. Take care to do as I have commanded them." Moses tells the people that the priests instructed them on another occasion about a series of laws relating to leprosy. Interestingly, the majority of the verses in Deuteronomy that reference the priests are concentrated in chapters 17–21 and 24–27.
12. See Weinfeld, *Deuteronomic School*, 179–189, 210–217. According to Weinfeld, the omission of the ritual laws teaches that the book of Deuteronomy regarded these laws as secondary.
13. Julius Wellhausen suggests another explanation for the absence of ritual law in the book of Deuteronomy. He argues that this omission is not a reflection of Deuteronomy's

What are we to conclude? It would not make sense to assume that Moses suspended a significant portion of the laws that were given to the nation in the previous four books of the Bible, since Deuteronomy is clearly aware that these laws exist and remain binding.[14] A simpler explanation emerges from a close look at the structure of the address and its purpose.

Moses's address has two components: the laws that must be followed, and the exhortation to follow them. Among the incentives Moses offers to obey the laws, one recurs with particular frequency. Actually, it is less an incentive than a threat. Moses warns that if the people do not follow the laws, God will expel them from the land that He has promised them: "And you will soon perish from the good land that the Lord is assigning to you" (Deut. 11:17).[15]

Moses hardly speaks to the nation about the real and immediate test they face, namely the conquest of the land. Rather, on the eve of their entry into the land, he speaks about punishment and expulsion. The real challenge, Moses seems to be suggesting, is not conquering the land but remaining in it.

This is the background necessary to understand the omissions in Moses's speech. Deuteronomy does not repeat the entire Torah, only those sections that are critical for the people to internalize if they wish to remain in their land – laws which, if not observed, will result in the

---

commentary on the preceding material, but rather indicates that Deuteronomy was unfamiliar with this material. He claims that therefore we can conclude that the book of Deuteronomy was written prior to the priestly source, which includes the majority of the material on the Tabernacle in the book of Exodus, the majority of Leviticus, and sizable portions of Numbers. See Wellhausen, *Prolegomena to the History of Ancient Israel* (Forgotten Books, 2008). Yehezkel Kaufmann refutes each of Wellhausen's claims and shows that the priestly material is older. See his monumental work *The Religion of Israel*, vol. 1 (Tel Aviv: 5697), especially chapters 5–7, pp. 113–184.

14. See note 11 above.

15. See also Deuteronomy 4:1, 4:23–24, and another eighty threatening verses. In the book of Deuteronomy, this threat is also stated in positive terms, such as, "Observe His laws and commandments, which I enjoin upon you this day, that it may go well with you and your children after you, and that you may long remain in the land that the Lord your God is assigning to you for all time" (4:40), as well as 5:28–29 and 11:8–9.

dissolution of society and the destruction of the nation. Moses's omission of the sacrificial laws suggests that even if he regarded these laws as important, he did not view them as critical in terms of avoiding the expulsion of the nation.[16]

As we have seen, Moses selectively repeats those parts of the Torah that are necessary for the people to observe in order to remain in the land. Deuteronomy indicates which laws are essential for the next stage of the people's history, and which are not. As such, the last book of the Torah is the first commentary on it, written by the man who first received it.[17]

MOSES AND THE PROPHETS

Not all sacrifices are omitted from the book of Deuteronomy. Reference is made to voluntary offerings, vow offerings, peace offerings, and festival-related sacrifices. Why these specifically? Unlike the sin offerings, which the priest alone consumes, or the burnt offerings, which are

---

16. Moses's address is directed to the people, and not to its priests or other members of the elite (with the exception of the laws about the king, which we will discuss below). Even when discussing ritual law, Moses directs his words to the people rather than the priests. See, for instance, Deuteronomy 17:1, 18:4, and 24:8. In his commentary on Deuteronomy 17:1, Nahmanides writes, "'You shall not sacrifice to the Lord your God an ox or a sheep that has any defect of a serious kind, for that is abhorrent to the Lord your God.' Now this is an explanatory commandment, for He has already admonished against slaughtering blemished offerings (Lev. 22:22), and here He repeated it in order to add the admonition against rendering it unfit by utterance. It is likely that He repeated this admonition in order that the Israelite who brings the offering should not render it unfit during the slaughter. The priests themselves, however, are scrupulous and careful; one warning suffices for them. Therefore, He did not repeat the prohibition against a blemished ministering priest performing a sacrifice." See *Ramban: Commentary on the Torah*, vol. 5, p. 200. Nahmanides argues that the book of Deuteronomy repeats selections from the priestly code but directs them to the Israelites, for whom a general warning to the priests was not enough. The Israelites need an additional admonishment that is addressed directly to them. This is what Moses does in his speech – warn all the Israelites, the future citizens of the land, about the laws they must observe if they wish to remain in it.
17. See *Peri Tzadok*, the commentary of Rabbi Tzadok HaCohen of Lublin, on the beginning of Deuteronomy, in which he identifies this book as a form of Oral Torah consisting of Moses's commentary. For more on inner-biblical interpretation, see Y. Zakovitch, *An Introduction to Inner-Biblical Interpretation* (1993), chapter 11.

entirely burnt on the altar, these are the sacrifices that the people, too, take part in eating.

The Sages regard those sacrifices which are consumed by their owners as being of lesser sanctity than sacrifices that are entirely consumed on the altar.[18] But in the book of Deuteronomy it is specifically those sacrifices of lesser holiness that figure most prominently, perhaps because they may be shared with the poor and the disadvantaged. It is a motif that is repeatedly emphasized: "And you shall rejoice before the Lord your God with your sons and daughters and with your male and female slaves, along with the Levite in your settlements, for he has no territorial allotment among you" (Deut. 12:12). Deuteronomy emphasizes not how sacrifices bring the individual closer to God, but how they bring people together.[19] Moreover, the repeated emphasis on the sacrifices that have a social dimension renders the omission of the others that much more noticeable.

When Moses describes the burnt offerings associated with the festivals, he notes that it is the blood that is placed on the altar: "You shall offer your burnt offerings, both the flesh and the blood, on the altar of the Lord your God. And for your other sacrifices, the blood shall be poured out on the altar of the Lord your God, and you shall eat the flesh" (Deut. 12:27). However, it is not just the flesh and blood that is offered to God, but also the fat. The blood and the fat are the parts of the sacrifice intended solely for God's consumption.[20] The prophet Ezekiel therefore refers to them as "God's bread" (Ezek. 44:7). Leviticus emphasizes the prohibition on eating the fat and blood, which must be offered to God. But the book of Deuteronomy does not mention the

18. See for instance, Mishna Zevaḥim 5:6.

19. See Deuteronomy 12:18–19, 14:27–29, 16:11–14, and 26:11–13. As Alexander Rofé noted, "The book of Deuteronomy is not particularly concerned with ritual detail, aside from one especially instructive exception. Deuteronomy is interested in ritual as an opportunity for communal feasting. The book repeatedly stresses that for the peace offerings and the feasts that are eaten in a state of ritual purity before God in the Temple, it is necessary to include the needy – Levites, converts, orphans, and widows." See Rofé, *Introduction to Biblical Literature* [Hebrew] (Jerusalem: 5766), 51.

20. Weinfeld, *Deuteronomic School*, 212.

prohibition on the fat at all, because Moses considers this detail relatively inconsequential. This is further evidence of the de-emphasis on ritual law in Moses's final address.

Moses's words in Deuteronomy constitute the first commentary on God's word, but this commentary often consists of omission. Moses does not explicitly say that the ritual laws are less important than other commandments, but he effectively subordinates them.

The de-emphasis on ritual law, which emerges from the silences in Deuteronomy, is given full voice by the prophets, who repeatedly stress that morality is more important than ritual. When Isaiah stands before the people, who are devoted wholeheartedly to Temple ritual, he cries out bitterly, "'What need have I of your sacrifices?' says the Lord. 'I am sated with burnt offerings of rams and suet of fatlings and blood of bulls, and I have no delight in lambs and he-goats. That you come to appear before Me, who asked that of you? Trample My courts no more'" (Is. 1:11–12). In Isaiah's prophecy, loving-kindness, charity, and justice are far more important to God than guilt and sin offerings. As Hosea puts it succinctly, "For I desire goodness, not sacrifice, obedience to God rather than burnt offerings" (Hos. 6:6).

The prophets express a hierarchy of values that they deduce from the text. Perhaps it is from Deuteronomy's omission of many of the ritual laws that the prophets conclude that these laws are of secondary importance to ethical norms. The Torah does not explicitly state that some commandments are more or less important than others. But the prophets do.[21]

And so the book of Deuteronomy is not just the first commentary on the Torah. It is a radical commentary as well.

THE DOUBLE OMISSION

The book of Deuteronomy, like the rest of the Torah, consists of laws and stories. These two kinds of texts comprise talmudic literature as well, in the form of halakha and Aggada. Just as Deuteronomy omits some of

21. On the relationship between Deuteronomy and the prophetic books, see Weinfeld, *Deuteronomic School*, 15–32. On Hosea and Deuteronomy, see appendix B, 366–370.

the laws, it also leaves out some of the stories. Not surprisingly, many of the omitted stories are related to the Tabernacle.

The story of the creation of the Tabernacle occupies a significant portion of the three preceding biblical books. After receiving the Ten Commandments, Moses goes up to Mount Sinai for the second time, where God shows him the structure of the Temple and demonstrates the assembly of its ritual objects, such as the Menora. The book of Exodus, despite popular misconceptions, has far more verses about the story of the building of the Tabernacle than the story of the Exodus from Egypt. This story includes the designation of Bezalel as the chief builder, the "wise-hearted" individuals who voluntarily assist him, the generous spirit of all those Israelites who donated the raw materials, and finally, the assembly of all the parts by Moses. This account also includes a sizable amount of ritual law, which is part and parcel of the story.

The story of the Tabernacle does not end with Exodus. After the construction of all the parts of the Tabernacle, the structure must then be dedicated. Leviticus devotes many verses to the dedication of the Tabernacle, a ceremony that involves a fatal tragedy – the deaths of Aaron's sons Nadav and Avihu. The book of Numbers also gives considerable attention to a description of the instructions for disassembling the Tabernacle and transporting its various ritual objects, as well as the arrangement of the people when they travel and camp around it.

How much of this story is repeated in Deuteronomy? Very little. Deuteronomy does away with most of the action surrounding the Tabernacle, leaving only the following verses:

> Thereupon the Lord said to me, "Carve out two tablets of stone like the first, and come up to Me on the mountain and make an Ark of wood. I will inscribe on the tablets the commandments that were on the first tablets that you smashed, and you shall deposit them in the Ark." I made an Ark of acacia wood and carved out two tablets of stone like the first. I took the two tablets with me and went up the mountain.... Then I left and went down from the mountain, and I deposited the tablets in the Ark that I had made, where they still are, as the Lord commanded me. (Deut. 10:1–3, 5)

Following the Golden Calf episode and the shattering of the tablets, Moses goes back up the mountain to receive the second set of tablets. But this time, unlike the previous occasion, he is commanded to build an Ark for the tablets. It is hard to believe, but that is all the book of Deuteronomy tells us about the Tabernacle.[22] What about the cherubs? The Ark covering? According to the book of Exodus, the Tabernacle was the place where Moses heard God's voice. But were we to read only Deuteronomy, we would never have known this. All the drama of the Tabernacle in the previous biblical books is absent from Deuteronomy. All that is left of Bezalel, the generous donations, the construction process, and the tragedy of Nadav and Avihu is a vague reference to the rather technical need for some sort of container for storing the tablets, perhaps so that they won't break again. The story of the Tabernacle is missing from Deuteronomy's narrative history.

The book of Numbers relates that the divine cloud of glory that rested on the Tabernacle served to guide the Israelites in their journey through the wilderness:

"And whenever the cloud lifted from the Tent, the Israelites would set out accordingly, and at the spot where the cloud settled, there the Israelites would make camp" (Num. 9:17). In the book of Deuteronomy, too, God leads the Israelites through the wilderness: "Who goes before you on your journeys to scout the place where you are to encamp, in fire by night and in cloud by day, in order to guide you on the route you are to follow?" (Deut. 1:33). This is almost an identical description, with just one difference: Deuteronomy omits the Tabernacle, that place where, according to Numbers, the cloud of God's presence rested. In Deuteronomy, the cloud does not need a resting place.

---

22. The only reference in Deuteronomy to the Tent of Meeting and the cloud that dwells upon it appears after the conclusion of Moses's address: "The Lord said to Moses: 'The time is drawing near for you to die. Call Joshua and present yourselves in the Tent of Meeting, that I may instruct him.' Moses and Joshua went and presented themselves in the Tent of Meeting. The Lord appeared in the tent, in a pillar of cloud, the pillar of cloud having come to rest at the entrance of the tent" (Deut. 31:14–15).

THE LOST ARK

The prophetic books of the Bible echo ideas that first appear in the book of Deuteronomy. We see this not just when it comes to the attitude toward sacrifice, but also with regard to the Tabernacle. The omission of the Tabernacle from Deuteronomy is best reflected in Jeremiah's prophecy. When he prophesies the exalted future that awaits the people of Israel, he describes a world in which the Ark does not play a major role in the religious consciousness of the nation:

> And when you increase and are fertile in the land, in those days – declares the Lord – men shall no longer speak of the Ark of the Covenant of the Lord, nor shall it come to mind. They shall not mention it, or miss it, or make another. (Jer. 3:16)

According to Jewish sources, the Ark disappeared at some point during the First Temple period. There were those who yearned to find it, but Jeremiah is not among them. He looks forward not to the return of the lost Ark, but to its disappearance from the people's religious life. He prophesies a consciousness that is not dependent on the Ark. The book of Deuteronomy diminishes the role of the Ark in the nation's past, and Jeremiah prophecies a future in which it plays no role at all.

THE PLACE OF GOD'S CHOOSING

Moses's omission of most of the sacrificial law and most of the stories about the Tabernacle seems strange when we consider Deuteronomy's emphasis on the Tabernacle's final resting place. According to the book of Deuteronomy, only in this place will it be permissible to engage in ritual sacrifice. Unlike previous books of the Bible, the book of Deuteronomy gives the Tabernacle (and the Temple that will replace it) a monopoly on sacrificial worship. This is a dramatic shift in Jewish religious life, a shift which is difficult to comprehend in light of our modern sensibilities. In the modern world, God is worshipped through prayer in any number of places. But in the ancient world, where worship meant sacrifice, confining sacrificial worship to the Temple meant that all religious activity was restricted to this one site.[23]

In Genesis, long before the Revelation at Sinai, the patriarchs built altars in various places.[24] Even after the Torah was given, Moses built an altar at the foot of Mount Sinai.[25] Was this permissible? The prohibition on building altars wherever one chooses may perhaps be implied somewhere in the various laws that were given prior to the book of Deuteronomy,[26] but this prohibition is not explicitly stated until Deuteronomy. Only when they reach the steppes of Moab does Moses tell the people that a fundamental aspect of their religious life is about to change. They will no longer be permitted to build altars and offer sacrifices wherever they choose. There may be just one altar,

---

23. Prior to the book of Deuteronomy, it was permissible to offer sacrifices anywhere, as we learn from one of the first commandments listed after the Revelation: "Make for Me an altar of earth and sacrifice on it your burnt offerings and your peace offerings, your sheep and your oxen. In every place where I cause My name to be mentioned, I will come to you and bless you" (Ex. 20:21). Most commentators maintained that this altar could not possibly be the altar in the Tabernacle, as that was not made of earth. Biblical scholars point out the difficulty with the phrase "every place where I cause My name to be mentioned," which was rendered in the Neofiti and Samaritan Targums as "every place where you cause My name to be mentioned." According to this rendering, people were permitted to build altars wherever they mentioned God's name. See Benjamin Oppenheimer, "The Question of the Centralization of Worship in Israel" [Hebrew], *Tarbiz* 28:2 (5719): 138–153. The Masoretic text suggests that sacrificial worship may not take place just anywhere, only where God causes His name to be mentioned. The Sages discuss this distinction in Sota 38a: "R. Oshaya says: Behold it says, 'In every place where I cause My name to be mentioned, I will come to you.' Can it possibly be that the text means every place? Rather, the text must be transposed thus: 'In every place where I come to you and bless you, I will cause My name to be mentioned.' And where will I come to you and bless you? In the Temple. That is where I will cause My name to be mentioned."
24. Genesis 26:25, 33:20, 35:7.
25. See Exodus 24. For a complete list of Bible references to sacrificial worship on altars, see S. R. Driver, *A Critical and Exegetical Commentary on Deuteronomy*, 3rd ed. (Edinburgh: Clark, 1973), 147–148 and B. M. Levinson, *Deuteronomy and the Hermeneutics of Legal Innovation* (New York: Oxford University Press, 1997), 34–35.
26. Leviticus 17:1–7. See Baruch Y. Schwartz, *The Holy Torah: Studies in the Priestly Law in the Torah* [Hebrew] (Jerusalem: Magnes, 5759), 73.

whose location will be chosen by God. Only there will it be permissible to offer sacrifices:[27]

> But look only to the site that the Lord your God will choose amidst all your tribes as His habitation, to establish His name there. There you are to go, and there you are to bring your burnt offerings and other sacrifices, your tithes and contributions, your votive and freewill offerings, and the firstlings of your herds and flocks. Together with your households, you shall feast there before the Lord your God, happy in all the undertakings in which the Lord your God has blessed you. You shall not act at all as we now act here, every man as he pleases, because you have not yet come to the allotted haven that the Lord your God is giving you. When you cross the Jordan and settle in the land that the Lord your God is allotting to you and He grants you safety from all your enemies around you and you live in security, then you must bring everything that I command you to the site where the Lord your God will choose to establish His name: your burnt offerings and other sacrifices, your tithes and contributions, and all the choice votive offerings that you vow to the Lord. (Deut. 12:5–11)

This is a significant change. It entails, for instance, a whole new approach to the Paschal sacrifice, which is offered each year on Passover in memory of the plague of the firstborn. On that fraught, dramatic night, God killed the Egyptian firstborns and passed over the homes of the Israelites, whose doorposts were marked with the blood of the sacrifices. While God was passing over their homes, the freed slaves ate the Paschal sacrifice within their homes.

---

27. Scholars who accept W. M. L. de Wette's claim that Deuteronomy was written in Jerusalem (see part one of this book's appendix) argue that "the place where God chooses" refers to Jerusalem as well. Others are not convinced. A similar debate appears in the Talmud. See Megilla 11a; Haim M. Y. Gvaryahu, "The Place Where God Chooses" [Hebrew], *Din VeḤeshbon: The World Congress on Jewish Studies*, vol. 1 (The World Congress of Jewish Studies, 5707), 211–216 and Mordechai Kogan, "The City I Chose – Jerusalem in Light of Deuteronomic Literature" [Hebrew], *Tarbiz*, vol. 55 (5746), booklet 3, p. 307.

In Exodus, the Paschal sacrifice that Jews are commanded to offer for all time is a way of commemorating that night, and more specifically, the sacrifice offered that night: "And when you enter the land that the Lord will give you, as He has promised, you shall observe this rite" (Ex. 12:25). This is a ritual in memory of a ritual. It is also a family practice: Just as in Egypt, the Paschal sacrifice was eaten within the family home (Ex. 12:7), so too in every generation, the Paschal sacrifice was to be slaughtered and eaten with family.[28] But not according to the book of Deuteronomy:

> You shall slaughter the Passover sacrifice for the Lord your God, from the flock and the herd, in the place where the Lord will choose to establish His name. (Deut. 16:2)

The book of Deuteronomy forbids the people, who know the Paschal sacrifice as a family affair, from continuing this tradition:

> You are not permitted to slaughter the Passover sacrifice in any of the settlements that the Lord your God is giving you. But at the place where the Lord your God will choose to establish His name, there alone shall you slaughter the Passover sacrifice, in the evening, at sundown, the time of day when you departed from Egypt. (Deut. 16:5–6)

The Passover sacrifice has changed. In Egypt, it was forbidden to leave home on that fateful night: "None of you shall go outside the door

---

28. German Bible scholars, along with others such as Robertson Smith, have argued that the Paschal sacrifice was originally a nomadic rite in which firstborn cattle were sacrificed each spring. This explains why Passover was a family ritual and why it took place at night. Wellhausen went so far as to suggest that the book of Deuteronomy linked this ancient rite with the Passover festival. This claim was challenged by Menahem Hern, who contended that the Paschal sacrifice is mentioned in sources that apparently predate the book of Deuteronomy. Cf. Menahem Hern, "Paschal Sacrifice" [Hebrew], *Seasons and Institutions in the Bible: Historical Studies* (Am Oved: 5732); Yaakov S. Licht, "Passover" [Hebrew], *Festivals of Israel* (Bialik Institute: 5748), 137–154; and Rofé, *Intro. to Deuteronomy*, 38–43.

of his house until morning" (Ex. 12:25). But in Deuteronomy, Moses requires the Israelites to leave their homes and go to "the place." From now on, Moses tells the people, the Paschal sacrifice must be offered in the national, not domestic, sphere.

The nationalization of the Paschal sacrifice is an example of the revolutionary nature of the book of Deuteronomy. This ritual, which originally took place wherever the nation found itself, is now concentrated in the one place that God chooses. Earlier, we discussed laws that were given prior to Moses's final address but were omitted from that address, such as the sin offering. Now we have just the opposite case – a prohibition that was not explicitly mentioned prior to Moses's address is presented to the people for the first time. They are no longer allowed to engage in sacrifice anywhere they choose. As a consequence of this prohibition, every place that is outside of the Temple walls becomes radically desacralized.[29] Sacrificial ritual loses some of its significance in Deuteronomy, but the place of worship becomes paramount. On the one hand, Moses takes the Tabernacle out of the story. On the other hand, he grants the Tabernacle a monopoly on ritual.[30] Is this an attempt to strengthen or weaken the place of the Tabernacle?

---

29. The meat that is permitted in Deuteronomy 12:15, which is referred to in the Talmud as *ḥullin* according to R. Yishmael (Ḥullin 16b), is permissible to eat from the moment the people enter the land. But Baruch Schwartz argues that the allowance to eat meat as food, even if it is not part of a sacrifice, was granted after the Flood (Gen. 9:3). From that point on, anyone who wanted to eat meat had to come to an altar. Prior to the building of the Tabernacle, such an altar could be built anywhere; after the Tabernacle was built, a person had to bring his meat there. Deuteronomy severed the link between eating meat and religious worship, thereby secularizing daily life while sanctifying the Temple. See *Talmudic Encyclopedia*, vol. 4, "Meat of desire" (column 5739). See also Schwartz, *Holy Torah*, 73.

30. Nonetheless, the biblical story relates that hundreds of years after Moses's final address, in which he commanded the people to build one central altar, they continued to build altars in other places as well, and there were multiple Temples (in Shiloh, Beit El, Dan, Gilgal, Shechem, Mizpeh in Gilad and Nahalat Binyamin, Nov, Hebron, Bethlehem, Har Efraim, and perhaps also Ofra and Givat Shaul). See M. Hern, "Temple, Temples in Israel" [Hebrew], *Biblical Encyclopedia*, vol. 5 (Jerusalem: Bialik Institute, 5728), 322–328.

The first prophet after Moses to mention the prohibition on building altars was Hosea, followed by Hizkiyahu, followed by Yoshiyahu. In the time between Hosea

NATIONALIZING RELIGION AND LIMITING OPPORTUNITIES FOR SACRIFICE

As part of his religious revolution, Moses limits all ritual worship to a single site. In so doing, he changes the meaning of "the place," as well as the meaning of all other places, a shift that had very practical implications in terms of the religious life of the Israelites.

Because our religious practice is so different today, it is hard to grasp how much this development shook the foundations of ancient Israelite worship. After the Second Temple was destroyed, the talmudic Sages recognized that in order to preserve Judaism, the religion had to be disassociated from Temple ritual. And so they instituted prayer. The Talmud states that prayer replaced sacrifice.[31]

But the transition from sacrifice to prayer was about more than just finding an alternative – when it was impossible to offer sacrifices, prayer would have to suffice. Rather, there are fundamental differences between these two forms of worship. Sacrifices may only be offered in the Temple, whereas prayers may be recited anywhere. The shift from sacrifices to prayer thus led to a diffusion of religious activity, which could now take place anywhere in the world. In addition, only priests may offer sacrifices, whereas any man or woman may pray. What was once the enterprise of a single family – the priests – now involved the entire nation. Religious activity was now democratized.

Before Moses's revolution, religious life also had been very democratic. Religious worship consisted primarily of sacrifices, which could be offered anywhere. Wherever there were people, there were altars. Any time a person wanted to eat meat, he would slaughter an animal on the

---

in the eighth century BCE and Yoshiyahu at the end of the third century BCE, the people gradually came to understand that God did not want them to build altars outside of the Temple. And so Moses's words on the eve of the people's entry to the land fully registered only on the eve of their expulsion from it. How to account for this total disregard for (or unfamiliarity with) Moses's injunction? Biblical scholar W. M. L. de Wette has argued that according to the book of Kings (II Kings 22), the book of Deuteronomy was lost and reappeared only during Josiah's time. For more on this theory, see this book's appendix.

31. See Berakhot 26b, *Pesikta Zutrata* [*Lekaḥ Tov*] *Bereshit, Toledot–Vayetzeh,* chapter 28; Maimonides, Prayer 1:5, 1:6; and *Shulḥan Arukh, Oraḥ Ḥayim* 98:4.

altar, offer part of the meat to God, and then eat the rest. The very act of eating meat was a religious activity, and there were periods in which people would only eat meat when they were prepared to include God as well.[32] Whereas today, observant Jews offer a blessing to God before eating, in those days they would actually offer part of their food to God.

This was a period in which the land was awash with altars, and life was rich with ritual. Against this historical backdrop, we can begin to appreciate the impact of Deuteronomy. Moses sought to limit the democratization of religion. He prohibited sacrificial worship outside of one sacred place, so that religious activity was no longer possible anywhere else.

In this sense, Moses's revolution was the opposite of the talmudic transformation in which prayer replaced sacrifice. The book of Deuteronomy curtailed autonomy and nationalized religion, such that worship was almost entirely removed from the people's daily lives. As we have seen, religious worship meant sacrifice in the ancient world. But when sacrifice was confined to one place, all worship was limited to those occasions when the people came to Jerusalem. Once Jerusalem had a monopoly on worship, all other places and times became devoid of religious significance. The Temple became holier, but life outside of the Temple became profoundly secular.[33]

Was this Moses's intention – to elevate the Temple to such status?

Judging from the rest of Deuteronomy, Moses did indeed want to concentrate religious activity in the Temple, but not so as to make the Temple paramount. This becomes clear when we realize that at the same time that Moses restricted all worship to the Temple, he also dismissed God from it.

GOD IS NOT IN THE TEMPLE

The book of Deuteronomy introduces a new story about the ritual worship of God, and about God as well. The book of Exodus (19:9) relates that God came down and rested on Mount Sinai, but in the account that

32. See *Talmudic Encyclopedia*, vol. 4, "Meat of desire" (column 5739). See also Schwartz, *Holy Torah*, 73.

33. Ibid.

appears in Deuteronomy, God remains in the heavens. In Deuteronomy, God does not appear in the big fire on Sinai; only His voice is heard: "From the heavens, He let you hear His voice to discipline you; on earth, He let you see His great fire; and from amidst that fire you heard His words" (Deut. 4:36).

Likewise, the two books differ in their accounts of God's relationship to the Tabernacle. Exodus relates that God entered the Tabernacle in a cloud:

> The cloud covered the Tent of Meeting, and the Presence of the Lord filled the Tabernacle. Moses could not enter the Tent of Meeting, because the cloud had settled upon it and the Presence of the Lord filled the Tabernacle. (Ex. 40:34–35)

According to the book of Leviticus, the cloud has a specific resting place. The Ark of the Covenant is covered by a thin gold layer, flanked by two cherubs. The cloud dwells in the space between the two cherubs: "For I appear in the cloud over the cover" (Lev. 16:2).[34] But Moses makes no mention in his final speech of God entering the confines of the Tabernacle. The only reference in Deuteronomy to God's physical location appears in the context of tithing, where there is an allusion to this theological shift. This commandment requires the person who brings the tithe to recite a short, scripted monologue:

> When you have set aside in full the tenth part of your yield – in the third year, the year of the tithe – and have given it to the Levite, the stranger, the fatherless, and the widow, that they may eat their fill in your settlements, you shall declare before the Lord your God.... Look down from Your holy abode, from heaven, and bless Your people Israel and the soil You have given us, a land flowing with milk and honey, as You swore to our fathers." (Deut. 26:12–13, 15)

34. Ibn Ezra offers a different interpretation of this verse. He holds that the cloud is not the Divine Presence, but rather the cloud of smoke from the incense.

This monologue includes the words "Look down from Your holy abode, from heaven." It doesn't get more explicit than this: God's holy abode is in the heavens, not in the Temple. Moreover, the individual bearing tithes makes the pronouncement while standing in the Temple itself![35] Thus, this is a paradoxical ritual, one that places man inside God's House and charges him to declare that God is not exactly there. God, according to Deuteronomy, did not descend to Sinai and did not enter the Tabernacle.

The paradox of standing in the Temple while declaring that it is not really God's House is also reflected in the prayer that King Solomon offered after building the Temple. The construction process lasted seven years and involved diplomatic negotiations, taxation, physical labor, and a significant investment of national resources. But at the end of the seven years, when the Temple was completed, the king delivered a speech which gives clear expression to the theology implicit in Moses's final address:

> But will God really dwell on earth? Even the heavens to their uttermost reaches cannot contain You – how much less so this House that I have built. (I Kings 8:27)

This is a strange address. No sooner does Solomon finish building God's House than he informs the people that it is not in fact God's House, because even the heavens cannot contain God, let alone a single building, no matter how magnificent.[36]

---

35. Deuteronomy 26:13 reads, "before the Lord your God," meaning in the Temple. Tithes may be offered anywhere, but this confessional monologue must be recited in the Temple. Per the halakha that developed, this confessional narrative is recited in the Temple on the seventh day of Passover. See the *Sifrei* on this verse; Maimonides, *Sefer Zera'im, Maaser Sheni*, chapter 11, halakha 2; *Tur Shulḥan Arukh, Yoreh De'ah, Laws of Terumot and Maasrot*, 331:140; and *Talmudic Encyclopedia*, vol. 11, "*Vidui Maaser*."
36. This tension is resolved in the following wonderful midrash: "It is written, 'Even the heavens to their uttermost reaches cannot contain You' (I Kings 8:27), and it is written, 'And the Presence of the Lord filled the Tabernacle' (Ex. 40:34). R. Yehoshua of Sikhnin said in the name of R. Levi: To what may the matter be compared? To a cave that opens to the seashore. The sea rages and the caves become full of water, but the sea has no less water. So too, even though it is written that God's glory filled the Tabernacle, the upper and lower realms were not lacking in the glory of the Holy

God does not dwell in the Tabernacle or in the Temple; only His name dwells there. It is difficult to understand the significance of a home in which only God's name dwells, but not God. Much ink has been spilled about this paradox.[37] For our purposes, one thing is certain: the book of Leviticus states that God dwells in the Tabernacle,[38] but the book of Deuteronomy qualifies this assertion. It is not God, but only God's name, that dwells in the Temple.[39] This is quite a novel idea. In Exodus, God descended to Sinai and then entered into the Tabernacle, but in Deuteronomy, when the story is retold anew, it seems that God did not descend to Sinai nor enter the Tabernacle but remained distant, in the heavens.

One, blessed be He, as it is written, 'For I fill both heaven and earth, declares the Lord' (Jer. 23:24). Therefore, it is written here that just as the Divine Presence was below, on earth, at the beginning of Creation but then fled upward, it returned now to be below once again 'on the day that Moses finished.'" See *Pesikta Rabbati* (*Ish Shalom*), *piska* 5, "On the day that Moses finished setting up the Tabernacle."

37. See note 39 below.
38. Israel Knohl distinguished between two priestly sources in the Torah, which he referred to as the Priestly Source and the Holiness Code. Both maintain that God dwells in the Tabernacle. But the Priestly Source avoids anthropomorphism and speaks simply of standing "before God" in the Tabernacle, with no mention of God consuming sacrifices. Sacrifices from living animals are offered on the outer altar, and the showbread is eaten by the priests. By contrast, the Holiness Code refers to God dwelling in the Tabernacle and describes sacrifices as the bread of the gods. See Knohl, *The Sanctuary of Silence*, trans. J. Feldman and P. Rodman (Minneapolis: Fortress Press, 1995). Unlike the priestly sources, the book of Deuteronomy does not accept the notion that God dwells on earth, and does not maintain that it is possible to see God or to commune with Him, as we have seen. On the differences between the conception of God in ritual in the Priestly Source as opposed to the conception of God in the book of Deuteronomy, see Weinfeld, *Deuteronomic School*, 191–224.
39. The references to God's name dwelling in the Tabernacle reflect a shift from the immanent God of earlier sources to the transcendent God of Deuteronomy. See Gerhard von Rad, "Deuteronomy's 'Name' Theology and the Priestly Document's 'Kabod' Theology," *Studies in Deuteronomy* (Chicago: H. Regnery Co., 1953), 37–44. On the differences between "dwell" and "establish His name," see Y. Zakovitch, "To Cause His Name to Dwell – To Establish His Name" [Hebrew], *Tarbiz* 41:3, Nisan–Sivan 5732, pp. 338–340.

CONCLUSIONS

Moses institutes two major changes. The first is the prohibition on ritual worship outside the Temple. The second is the avowal that God is not present in the Temple. The first magnifies the Temple, granting it a monopoly on ritual. The second limits the role of the Temple by removing God and attributing less significance to the rituals that take place within it. Previously, we asked whether the prohibition on ritual outside of the confines of the Temple springs from a greater sense of the Temple's holiness. It seems that this is not the case. After all, the book of Deuteronomy does not just diminish the importance of Temple ritual; it also diminishes the significance of the Temple itself.

But if so, why does Moses insist that all sacrifice take place within the confines of the Temple? In order to answer this question, we must return to the omissions discussed above. Deuteronomy omits the majority of the laws pertaining to sacrifice and the stories about the building of the Tabernacle.[40] How could it be, then, that the purpose of the book is to emphasize the Temple's significance?

The book of Leviticus refers on two occasions to a commandment that is not in the book of Deuteronomy, namely the commandment to revere the Temple (Lev. 19:30; 26:2). How is it possible that Deuteronomy, which moves all religious activity to the Temple, does not include this commandment? Deuteronomy does not emphasize the Temple. Instead, it seems that the point of concentrating all ritual in the Temple is not to make the Temple more salient, but rather to make ritual less so.[41]

This idea is not original. In *Guide for the Perplexed,* Maimonides tries to explain why non-priests were barred from sacrifice and why it is forbidden to offer sacrifices outside the Temple. According to Maimonides, the answer is related not to any heightened sanctity of the priests or the Temple, but rather to a devaluation of ritual activity. The purpose of these prohibitions is to limit sacrificial ritual.[42]

---

40. Moses informs the nation that there are ritual laws with which the priests are familiar. See Deuteronomy 24:8.

41. See Weinfeld, *Deuteronomic School,* 210–224.

42. *Guide for the Perplexed,* III:32, trans. Michael Schwartz (Tel Aviv University, 2002).

The following analogy is not exact, but it seems nonetheless instructive. Herzl, in his book *The Jewish State,* outlined the role he envisioned for synagogues in the Jewish state. He said that synagogues would serve an important function: they would provide a place for rabbis so that the public sphere would be free of religious influence.

> Shall we end by having a theocracy? No, indeed. Faith unites us; knowledge gives us freedom. We shall therefore prevent any theocratic tendencies from coming to the fore on the part of our priesthood. We shall keep our priests within the confines of their temples in the same way as we shall keep our professional army within the confines of their barracks. Army and priesthood shall receive honors high as their valuable functions deserve. But they must not interfere in the administration of the State which confers distinction upon them, else they will conjure up difficulties without and within.[43]

Theodor Herzl, the visionary of the Jewish state, asks how the priests can be denied influence in the public sphere. His answer: by building synagogues and centers of religious worship. This way, religious activity will be confined to these institutions, and it will not infiltrate the public space. Like an army that must remain in its barracks so that society does not become militaristic, religion must be confined to synagogues so that society does not become theocratic.

Herzl's proposal is reminiscent of the theological logic of Deuteronomy. The book that confines all religious activity to the Temple does so not out of reverence for the Temple, but out of a conscious effort to rid the public space of sacrifice.

This brings us to the question of whether the book of Deuteronomy, which places limits on the ritual worship of God, comes out against all worship of God. The answer is a resounding no. Deuteronomy is the first book that emphasizes man's total responsibility to God: "And you shall love the Lord your God will all your heart and all your soul and all your

43. Theodor Herzl, *The Jewish State,* trans. Sylvie D'Avigdor (American Zionist Emergency Council, 1946).

might" (Deut. 6:5).[44] The phrase "with all your heart" recurs nine times throughout the book.[45] When it appears in other biblical books,[46] it is as an echo of the phrase in Deuteronomy, which serves as the source and the inspiration. And so the book that de-emphasizes ritual does not detract from man's responsibility to worship God. In Moses's reformed spirituality, there is more love of God and fewer rituals in God's honor.[47] But how could love for God be expressed if not by means of religious ritual? The book of Deuteronomy offers one answer: shift the religious emphasis from sacrifice to language.

Jews and Words

The most well-known line in Moses's final speech is "Hear O Israel, the Lord is our God, the Lord is one" (Deut. 6:4). Not everyone who recites the *Shema* is aware of it, but it is Moses who speaks these words to the people. Moses informs them of God's unity and commands them to devote themselves wholeheartedly to Him: "And you shall love the Lord your God with all your heart and all your soul and all your might" (Deut. 6:5).

How is such total devotion possible? The answer appears shortly thereafter: "Take to heart these instructions with which I charge you this day. Impress them upon your children. Recite them when you stay at home and when you are away, when you lie down and when you get up"

---

44. On the significance of these phrases in light of ancient Near Eastern contracts, see the works cited in the introduction, note 18: George E. Mendenhall, "Covenant Forms in Israelite Tradition," *The Biblical Archaeologist*, vol. 17, no. 3 (September 1954), 49–76; Erica Reiner, "The Vassal Treaties of Esarhaddon," *Ancient Near Eastern Texts Relating to the Old Testament*, 3rd ed., ed. J. B. Pritchard (Princeton University Press, 1969), 534–541; Joseph A. Fitzmyer, SJ, "The Inscriptions of Bar-Ga'yah and Mati'el from Sefire," *The Context of Scripture: Monumental Inscriptions from the Biblical World* 2, ed. William W. Hallo and K. Lawson Younger, Jr. (Leiden, Netherlands: Brill, 2003); Haim Tadmore, *Assyria, Babylonia, and Judea: Studies in the History of the Ancient Near East* [Hebrew], ed. Mordechai Kogan (Bialik Institute, 5766), 183–213; Weinfeld, *Deuteronomic School*, 59–157 and especially 116–128; and Tigay, *JPS: Deut.*, xiii–xv.

45. Deuteronomy 4:29; 6:5; 10:12; 11:13; 13:4; 26:16; 30:2, 6, 10.

46. Joshua 22:5, 23:14; I Samuel 7:3, 12:20, 24; I Kings 2:4, 8:48, 14:8; II Kings 10:31, 23:25; Jeremiah 29:13; Joel 2:12.

47. Weinfeld traces Deuteronomy's emphasis on morality over ritual to the wisdom literature. See Weinfeld, "The Shift in the Concept of Divinity and Ritual in the Book of Deuteronomy" [Hebrew], *Tarbiz* 31:1 (Tishrei 5722), 1–17.

(Deut. 6:6–7). Devotion to God is expressed by reviewing God's words. Moses's final address, or at least parts of it, need to be recited every day, all day, by all of the Jewish people. Upon entering the land, the words of the address must be carved onto a rock.[48] Moreover, the king must write down Moses's address in a book and study it his whole life.[49] And once every seven years, the people are commanded to gather together to read the speech again.[50] In other words: The book that rids the public space of ritual is the same book that fills the public space with words. And the holy words to which the people need to keep coming back will replace ritual sacrifice as the focal point of religious life.[51] The book of Deuteronomy thus heralds the talmudic transformation from sacrifice to Torah study.[52]

The Mishna states explicitly that those who study Torah are superior to those who bring sacrifices:

> If there was a bastard Sage and an unlearned high priest, the bastard Sage would come before the unlearned high priest.[53]

Torah scholars are more important than priests because in the world of the Sages, Torah study trumps ritual sacrifice. In the society that the Sages founded after the destruction of the Temple, Torah study became the center of religious life. There was a shift from the Temple to the study house, and from ritual to reading, reciting, and reviewing.[54]

---

48. Deuteronomy 27:4.
49. Ibid. 17:18–19.
50. Ibid. 31:12–13.
51. Israel Knohl described the theological turn of Deuteronomy. Knohl, "The Torah Replaces the Cherubs as a Symbol for God," [Hebrew], *Biblical Beliefs* (Jerusalem: Magnes, 2007).
52. The book of Deuteronomy heralds the talmudic revolution in another way as well: It is the first book that offers a fixed liturgy. As Weinfeld noted, Deuteronomy provides fixed liturgy for those who bring a broken-necked calf, those who offer tithes, and those who bring first fruits. Weinfeld showed that our liturgy today is very strongly influenced by Deuteronomy. See Weinfeld, "The Biblical Origin of the Shabbat and Festival *Amida*" [Hebrew], *Tarbiz* 65:5 (Tamuz–Elul 5756), 547–563. Also see Weinfeld, *Deuteronomic School*, 43.
53. Mishna Horayot 3:8.
54. As Alexander Rofé demonstrated, this shift was gradual and began back in the Persian period. See II Chronicles 17:7–9.

Moses, who omits most of the sacrifices from his final address and instead places the emphasis on reviewing God's laws, replaces ritual with text as the focal point of religious life. In so doing, he marks a turning point in the Jewish story that heralds the talmudic transformation. Prior to Moses's final address, ritual was paramount. In Moses's address, the text takes precedence.[55]

And so perhaps we should revisit the analogy to Herzl. Herzl wanted to confine Judaism to the Temple so as to rid the public space of religion. But Deuteronomy has the opposite goal – to confine sacrifice to the Temple not to rid public space of religious activity, but to replace one form of religious activity with another. The world that preceded the book of Deuteronomy was a world full of sacrifice; the world that Deuteronomy tries to found is full of Torah. Instead of a religion of ritual, it is a religion of loving God with all one's heart and soul and might.

God's word is one, but it is heard in many voices. In the words of Psalms, "God has spoken once, twice have I heard" (Ps. 62:12). The multivocality of the Bible is reflected in the religious gulf between Leviticus and Deuteronomy. The Judaism that springs forth from Deuteronomy is very different from that which emerges from Leviticus. The world of Leviticus is full of sacrifice; the world that Deuteronomy seeks to found is full of words. And so a Judaism of ritual is replaced by a Judaism of words. At the same time, the Torah did not choose one over the other; it included them both in the five books of the Torah. The voice of God is heard, as Rav Kook taught, not in one voice, but in a polyphony of voices.

FINAL THOUGHTS

We have enumerated four significant developments in Moses's last address:

1. The omission of sacrifices from the list of laws
2. The omission of the Tabernacle from the narrative

55. In the book of Deuteronomy, the word "Torah" as a reference to law appears twenty-two times, more than in any other biblical book. It appears once in Genesis, seven times in Exodus, sixteen times in Leviticus, and ten times in Numbers. In Leviticus and Numbers, most of the incidents refer to a collection of specific laws, such as *Torat HaOlah* as a reference to the laws of the burnt offering (Lev. 6:2).

3. The removal of God from the Tabernacle
4. The confining of all ritual activity to the Tabernacle

Taken together, these four developments lead to the following conclusion: Moses did not just limit the place of the Tabernacle in the narrative, he also limited its role in the religious life of the people. Once the landscape was rid of sacrifices, Moses commanded that it be filled with the study of God's word.

The place of ritual in Jewish life remains an open question in our time. The modern Jewish world sometimes seems caught between two conflicting ideologies: one stringently devoted to religious ceremonies, and one that downplays such ceremonies or does away with them entirely. Moses offers a middle ground.

The role of ritual that is implied in Moses's address is more clearly articulated in the book of Psalms. The fiftieth chapter of Psalms describes a revelation:

> From Zion, perfect in beauty, God appeared – let our God come and not fail to act! Devouring fire preceded Him; it stormed round Him fiercely. He summoned the heavens above and the earth for the trial of His people. (Ps. 50:2–4)

God reveals Himself inside the Temple and calls out to all those offering sacrifices to gather and listen:

> Bring in My devotees, who made a covenant with Me over sacrifice. Then the heavens proclaimed His righteousness, for He is a God who judges, Selah. (Ps. 50:5–6)

What does God have to say to people who express their devotion through sacrifice? That He is not interested in sacrifice!

> I censure you not for your sacrifices and your burnt offerings made to Me daily. I claim no bull from your estate, no he-goats from your pens. For Mine is every animal of the forest, the beasts on a thousand mountains. I know every bird of the mountains.

> The creatures of the field are subject to Me. Were I hungry, I would not tell you, for Mine is the world and all it holds. Do I eat the flesh of bulls or drink the blood of he-goats? (Ps. 50:8–13)

But the next verse takes a surprising turn: God commands that a sacrifice be brought:

> Sacrifice to God a thanksgiving offering and pay your vows to the Most High. (Ps. 50:14)

Why does God command the bringing of a sacrifice after denouncing sacrifice? A similar development takes place in the next chapter in Psalms, where once again God reiterates that sacrifices do not interest Him:

> You do not want me to bring sacrifices. You do not desire burnt offerings. True sacrifice to God is a contrite spirit. God, You will not despise a contrite and crushed heart. (Ps. 51:18–19)

Again, the Psalm then goes on to contradict itself:

> Then You will want sacrifices offered in righteousness. Burnt and whole offerings, then bulls, will be offered on Your altar. (Ps. 51:21)

Once again, after denouncing sacrifice, God suggests that the people bring an offering. The message of this Psalm resonates with that of Deuteronomy, namely that religious ritual has significance only if it is clear to the one engaging in such ritual that it is a means to an end.

The distinction remains relevant to this day. Many of our Jewish practices today, such as prayer and blessings, arose as an alternative to sacrifice. The same temptation that applies to sacrifice applies also to these practices, namely elevating their significance so that they become ends in themselves. But it is this temptation that Moses's Torah calls on us to resist. Religious practices lose their force when we overvalue them. This is one of the great paradoxes of religious consciousness. Ritual commandments have significance only if they are regarded as means, not ends.

Chapter 2

Monarchy Without Power

WHERE IS THE KING?

In the historical biblical books of Samuel and Kings, the king is depicted as a figure who shapes the course of history. Good kings like David redeemed the nation; bad kings like Menashe ravaged it. The state of the nation was dependent on the state of its leaders. But kings play almost no role in the five books of Moses.[1] In all four books of Moses that precede Deuteronomy, there is no reference to the role of the king of Israel, not even where we would most expect to find it.

For instance, the opening chapters of the book of Leviticus detail the sacrifices that must be brought by leaders who sin:

> If it is the anointed priest who has incurred guilt, so that blame falls upon the people, he shall offer for the sin of which he is guilty a bull of the herd without blemish as a sin offering to the Lord. (Lev. 4:3)

1. The king of Israel is mentioned prior to the book of Deuteronomy, in the book of Genesis: "And these are the kings who reigned in the land of Edom before any king reigned over the Israelites" (Gen. 36:31).

> In case it is a chieftain who incurs guilt by doing unwittingly any of the things which by the commandment of the Lord his God ought not to be done, and he realizes his guilt, or the sin of which he is guilty is brought to his knowledge – he shall bring as his offering a male goat without blemish. (Lev. 4:22–23)

The Torah refers to a sin offering brought by a priest and a sin offering brought by a chieftain. But what about a king? In the book of Leviticus there is no mention of any king. Moreover, the book of Exodus relates that one must respect authority figures, and that it is forbidden to curse them or swear by them: "You shall not revile God, nor put a curse upon a chieftain among your people" (Ex. 22:27). But what about the king? The Torah does not mention one.

In the Torah, law and kingship are distinct from one another. But in the ancient Near East the king also functioned as a legislator. Ancient Near Eastern collections of law generally began with praise for the king who created the law.[2] This is how Hammurabi speaks of himself in the introduction to the most famous Mesopotamian collection of laws from the second millennium BCE:[3]

> Then Anu and Bel [the gods] called by name me, Hammurabi, the exalted prince who feared God, to bring about the rule of righteousness in the land, to destroy the wicked and the evil-doers, so that the strong should not harm the weak.... Hammurabi who conquered the four quarters of the world made great the name

2. See Haim Tadmor, "Mystery, Literature, and Historiography: Cracking the Code of the Inscriptions of the Assyrian Kings" [Hebrew], in *Assyria, Babylonia, and Judea*, ed. Mordechai Kogan (Jerusalem: Bialik, 5766), 1–19. Also see the prologues to ancient Near Eastern legal collections in Meir Malul, *Compilations of Laws and Other Legal Collections from the Ancient Near East* [Hebrew] (Haifa: Pardes, 5770), 42–43 and 63–65. Also see introduction, note 19.
3. Hammurabi was king of Babylonia from 1792–1750 BCE. During his reign, the borders of the kingdom expanded significantly, and Babylonia became a center of learning, wisdom, and literature. See Elkana Bialik, "Hammurabi," *Biblical Encyclopedia*, columns 171–181. I am indebted to Yoshi Fargeon for teaching me some of the secrets of the ancient Near East.

> of Babylon...who made his kingdom everlastingly great – the princely king of the city."[4]

In the ancient Near East, the king was the center of the world. In Moses's Torah, however, the king is a marginal figure. The only book in which he is mentioned is Deuteronomy, and even there the king remains peripheral and does not appear where we would expect to find him. When the book discusses the punishment meted out to sinners, there is no mention of who is responsible for administering justice. For instance, the following is the book of Deuteronomy's description of the punishment given to anyone who preaches idolatry:

> As for that prophet or diviner of dreams, he shall be put to death, for he urged disloyalty to the Lord your God – who freed you from the land of Egypt and who redeemed you from the house of bondage – to make you stray from the path that the Lord your God commanded you to follow.... Do not assent or give heed to him. Show him no pity or compassion and do not shield him. (Deut. 13:6, 9)

Who is responsible for killing an individual who preaches idolatry? The Torah does not say. Throughout the entire book of Deuteronomy, there are descriptions of crimes and punishments, but the law-enforcing body is rarely identified.[5] Those few verses that do describe an executive arm do not reference a king, as we see from the laws of the rebellious son and the blasphemed woman:

---

4. The Code of Hammurabi, trans. L. W. King, https://avalon.law.yale.edu/ancient/hamframe.asp. See also the praise lavished on Hammurabi in the epilogue.
5. We sometimes make the mistake of thinking that the magistrates who are mentioned in the book of Deuteronomy (1:15; 16:18; 20:5, 8–9; 29:9; 31:28) are responsible for punishment, but that is not the case. If we read these verses carefully, along with the verses about the magistrates in Joshua (1:10; 3:2; 8:33; 23:2; 24:1), the reference in Proverbs (6:7), and the references in the books of Chronicles (I Chr. 23:4, 26:29, 37:1; II Chr. 19:11), it becomes clear that these magistrates are mostly mentioned alongside officials, elders, and rulers. The Hebrew word for "magistrates" (*shotrim*) comes from the Akkadian word *sataru*, meaning "writing." It appears that they were clerks and not a law-enforcing body. See the entry for *shoter* in the *Biblical Encyclopedia*, vol. 7, 534–535.

> His father and mother shall take hold of him and bring him out to the elders of his town at the public place of his community. They shall say to the elders of his town, "This son of ours is disloyal and defiant; he does not heed us. He is a glutton and a drunkard." Thereupon the men of his town shall stone him to death. Thus you will sweep out evil from your midst; all Israel will hear and be afraid. (Deut. 21:19–21)

> The elders of that town shall then take the man and flog him, and they shall fine him one hundred [shekels of] silver and give it to the girl's father, for the man has defamed a virgin in Israel. Moreover, she shall remain his wife; he shall never have the right to divorce her. But if the charge proves true, the girl was found not to have been a virgin. (Deut. 22:18–19)

It is the elders of the town who enforce and execute the Torah's laws, not the king. Likewise, the king does not play a significant role when the people go out to battle. The book of Deuteronomy offers the following description of the activities that are supposed to take place on the eve of battle:

> When you take the field against your enemies and see horses and chariots – forces larger than yours – have no fear of them, for the Lord your God, who brought you from the land of Egypt, is with you. Before you join battle, the priest shall come forward and address the troops. He shall say to them, "Hear, O Israel! You are about to join battle with your enemy. Let not your courage falter. Do not be in fear, or in panic, or in dread of them." (Deut. 20:1–3)

Just before the war, the priest must stand before the people and address the troops, offering them words of encouragement. When the priest finishes doing so, the magistrate[6] comes along and adds his own instructions:

6. See previous note.

> Then the magistrates shall address the troops, as follows: "Is there anyone who has built a new house but has not dedicated it? Let him go back to his home, lest he die in battle and another dedicate it." (Deut. 20:5)

The priests have a role to play, the magistrates have a role to play – but what about the king? Surely, we would expect to find the king out on the battlefield.[7] But the book of Deuteronomy, which does not mention the king as a punitive body, also makes no mention of the king as a military leader.[8] In fact, throughout the entire Torah there is only one verse that describes the king's activities.

> When he is seated on his royal throne, he shall write a copy of this Torah on a scroll before the Levitical priests. Let it remain with him and let him read it all his life, so that he may learn to revere the Lord his God, to observe faithfully every word of this Torah as well as these laws. (Deut. 17:18–19)

The king is absent from the books of Exodus, Leviticus, and Numbers. He does not appear until the book of Deuteronomy, but even there, his

7. Throughout the Bible, the king is mentioned with reference to war. See Genesis 14; I Samuel 18:13, 17; II Samuel 2:5; I Kings 3:7, 15:17; and II Kings 11:8. Likewise, in every royal inscription from the ancient Near East, from the northern kingdom of Het to the southern kingdom of Egypt, the king is described as a fighter and a military leader. For instance, see the famous royal inscription in Mordechai Kogan, *Collections of Historical Inscriptions from Assyria and Babylonia* [Hebrew] (Jerusalem: Bialik, 5764).
8. The elimination of the king from the field of battle in Deuteronomy is even more striking if we compare the laws that apply to kings in Deuteronomy to the people's request for a king in the book of Samuel: "And they said to him: 'You have grown old and your sons have not followed your ways. Therefore appoint a king for us, to govern us like all the other nations…that we may be like all the other nations. Let our king rule over us and go out at our head and fight our battles'" (I Sam. 8:5, 20). The language in Deuteronomy is similar, except there is no mention of the king fighting battles: "After entering the land that the Lord your God has assigned to you, and taking possession of it and settling in it, if you then decide, 'I will set a king over me, as do all the nations around me'" (Deut. 17:14).

role is described in a single verse – he must study. The Bible's vision of a king is thus a sort of Torah scholar.[9]

THE COMMANDMENT THAT IS NEVER SPOKEN

The king does not learn for the sake of enlightenment, but for the sake of his own moral education:

> Let it remain with him and let him read in it all his life, so that he may learn to revere the Lord his God, to observe faithfully every word of this Torah as well as these laws. Thus he will not act haughtily toward his fellows or deviate from the commandment to the right or to the left, to the end that he and his descendants may reign long in the midst of Israel. (Deut. 17:19–20)

In the ancient world, the king was never depicted as obedient, but rather as someone who commands the obedience of others.[10] But Deuteronomy offers a radically different view of kingship, because the nation is never commanded to obey the king. The people are commanded to obey the authority of the courts and to obey any true prophets who arise – but they are never told to obey the king. Though we would expect to find such a verse, it does not appear.

Political history is rife with examples of kings who ruled by divine right. In all such cases, the authority of the ruler rested on a religious foundation, and the people were religiously obligated to obey him. In

9. The king who studies is a familiar image from other ancient Near Eastern kingdoms. But for other nations, learning was not an end in itself but a means of training for military and political roles that were forbidden to Jewish kings as per the book of Deuteronomy. See Moshe Weinfeld, "The Temple Scroll or the King's Law," *An Annual for Biblical and Ancient Near Eastern Studies*, vol. 3 (5739), 224–226, 231–232.

10. In all the ancient Near Eastern kingdoms, the king had a direct link to God, whether he was regarded as a god himself – as the Egyptians believed – or whether he was God's representative on earth, as the Assyrians, Babylonians, and Hittites believed. Thus, as we saw, Hammurabi presented himself as the gods' chosen one, a king whom the gods charged with ruling on earth. With such divine right, no one could challenge him. See the Codex Hammurabi referenced above in note 4. Another example can be found in the Kalhu inscription by Adad Nirari III, referenced below in note 12.

European society, God played a significant political role. In the Middle Ages, as in the ancient world, it was commonly accepted that it was God who invested kings with the divine right to rule over their subjects. The notion of divine right secured the king's authority. So long as God conferred on the king the authority to rule, obeying the king was a way of obeying God. The religious feelings that would lead a person to submit to God would also cultivate submission to the king. This is one of the most ancient forms of manipulation, and one of the most effective. But the Torah does not do this. In the Torah, the people are not commanded to obey the king. They are not told that obeying the king is a way of obeying God. Instead, the Bible's kings, like their subjects, are commanded to submit to the Torah. And so the Bible's king does not just rule – he is ruled.[11]

Deuteronomy's politics are unprecedented. In order to understand them better, we will take a careful look at the laws pertaining to monarchy in the book of Deuteronomy.

THE LAWS OF MONARCHY

> If after you have entered the land that the Lord your God has assigned to you, and taken possession of it and settled in it, you decide, "I will set a king over me, as do all the nations about me." (Deut. 17:14)

Moses tells the people that a king may be appointed only if the people request one, and such a request may be made only after the people are already in the land ("after you have entered the land"), and have conquered it ("taken possession of it"), and have made their home in it ("settled in it"). That is, only after these three historical developments may the king appear on the stage of Jewish history. This is a very strange sequence of events. According to Moses, there is no need for a king

11. See Moshe Weinfeld, "The King as the People's Servant: On the Origins of an Idea" [Hebrew], in *Eshel Be'er Sheva: Episodes in Jewish Thought Through the Generations*, vol. 2 (Be'er Sheva: Reuven Mass, 5736), 19–25. This essay was also published in *Thoughts on Jewish Democracy*, ed. Benny Porat with Aviezer Ravitzky [Hebrew] (Jerusalem: Israel Democracy Institute, 5770), 461–465.

during the conquest of the land; the king will be crowned only after the war has concluded. That is, the king does not regard himself – and in the future, he will not be able to regard himself – as the founder of the nation. In other nations, strong kings cloak themselves in ennobling myths. One of the most common myths is that the king founded the nation, or at least that the king was chosen by God, who founded the nation so that the king might rule over it.[12] But the verses in Deuteronomy do not allow for this possibility. The king is not the founder of society; rather, it is society that establishes the kingship.

By postponing the appointment of a king until after the nation has already been founded, the monarchy is weakened and the myth of the king as founder is shattered. After all, before the king comes on the scene, non-royal systems of power would have to be developed. They would continue to operate even after the king is appointed, and would check and restrain the king's power.

This is exactly what happened with the elders, according to the continuation of the biblical story. The elders appeared alongside David on the day of his coronation: "All the elders of Israel came to the king at Hebron, and King David made a pact with them in Hebron before the Lord. And they anointed David king over Israel" (II Sam. 5:3). These elders also appear alongside King Josiah: "At the king's summons, all the elders of Judah and Jerusalem assembled before him" (II Kings 23:1). According to scholar Benjamin Mazar, the elders were there before the king appeared on the scene, and the king was required to stand before

12. This is what Ahad Nirari III, king of Assyria from 810–783 BCE, reports on himself in the Kalhu inscription, in which he recounts his victories in the West, including the victory over the land of Imri. At the beginning of the inscription, he writes: "Adad Nirari the great king, the strong king, the king of the world, the king of Assyria, the king whom the god Assur... chose in his youth and gave him this kingdom with no other competitor for the throne... he goes out to war with the support of his master Assur, who subjugated the kings from the four corners of the world and brought them to his feet." See Mordechai Kogan, *Collections of Historical Inscriptions from Assyria and Babylonia* [Hebrew] (Jerusalem: Bialik, 5764), 24. For other examples of kings who depict themselves or their dynasties as divinely chosen, and their lands as founded by the gods at the beginning of time, see Malul, *Compilations of Laws and Other Legal Collections from the Ancient Near East* [Hebrew] (Haifa: Pardes, 5770), 42 (the laws of Ur-Namma), 63 (the laws of Lipit Ishtar), 105 (Hammurabi).

them and make a covenant with them.[13] The elders diminish the power of the king and prevent him from concentrating all the political power in his palace.

But this restraining power is not enough for Moses. After Deuteronomy postpones the foundation of the monarchy until after the war and the conquest of the land, Moses levels one more blow at the figure of the future king: he describes him derisively as an imitation of foreign kings.

> You decide, "I will set a king over me, as do all the nations about me." (Deut. 17:14)

One of Moses's chief fears on the eve of the entry into the land is that the Israelites will begin to worship the gods of the Canaanites. Moses returns again and again to the same piercing question: Will the nation succeed in living in the land without becoming like its inhabitants? And then the subject of monarchy arises, and Moses interprets the people's request for a king as the desire to resemble the other Canaanite nations.[14]

The verses continue:

> You shall be free to set a king over yourself, one chosen by the Lord your God. Be sure to set as king over yourself one of your own people; you must not set a foreigner over you, one who is not your kinsman. (Deut. 17:15)

Ostensibly, Moses is charging the people to appoint a king: "You shall be free to set a king over yourself." The talmudic Sage R. Yehuda used this verse as the basis for his claim that appointing a king is a positive

13. Benjamin Mazar, "Monarchy in Israel" [Hebrew], in *Types of Leadership During the Biblical Period* (Jerusalem: National Israeli Academy for the Sciences, 5733), 31–33. Also see J. H. Tigay, "The Role of the Elders in the Laws of Deuteronomy," in *A Common Cultural Heritage: Studies on Mesopotamia and the Biblical World in Honor of Barry L. Eichler* (CDL Press, 2011), 96–98.
14. Rofé, "Historiography," 20.

commandment,[15] as Maimonides ruled as well.[16] But given that Moses speaks of the request for a king as an imitation of the practices of other nations, can it be that the appointment of a king is a positive commandment? It seems more compelling to maintain – like Abrabanel, Targum Yonatan, and Ibn Ezra – that the Torah does not command that a king be appointed. It merely grants dispensation to do so.

The verses continue:

> Moreover, he shall not keep many horses or send people back to Egypt to add to his horses, since the Lord has warned you, "You must not go back that way again." And he shall not have many wives, lest his heart go astray; nor shall he amass silver and gold in excess. (Deut. 17:16–17)

These verses, too, reflect a drive to limit the power of the king. We have already said that the elders limit the king, but these additional proscriptions serve a similar purpose. In the ancient world, nations would forge alliances by means of diplomatic marriages between kingdoms.[17] The network of relationships between countries was forged and solidified by means of family ties. And so a king who was commanded not to have too many wives was limited in his ability to forge alliances with other nations.[18]

---

15. Sanhedrin 20b: "R. Yehuda says: Three commandments were commanded to Israel when they entered the land: to appoint a king, to destroy the seed of Amalek, and to build the Temple." For an overview of this exegetical dispute throughout the generations, see Elhanan Samet, *Studies in the Weekly Torah Portion*, vol. 2, 348 ff.
16. *Mishneh Torah, Shofetim*, in the list of the commandments pertaining to kings and their wars.
17. This was the case between the Egyptians and the Hittites, the two great empires at the end of the first millennium BCE. After a long war, the two empires finally decided to forge an alliance by means of a diplomatic marriage between the kingdoms. See Alan R. Schulman, "Diplomatic Marriage in the Egyptian New Kingdom," *Journal of Near Eastern Studies*, 38:3 (July 1979): 177–193. See also A. Malamat, "Aspects of the Foreign Policies of David and Solomon," *Journal of Near Eastern Studies*, 22:1 (January 1963): 8–10.
18. See Roni Megidov, "The Law of Kingship," Center for Educational Technology [Hebrew].

And it is not just the king's diplomatic power that is limited in Deuteronomy, but his military power as well. This is the significance of the stipulation that "he shall not keep many horses." Without horses, there can be no usable chariots, which were the primary weapons of war. In limiting the king's horses and wives, the Torah reduces the space within which the king can maneuver. The Torah adds a third prohibition as well: "Nor shall he amass silver and gold in excess." That is, the king cannot drain the nation of its resources.

If the people request a king, the Torah stipulates, their request must be granted, but only on certain terms and conditions. The Torah's king will have limited sovereignty. He will not be able to expand his borders and amass riches without restraint. He will be a king, yes. But a king like the other nations have, no.[19]

> When he is seated on his royal throne, he shall write a copy of this Torah on a scroll before the Levitical priests. (Deut. 17:18)

It is hard to know the precise significance of writing this scroll before the Levitical priests.[20] The verse seems to suggest some sort of ceremonial event. But one thing is certain: If the king is writing before the Levitical priests, then he is not one of them. The king is not a religious leader, and the kingship is distinct from the priesthood. Not only is the king limited diplomatically and militarily, he also does not have unbounded religious authority.[21] Religious matters lie beyond his purview.[22]

---

19. On the differences between the laws of the book of Deuteronomy and their ancient Near Eastern counterparts, see Joshua Berman, *Created Equal: How the Bible Broke with Ancient Political Thought* (New York: Oxford University Press, 2008), 51–80.
20. It is unclear whether the scroll must be written in the presence of the priests, or whether they supervise the writing in a manner similar to I Samuel 10:25. See Nelson, *Deuteronomy*, 213.
21. See Berman, *Created Equal*, 91.
22. One of the roles of ancient Near Eastern kings was to lead the religious cult and to act as the nation's high priests. See Yaakov Liever, "King, Kingship," *Biblical Encyclopedia*, vol. 4, 1080–1085. The law of kingship in Deuteronomy and the stories of the Bible teach us that whenever the king tries to be a priest or to participate in the religious cult as a priest, he is punished. This may be the lesson of the story of Saul in Mikhmas (I Sam. 13:5–14). And perhaps the story of the altar in Beit El that

For as long as the king reigns, his power is circumscribed. He is constantly reminded that his power is limited. The Torah brings the king back down to earth so that he feels no loftier than the people from among whom he arose. Why? The following verse describes the recompense due to the king if he takes care to observe the Bible's laws of kingship:

> To the end that he and his descendants may reign long in the midst of Israel. (Deut. 17:20)

The king thus will remember that he does not rule but is ruled over, and that he is not above the nation but a part of it. If he bears this in mind, he will remain the true king of the people.[23] This is the paradox of kingship: if the king thinks that he is an absolute ruler, he and his successors will lose their power. The book of Deuteronomy asserts that only someone who is prepared to accept his limited rule will remain ruler of the people.

STRONG CITIZENS

The notion of limited monarchy has tremendous historical significance. The ideal of a king who obeys the Torah and rules according to the Torah – without any political, diplomatic, or military power, and without being regarded as the founder of his nation – is Deuteronomy's great contribution to political discourse and Western culture. But this is

---

appears in I Kings 13 reflects a similar principle: Jeroboam offers a sacrifice and is then punished. This may also be the lesson of the leprosy that inflicted King Uzzia after he appointed himself as priest: "When he was strong, he grew so arrogant that he acted corruptly: he trespassed against his God by entering the Temple of the Lord to offer incense on the incense altar. The priest Azariah, with eighty other brave priests of the Lord, followed him in and, confronting King Uzziah, said to him, 'It is not for you, Uzziah, to offer incense to the Lord, but for the Aaronite priests, who have been consecrated, to offer incense. Get out of the Sanctuary, for you have trespassed. There will be no glory in it for you from the Lord God.' Uzziah, holding the censer and ready to burn incense, got angry, but as he got angry with the priests, leprosy broke out on his forehead in front of the priests in the House of the Lord beside the incense altar" (II Chr. 26:16–21).

23. On the notion of the king as the servant of God, see Weinfeld, "King as the People's Servant," 19–25. This essay was also published in *Jewish Democracy*, ed. Benny Porat, 461–465.

not the only notion of monarchy that appears in the Bible.[24] The Bible contains many views, occasionally contradictory, regarding the status of kingship. There are chapters in Psalms, Chronicles, and other biblical books that glorify monarchy.[25] Still, in its emphasis on weakening the monarchy, Deuteronomy reflects an important biblical strain. Other biblical books try to reach a similar end, not by limiting the power of the king, but by empowering the nation's citizens. We find an example of this phenomenon in the story of Gideon in the book of Judges.

Gideon could have been the founder of the monarchy. The people wanted to make him king, but he refused. He is one of the most respected figures in the book of Judges and in the Bible in general. When he first comes on the historical stage, he is introduced as follows:

> An angel of the Lord came and sat in the terebinth at Ophrah, which belonged to Joash the Abiezrite. His son Gideon was then beating out wheat inside a winepress in order to keep it safe from

24. For more on the gap between the king described in the book of Deuteronomy and descriptions of kingship in other books, see Israel Knohl, "Biblical Faith: A Dialogue with Yehezkel Kaufmann" [Hebrew], *Biblical Literature: Introductions and Studies,* 142–146.
25. In biblical scholarship, these contradictory views are generally regarded as a product of the synthesis of two different sources, one that is anti-monarchy and one that is pro-monarchy. We can see an example of this in the book of Judges, which was originally an anti-monarchic work. Its charismatic leaders are chosen by God and are not part of a hereditary dynasty, and God is regarded as the true king, as the prophet Gideon asserts (Judges 8:23). But this book contains an additional editorial layer that is captured by the familiar verse "In those days, there was no king in Israel; everyone did what was right in his eyes." This is the pro-monarchic strain. Alexander Rofé posited an explanation for this tension: The anti-monarchic strain originated in the northern kingdom, in Israel, from the beginning of the days of kingship until the destruction of the Israelite kingdom, and it was composed by the "Efrat School." The later layer, which accepts the notion of monarchy albeit not without reservation, consists of the book of Deuteronomy, which was added to the Efrat School in the seventh century BCE in Jerusalem. These writings served as the legal basis of the books attributed to the Deuteronomic School, scribes in Jerusalem in the seventh and sixth centuries BCE who were responsible for the pro-monarchic strain in the Bible. See Rofé, "Historiography," 14–26. Also see a more comprehensive explanation in Rofé, *Intro. to Biblical Literature,* 154–162.

> the Midianites. The angel of the Lord appeared to him and said to him, "The Lord is with you, valiant warrior!" (Judges 6:11–12)

God reveals Himself to Gideon by crying, "The Lord is with you, valiant warrior!" Gideon does not respond with fear, awe, or submissiveness. Rather, his response is almost adversarial:

> Gideon said to Him, "Please, my lord, if the Lord is with us, why has all this befallen us? Where are all His wondrous deeds about which our fathers told us, saying, 'Truly the Lord brought us up from Egypt'? Now the Lord has abandoned us and delivered us into the hands of Midian." The Lord turned to him and said, "Go in this strength of yours and deliver Israel from the Midianites. I herewith make you My messenger." (Judges 6:13–14)

Gideon responds to God's revelation by criticizing God. Where are all the wondrous deeds the people were told about? Where has God been?

And how does God react to Gideon's rebuke? God's response, too, is surprising. Gideon is not punished for his audacity. It seems, in fact, that he is chosen for this very trait: "Go in this strength of yours." This same strength that enables him to stand brazenly before God is the very strength that will enable him to redeem Israel. Those who are submissive and obedient do not have what it takes to deliver God's people.

But we know this already from the famous story of Abraham and the destruction of Sodom. Before He destroyed Sodom, God informed Abraham of His plans:

> Now the Lord had said: "Shall I hide from Abraham what I am about to do, since Abraham is to become a great and populous nation and all the nations of the earth are to bless themselves by him? For I have singled him out that he may instruct his children and his posterity to keep the way of the Lord by doing what is just and right, in order that the Lord may bring about for Abraham what He has promised him." (Gen. 18:17–19)

Abraham's sensitivity to what is right and just is the reason that God informs him of the destruction He has planned for Sodom.[26] In other words, God tells Abraham about an event that is likely to seem unjust to a man of justice. Their encounter becomes increasingly charged and dramatic when Abraham responds:

> Far be it from You to do such a thing, to bring death upon the innocent as well as the guilty, so that innocent and guilty fare alike. Far be it from You! Shall not the Judge of all the earth deal justly? (Gen. 18:25)

On the threshold of Sodom's destruction, God and man reverse roles. God does not rebuke man; rather, man rebukes God.[27]

---

26. See Nahmanides's commentary on Genesis 18:18: "God, blessed be He, spoke of the honor of Abraham, saying, 'Behold, he is destined to become a great and mighty nation…' Therefore, I shall not conceal it from him, for all the future generations will say, 'How could He hide it from him?' or 'How could the righteous one be so callous about his close neighbors and have no mercy on them, not praying at all on their behalf, and that which was known to him was good and pleasing!' For I know that he recognizes and is cognizant that the Eternal loves righteousness and justice." See *Ramban: Commentary on the Torah*, vol. 1, p. 241.
27. Abraham's response may be puzzling. How can he rebuke God regarding Sodom but accept God's commandment to sacrifice his son unquestioningly? A common modern answer is that Abraham did indeed fail the test; he should have opposed God's directive. Although the text suggests that Abraham demonstrated his loyalty to God and thus passed the test, the subtext suggests the opposite. Before the story of the binding of Isaac, God speaks to Abraham directly, but this event marks the end of their direct communication. As Abraham is about to sacrifice his son, an angel appears to him and prevents him from going ahead with the act, and he is subsequently blessed by an angel. From this point on, Abraham does not experience any revelations, either from God or from His angel. This has become a popular modern reading of the story. See, for instance, Abraham Burg's *Very Near to You: Human Readings of the Torah* (Gefen, 2012). See also the opening of Aviezer Ravitzky, "The Binding of Isaac and the Covenant: Abraham and His Sons in Jewish Thought," and Efraim Meir, "The Binding of Isaac in the Dialogic Thought of Mordechai Martin Buber: Between Kierkegaard and Hasidism," in *Abraham the Father of the Faithful: The Figure of Abraham Through the Lens of the Generations*, ed. Moshe Halamish, Hannah Kasher, and Yohanan Silman (Bar-Ilan, 5763), 11–38 (Ravitzky), 281–293 (Meir).

Throughout the history of religion, there have been countless attempts to prove God's absolute goodness. Even in light of all the terrible atrocities that happen in the world, religious thinkers have tried to account for the existence of evil and to explain that God cannot act unjustly because injustice contradicts His very nature. The term theodicy refers to the vindication of divine goodness and providence in light of the existence of evil. But the Bible's heroes are not seduced by theodicy. They give painful expression to the gulf between the notion of God as entirely just and the unjust world they see before them.

The Bible's respect for individuals who are not merely docile followers, for those who engage and struggle with God, encourages a citizenry that is stubborn and hard to govern. If Jewish role models include Abraham and Gideon, how can Jews be expected to be obedient and submissive to their political leaders?

Two complementary biblical tropes – speaking truth to power and the limiting of the ruler's power – transform the biblical nation into something anachronistic in the ancient world. In the great kingdoms of Mesopotamia and Egypt, there was a wide gulf between rulers and subjects. In the Bible's ideal nation, the rulers are less powerful and the subjects are less obedient.

The first chapter of the Bible teaches that the human being was created in God's image.[28] This means that there is an element of the divine in each person. Any ruler who tramples on the individual and erases his humanity is contravening the divine will. Two theological foundations underlie the power structure of the biblical nation: the sovereignty of God[29] and the divine within each individual. On account of the sovereignty of God, there is a limit to the degree to which a person may rule over others, and on account of the divine in man, there is a limit to the degree to which a person may be ruled by others.

---

28. Levinstamm honed the distinction between the ancient Near Eastern political model and the biblical political model by comparing Genesis 1:27 ("And God created man in His image, in the image of God He created him") to ancient Near Eastern sources in which only the king is created in the divine image. See S. A. Levinstamm, "Beloved Is Man Who was Created in the Image" [Hebrew], *Tarbiz* 27:1 (Tishrei 5718): 1–2.
29. See introduction, note 19, on the notion of God as king and its implications for the attitude toward human rulers.

WEAKENED KINGS?

The hunger for power is difficult to sate. Thomas Hobbes described it fittingly:

> So that in the first place, I put for a general inclination of all mankind, a perpetual and restless desire of power after power that ceases only in death.[30]

Is the model of a king who limits his reign realistic? Is it possible to subject a power-hungry king to the kingdom of heaven? These are questions that arise from a reading of the verses on kingship in the book of Deuteronomy, but the answers cannot be found in Deuteronomy itself. In order to learn if Deuteronomy's notion of a weakened king was ever realized, we must skip forward in time to the later books of the Bible, in which there is an attempt to found a limited monarchy.

The first individual who tried to present the people with a weakened king was the prophet Samuel. In Samuel's day, the people requested a king like all the other nations, as if in fulfillment of the prediction in the book of Deuteronomy. The people turn to the prophet Samuel, who is chosen to found the monarchy and install the first king:

> All the elders of Israel assembled and came to Samuel at Ramah, and they said to him, "You have grown old, and your sons have not followed your ways. Therefore, appoint a king for us to govern us like all the other nations." (I Sam. 8:4–5)

Samuel was one of the foremost opponents of kingship monarchy, which he considered a rebellion against God's kingship. Paradoxically, the leading antagonist against kingship is the one who establishes the institution in Israel.

Samuel tells the nation that he is appointing a king over them, but he does not command the people to obey him. Rather, he reminds the people of their obligation to obey God.

---

30. Thomas Hobbes, *Leviathan*, www.gutenberg.org.

> Well, the Lord has set a king over you! Here is the king who you have chosen, who you have asked for. If you will revere the Lord, worship Him, and obey Him, and will not flout the Lord's command, if both you and the king who reigns over you will follow the Lord your God, well and good. But if you do not obey the Lord and you flout the Lord's command, the hand of the Lord will strike you as it did your fathers. (I Sam. 12:13–15)

The nation is not charged to obey the king. Rather, the nation is charged – along with the king – to obey God. The speech to coronate the king serves to remind the people that the king is not really king. Samuel aspires to appoint a king who is ruled rather than one who rules, a king who is subservient to God. This is his aspiration, but he fails. Twice Saul makes his own judgment call, contravening God's will: first on the eve of the war with the Philistines (I Sam. 13), and then during Israel's war with Amalek (I Sam. 15). Both times, Saul shows that he is heedless of God's will, as Samuel puts it (I Sam. 15:19), and the result is that Saul loses his kingship. Saul insists that he is king and he is the one in charge, and so he is ousted from the throne. Once again, power is the exclusive province of those who understand that they are not the true masters of their own power.

Saul, of course, was not the first king who refused to submit to God's will. Most kings did not subjugate themselves to God. Most simply wished to be kings. Does this mean that Deuteronomy's model was unrealistic? Will the human desire for power always win out in the face of all attempts to rein it in?

Not necessarily. Perhaps Deuteronomy's model need not be dismissed as unrealistic. Perhaps it was simply never truly put to the test. Samuel wished to subjugate the king to God's word, but Samuel himself was the conduit of God's word. The model that failed during Samuel and Saul's time was a model in which the king was expected to pay heed to the prophet. Like Saul, other kings also failed to obey the prophets. They avoided them at best and executed them at worst.[31]

31. See, for instance, Jeremiah 26:20–23.

But the king who is subservient to the prophet is not exactly the model that Moses proposes in Deuteronomy. Moses seeks a king who will read the book – the Torah – that will expose him to God's will directly, rather than by means of the prophet. Perhaps the clearest attempt to realize this ideal was during the reign of King Josiah.[32]

After Josiah oversees the Temple's repairs, a priest named Hilkiah finds a scroll in the Temple that had been unfamiliar to the people until that point. This scroll is generally identified as Deuteronomy.[33] King Josiah accepted its prohibition on idolatry and on the worship of God outside of the Temple. He submitted himself to this text, devoting himself to fulfilling its dictates. King Josiah rooted out idolatry from the land and destroyed all other altars. No other king was as responsive to prophetic rebuke as Josiah. No other king acted as he did. Perhaps Moses's model of limited monarchy is possible only when the king is subservient directly to God's Torah, and not to God's prophet.

In the previous chapter, we saw how the book of Deuteronomy de-emphasized ritual. Moses confined all ritual to the Temple, while at the same time scaling back the centrality of the Temple in the life of the people. In this chapter, we saw how Moses set limits on the monarchy as well as on ritual. In the first four books of the Bible, there was no mention of a Jewish king. Among the verses about sacrifice, there is no sacrifice which the king must bring; among the verses on punishment and law enforcement, there are no laws that the king is responsible for enforcing; and in the verses on war, there is no mention of the king's role on the battlefield. The only reference to monarchy is Deuteronomy's description of the limitations placed on this institution. The king plays only a marginal role in the Torah. Just as religious ceremonies are only a means to an end, so too the monarchy is justified only if it is limited. These are Moses's two revolutions.

SUMMARY: TWO REVOLUTIONS, TWO FAILURES

As we saw in chapter 1, Moses narrated the Torah's story anew, removing himself from Jewish history. In this chapter, we saw that just as Moses

32. II Kings 22:8–13.

33. See part one of this book's appendix.

removed himself from the story, he also ensures that no future ruler will be able to set himself at the center of the people's narrative. Moses is the founding father of the Jewish nation and of its rulers, and he shapes the figure of all future kings in his own image. He disappears from the story, leaving no grave as a reminder of his rule, nor any sons to continue his lineage. So too, no future king will have absolute power, nor will he be able to tell ennobling and aggrandizing national myths about himself. Moses thus converts his humility into a national ethos. And he transforms psychology into politics.

The Bible grants the people a king, but only within the confines of the Torah's laws of monarchy. At the same time, the Bible's monarchies do not necessarily reflect this Deuteronomic ideal, since they manifest real human character.

This is how Maimonides explained the role of ritual in the Torah in his *Guide for the Perplexed*. There is a deep human need to come close to God through ritual. According to Maimonides, the Torah took this need into consideration and gave people a way of expressing their religious feelings by means of Temple worship.

Organizing politics around kingship and organizing religion around the Temple are two compromises that the Torah makes to accommodate human nature, which naturally yearns for a strong ruler and for ritualized practice.

Did Moses's twofold project succeed? After entering the land, the people established a Tabernacle in Shiloh and then in other places, and finally in Jerusalem. Monarchy arose in Benjamin during the time of Saul, and in Jerusalem during the time of David. In Solomon's era, both monarchy and ritual reached their zenith. The kingdom was vast but unified, and the new Temple was magnificent. It took the Bible three books and 440 years, but in the end there was a religion based on the Temple and a political system grounded in monarchy. No sooner had these institutions been put into place than they began to fall apart. Solomon died, the kingdom split into two, Israel was exiled, Jerusalem was destroyed, and all that had been built so painstakingly began to crumble. Why?

The Temple was destroyed for the same reason the monarchy dissolved. The two compromises that the Torah made with human nature failed when the people elevated the Temple and the monarchy to ideologies. The people glorified the monarchy, and it became so powerful that it broke through all the obstacles the Torah had set in its path. The kings acquired too many horses and women and stockpiled too much silver and gold. The kings also appropriated the priesthood. The monarchy refused to limit itself, and so it collapsed under its own weight, once again proving that power is the rightful province only of those who are not addicted to it.

This is also true of the Temple. According to prophets like Hosea and Jeremiah, the Temple was destroyed because the people became too devoted to it. They believed that the Temple would protect them. Faith in the Temple became the central focus of the religious lives of the residents of Judea and Jerusalem, to the exclusion of the development of authentic spiritual consciousness or social responsibility. The Temple was not destroyed because the people did not take it seriously, but because they took it too seriously.

The removal of God from the Temple was a revolution relative to the rest of the five books of Moses. The limiting of the ruler's power was a revolution relative to all the surrounding pagan cultures of the time. But both originated in the same source – an even greater, more significant, and more far-reaching idea than those relating to ritual and monarchy, namely a new conception of God.

Chapter 3

God

GOD IS ONE

Monotheism is one of the Bible's profound contributions to the world of ideas. The children of Israel, it is commonly claimed, taught the world how to think about God in a new way. The various books of the Bible are regarded as the first expression of the belief in one God. This idea then spread to the rest of the world, transforming it. And so it is surprising that most of the Bible's books make no mention of monotheism at all. Anyone who studies the text closely will discover that Abraham, whom many regard as the founder of monotheism, never issued a single monotheistic proclamation. Among all the stories of the forefathers and in all of Genesis, there is not a single explicit expression of God's unity. In the next three books, Exodus, Leviticus, and Numbers, there is much discussion of one God, but there is never any mention of the exclusivity of this God.

In recent generations, there have been those who found hints in the Torah of the existence of other gods. For instance, the verse "Who is like You, O Lord, among the gods" (Ex. 15:11) has been understood as positing God's superiority, but not God's uniqueness. According to this understanding, the verse proclaims that there are many gods, and the greatest of them is the God of Israel.[1]

Among the various collections of laws scattered throughout the first four books of the Torah, there is no commandment to believe that God is one, but only to worship one God alone. "I the Lord am your God...You shall have no other gods besides Me" (Ex. 20:2–3). The first commandment does not assert that there are no other gods, only that it is forbidden to worship them. Theologians call this idea monolatry.

1. These scholars base their claims on verses such as Exodus 15:11 and on the poem that appears at the end of Deuteronomy: "When the Most High gave nations their homes / And set the divisions of man, / He fixed the boundaries of peoples / In relation to the sons of Israel's number. / For the Lord's portion is His people, / Jacob His own allotment" (Deut. 32:8–9). Verse 8 is not sufficiently clear in the masoretic text; it seems to suggest that God divided the nations of the world according to the sons of Israel's number, and God's portion is the sons of Jacob. This raises two questions. First, what is the number of the sons of Israel? Second, why should God divide the nations according to this number? A tannaitic midrash that is quoted in Rashi's commentary on this verse states that this number is seventy, that is, the number of Israelites who went down to Egypt at the end of Genesis (Gen. 46) and the number of Noah's descendants who are mentioned in Genesis 10. But this interpretation is not the simple meaning of the verse. The other matter that requires explanation is the claim in verse 9 that God received the portion of Jacob's sons, just as others received their portions. But who are these others who received the portions of the other nations? The answer appears in the scroll of Deuteronomy found in Qumran (4QDeutj, Ulrik [DJD 14], p. 90), in which we find an alternative version to the masoretic text: Instead of "the sons of Israel" it says "the sons of God." And the Septuagint reads, "the angels of God." According to these versions, there were additional celestial beings along with the God of Israel, and God divided the nations among them but chose Israel for Himself. See also later verses in this poem, namely Deuteronomy 32:12, "The Lord alone did guide him, / No alien god at His side," and Deuteronomy 32:39, "See then that I, I am He; There is no god beside Me. I deal death and give life; I have wounded and I will heal. None can deliver from My hand." These verses suggest that God is superior to all other gods; He alone runs the world, and others gods are powerless to intervene. This is also what emerges from Psalms 82: "God stands in the divine assembly; among the divine beings He pronounces judgment.... I had taken you for divine beings, sons of the Most High, all of you." Also see Psalms 89:6–7: "Your wonders, O Lord, are praised by the heavens, Your faithfulness too, in the assembly of holy beings," and Psalms 77:14. Cf. Israel Knohl, *Biblical Beliefs: The Borders of the Biblical Revolution* [Hebrew] (Jerusalem: Magnes, 2007), 9–23.

The first four books of the Bible are concerned with religious behavior rather than religious faith. They focus on actions rather than intentions. As such, they stipulate that Israel may not worship other gods, but they contain no explicit commandment not to believe in other gods. Deuteronomy contains the first clear and explicit articulation of monotheistic faith: "It has been clearly demonstrated to you that the Lord alone is God; there is none beside Him" (Deut. 4:35). The book of Deuteronomy replaces monolatry with monotheism. Moses is not satisfied with the superiority of God; he must also eliminate the competition. In addition to the prohibition on worshipping other gods, he insists that it is prohibited to believe in them. This is an instance of Moses adding commentary to the earlier books of the Torah.[2]

This is an interesting development. The divine books of the Bible do not deal with God's uniqueness. It is only the first human book of the Torah that describes God as one. The unity of God is first articulated not by God, but by man.

LEST YOUR HEART GROW HAUGHTY AND YOU FORGET

Deuteronomy expresses a deep connection between man's self-perception and his faith. The secret of this connection is laid bare in Moses's warning to the people:

> Take care lest you forget the Lord your God and fail to keep His commandments, His rules, and His laws, which I enjoin upon you today. When you have eaten your fill and have built fine houses to live in, and your herds and flocks have multiplied, and

2. The shift in the concept of God that takes place with the book of Deuteronomy is not the only theological turning point in the Torah. In his book *Where Are We From?*, Israel Knohl presents all the shifts that faith in God underwent, according to the priestly source. In Genesis, faith in God is described in anthropomorphic terms. God watches over His creatures providentially, and He reveals Himself again and again to multiple individuals. But in Moses's time, something shifted. God began revealing Himself by the tetragrammaton, devoid of bodily form or function. God also became disconnected from the mechanisms of sexuality and procreation. He was no longer a providential God promising reward and punishment to the individual. And He revealed Himself only to Moses. See Israel Knohl, *Where Are We From?: The Genetic Code of the Bible* [Hebrew] (Tel Aviv: Dvir Press, 2008).

> your silver and gold have increased, and everything you own has prospered, beware lest your heart grow haughty and you forget the Lord your God, who freed you from the land of Egypt, the house of bondage. (Deut. 8:11–14)

The success that awaits the Israelites who conquer the land is liable to change the people's self-image. They may fall prey to the belief that their success is a testament to their own powers. "Lest your heart grow haughty and you forget the Lord your God." Forgetting God is a consequence of haughtiness.

What does it mean to forget God? A few verses later, Moses explains:

> If you do forget the Lord your God and follow other gods to serve them or bow down to them, I warn you this day that you shall certainly perish. (Deut. 8:19)

Forgetting God is expressed by worshipping other gods.[3] And so now we can tie these three ideas together: Haughtiness leads to forgetting God, which is expressed through idolatry. Moses identifies the spiritual state in which a person is blinded by his own power with the religious sin of idolatry. When a person understands himself anew, he also understands God anew. When he is blinded by his power, he worships idols.

We can also understand it this way: If idolatry is the Torah's worst offense, and if idolatry is a consequence of an inflated sense of self, then according to Deuteronomy, one of man's greatest struggles is against his own ego. The individual's self-image is thus a primary concern of the Torah.

Is this too bold and sweeping a conclusion? Let us look more closely at the confounding relationship between haughtiness and idolatry. At first blush, we would not expect to find a connection between the two. After all, why should haughtiness necessarily lead

3. In his discussion of the legend about the generation of the Tower of Babel, Yehezkel Kaufmann links forgetting God with idolatry. See Kaufmann, *The Religion of Israel*, vol. 2 (Tel Aviv: 5697), 414.

to idolatry? It might be just the opposite: We might expect that someone who is haughty would choose not to subject himself to any god, even to a single god. So why would such person begin worshipping multiple gods?

It is not just in Deuteronomy that we find a description of the surprising causal connection between the spiritual state of haughtiness and the religious activity of idol worship. We find it also in prophetic books, including Habakkuk.

Habakkuk foresaw the rise of the Chaldean kingdom and its aggressive military ambitions:

> For lo, I am raising up the Chaldeans, that fierce, impetuous nation who cross the earth's wide spaces to seize homes not their own. (Hab. 1:6)

The Chaldeans – another name for the Babylonians – began by conquering lands that were not theirs. Habakkuk compares them to fishermen who fish for other nations and enslave them with their might: "You have made mankind like the fish of the sea, like creeping things that have no ruler. He has fished them all up with a line, pulled them up in his trawl, and gathered them in his net. That is why he rejoices and is glad" (Hab. 8:14–15). In this imagery, the Chaldeans' trawl and line are weapons of war, and they lift the other nations out of their waters. They are very good at it, too: by means of their weapons, the Chaldeans manage to subdue and conquer the surrounding nations.

Habakkuk focuses on the Chaldeans' reaction to their own success:

> That is why he sacrifices to his trawl and makes offerings to his net; for through them, his portion is rich and his nourishment fat. (Hab. 1:16)

They worship their line and trawl, that is, their weapons of war. As the prophet sees it, the Chaldean religion is all about worshipping the symbols of their own power. Paganism, according to Habakkuk, is man's worship of himself.

This is how the prophet Ezekiel describes the idolatry of the Phoenician kingdom:

> O mortal, say to the prince of Tyre: Thus says the Lord God, "Because you have been so haughty and have said, 'I am a god; I sit enthroned like a god in the heart of the seas,' whereas you are not a god but a man, though you deemed your mind equal to a god's. Yes, you are wiser than Daniel; in no hidden matter can anyone compare to you. By your shrewd understanding you have gained riches and have amassed gold and silver in your treasuries. By your great shrewdness in trade, you have increased your wealth and you have grown haughty because of your wealth." (Ezek. 28:2–5)

The idolatry of the prince of Tyre resembles the idolatry described by Habakkuk. Both reflect the same underlying psychological process. Success – whether military or commercial – strengthens a sense of dominance, which transforms a person's self-image, ultimately leading to idolatry.

The intuition of the prophets echoes Moses's words in Deuteronomy. On the most fundamental level, idolatry is apt to be the worship of oneself. The prophets do not elaborate on why this is so. But thousands of years later, modern anthropologists propose an answer to the question.

THE CONCEPT OF MAGIC AND THE SENSE OF CONTROL

Paganism is the belief that there is nothing beyond nature, and that all gods, even the most powerful, are subject to the natural order.[4] The natural order is governed by impersonal powers that control the gods as well. As Yehezkel Kaufmann put it, "The distinguishing mark of pagan thought [is] the idea that there exists a realm of being prior to the gods and above them, upon which the gods depend, and whose decrees they

4. Yehezkel Kaufmann, *The Religion of Israel*, vol. 1 (Tel Aviv: 5732), 299–300. When I speak of nature, I am referring to what Kaufmann describes as "a realm of being prior to the gods and above them," to which the gods are bound.

must obey."[5] Through symbolic and ritual acts, it is possible to come into contact with these governing powers. And by means of this contact, the worshipper can influence the gods to work on behalf of man. This, according to Kaufmann, is the link between pagan faith and magic.[6]

Paganism posits an underlying reciprocal relationship between the rites that a person performs and the forces that control the gods. The belief in the existence of such a relationship furnishes the worshipper with a sense of control – also known as magic – over cosmic forces. Magic is a technique for manipulating the gods. It enables human beings to cause rain to fall, to win wars, and to ward off disaster.

Paganism holds that magicians initiated into the secret know how to convert knowledge into power. Believers in magic maintain that there are intricate and intimate relationships between signifier and signified, and that the former contains an element of the latter.[7] Someone who succeeds in making, for instance, a precise symbol of Mars can imbue that symbol with some of the energy of Mars itself. And someone who makes a precise model of a particular person can control that individual. The stabbing of a voodoo doll that represents a person can cause that person physical harm. The signified is inherent in the signifier. Part of the person is present in the doll that symbolizes him or her. The English language expresses this notion in the term "represent," which contains within it the word "present." To represent something is to render it present.

This is the source of the tremendous power that the magical world associates with imitation. Anthropologist James Frazer explained that in

5. Yehezkel Kaufmann, *The Religion of Israel*, trans. Moshe Greenberg (Jerusalem: Sefer veSefel, 2003), 21. I am using Kaufmann's distinctions as the basis for my theological discussion. It is true, however, that several of Kaufmann's claims have been rejected by the majority of scholars today. Kaufmann argued that biblical monotheism was not just the Bible's theological innovation; it was also the faith practiced by the Israelites in the Bible. Today it is more commonly held that while pure monotheism is given expression in the Bible, it is not the only biblical belief system, and moreover, the Israelites' faith was not at all pure monotheism. However, Kaufmann succeeded in capturing the philosophical intuition underlying the dominant strain of biblical faith.
6. Yehezkel Kaufmann, *The Religion of Israel*, vol. 1 (Tel Aviv: 5732), 350–351.
7. Historian Hans Belting demonstrated just how pervasive this notion is. See Hans Belting, *Likeness and Presence: A History of the Image Before the Era of Art*, trans. Edmund Jephcott (Chicago: University of Chicago Press, 1994).

magic, the successful imitation of a phenomenon brings about its occurrence.[8] For instance, before heading out for the hunt, primitive tribes would engage in a dance that included an imitation of the wounding and killing of the animals that the tribe sought. By imitating the death of the animals, the hunters believed that they were guaranteeing the success of the hunt. Likewise, a dance mimicking the croaking of frogs was believed to cause rain to fall, since frogs croak after a rainfall.

Aristotle called art the imitation of nature. In magic, things work the other way around: nature replicates human ritual. This dynamic applies to the gods as well. The symbol of a god renders that god present in the world. In their study of idolatry, Moshe Halbertal and Avishai Margalit explain that the idols that symbolize the gods are regarded by their worshippers as containing some aspect of the gods. By making representations of the gods, it is possible to channel some of their energy.[9]

Magic gives voice to man's fantasy of control. Man's unwillingness to accept the uncertainty of the world and his own lack of control leads to fear. And fear, according to Spinoza, is the source of all superstitious beliefs.[10] A belief in magic is a calming force in the face of nature's unpredictability and capriciousness. In a fearful and threatening world, rites and beliefs are reassuring.[11]

---

8. Frazer called this form of magic "sympathetic magic." See James Frazer, *The Golden Bough*, part I (1890), 19–46.
9. Moshe Halbertal and Avishai Margalit, *Idolatry* (Cambridge, Mass.: Harvard University Press, 1992), 83–95.
10. Baruch Spinoza, *Theologico-Political Treatise*, trans. C. Warshavsky (Jerusalem: Magnes, 5722), 1–3.
11. An interesting example of this phenomenon is man's way of dealing with anxiety about both infertile land and infertile women. Ancient pagans would create images of fertility goddesses and mate them with the local deity. This was believed not just to represent fertility, but also to create the conditions for it. All ancient Near Eastern cultures had fertility rites involving fertility goddesses and their male counterparts. In Egypt, the sun god Ra was at the center of the cult, along with the Nile, represented by Osiris. In Mesopotamia, the two key players were Inanna/Ishtar, the goddess of war and fertility, and her husband Dumuzid/Tammuz. From Ugaritic sources we know that there was a similar fertility rite in Canaan centering on the goddess Astarte. These fertility rites were symbolized by figurines in the shape of women, who were probably associated with the main god in the pantheon.

MONOTHEISM

Monotheism controverts the assumptions of the magical idolatrous worldview and it denies the existence of a multiplicity of gods. But this is not its essence. The main point of monotheism is not the unity of God, but rather the uniqueness of God. Yehezkel Kaufmann, one of the great scholars of biblical religion, asserted that monotheism is not a matter of quantity but of quality: God is a different type of god entirely, one that is not part of the natural world. At its heart, the monotheistic revolution is not about reducing the number of gods to just one, but rather about removing God from nature. As Kaufmann put it, "The foundation of biblical faith is bound up, from the outset, in the separation of God from the world."[12]

If, in the pagan world, the gods were regarded by their worshippers as part of the natural order, monotheism posits the existence of a God above and beyond nature. This God is not subordinate to the laws of nature, nor is He subject to its cycles. "In the beginning, God created the heavens and the earth" (Gen. 1:1). The first verse of the Bible teaches that God is not part of the world between heaven and earth. God created nature, and God exists outside of it. We might say that before monotheism was a faith, it was a heresy against the gods of nature.[13]

As the sociologist Peter Berger put it, monotheism is the desacralization of nature.[14] In the monotheistic worldview, man is part of nature but God is not. Man aspires to control nature, but he cannot control God, because God is beyond nature. Monotheism places God out of the reach of man's dominion.

---

12. Yehezkel Kaufmann, *The Religion of Israel*, vol. 1 (Tel Aviv: 5732), 245. Kaufmann emphasized the antinomy between the magical world and biblical faith. Unlike idolatry, which believed in the human power to influence the gods and, by extension, the world, the Israelite religion held that "God is supreme over all. There is no realm above or beside Him to limit His absolute sovereignty. He is utterly distinct from, and other than, the world; He is subject to no laws, no compulsions, or powers that transcend Him. He is, in short, non-mythological." See Yehezkel Kaufmann, *The Religion of Israel*, trans. Moshe Greenberg (Jerusalem: Sefer veSefel, 2003), 60.
13. See Heschel, *God in Search of Man*, chapter 9.
14. Peter Berger, *The Sacred Canopy: Elements of a Sociological Theory of Religion* (New York: 1967), 105–126.

One of the strongest expressions of man's lack of control over the Divine is the removal of God from the world of representation. According to Jewish monotheism, God may not be represented iconographically.[15] There is no statue that can symbolize God, nor is there any icon that contains a trace of divinity. This makes sense. If it is impossible to represent God, then it is also impossible to render God present and control Him.

Moses seeks to transmit an unprecedented religious worldview.[16] The greatest, boldest ambition contained in Moses's parting address may be the charge to worship a God who is not present.[17] How does Moses try to persuade the people to overcome the temptation to represent God?

15. See Deuteronomy 4:15–19.
16. There are scholars who regard the archaeological findings from the Samarian hills as evidence of Moses's success in transmitting this worldview to the generation of Israelites who conquered the land. In the early Iron Age (the archaeological period corresponding to the Israelites' conquest of the land and the period of the Judges, around the tenth to twelfth centuries BCE), the number of settlements in this region rose to the hundreds. The material culture unearthed was identified with the first Jewish settlers, in large part based on the unique construction and weapon design, but also because of the absence of pig bones, which were common in the adjacent settlements. Archaeologists also found no figurines of gods and goddesses in this region, in contrast to the many horses' heads and figurines of naked women identified as images of Astarte that were found from the following period. These were presumably used in religious rites that also involved the worship of God. See Y. Finkelstein, "Excavations of Azvat Tzarta and the Israelite Settlement on the Mountain" [Hebrew] (PhD diss., Tel Aviv University, 5743); Y. Magen and Y. Finkelstein, eds., *An Overview of Archaeological Findings in the Region of Binyamin* [Hebrew] (Jerusalem: 5753); A. Ofer, "A Survey of the Judean Hills" [Hebrew], in *The New Encyclopedia of Archaeological Excavations in the Land of Israel*, vol. 1, ed. A. Stern (Jerusalem: 1993), 575–576; A. Zartal, *A Nation Is Born: The Altar on Mount Ebal and the Beginnings of Israel* [Hebrew] (Tel Aviv: 2000); Y. Maytalis, *Excavating the Bible* [Hebrew] (Jerusalem: Reuven Mass, 2008), 242.
17. In this regard, there is a stark difference between Deuteronomy and the preceding books of the Bible. In the book of Exodus, God is indeed present: "And the glory of God filled the Tabernacle" (Ex. 40:34). But in Deuteronomy, God is nowhere to be found; He has no contact with the physical world. Within Deuteronomy, we witness a gradual disappearance of God in the shift from the phrase "to indwell His name there," which appears in the earlier parts of this composition, to "to establish His name there," which appears in the later textual layers. See Y. Zakovitch, "To Cause

In Moses's final address, he asks the people to remember the dramatic event that transpired almost forty years earlier:

> But take utmost care and watch yourselves scrupulously, so that you do not forget the things that you saw with your own eyes and so that they do not fade from your mind as long as you live. And make them known to your children and to your children's children, the day you stood before the Lord your God at Horeb, when the Lord said to me, "Gather the people to Me that I may let them hear My words, in order that they may learn to revere Me as long as they live on earth, and may so teach their children." (Deut. 4:9–10)

The emphasis is on what the people saw. They are commanded not to forget everything they saw with their own eyes.[18] But what did they see?

> For your own sake, therefore, be most careful, since you saw no shape when the Lord your God spoke to you at Horeb out of the fire. (Deut. 4:15)

The people did not see God. This is a moment of great rhetorical subtlety in Moses's address. The people are asked to remember what they saw. Moses reminds them that they saw the mountain ablaze, the lightning streaking across the sky. But all of this drama was accessible exclusively as a natural phenomenon, a manifestation of God's revelation. The Revelation at Sinai was a drama highlighting what the people did *not* see, namely God Himself. The people saw the effects of Revelation, but not Revelation. It was like hearing the music accompanying the appearance of a king without ever catching sight of the king himself.

Moses invokes the memory of Revelation in order to persuade the people to abandon all attempts to represent God, "lest you act wickedly

---

His Name to Dwell – to Establish His Name" [Hebrew], *Tarbiz* 41:3 (Nisan–Sivan 5732): 338–340. See also chapter 1, note 39.

18. On the concept of forgetting God, see Kaufmann, *The Religion of Israel*, vol. 2 (Tel Aviv: 5697), 414.

and make for yourselves a sculptured image in any likeness whatsoever – the form of a man or a woman" (Deut. 4:16). The prohibition was stated prior to Moses's address, but the reason is given only in Deuteronomy. According to Moses, it is forbidden to represent God because God is not representable. And a God that lies beyond man's representational capacities also lies beyond man's control.

FROM THE ANTHROPOLOGISTS BACK TO THE PROPHETS

The prophets cautioned that haughtiness leads to idolatry. Haughtiness – hubris – is man's sense that he is in control of his environment and his fate. This haughtiness is manifested in idolatry, the prophets cried out, but they did not explain why. Perhaps modern anthropology has provided the explanation.

The Egyptian and Babylonian rulers worshipped themselves:

> Speak these words: Thus said the Lord God: I am going to deal with you, O Pharaoh king of Egypt, mighty monster, sprawling in your channels, who said, "My Nile is my own; I made it for myself." (Ezek. 29:3)

> You thought in your heart: I will climb to the sky. Higher than the stars of God I will set my throne. I will sit in the mount of assembly in the farthest end of the north. I will mount the back of a cloud; I will match the Most High. Instead, you are brought down to Sheol, to the bottom of the pit. (Is. 14:13–15)

Those cultures that sprang up on the great rivers –the Nile, the Euphrates, and the Tigris – were rich and multifaceted. They also worshipped their own power. Their magic was the ultimate expression of their illusion of control. The Bible suggests an alternative, according to which man's faith in God is the faith that man is not God. The monotheistic revolution is not just a theological revolution, but a psychological one as well.

In chapter 1, we discussed the paradox that Deuteronomy channels all the sacrifices to a single place, the "place" of God's choosing. Since sacrifice was the primary way of worshipping God in the ancient world, this injunction served to confine all religious worship, too, to a single place, thus barring it everywhere else. But alongside the drastic constraints placed on religious life, i.e., its localization in the Temple, the book of Deuteronomy demands total religiosity: "And you must love the Lord your God with all your heart and all your soul and all your might" (Deut. 6:5). The book that limits the opportunities to worship God is also the book that demands total devotion. We resolved this paradox by positing that the book of Deuteronomy offers an alternative to sacrifice, namely the study of God's word. Heralding the talmudic revolution, Deuteronomy replaced ritual with words.

But this was only a partial answer, and now we can fill in the gaps. The love of God cannot be expressed only in the study of God's word. It is also expressed through an act of self-discipline, namely the avoidance of worshipping other gods. By rejecting idolatry, man accepts his own lack of control over reality, as well as his own weaknesses and limitations.

The connection between the new system of belief – monotheism – and a new religion – a religion devoid of magic – as well as a new psychology, in which man overcomes his fantasy of control, paves the way for our summary and integration of all the ideas that comprised part one of this book.

CONCLUSION TO PART ONE: TWO REVOLUTIONS, ONE GOD

Fear, Religion, and Politics

The human condition is one of existential fear. An awareness of two realities gives rise to this fear. The first is the reality that there is a future. People, perhaps unlike animals, are aware of the existence of the future. Their consciousness is not rooted only in the present, but is free to consider the future as well. The second reality is our inability to know the future. The knowledge that there is a future but we cannot know what it will bring is the source of our fear, as well as the foundation for the two human projects that arose to overcome that fear, namely religion and politics.

Religion and politics help us gain control over an uncontrollable future. Religion, when it takes the form of magical beliefs, furnishes man with a sense of control. Politics, when it takes the form of tyrannical rule, furnishes the ruler with physical control over his subjects. Moses's double revolution abrogates both. Moses shifts the dynamics of power in religion and severely limits it in political life. He describes a religion that is not magical and a system of politics that is not tyrannical. Moses's religion does not furnish its adherents with a sense of control, and his politics do not involve subjugation – and as such, both are revolutionary.

Great ideas give rise to other great ideas. Moses's revolutions – a Temple without God and a kingdom without power – are outgrowths of the new idea that preceded them, namely a new conception of God. Monotheism is an idea that changed the world. According to the monotheistic worldview, only God has total power; human beings can aspire to limited power at best. Before Moses, religion imbued people with the illusion of control. But Moses's more exalted concept of religion taught people to accept their own lack of control.

Moses's notions of power, too, were revolutionary. It is commonly thought that democracy arose in Athens. It did, but not liberal democracy. The liberal part of "liberal democracy" arose in Jerusalem.[19] The Greeks gave the world the concept of "government by the people," but the Jews gave the world the notion of limited rule.[20] The notion of limited government is just one element of liberalism. Even so, it would be difficult to exaggerate its contribution to the development of liberal democracy.

The Voice That Is Not Heard

The story we have told until this point is the story of an idea, but it is not the Bible's only story. Consider, for instance, the book of Leviticus.

---

19. Biblical and ancient Near Eastern scholars have pointed out that the Bible describes the "first democracy." Amnon Shapira provided a comprehensive presentation of all the relevant ideas in biblical studies and Assyriology. See A. Shapira, *Early Democracy in the Bible* (Tel Aviv: Hakibbutz Hameuchad, 5769), 188–191. Also see Shapira's introduction, pp. 9–34, which deals with issues discussed throughout this part of the book.
20. Much has been written about the relationship between ancient biblical philosophy and the modern liberal state. For a survey of some of these articles, see Jonathan Sacks, *The Great Partnership: God, Science and the Search for Meaning* (New York: Schocken, 2012).

In the Tabernacle in Leviticus, God is very present. The religious rites described in Leviticus are not about controlling God, but they are a response to God's presence. These rites are essential to making God manifest in the Temple, and by extension in all of Israel. They are not meant to be marginal; they are the focus of the people's spiritual consciousness. The priestly religious world is rich and mysterious. We have not analyzed it, nor have we even touched upon it. But it is not hard to notice all of the disparities between the world of Leviticus and the world of Deuteronomy.

How can such different beliefs coexist in a single Torah? For the sake of the unity of the Torah, should we ignore these differences and search for coherence, even if it is forced? Is the role of biblical exegesis to identify the harmony that is inherent in the Torah? One of the major twentieth-century scholars and commentators on the Bible, Rabbi Mordechai Breuer, argued that we must not try to resolve the internal tension within the Bible because some of these tensions and contradictions are the source of the Torah's greatness and brilliance. Breuer's point is that we need not deny reason for the sake of faith. As Breuer put it, "Even we, the most faithful to the tradition of Israel, will not deny that which our human reason shows us with certainty. We cannot tell lies so as to make lies into truth, and truth into lies."[21]

Breuer's ideas expand upon those of Rabbi Abraham Isaac Kook, whom we quoted previously.[22] According to Rabbi Kook, the contradictions in the Torah do not undermine faith. Perhaps, he suggests, the Torah presents the many voices of God because God's word can only be heard amidst this multivocality. "God has spoken once, twice have I heard" (Ps. 62:12). Divine truth, unlike human truth, cannot be expressed coherently to man except by means of a multiplicity of versions that are varied and at times contradictory.[23]

---

21. Yosef Ofer, ed., *Shitat HaBeḥinot* (Alon Shevut: Tvunot, 2005), 112.
22. See the introduction to this book.
23. This point is made by Israel Knohl. In response to Breuer, Knohl shows that Jewish tradition from the Bible to the medieval exegetes allows for multiple views and voices within the Torah. These voices come not from a single author, but from several. See Knohl, "From Belief to Criticism" [Hebrew], https://www.daat.ac.il/daat/kitveyet/deot/kanohel.htm. On the different beliefs that coexist in the Bible, see

Although the ideas in Deuteronomy are not the only ideas expressed in the Torah, they are part of the Torah's message. And I would contend that among the various biblical voices that are expressed within Israeli discourse today, the voice of Deuteronomy as we have described it is not always heard.

Just before the destruction of the First Temple, according to the testimony of the prophets, religion became increasingly magical. The people believed in the protective power of the Temple. Sacrifices became rites for exerting control and gaining protection. The people became caught up in an illusion of certainty, based on the protection that the Temple and its rituals ostensibly conferred. And as religion became magical, politics became tyrannical. The kings had many wives, horses, silver and gold. The kingdom expanded its borders and knew no limits. I will discuss this at greater length in part three of this book, where we will see the realization of the paradox that emerges from all these discussions: Faith in the Temple leads to the destruction of the Temple, and faith in the monarchy leads to the collapse of the monarchy. In both cases, striving for excessive control leads to a loss of control.

Moses was not naïve. He knew the extent of the challenge and the unlikeliness of overcoming it, and in his address, he gave voice to his trepidation. Moses knew that the type of monotheism he was presenting to the people would not be easy for them to accept. At the same time, he believed that the proper education could give rise to a society that is not materialistic or drunk on power. The next part of the book will be devoted to the practical dimension: How did Moses propose to fashion society so as to implement these two revolutions?

Biblical Beliefs: The Borders of the Biblical Revolution [Hebrew] (Jerusalem: Magnes, 2007). See also Uriel Simon, *The Ear Discerns Wisdom: Studies in Ibn Ezra's Exegetical Methodology* [Hebrew] (Bar-Ilan University: 5773), 421–425.

Part Two

The Power Trap

Chapter 4

The Challenge of Power

A few years ago, on a stormy winter's day, I had an uneasy conversation with students from Beit Prat Academy. The students at the academy are young Israelis in their twenties, some secular and some religious. They have already completed their military or national service, but they think of themselves as being in that "before" stage – before real life, as they put it. Nothing has been decided and everything remains open to them: family, career, and, as they see it, the type of men and women they will become.

It was election season, and the *beit midrash* was awash with political debate. That evening I asked the students who among them was interested in a career in politics. A few hands went up. I asked one student why she raised her hand. What was she looking for in a political career? She responded with ideological fervor, "We can't leave politics to the politicians." I countered that there are honest politicians too. She angrily summoned from memory a list of politicians who had been implicated in corruption or sex scandals. Other students chimed in, adding more names to the list. I looked out at them, observing their burning innocence, and in a burst of cynicism, I threw back, "Even the politicians you listed were once young and idealistic like you, and they too went into politics so as to make a change. But with time, they did not change politics – politics changed them. Why do you think you are any better? How can you be so sure that what happened to them won't happen to you?" A sad silence descended on the room.

From time to time, I am reminded of that evening and of my surprising outburst of cynicism, a cynicism that recalls criticism of Zionism a century ago. Theodor Herzl, Berl Katznelson, Rabbi Abraham Isaac HaCohen Kook, and other thinkers believed that when the Jews entered the international political scene, they would transform it. But there were those who dismissed what they considered the blind idealism of the founders of the Jewish state. Hermann Cohen, Franz Rosenzweig, Simon Dubnow, and others predicted that Zionism would not change global politics. With time, they argued, politics would change Zionism. Hermann Cohen maintained that the moral sensitivity of Jews was a product of exile. Without power to corrupt them or politics to defile them, Jews could cultivate a unique national-moral ethos. Zionism, he thought, threatened to undermine that ethos. The words I hurled at my students that night were similar to the critique of the fathers of Zionism: Your ideals have led you to think of yourself as a light unto the nations, but you'll end up just like all the rest of them.

Zionism changed the situation of the Jewish people. It changed the geography of Jewish life, bringing more than 40 percent of Jews to the State of Israel, and it changed their status, converting a weak people into a strong one.[1] Power is Zionism's great gift to the Jewish people, as well as its greatest challenge. But the dramatic shift from a position of weakness to one of strength is not just the Zionist narrative but also

---

1. Historian David Biale challenged this prevailing narrative. He contended that the history of the Jews is not a history of a powerless nation, and in any case, Zionism is not the story of transforming a weak nation into a strong one. Jews in exile had political power even though they did not have a state. Jewish political power was expressed in the self-government of the autonomous communities in which they lived. Ruth Wisse supported this argument, though she held that Jews in exile had political power, but they did not have a central government or military power until the establishment of the Jewish state. See David Biale, *Power and Powerlessness in Jewish History* (New York: 1986) and Ruth Wisse, *Jews and Power* (New York: 2007).

the biblical narrative. At the Bible's heart is the story of slaves in Egypt who became a nation of fighters that conquered and settled Canaan.

Zionism echoes the biblical revolution, and the book of Deuteronomy captures the moment of transformation. The Jews have left Egypt but they have not yet entered the land. The focus of Moses's address is his concern that power will corrupt the people. But Moses does not urge the people to shun power. Moses, like the humanist intellectuals who criticized Zionism, knew that power is dangerous – but unlike them, he was prepared to take the risk.

THE THREAT OF BECOMING EGYPT

At the heart of Moses's address lies a threat: If the Israelites do not obey the Torah's laws, they will be expelled from the land. This threat recurs several times in his address, in general terms. At the end of Deuteronomy, Moses becomes more specific. He describes in frightening details what the expulsion will look like. Here is an example:

> The Lord will strike you with consumption, fever, and inflammation, with scorching heat and drought, with blight and mildew; they shall hound you until you perish. The skies above your head shall be copper and the earth under you shall be iron. (Deut. 28:22–23)

The images are graphic and harsh, and they extend for many verses.[2] At one of the rhetorical climaxes of this section, Moses threatens the people with a loss of sovereignty and describes their expulsion from the land (Deut. 28:36–37, 63–68). A close look at the verses consisting of Moses's rebuke indicates that some of the images that Moses invokes so as to intimidate the people are meant to sound familiar:

---

2. These threats are part of the contract between the sovereign God and His vassal nation. As discussed in note 18 of the introduction, there are many comparable ancient Near Eastern treaties, most notably the treaty of Esarhaddon, the son of Sennacherib, which is similar in its language and in the order of its curses. See Weinfeld, *Deuteronomic School*, 116–128. For an illuminating comparison in English, see *The World of the Tanakh* [Hebrew], Deuteronomy, 204–205.

> The Lord will make pestilence cling to you until He has put an end to you in the land that you are entering to possess. (Deut. 28:21)
>
> You shall grope at noon as a blind man gropes in the dark; you shall not prosper in your ventures, but shall be constantly abused and robbed, with none to give help. (Deut. 28:29)
>
> The Lord will afflict you at the knees and thighs with severe boils from which you shall never recover, from the sole of your foot to the crown of your head. (Deut. 28:35)
>
> Though you take much seed out to the field, you shall gather in little, for the locust shall consume it. (Deut. 28:38)

Boils will afflict their skin, darkness will blind their eyes, pestilence will wreak havoc upon them, and locusts will consume their crops. These are reminiscent of the plagues in Egypt, and Moses's shrewd intimations are meant to be painful for his audience.[3] The boils, locusts, darkness, and pestilence seem to warn that the drama of the Exodus from Egypt is going to happen again, but in reverse. The biblical story that began with the Exodus from Egypt will end with the exodus from Canaan. Both are dramatic miracles, and both will involve divinely inflicted plagues. During the Exodus from Egypt, the plagues skipped over the children of Israel and afflicted the Egyptians, but during the expulsion from Canaan, the Israelites will not be spared. Moses warns that God will treat the descendants of those who left Egypt as if they are Egyptians themselves.

On Passover, the nation celebrates the fact that the Israelites were miraculously spared. God skipped over the houses of the Israelites when He killed the Egyptian firstborns. This is another miraculous characteristic of the Egyptian plagues: not only did they afflict the Egyptians, but they skipped over the Israelites. But during the exodus from Canaan, this

3. At the end of his address, the echoes become vivid: "The Lord will inflict extraordinary plagues upon you and your offspring, strange and lasting plagues, malignant and chronic diseases. He will bring back upon you all the sicknesses of Egypt that you dreaded so, and they shall cling to you" (Deut. 28:59–60).

miracle will not happen again. The plagues will not skip over the people of Israel. On the contrary, they will be directed at them.

THE POWER TRAP

The history of political philosophy is the history of ideas about power. What is the source of the authority of those in power? How does one attain a position of power? How should power be distributed? How is power administered? The book of Deuteronomy touches upon the effect of power on those who command it. When people become powerful, they change. As Lord Acton famously put it in the late nineteenth century, "Power tends to corrupt, and absolute power corrupts absolutely. Great men are always bad men." There is a direct connection between the amount of power a person has amassed and the moral corruption that overtakes his soul. The more powerful the person, the less moral. In other words, as Moses intimated, power can turn those who fled Egypt into Egyptians themselves.

Why is this so? How does power change those who possess it? Here is one possible explanation. Morality is an external limitation on the use of power. But it is an artificial limitation. It stems from the conscious choice of the person in power. Imagine two people together on a desert island. One has a black belt in karate, and the other has a degree in philosophy. The karate master holds the keys to a storehouse full of food and drink. The weak intellectual has to forage in nature. He is aware of the existence of the storehouse, and he wishes he could enjoy its delicious contents. When he is asked why he doesn't fight the man who has the keys, break into the storehouse, and eat to his heart's content, he submits that he is an ethical person. But more likely, what holds him back is not his high moral standards but his understanding of the dynamics of power.

What would happen if the philosopher were the one in possession of the keys, and the karate master were the hungry one? What if the strong man were the one who restrained himself from breaking into the storehouse and stealing the delicious food? What if it were he who professed that he avoided the use of force on ethical grounds? Obviously, it would be much easier to believe that he avoided striking his fellow because he held himself to a certain moral standard. We would understand that what held him back from using force was not the limits of his own power, but the restraining power of morality, that artificial limitation placed on man's power. A moral person is one who chooses to be weaker than he really is.

And so power can be the enemy of morality. Strong men wish to use their power to push every limit. And the limits that are easiest to violate are those that man places on himself. Power tempts a person to forsake his values. This raises the question: Is it possible, psychologically speaking, to be both powerful and ethical at the same time?

There is a reason that society entrusts some of its members with power. Rulers are invested with power because without it, they cannot act on behalf of society, fixing its ills and healing its sick. Without power, it is impossible to change and better the world. The more a society expects of its rulers, the more it needs to give them the power to realize those expectations. The problem is that those who are invested with the power to act for the good of society may be changed for the worse because of that power. It becomes a Catch-22: a ruler needs power to change the world, but as a consequence of this power, he becomes incapable of ruling fairly. The challenge, then, is how to give rulers enough power to transform the world for the better without being transformed for the worse.

Plato dealt with this question in an original but theoretical manner. The founding fathers of the United States of America dealt with this question in an original and practical way. A combination of these two approaches may illuminate the way in which Deuteronomy confronts the power trap.

PLATO AND POWER

Plato is interested in maximal rule, so he is prepared to entrust the ruler with maximal power.[4] But not without reservation. On the contrary, Plato is concerned about the power trap. The way out, he thinks, is education. The Greek philosopher proposes an intensive, all-encompassing,

4. Thom Brooks, "Knowledge and Power in Plato's Political Thought," *International Journal of Philosophical Studies* (2006): 14:1, 51–77.

decades-long curriculum to identify and train future rulers and immunize its successful graduates against the seduction of power.

There are several components of the Platonic education. There is a specific type of music to listen to, a specific type of drama to read, a specific type of physical training.[5] The Platonic education also involves the renunciation of self-love and the cultivation of true love.

The Renunciation of Private Property

Plato referred to a class of citizens known as guardians, responsible for the governance of society. They are soldiers from whom the future ruler will be chosen in Plato's ideal republic. The guardians have no private property. Everything that is theirs is communally owned. Plato maintained that without private property, there are fewer private interests. But Plato does not deny his future rulers just private property; he also denies them family. The future ruler has, in essence, no parents or children of his own. Everything is communal. Plato assumes that someone who grows up without his own family or property will develop a selfless personality. He will regard society's interests as his own. And he will believe that any insult to society is an insult to his own person, just as any of the achievements of society are also his own.[6]

Plato was not the only one to advocate the renunciation of the ego. This is also the spiritual goal of Buddhism. But there is a significant difference between Greek and Eastern cultures. Whereas in the Eastern tradition, the "I" is subsumed through meditation, Plato tries to attain this goal by political means – by dismantling the ego of its rulers.[7] Plato did not try to replace the "I" with nothingness, but with the collective "we."

Philosophical Education

Following his military training, the ruler must also undergo philosophical training. The Platonic ruler is a soldier-turned-philosopher.

---

5. Amelie Oksenberg Rorty, "Plato's Counsel on Education," *Philosophy* 73:284 (April 1998): 157–178.
6. Plato, *The Republic*, trans. Benjamin Jowett, Internet Classics Archive, http://classics.mit.edu//Plato/republic.html.
7. Plato did not challenge the metaphysical existence of the ego; he merely tried to limit its influence on the soul of those in power.

Why must society be led by a philosopher? One of the reasons that Plato suggests (albeit not the main reason)[8] is that the philosopher has no self-interest in leading society. According to Plato, only someone who recoils from government should be charged with this role. "Those who govern ought not to be lovers of the task.... The only life which looks down upon the life of political ambition is that of true philosophy. Do you know of any other?"[9] The philosopher is a man in love with wisdom. Because he is not enamored of power or honor, he can withstand the allure of both.

Philosophy is a prophylactic against total power and therefore – at least according to Plato's dialogue *The Republic* – the philosopher should be the one entrusted with this power.[10] The combination of Plato's two major pedagogical activities, the renunciation of private property and political education, shape an individual who is not focused on himself and yearns only for truth. Such an individual is immune to the corrupting influence of power, and therefore he can be invested with power over society. As Plato put it, "You must contrive for your future rulers another and a better life than that of a ruler, and then you may have a well-ordered State."[11]

FROM ATHENS TO WASHINGTON

The founding fathers of the United States of America also believed that untrammeled power corrupts, and that everything must be done to safeguard against its abuse. But in contrast to Plato, the American founding fathers were not primarily concerned with how to protect the ruler from his own power, but with how to protect citizens from the excesses of the ruler.

The intuitions of the American founding fathers were rooted in the Christian tradition, with its doctrine of original sin: Adam sinned, and all of his descendants inherited the impulse to sin. Sin is not an obstacle over which man stumbles, but an inherent, even organic, part

8. The main reason is the philosopher's deep familiarity with these ideas, which enables him to fashion society in accordance with them.
9. Plato, *The Republic.*
10. In his dialogue *The Laws,* Plato suggests limiting the ruler by making him subordinate to the rule of law.
11. Plato, *The Republic.*

of being human. For the thinkers who articulated the American ethos, it seemed absurd that a person could be immunized against sin and the temptation to sin. There is no way to extirpate the natural human tendency, whether it is of the ruler or the subject. Unlike Plato, most of the founding fathers did not consider how to heal the souls of their rulers. Instead they sought to limit and weaken the powers of the government.

Three ideas relevant to this discussion significantly shaped the American consciousness during the early years of the nation: the belief in the natural rights of man, the lack of faith in a strong central government, and the importance of the free market.

1. *Natural Rights*

Among the American founding fathers there was a pervasive notion that basic liberties derive not from the government, but from God. The government cannot take away these natural rights, as they are inalienable. According to John Locke, a philosophical inspiration for the American Revolution,[12] the role of government is to safeguard human liberties. When government threatens these liberties, it loses legitimacy. According to the American historical understanding, this is what happened to the British government that ruled the North American colonies during the second half of the eighteenth century. The British overstepped their bounds in the American Colonies and lost the right to rule.

2. *The Division of Power*

The founding fathers maintained that too much power may not be placed in the hands of too few. Power must be divided among various political bodies such that each checks and balances out the others. The distribution of power leads to power struggles, but a system of checks and balances prevents or at least inhibits the emergence of an all-powerful

12. Locke is the philosopher most frequently quoted by the American founding fathers. See David S. Lutz, "The Relative Influence of European Writers on Late Eighteenth-Century American Political Thought," *The American Political Science Review* (78:1) (March 1984), 189–197.

central authority. This idea, developed by Charles-Louis Montesquieu, had a powerful influence on the shaping of the American Constitution.[13]

3. *The Free Market*

The marketplace is a locus of interpersonal relationships: employers and employees, consumers and producers, investors and entrepreneurs. Economist Adam Smith maintained that the less the government gets involved in these relationships, the more apt they are to flourish. Perhaps surprisingly, Smith based his economic views not on man's inherent goodness but rather man's egotism.

We might have thought that the selfishness would be a reason for more governmental intervention and more governmental supervision of civilian life. We might have thought that there is a need for government to force people to overcome their human nature and contribute to society. Smith, on the other hand, maintained that when each individual pursues his own self-interest, the wealth of society increases. This is the miracle of the free market, which captured the hearts of the American people.

John Locke and Charles-Louis Montesquieu were the philosophers most often quoted by the American founding fathers. They did not know of Adam Smith. But his ideas gave voice to one of their fundamental intuitions. The idea that a government that intervenes less is more effective accorded with their belief in the natural rights of man, including the right to private property.

The founding fathers divided governmental power among three branches in order to prevent any single body from amassing too much power. The outlook that lies at the heart of the American Constitution is captured by an ancient Chinese proverb: "The best ruler is the one who rules the least."

We have now outlined in the most general terms two approaches to government: Plato's notion that rulers must be educated, and the American notion that rulers should have only limited power. These two ideas both

13. Montesquieu, *The Spirit of the Laws*, trans. Thomas Nugent (New York: 1949), lix–lxiv. See Franz Neumann's introduction on the degree to which the American founding fathers were familiar with and shaped by Montesquieu's ideas.

emerge from the assumption that power is dangerous and corrupting. Plato cautioned about what would happen to the rulers; the founding fathers were concerned about what would happen to civil liberties. Plato tried to defend the ruler's human nature from his own power, whereas the American founding fathers tried to protect citizens from the power of the ruler.

DEUTERONOMY'S SYNTHESIS

In his final address, Moses identifies two developments on the path to power: the people's entry into the land and the individual's appointment as king. The people who enter the land, conquer it, and settle in it will become a rich and powerful nation. The man who is crowned king will become a rich and powerful individual. Moses discusses these two developments, one involving the collective and one involving the ruler. He is wary of both. He cautions that the people's success is likely to transform their own self-image: "You will say to yourselves, 'My own power and the might of my own hand have won this wealth for me'" (Deut. 8:17). Such haughtiness will lead to idolatry, which is a more sophisticated version of worshipping oneself: "Beware lest your heart grow haughty and you forget the Lord your God, who freed you from the land of Egypt, the house of bondage" (Deut. 8:14). Worshipping oneself was the great sin of the major kingdoms of the ancient world. This is exactly the spiritual danger that threatens those who enter the land: those who left Egypt are liable to become like Egypt themselves.

Even a good person who enters into politics is likely to be tarnished. But Moses has different strategies for dealing with the psychological challenges confronting the people and the ruler. He does not wish to deny power and prosperity to the collective; rather, he tries to educate them in how to assimilate their successes. With the ruler, by contrast, he argues for limited power. He forbids the ruler from amassing too many wives and horses and too much silver and gold, and he limits the extent of the ruler's control. In its approach to the collective, Deuteronomy resembles Plato; in its approach to the ruler, it resembles American political philosophy.[14]

---

14. The similarity of American political philosophy to the book of Deuteronomy is not accidental. In many ways, the American founding fathers drew directly from Moses's

The parallel between these two paths to power – that of the people and that of the ruler – is alluded to in the biblical verses. The text points to the similarity between the individual who becomes king and the nation that rises to power. Here is how the rise of the nation is described:

> When you have eaten your fill and have built fine houses in which to live, and your herds and flocks have become many, and your silver and gold have become many, and everything you own has become many, beware lest your heart grow haughty and you forget the Lord your God who freed you from the land of Egypt, the house of bondage. (Deut. 8:12–14)

The word that recurs is "many." The herds and flocks will become many; the silver and gold will become many. But prosperity will lead to haughtiness. Abundance will lead to arrogance.

Moses describes the hazards of the nation's strength and success in similar terms:

> He shall not keep many horses or send people back to Egypt to add to his horses, since the Lord has warned you, "You must not go back that way again." And he shall not have many wives, lest his heart go astray; nor shall he amass silver and gold to excess. (Deut. 17:16–17)

Here too, the word "many" is repeated. Success and abundance will have a bad influence on both the king and the nation, and it is this influence that must be avoided "lest he act haughtily toward his fellows" (Deut. 17:20). Once again, the concern is that having too much will lead to haughtiness.

In both descriptions, prosperity can lead to haughtiness. Success threatens to corrupt the individual, just as it threatens to corrupt the nation. But Moses's strategy is different in each case. Moses chooses

---

final address. The book most commonly quoted by the founding fathers was not the work of any European intellectual, but the book of Deuteronomy: "If we ask what book was most frequently cited by Americans during the founding era, the answer somewhat surprisingly is the book of Deuteronomy." See Lutz, "Relative Influence," 192.

to educate but primarily to limit the individual, forbidding him from amassing too much. The verses limiting the king's power anticipate the clauses in which the Americans limit their rulers. We considered Moses's desire to limit the monarchy in part one of this book. It is worth noting that unlike the dictates of the American Constitution, Moses does not propose a mechanism for curbing the king's power. The verses simply describe the goal of limited rule without explaining how this can be implemented. In this sense, modern political philosophy served to realize the biblical ideal.

In part one, we discussed limited monarchy. In part two, we will consider the education of the people. In the case of society, wealth is not a sin but a reward for doing God's will. If the people are faithful to God's word, they will merit abundance and prosperity. Wealth is dangerous,[15] but Moses believes that it is possible to shape a national consciousness in which material surplus does not lead to a materialistic society. He believes that there is a way to fashion a society that will not translate economic and military success into excessive national pride.

What is the core of an education that safeguards against power? In the next chapter we will see how Moses fortifies the nation's soul with a protective wall – a wall of memory – to guard against the dangers of power.

15. Hosea spoke of the connection between success, wealth, and haughtiness on the national level: "And she did not consider this: It was I who bestowed on her the new grain and wine and oil, I who lavished silver on her, as well as gold, which they used for Baal" (Hos. 2:10); "Ephraim says, 'Ah, I have become rich; I have attained power! All my gains do not amount to an offense that is real guilt'" (Hos. 12:9); "When they grazed, they were sated; when they were sated, they grew haughty; and so they forgot Me" (Hos. 13:6). On the connection between Hosea's prophecy and the book of Deuteronomy, see Weinfeld, *Deuteronomic School*, 366–370.

Chapter 5

Protective Memory

Moses speaks to the people in the midst of war. The Israelites have already fought two great battles, defeating the Amorite kings Sihon and Og. They have yet to conquer the western side of the Jordan. Now Moses stands before the people, about to take their leave. He does not describe the military tactics that the Israelites will need to use in order to continue to prevail. The people may be concerned about the possibility of defeat, but Moses is not worried that the people may lose the war. He knows that they will win, and that is what seems to worry him: that victory will confound their moral and spiritual consciousness. And so he works to cultivate a national moral sensibility.[1]

1. The cultivation of a national moral sensibility is one of the foci of the book of Deuteronomy, but the book has another, less savory aspect. This is the most violent and most graphic book in the Torah. It commands brutal aggression against the inhabitants of the land, all of whom must be wiped out. The contrast between the book's moral sensitivity and its intense violence presents the most difficult and complex tension in Moses's final address. I will discuss that at the end of this book.

THE NATIONAL STORY AND THE NATIONAL CHARACTER

The stories that a nation tells not only reflect its character but also shape it. In *The Republic,* Plato saw the ruler as overseer of the stories that people tell one another. Plato thought that stories that weaken the nation should be censored, whereas stories that strengthen the nation should be promulgated.[2] Moreover, the rulers themselves must become storytellers. The ruler must instill a single foundational narrative in the nation's consciousness so as to forge a more committed populace and educate braver and more loyal fighters. This foundational narrative is the story of the birth of the nation out of the earth. A long time ago, the nation lay buried in the earth – so begins the story that must be instilled in the hearts of all citizens. After a while, the land sent the inhabitants up from its depths, "and so, their country being their mother and also their nurse, they are bound to advise for her good, and to defend her against attacks."[3]

Citizens and soldiers must believe that they are indigenous to the place where they live and for which they are fighting. They must believe that they received their lives from the place where they make their home. The land birthed them and they will sacrifice their lives to defend her, should they be called upon to do so. The deeper this story is embedded in the national consciousness, the greater the sense of solidarity and valor the soldiers will feel. The notion that the land is a homeland, the earth is a mother, and national identity arises from one's place of residence transcends cultures and generations. Nations derive their identity from the land. Even if citizens don't believe literally in Plato's myth and do not think that their bodies were born from the earth, they still imbibe their identity from the ground beneath them. This is how patriotic and nationalistic sentiments are cultivated, and this is how the myth of indigenousness is strengthened. *We are from here,* the loyal citizens of the nation tell themselves.

On the eve of the Israelites' entry into the land, Moses proposes a surprising ethical alternative to this myth. He too tells the people a story, but it is a different story – actually, the mirror image of the indigenous

---

2. Plato, *The Republic.*
3. Ibid.

story. Moses tells the people that they did not come from the land. They are not natives or locals, and the holy earth did not give birth to them. Moses commands the people to repeat this aloud each year, when they bring the first fruits of the land to the priest:

> You shall take some of every first fruit of the soil, which you harvest from the land that the Lord your God is giving you, put it in a basket and go to the place where the Lord your God will choose to establish His name. You shall go to the priest in charge at that time and say to him, "I acknowledge this day before the Lord your God that I have come to the land that the Lord swore to our fathers to assign us." (Deut. 26:2–3)

At the annual ceremony of the bringing of the first fruits to the Temple, the Israelite informs the priest that he has come *to* the land, meaning that he does not come *from* it. As he presents his fruits that grew forth from the land, he informs that priest that he himself is not one of those fruits.

After presenting the first fruits to the priest in the Temple, the Israelite is then to make an additional declaration:[4]

4. In 1938, biblical scholar Gerhard von Rad argued that these words were originally recited aloud when bringing gifts to the Temple. He contended that this is the historical kernel that gave rise to the rest of the Bible. See Rofé, *Intro. to Deuteronomy*, 89–90. Rofé explains that the designation of one father for the nation, as opposed to the three fathers familiar from Genesis, supports von Rad's claim regarding the historical primacy of this passage, which documents the national story before the development of the tradition of three fathers.

   Another scholar, Yair Zakovitch, maintains that the narrator who included this passage about the bringing of first fruits in the book of Deuteronomy modified the original version so that it corresponded to his political views. The original version read, "Edom served my father," an allusion to Esau's subordination to Jacob. The version focusing on the hubris of the father was changed to a version that shatters this hubris by mentioning both foreignness and servitude. See Yair Zakovitch, "'My Father was a Wandering Aramean' (Deut. 26:5) or 'Edom Served My Father'?" in *Mishneh Todah: Studies in Deuteronomy and its Cultural Environment in Honor of Jeffrey H. Tigay*, ed. M. J. Williams, D. A. Glatt-Gilad, N. S. Fox (Winona Lake, IN: Eisenbrauns, 2009), 133–137.

> You shall then recite as follows before the Lord your God: "My father was a wandering Aramean. He went down to Egypt with meager numbers and sojourned there, but there he became a great and very populous nation. The Egyptians dealt harshly with us and oppressed us; they imposed heavy labor upon us. We cried to the Lord, the God of our fathers, and the Lord heard our plea and saw our plight, our misery, and our oppression. The Lord freed us from Egypt by a mighty hand, by an outstretched arm and awesome power, and by signs and portents. He brought us to this place and gave us this land, a land flowing with milk and honey. Wherefore I now bring the first fruits of the soil which You, O Lord, have given me." (Deut. 26:5–10)

The entire national story is condensed to sixty-three Hebrew words. "My father was a wandering Aramean," that is, we carry the national genes of the Arameans, since that is where we set off on our journey. Then we came to Egypt. We were set free from Egypt, and only at the end of our journey did we come to Canaan, the land between Aram (now Syria) and Egypt. According to this narrative, the story of the Hebrews is one of two exoduses: the exodus from Aram and the Exodus from Egypt.

It is worth noting, too, what is absent from this text. The period of the forefathers goes unmentioned. It is as if the forefathers went straight from Aram to Egypt, without stopping first in Canaan in the days of Abraham, Isaac, and Jacob. Hundreds of years of history are thus excised from the national story. It is not incidental that it is specifically these stories that were omitted from the text recited while presenting the first fruits. The stories of the forefathers and foremothers in Genesis are what imbue the Exodus story with a sense of returning home: Our ancestors were in Canaan and their descendants returned to Canaan, the land of their fathers. By contrast, the text about the first fruits implies that the Jews are not indigenous to the land. We are not from here – this is what Moses commands the people to recite each year anew.

The ancient text recited while bringing the first fruits is the opposite of the Declaration of Independence written by the founders of the Jewish state:

> The Land of Israel was the birthplace of the Jewish people. Here their spiritual, religious, and political identity was shaped. Here they first attained statehood and created cultural values of national and universal significance.

Inspired by David Ben-Gurion, the framers of Israel's Declaration of Independence sought to forge a new national consciousness according to the Platonic model, presenting a narrative in which the Jewish nation arose in the Land of Israel. But there is an obvious disparity between the Zionist and biblical narratives. The Declaration of Independence is the opposite of the biblical passage about the first fruits. The latter excises the forefathers who settled in the land. Ben-Gurion, by contrast, omitted the fact that the nation was forged outside of the land. The Zionist aspiration to normalize Jewish consciousness demanded a new interpretation of the Torah, one in which the nation sprung from the land.[5] As with other normal nations, Zionism advanced a story about the birth of the nation from the land for which it was destined. According to this narrative, Zionism is the return to this land.

Plato described a normative national consciousness: the nation arose from the land. Moses tried to forge a non-normative national consciousness: we came to a land in which we were not born. The non-normative national story is a means of shaping and elevating the national consciousness. Why is it important to Moses to emphasize that the nation is not indigenous to the land? Because the story according to which we, the people of Israel, are immigrants to the Land of Israel is supposed to instill in our consciousness a keen sensitivity to other foreigners and an empathy for the strangers in our midst.

The sense of foreignness that the Torah implants in the Jewish consciousness is the most important means of cultivating sensitivity to strangers. The Torah frequently juxtaposes the reminder of our

5. Micha Josef Berdichevsky was one of the architects of the "indigenous" interpretation of the Bible. See *Sinai and Gerizim* [Hebrew] (Israel: 5722), 143–226. The search for evidence that the nation was born and forged in the land is reflected in a conversation between David Ben-Gurion and Yehezkel Kauffman in Jerusalem in 1962. See David Ben-Gurion, *Biblical Studies* (Tel Aviv: 5730), 104–125.

foreignness and our enslavement with the commandments that deal with the rights of strangers and slaves. "You shall not wrong a stranger or oppress him, for you were strangers in the land of Egypt" (Ex. 22:20). "You shall not oppress a stranger, for you know the feelings of the stranger, having yourselves been strangers in the land of Egypt" (Ex. 23:9). The book of Deuteronomy repeats this demand for sensitivity more than any other book in the Torah.[6] Cultivating the memory of the Israelites' own experience as foreigners serves to develop the nation's moral character. Plato, as a proponent of the normative national consciousness, shapes a national story that cultivates nationalistic valor. Moses, as the founder of a non-normative consciousness, shapes a national story that cultivates moral sensitivity.

Plato and Moses have the same goal – safeguarding the nation on its land – and both believe that they have found the means of doing so. Plato believed that the people would be able to remain in the land so long as their soldiers felt driven to defend it valiantly. Moses believed that the ability to survive in the holy land was dependent on the people's sensitivity to its weakest residents. If the people recognize that they themselves are strangers, and if they develop a sensitivity to other strangers, they will merit to inherit the land. Only if the people believe that they are not from the land will the land remain theirs.

ALL IN THE PRESENT TENSE

Moses's efforts to cultivate an awareness that the Israelites are strangers and his challenge to the notion that the people are indigenous to the land are part of a larger effort to shape the relationship between the people and their past. When Moses reminds the nation of the giving of the Torah, he refers to the past as if it were taking place in the present. He turns to the children of those who left Egypt as if they are their parents, as if it is they themselves who fled.[7]

6. See Deuteronomy 10:9, 16:11–12, and 24:17–22.
7. In the ancient Near East, a ruler would often make a treaty with those who were actually present and with their future descendants, similar to Deuteronomy 4:9. But Moses does something else entirely, which is without precedent in contemporaneous treaties: He turns to those who are immediately present as if they are the ones who contracted the treaty in the past. See Weinfeld, *Deuteronomic School*, 105. Also see

> The Lord our God made a covenant with us at Horeb. It was not with our fathers that the Lord made this covenant, but with us, the living, every one of us who is here today. (Deut. 5:2–3)

Moses does not seem to distinguish between the present generation and the preceding one.[8] As he sees it, the generation that received the Torah at Horeb and the generation that stands poised to enter the land are one and the same. It is as if forty years have not elapsed, as if one generation has not given way to another, and as if the audience he stands before and addresses consists of the Israelites who left Egypt. He relates to them as if they witnessed the Exodus with their very own eyes:

> Take thought this day that it was not your children, who neither experienced nor witnessed the lesson of the Lord your God – His majesty, His mighty hand, His outstretched arm; the signs and the deeds that He performed in Egypt against Pharaoh king of Egypt and all his land; what He did to Egypt's army, its horses and chariots; how the Lord rolled back upon them the waters of the Sea of Reeds when they were pursuing you, thus destroying them once and for all; what He did for you in the wilderness before you arrived in this place; and what He did to Datan and Abiram, sons of Eliab son of Reuben, when the earth opened her mouth and swallowed them, along with their households, their tents, and every living thing in their train, from amidst all Israel, but that it was you who saw with your own eyes all the marvelous deeds that the Lord performed. (Deut. 11:2–7)

---

introduction, note 18. One possible explanation is that according to Deuteronomy, Moses received the commandments at Sinai (Horeb), but he did not pass them on to the people until he delivered his final address. That is, the sense of being in the present stems from the fact that Moses is now completing the covenant by passing on the laws to the people. See Yaakov Schwartz, "The Torah: Its Five Books and Four Documentations" [Hebrew], in *Biblical Literature: Introductions and Studies*, ed. Tzipora Talshir (Jerusalem: Yad Ben Zvi, 5771), 181 and note 79. Also see above, chapter 4, note 2.

8. In the course of his address, it happens eleven times that Moses addresses the people standing before him as if they themselves went forth from Egypt: 1:30, 4:3, 9, 34, 6:22, 7:19, 9:17, 10:21, 11:7, 29:1–2.

Moses tells this generation of Israelites that they are different from subsequent generations because the members of this generation witnessed the miracle of the Exodus from Egypt with their own eyes. But the reader knows very well that these Israelites – the generation that is listening to Moses on the eve of its entry into the land – did not in fact witness the Exodus, because the generation of Sinai died out in the wilderness.

In his address, Moses blends the past and the present. The past, which starred the generation delivered from Egypt, is conflated with the present, in which their children stand poised to enter the Promised Land. This chronological blurring reaches its climax when Moses speaks of how he anticipates that future generations will experience time. At this point it becomes clear that it is not just those who left Egypt who are entering the land, but also their descendants:

> When, in times to come, your children ask you, "What mean the decrees, laws, and rules that the Lord our God has enjoined upon you?" you shall say to your children, "We were slaves to Pharaoh in Egypt and the Lord freed us from Egypt with a mighty hand. The Lord wrought before our eyes marvelous and destructive signs and portents in Egypt, against Pharaoh and all his household, and us He freed from there that He might take us and give us the land that He had promised on oath to our fathers. Then the Lord commanded us to observe all these laws, to revere the Lord our God, for our lasting good and for our survival, as is now the case." (Deut. 6:20–24)

Memory has the extraordinary power to transform the past into the present. Memory can make the events of the distant past seem immediately present before our eyes, as if they are taking place at this very moment. The great cultural act that Moses suggests is one of erasing the past, erasing the future, and collapsing all time into the present. This is the basis for the covenant that Moses makes with the people at Horeb:

> You stand this day, all of you, before the Lord your God – your tribal heads, your elders, and your officials, all the men of Israel, your children, your wives, even the stranger within your camp,

> from woodchopper to water-drawer – to enter into the covenant of the Lord your God, which the Lord your God is concluding with you this day, with its sanctions, to the end that He may establish you this day as His people and be your God, as He promised you and as He swore to your fathers, Abraham, Isaac, and Jacob. I make this covenant, with its sanctions, not with you alone, but both with those who are standing here with us this day before the Lord our God and with those who are not with us here this day. (Deut. 29:9–14)

Moses makes this covenant with all future generations, those who are present and those "who are not with us here this day." The expanse of time has no effect on who is present and who is absent. Everything takes place on "this day": the address is given on "this day," the laws are transmitted on "this day," and the entry into the land takes place on "this day." Moses knows that the people will enter the land shortly, in the not-too-distant future. But for him, even that future takes place "today." In Deuteronomy, all the generations are one, and every day is "this day."

ALL IN THE PAST TENSE

Moses's address does not begin with the Exodus from Egypt, but with the departure from Horeb, when the people leave Sinai to continue wandering through the desert. "The Lord our God spoke to us at Horeb, saying: 'You have stayed long enough at this mountain'" (Deut. 1:6). The first revelation documented in the book of Deuteronomy is one in which God propels the people to leave Horeb at last and to make their way toward the Promised Land. The next historical moment that Moses recounts is the sin of the spies. The people whom God had to encourage to enter the land get cold feet and ask not to go in. Their punishment, as is well known, is that their request is granted: This timorous generation will not enter the land.

Forty years later, when the people are standing at the foothills of Mount Seir, they experience another revelation that echoes the previous one: "You have been skirting this hill country long enough; now turn north" (Deut. 2:3). God again exhorts the people to continue their journey to the land. The verses emphasize that it is a new generation now being addressed:

> The time that we spent in travel from Kadesh-barnea until we crossed the wadi Zered was thirty-eight years, until that whole generation of warriors had perished from the camp, as the Lord had sworn concerning them. Indeed, the hand of the Lord struck them, to root them out from the camp to the last man. When all the warriors among the people had died off… (Deut. 2:14–16)

It may be that they are referred to as a generation of warriors because of their ages when they sinned. But it is ironic to refer to the generation that was too frightened of their adversaries as the generation of warriors. In any case, when this generation has died out, the war for the land begins. And it begins with the attack on Sihon king of the Amorites and Og king of the Bashan.[9] The figure of Og has tremendous significance in Moses's narrative. This significance is explained almost as an aside, as if in a footnote; it appears in the text but seems marginal to it. This aside describes the nations who resided across the Jordan before the present inhabitants, the ancestors of Lot. "It was formerly inhabited by the Emim, a people great and numerous and as tall as the Anakites" (Deut. 2:10).

This is not merely a point of information. The text is telling us that in the past, there were giants who lived in the land. These giants were so terrifying and intimidating to the children of Israel that they did not want to enter the land at the time of the sin of the spies. But as the text also suggests, these giants were not unassailable. The Moabites defeated such giants,[10] leaving only one alive.[11] "Only King Og of Bashan

9. On the wars against Sihon and Og through the lens of Deuteronomy, see W. A. Sumner, "Israel's Encounters with Edom, Moab, Ammon, Sihon, and Og According to the Deuteronomist," *Vetus Testamentum* 18:1 (1968): 216–228.
10. The Moabites defeated the Emim.
11. Og was a mythological hero. A Phoenician coffin from the fifth to sixth centuries BCE contains an inscription that refers to Og as the protector of the Rephaites, who went down to hell. The dead person proclaims that if anyone desecrates his grave, the great Og will take vengeance. See Zvi Ron, "The Bed of Og," *Jewish Bible Quarterly* 40:1 (January–March 2012): 32–33. Also see Weinfeld, *The World of The Bible: Deuteronomy* [Hebrew] (Tel Aviv: Yedioth Ahronoth, 5762), 49. It seems that later Jewish tradition preserved these mythological associations. The Targum Pseudo-Jonathan on Deuteronomy 3:11 adds a comment explaining that Og was the only one remaining of all the heroes who survived the flood. Compare this to

was left of the remaining Rephaites" (Deut. 3:11).[12] It is the job of the new generation of Israelites to defeat this giant. Moses explains that this new generation does not suffer from its predecessors' complexes – they are not afraid of giants and will be able to defeat even Og. Unlike the preceding "generation of warriors," the new generation has faith in God, who will conquer the land for them and with them. A refreshing new chapter is beginning in the history of the Jewish people.

But the assertion that the generation that enters the land is not the generation that left Egypt contradicts Moses's statement elsewhere that they are one and the same. The desire to be liberated from the past – expressed in the story of Sihon and Og – contradicts Moses's affirmation that there is no past, expressed in the story of the Exodus from Egypt about which every generation is supposed to say, "And us He freed from there" (Deut. 6:23). Moses tells the nation that they do not belong to the generation that was terrified of entering the land and conquering it, but that they are part of the same generation that received the Torah and witnessed all the miracles.

Implicit in Deuteronomy is the idea that the past is within our control because we can decide how it will shape us. Moses tells the people how to employ the technique of selective memory. There are parts of the past which the people must renounce and from which they must liberate

---

Reish Lakish's statement in Genesis Rabba, *Lekh Lekha* 42:8: "'A fugitive came and brought the news to Abram' – Reish Lakish said in the name of Bar Kappara that this was Og." This tradition found its way into the Talmud as well: "But did not R. Ḥisda say, 'The people in the generation of the flood sinned with hot passion, and with hot water they were punished'? ... How did Og king of Bashan stand? Rather, a miracle was performed for it [the water], and it was cooled at the side of the Ark" (Zevaḥim 113b). "A fugitive came and brought the news to Abram – R. Yoḥanan explained: This refers to Og, who escaped the fate of the generation of the flood" (Nidda 61a).

Regarding the Phoenician association with Og as the defender of hell, there is a story cited by Abba Shaul in the Babylonian Talmud: "It was taught: Abba Shaul, or as some say, R. Yoḥanan stated: 'I was once a gravedigger. On one occasion, while pursuing a deer, I entered the thigh bone of a corpse and pursued it for three parasangs but neither reached the deer nor the end of the thigh bone. When I returned, I was told that it was the thigh bone of Og king of Bashan'" (Nidda 24b). Also see the tradition preserved in Genesis Rabba (Vilna), *Noaḥ* 34:12: "Og the king of the Bashan died. He is preserved from the rats and mice so that they don't peck out his eyes."

12. Compare this verse to Genesis 14:5 and 15:20 and to Joshua 12:4 and 13:12.

themselves so that they do not become part of the national character. And there are other parts of the past which the people must incorporate and assimilate deep into their national consciousness. The sin of the spies is relegated to the past, but the revelation at Horeb becomes the present. Moses shows that we have the power to activate memory intelligently and selectively so as to reshape the past, thereby safeguarding our moral character in the present.[13]

THE MEMORY SECTION

Moses devotes a long section of his address – from Deuteronomy 7:17 until the end of Deuteronomy 9 – to memory. He reviews many of the major events that the children of Israel experienced. But he does not review them for the sake of documentation. Moses has no interest in describing past events so as to maintain a database of national memories. Rather, he instructs the people in how to use their memories so that they will have a positive influence on the national character. Memory can have this influence only if the right memory is invoked at the right time. Toward this end, Moses presents three categories of national memories: the period of the wilderness, the major sins, and the miracles of war.

The Period of the Wilderness

The memory of slavery and alienation in Egypt recurs throughout the book of Deuteronomy, but the section on memory focuses primarily on the challenges of the wilderness experience, a time of total dependence on God.

> Remember the long way that the Lord your God has made you travel in the wilderness these past forty years, that He might test you by hardships to learn what was in your hearts: whether you would keep His commandments or not. He subjected you to the

13. On the power of memory to shape national character, particularly in the book of Deuteronomy, see Jan Assmann, "Communicative and Cultural Memory," in *Cultural Memory Studies: An International and Interdisciplinary Handbook*, ed. Astrid Erll and Ansgar Nunning (Berlin: Walter de Gruyter, 2008), 109–118. Also see Assmann's comprehensive study of cultural memory in ancient cultures: Jan Assmann, *Religion and Cultural Memory: Ten Studies* (Stanford, 2006).

> hardship of hunger and then gave you manna to eat, which neither you nor your fathers had ever known, in order to teach you that man does not live on bread alone, but that man may live on anything that the Lord decrees. The clothes upon you did not wear out, nor did your feet swell these forty years. Bear in mind that the Lord your God disciplines you just as a man disciplines his son. Therefore, keep the commandments of the Lord your God: walk in His ways and revere Him. (Deut. 8:2–6)

The memory of the people's dependence on God in the desert should and must shape their experience of the success that awaits them. This is a memory that can inhibit success from metamorphosing into pride, because it reminds them that their accomplishments are not really their own. When the Israelites were poor and weak, everything came from God; when they are rich and successful, so too everything will come from God.

Moses recognizes that the influence of memory is dependent on the time in which a particular memory is activated. When we are with strangers, we should recall when we were strangers. In times of success, we must remember our experience of deprivation and dependence. Memory influences the individual, and Deuteronomy emphasizes that a particular memory ought to be juxtaposed with the opposite experience: When a person is in control, he should remember his servitude. When she is successful, she should remember her dependence.

Self-Righteousness and the Memory of Sin

Hubris, the sin of overweening pride, generally involves one forgetting the limits of his own power. But the Torah depicts another kind of pride: moral self-righteousness. Just as the proud are blind to their own weaknesses and limitations, the self-righteous are blind to their own sins.

> And when the Lord your God has thrust them from your path, say not to yourselves, "The Lord has enabled us to possess this land because of our virtues." It is rather because of the wickedness of those nations that the Lord is dispossessing them before you. It is not because of your virtues and your rectitude that

> you will be able to possess their country, but it is because of their wickedness that the Lord your God is dispossessing those nations before you, and in order to fulfill the oath that the Lord made to your fathers, Abraham, Isaac, and Jacob. Know, then, that it is not for any virtue of yours that the Lord your God is giving you this good land to possess, for you are a stiff-necked people. (Deut. 9:4–6)

The great success of conquering the land is liable to lead the Israelites to a conviction of their own uprightness. Often, success is transformed into a sense of moral superiority. But success does not necessarily bespeak righteousness. Moses appeals to memory:

> Remember, never forget, how you provoked the Lord your God to anger in the wilderness: from the day that you left the land of Egypt until you reached this place, you have continued defiant toward the Lord. At Horeb, you so provoked the Lord that the Lord was angry enough with you to have destroyed you. I had ascended the mountain to receive the tablets of stone, the Tablets of the Covenant that the Lord had made with you, and I stayed on the mountain forty days and forty nights, eating no bread and drinking no water. And the Lord gave me the two tablets of stone inscribed by the finger of God, with the exact words that the Lord had addressed to you on the mountain out of the fire on the day of the Assembly. At the end of those forty days and forty nights, the Lord gave me the two tablets of stone, the Tablets of the Covenant. And the Lord said to me, "Hurry, go down from here at once, for the people whom you brought out of Egypt have acted wickedly. They have been quick to stray from the path that I enjoined upon them; they have made themselves a molten image." The Lord further said to me, "I see that this is a stiff-necked people. Let Me alone and I will destroy them and blot out their name from under heaven, and I will make you a nation far more numerous than they." I started down the mountain, a mountain ablaze with fire, the two Tablets of the Covenant in my two hands. I saw how you had sinned against the Lord your God.

> You made yourselves a molten calf; you were quick to stray from the path that the Lord had enjoined upon you. (Deut. 9:7–16)

Moses reminds the people of their sins. He asks the people to remember their less savory moments. The memory of sin is not intended to instill in the people a lasting sense of guilt about their past offenses, but rather to prevent them from developing a sense of moral superiority.

The three types of memory that we have listed have healing properties. In order to overcome the temptation to oppress a stranger, we must remember our own experience of being strangers in a strange land. In order to prevent victory from turning into hubris, we must remember our period of dependence on God in the wilderness. In order to resist an attitude of moral superiority, we must remember our past sins. The people must selectively remember those experiences that arouse feelings opposite to whatever emotions they are having in the present. And it is not just in times of strength that the people must summon the countervailing memory, but in times of weakness too.

The Fear of Failure

The fear of war is likely to be paralyzing, as Moses is well aware: "Should you say to yourselves, 'These nations are more numerous than us; how can we dispossess them?'" (Deut. 7:17). But Moses also teaches how to enlist memory to overcome this paralysis.

> You need have no fear of them. You have but to bear in mind what the Lord your God did to Pharaoh and all the Egyptians: the wondrous acts that you saw with your own eyes, the signs and the portents, the mighty hand, and the outstretched arm by which the Lord your God liberated you. Thus will the Lord your God do to all the peoples you now fear. The Lord your God will also send a plague against them, until those who are left in hiding perish before you. Do not stand in dread of them, for the Lord your God is in your midst, a great and awesome God. (Deut. 7:18–21)

Memory can help the people not only when they have a surplus of self-confidence, but also when they are in a crisis of confidence. Memory serves as a ballast, counteracting the intoxication of power or the fear of failure.

THE TEXTUALIZATION OF ISRAELITE LIFE

The enlightened use of memory safeguards Moses's two revolutions, i.e., the religious and the political. Both revolutions deal with power. They herald a religion devoid of power and a politics with limited power. Memory safeguards people from the misunderstanding and misuse of power.

Moses is afraid of forgetting.[14] He worries that after the people enter the land, they will forget all that they went through and all the laws they received from him. Moses's way of dealing with the threat of forgetting begins with recording his address. At the end of the book of Deuteronomy, he describes how he writes down his address, or at least the section in which he transmits the commandments to the people:[15] "When Moses had put down in writing the words of this Torah in a book to the very end" (Deut. 31:24). The book of Deuteronomy is the only book in the Bible that is identified as a book.[16] The book that consists mostly of an oral address is the only one explicitly described as a written book. Moses exhorts the people to read this book again and again. Their first encounter with the text happens immediately after they enter the land, when they must write it on one of the stones on Mount Ebal.[17]

14. The phrase "lest you forget" appears four times in Moses's address alongside three additional warnings against forgetting the address and the covenant. See Deuteronomy 4:9, 23; 6:12; 8:11, 14, 19; 9:7.
15. Rashi interprets the verse from Deuteronomy (4:44) that reads, "This is the Torah that Moses set before the Israelites" as meaning "This is the Torah, this one that he is about to set down after this chapter."
16. On several occasions, Deuteronomy is referred to as "this Torah" (1:5; 4:8; 17:18–19; 27:3, 8, 26; 28:58, 61; 29:28; 31:9, 11–12, 24; 32:46). There is also "in this book" (28:58; 29:19, 26) and "this book of the Torah" (29:20; 30:10; 31:26). See Schwartz, "The Torah," 163.
17. Biblical scholars disagree as to what exactly Moses commands the people to write on the stones. All scholars agree that it is a text from Deuteronomy, but they disagree about which one it is. Some argue that it is only the laws that must be recorded on the stones, whereas others hold that it is also the addresses. See Tigay, *JPS: Deut.*, 248.

> As soon as you have crossed the Jordan into the land that the Lord your God is giving you, you shall set up large stones. Coat them with plaster and inscribe upon them all the words of this Torah. When you cross over to enter the land that the Lord your God is giving you, a land flowing with milk and honey, as the Lord, the God of your fathers, promised you – upon crossing the Jordan, you shall set up these stones, about which I charge you this day, on Mount Ebal, and coat them with plaster. There too, you shall build an altar to the Lord your God, an altar of stones. Do not wield an iron tool over them; you must build the altar of the Lord your God of unhewn stones. You shall offer on it burnt offerings to the Lord your God, and you shall sacrifice there offerings of well-being and eat them, rejoicing before the Lord your God. And on those stones you shall inscribe every word of this Torah most distinctly. (Deut. 27:2–8)

Furthermore, after the people settle in the land, they must congregate every seven years and listen to the words of the Torah:

> And Moses instructed them as follows: Every seventh year, the year set for remission, at the Feast of Sukkot, when all Israel comes to appear before the Lord your God in the place that He will choose, you shall read this Torah aloud in the presence of all Israel. Gather the people – men, women, children, and the strangers in your communities – that they may hear and so learn to revere the Lord your God and to observe faithfully every word of this Torah. Their children, too, who have not had the experience, shall hear and learn to revere the Lord your God as long as they live in the land that you are about to cross the Jordan to possess. (Deut. 31:10–13)

Every seven years, there is a year of remission, a sabbatical in which economic hierarchies are blurred as some of the debts that the poor owe to the rich are forgiven. But now we learn that the spiritual hierarchy is blurred as well. Men, women, and children gather to listen to words of the Torah. The section of the Torah that is read aloud on this occasion is thought to be several chapters from the book of Deuteronomy.[18]

But it is not just when the people are entering the land and not just once in seven years that they are obligated to read Moses's address. The address must be read, in an abridged version, every day. "Take to heart these instructions with which I charge you this day. Impress them upon your children. Recite them when you stay at home and when you are away, when you lie down and when you get up" (Deut. 6:6–7). Moses embeds within his address the mechanism that is supposed to prevent forgetting. Anyone who listens to the address and accepts its teachings will keep listening to it all the days of his life.

If we listen carefully to the words of Moses's address, we will discover that Moses is concerned about the weakened commitment not of the generation that enters the land, but rather of the subsequent generations.

> When you have begotten children and children's children and are long established in the land, should you act wickedly and make for yourselves a sculptured image in any likeness, causing the Lord your God displeasure and vexation. (Deut. 4:25)

Moses cautions that as the next generations become increasingly prosperous and complacent, they will lose the drive that characterized the generation of founders and fighters, leading to forgetting and moral decline. Moses's challenge is not just educating the next generation but educating subsequent generations as well. He tells the people to teach Torah to their children, but he emphasizes that they must also teach it to their grandchildren.

> But take utmost care and watch yourselves scrupulously, so that you do not forget the things that you saw with your own eyes and so that they do not fade from your mind as long as you live. And make

18. See Sota 7:8. The midrash in *Sifrei* teaches that all of Deuteronomy is read aloud: "*Mishneh* – There is no *Mishneh* [Torah] except Deuteronomy.... They read before the congregation only the *Mishneh Torah*" (*Sifrei* on Deuteronomy, *Shofetim* 160). Also see Rofé, *Intro. to Deuteronomy*, 22, and Schwartz, "The Torah," 163.

> them known to your children and to your children's children: the day you stood before the Lord your God at Horeb. (Deut. 4:9–10)

And indeed, what follows Deuteronomy proves that Moses's concerns were justified. In the book of Joshua, the Israelites remain faithful to God and even renew their covenant with Him.[19] But the moral and spiritual decline begins with the children of those who conquered the land. "And all that generation were likewise gathered to their fathers. Another generation arose after them that had not experienced the deliverance of the Lord or the deeds that He had wrought for Israel" (Judges 2:10). The inhabitants of the land and their culture have no appeal to a conquering army. So long as the Israelites are fighting against them, and so long as the inhabitants of the land are regarded as enemies, their power to influence the Israelites is limited. But when the fighting ends and the era of conquest draws to a close, the nation begins to see the inhabitants of the land through new eyes. Their culture becomes more alluring. Moreover, by the end of the conquest, the nation is that much more removed from the founding generation, and their sense of commitment to the covenant made at Sinai and renewed in Moab begins to waver.

Moses works to prevent the people from feeling that Sinai is a bygone event and that his injunctions were meant for another time. He hopes that just as the Revelation at Sinai will be regarded as taking place "on this day," so too the covenant at Moab will feel part of an eternal present. How will this goal be attained? By study and review.

Deuteronomy instructs that adherence to the Torah's laws will enable the people to remain in the land, and this steadfastness is in turn dependent on the continual study of those laws. Deuteronomy joins form and content. Those who listen to the book of Deuteronomy do not just listen to the ongoing commandment to study Torah; they also

---

19. Alexander Rofé and others have suggested that the covenant in chapter 24 of the book of Joshua is not a renewal of the prior covenant, but an alternative to the covenant at Sinai/Moab from the Efrati school. See Rofé, "The Story of the Gathering at Shechem (Josh. 24:1–28, 31) – Version, Literature, and History" [Hebrew], *World Congress of Jewish Studies*, vol. 12: The Bible and its World (5757): 17–25. On the nature of the Efrati composition, which is also reflected in Joshua 24, see Rofé, "Historiography," 18–23. And see note 25 in chapter 2, above.

experience it firsthand, since the book itself repeats much of what was already narrated and commanded in previous books.

In part one of this book, we dealt with the textualization of Jewish life. We saw how Moses confines all the religious drama to the Temple, while at the same time removing God from the Temple. We also saw how Moses plants the seeds of Torah in all those places from which he uproots religious worship. Now we will see that these efforts are part of his battle against forgetting. Moses tries to transform his final address from a valedictory into words that will stay with the people forever.

CONCLUSION: HALAKHA AND AGGADA

Moses reshapes the political and religious life of the Israelites. He suggests a political structure with attenuated control over the governed and a religion with no claim of control over nature. But there were difficult psychological circumstances to contend with. Moses asks a nation on the verge of military victory – an experience that awakens a hunger for power and control – to fashion a society with limited power and control. He tries to educate the people to accept a new model of society in order to protect themselves from moral and religious decay. We considered the two approaches that stand at the heart of his educational philosophy:

1. *The Full Textualization of Life*

The book of Deuteronomy is the first book of the Torah that refers to itself as a book. "If you fail to observe faithfully all the terms of this Torah that are written in this book, to revere this honored and awesome Name, the Lord your God" (Deut. 28:58). The people are given the opportunity to devote themselves to God not by obeying His messenger, but by dedicating themselves to His Torah.[20] God's laws must be studied and understood. They have a rational basis and make sense. "Observe them faithfully, for that will be proof of your wisdom and discernment to other peoples, who on hearing of all these laws will say, 'Surely, that great nation is a wise and discerning people'" (Deut. 4:6).

20. On the commandment to learn and to teach, see Deuteronomy 4:9–10; 6:7; 11:19; and 31:12–13.

In the book of Exodus, the leaders of the people are to be "capable men who fear God, trustworthy men who spurn ill-gotten gain" (Ex. 18:21). In Deuteronomy, they must be "men who are wise, discerning, and experienced" (Deut. 1:13). The characteristic of wisdom is now a prerequisite for leadership. The leaders and the people who follow them must be wise, as are the laws themselves: "Observe them faithfully, for that will be proof of your wisdom and discernment to other peoples, who on hearing of all these laws will say, 'Surely that great nation is a wise and discerning people'" (Deut. 4:8).[21] This is a revolution. The glorification of learning is one of the most significant turning points in Jewish history, and it occurs in the book of Deuteronomy.

2. *The Selective Fashioning of Memory*

Every nation tells itself stories about its past, and these foundational narratives serve to shape national identity and character. But not every nation uses its stories as a remedy for psychological imbalance. This is what is so novel about Moses's approach to the selective fashioning of memory. The story of slavery should be told in a period of dominance; the story of being dependent on God in the wilderness should be told in periods of success; the story of the miraculous victories should be told in a time of national fear; the stories of sin should be told in times of moral righteousness. The right story at the right time serves to create the proper national balance.

Forgetting is the greatest threat to national survival. According to Moses, it is far worse than any Canaanite, Assyrian, or Egyptian enemy. The greatest danger is not physical but psychological, and thus Moses is less concerned about an external attack than about the loss of national identity. He presents the people with two means of preserving their national identity: They must review the Torah's laws and retell its stories. To use terms that would become popular later, they must engage with halakha and Aggada.

21. Moshe Weinfeld demonstrates the strong link between wisdom literature and the attitude toward wisdom in the book of Deuteronomy. See Weinfeld, *Deuteronomic School*, 244–274.

Chapter 6

A New Consciousness of Success

A famous story by one of the greatest Jewish storytellers, Rabbi Nachman of Breslov, tells of a king who made a great party to celebrate the end of his reign. He was stepping down from the throne because he decided to pass on the mantle of leadership to his son. But during the party, the king informs his son that he has seen in the stars that his son will one day lose the kingdom. He tells his son:

> Since I am an astrologer, I can see from the stars that in the future you are going to lose the monarchy, and when that happens, I want you to be very careful not to fall into depression. Rather, you must force yourself to remain happy. And if you do succeed in remaining happy, then I will also be happy. In fact, even if you become depressed, I will still be happy. I will be happy that you are no longer king. For if you cannot remain happy despite

> losing the kingship, that will be a sign that you were not worthy of being king.[1]

Why is the father glad to know that the son will someday lose the kingship. Because if the son is happy when he loses the kingship, then the father will delight in his happiness. And if the son becomes depressed when he loses the kingship, it will be a sign that he was not fit to be king in the first place, and so the father will be happy that justice was served. Power, Rabbi Nachman is saying, befits only those who are not dependent on it. A truly honorable person is one who knows how to deal with failure and the loss of power. The sign that a person is not dependent on power is that he remains happy even when he loses that power. Only someone who does not become emotionally dependent on power and success deserves to merit both.

MY OWN POWER AND THE MIGHT OF MY HAND HAVE WON THIS WEALTH FOR ME

Successful people are apt to identify with their success, believing that success is something that defines them rather than befalls them.

Seasoned Wall Street investors are all too familiar with this psychological phenomenon. They watch as people study the value of a stock, watch it rise, invest in it, and profit. These investors are seduced into thinking that their own intelligence and skills led them to invest in the "right" stock. The problem is that it doesn't take unusual intelligence to earn money when the entire stock market is climbing. As one sober and seasoned investor told me, "Success leads the successful astray."[2] Success causes the successful to tell his own story inaccurately. It leads him to think that he is much greater than he is.

Moses's final address is a sobering one in which he warns his listeners about the dangers of success. The nation that enters the land, and that will enjoy military and economic success, is likely to identify with

---

1. "The Story of the Seven Beggars," by Rabbi Nachman of Breslov. Yeshivat Shuvu Bonim, 2000. http://www.shuvubonim.org/storysb.html.
2. From Jay Pomrenze's book in progress on the psychological influence of wealth on the wealthy.

its success and to think itself the embodiment of that success: "And you say to yourselves, 'My own power and the might of my own hand have won this wealth for me'" (Deut. 8:17). But at the same time, Moses is not altogether dismissive of success, as we shall see.

THE PARADOX OF PLENTY

Moses's concerns about the risks of success, power, and prosperity do not lead him to advocate asceticism and self-denial. One does not have to run away from success and abundance; one should rather benefit from them. Prosperity is the recompense granted to those who devote themselves wholeheartedly to God.

> If, then, you obey the commandments that I enjoin upon you this day, loving the Lord your God and serving Him with all your heart and soul, I will grant the rain for your land in its season, the early rain and the late. You shall gather in your new grain and wine and oil – I will also provide grass in the fields for your cattle – and thus you shall eat your fill. (Deut. 11:13–15)

But prosperity is not just the reward for devotion to God. It is also the greatest threat to that devotion.

> When the Lord your God brings you into the land that He swore to your fathers, Abraham, Isaac, and Jacob, to assign to you – great and flourishing cities that you did not build, houses full of all good things that you did not fill, hewn cisterns that you did not hew, vineyards and olive groves that you did not plant – and you eat your fill, take heed that you do not forget the Lord who freed you from the land of Egypt, the house of bondage. (Deut. 6:10–12)

> When you have eaten your fill, give thanks to the Lord your God for the good land which He has given you. Take care lest you forget the Lord your God and fail to keep His commandments, His rules, and His laws, which I enjoin upon you today. When you have eaten your fill and have built fine houses to live in, and your herds and flocks have multiplied, and your silver and gold

> have increased, and everything you own has prospered, beware lest your heart grow haughty and you forget the Lord your God who freed you from the land of Egypt, the house of bondage. (Deut. 8:10–14)

Prosperity is the reward for keeping the covenant, but it is also the reason for violating it. The recompense for loyalty to God threatens to undermine that loyalty. How to overcome this paradox?

Unlike other religious preachers throughout history, Moses does not glorify poverty or call for a renunciation of sovereignty and power. Instead, Moses seeks to cultivate a national consciousness that understands how to use power in order to change reality for the better, without enabling that power to change reality for the worse. This is where Moses's speech is at its most ambitious.

FROM THE WILDERNESS TO CANAAN

Life in Canaan needs to be informed by the journey to Canaan. The people are charged to remember their trek to the land: "Remember the long way that the Lord your God has made you travel in the wilderness" (Deut. 8:6). This memory must become assimilated into the national character.

As Moses knows, the haughtiness that the Israelites who conquer the land are liable to develop threatens to overwrite the memories of the wilderness journey.[3] Moses's concern is that the strong nation will forget its period of weakness. But the dynamic between memory and pride is even more complicated. Pride will lead to forgetting the wilderness period, but preserving the memory of the wilderness will immunize the people against pride. The story of the manna is instructive:

> He subjected you to the hardship of hunger and then gave you manna to eat, which neither you nor your fathers had ever known,

3. As the Midrash suggests, "'Who led you through the great and terrible wilderness' – This is a hint to the people that one day they will rebel against God and worship idols instead of the goodness that influenced them" (Midrash Aggada [Buber], Deuteronomy, *Ekev*, chapter 8).

> in order to teach you that man does not live on bread alone, but that man may live on anything that the Lord decrees. (Deut. 8:3)

The manna given to the people who were without bread reminds a nation that now has plenty of bread that they remain dependent on God. When the people have bread to eat, they can still appreciate that bread as if it were manna falling from heaven. This is the psychological challenge that Moses puts forth: to experience their success as if it is not theirs.

ON BREAD FROM THE GROUND AND FIRE FROM THE GODS

In retelling the story of the manna, Moses challenges the people to reach a level of consciousness in which even after harvesting wheat and making bread with their own hands, they can still regard bread as manna from heaven. The Sages of the Talmud posed the same challenge when they formulated the blessing recited over bread.

Jews are commanded to bless God, the king of the universe, for bringing forth bread from the earth.[4] But it is man who plants, waters, cultivates, and cuts the wheat. Bread is not manna. Manna falls from heaven, already made and ready to eat. Bread, on the other hand, is the final product of a long process of human labor. Even so, the blessing over the bread transforms it into a kind of manna. This blessing requires people to regard the bread they toiled to prepare as created by God, as if bread indeed came forth from the earth. We are supposed to experience our own creations as if they are divine.

Compare the story of the discovery of fire in Genesis Rabba with the myth of Prometheus. In Greek mythology, Prometheus steals fire from the gods, for which he is eternally chained to a rock. Fire symbolizes power and belongs to the gods; all human power is a form of

4. The blessing is based on a verse from Psalms which describes God's glory and God's works: "He makes grass grow for the cattle and makes plants for people to cultivate, bringing forth bread from the earth" (Ps. 104:14). According to this verse, God does not bring forth bread directly; He makes grass grow for cattle and makes plants for people to cultivate, but it is human labor that ultimately brings forth bread. The blessing changes the meaning of the verse on which is it based.

theft. By contrast, in the midrashic tradition, Adam rubbed two stones together and fire came forth.

> When the sun sank at the end of the Shabbat and darkness began to set in, Adam was terrified, as it is written, "Surely the darkness will bruise me, and the light become night around me" (Ps. 139:11). Shall he of whom it was written, "He shall bruise your head and you shall bruise his heel" (Gen. 3:15) now come to attack me? What did the Holy One, blessed be He, do? He made him find two flints, which he struck against each other. Light came forth and he blessed over it, as it is written, "And the light became night around me" (Ps. 139:11). What did he bless over it? "Creator of the lights of fire."[5]

After completing Creation, God blesses man. After discovering fire, man blesses God: "Creator of the lights of fire." This is the opposite of the Prometheus myth, in which fire originally belonged to the gods, but it was stolen from them and passed to human beings. In the Midrash, fire is man's creation, but man chooses to attribute this creation to God. The Midrash relates that fire was discovered on Saturday night after the conclusion of Shabbat – after God had rested from Creation and after man had begun his own activities within the created world. But even after God finished creating the world and man took over, God continued to create as well – this time not for man, but by means of man. Man, in turn, identifies each of his creations as divine.

The blessings over the bread and the fire are the rabbinic expression of the Deuteronomic ideal. Adam discovers fire and refers to God as "Creator of the lights of fire." And when human beings prepare bread, they refer to God as He who "brings forth bread from the earth." In so doing, they fulfill the charge put forth by Moses: to preserve the consciousness of the wilderness journey even while no longer in the wilderness, and to remember the journey to the land even while already living within its borders. Deuteronomy also requires the same reshaping of the experience of success when it comes to military victory.

5. Genesis Rabba 11:2.

THE WAR

Moses tries to strengthen the self-confidence of a nation on the eve of war by promising them divine assistance.

> Hear, O Israel! You are about to cross the Jordan to go in and dispossess nations greater and more populous than you: great cities with walls sky-high; a people great and tall, the Anakites, of whom you have knowledge; for you have heard it said, "Who can stand up to the children of Anak?" Know then this day that none other than the Lord your God is crossing at your head, a devouring fire; it is He who will wipe them out. He will subdue them before you, that you may quickly dispossess and destroy them, as the Lord promised you. (Deut. 9:13)

With the trauma of the sin of the spies as backdrop, Moses seeks to fortify the people's confidence so that they will not be terrified by the winds of war.[6] He also is concerned about the opposite possibility – that they will become overly haughty after their anticipated victory, take credit for all of their successes, and become drunk with power.

Moses describes to the Israelites that God is present in the military camp:

> When you take the field against your enemies, and see horses and chariots – forces larger than yours – have no fear of them, for the Lord your God, who brought you from the land of Egypt, is with you. Before you join battle, the priest shall come forward and address the troops. He shall say to them, "Hear, O Israel! You are about to join battle with your enemy. Let not your courage falter. Do not be in fear, or in panic, or in dread of them. For it is the Lord your God who marches with you to do battle for you against your enemy, to bring you victory." (Deut. 20:14)

6. See also Deuteronomy 7:7–23.

> Since the Lord your God moves about in your camp to protect you and to deliver your enemies to you, let your camp be holy. Let Him not find anything unseemly among you and turn away from you. (Deut. 23:15)[7]

The idea that God moves about the Israelite military camp is inconsistent with other parts of Deuteronomy. According to Deuteronomy, God did not descend to Mount Sinai, and He does not dwell even in the Temple. The God of Deuteronomy dwells in the heavens. And yet here He is described as part of the Israelite military camp.[8]

But there is a deep tension when it comes to the religious status of warfare in Deuteronomy, because notwithstanding God's presence in the military camp, the book makes no mention of the rites associated with going out to war. In the ancient world, soldiers customarily held religious ceremonies on the eve of battle in order to ensure their victory.[9] A ceremony of this sort may be alluded to in the book of Numbers, in which the people are commanded to blow trumpets on the eve of battle.

> When you are at war in your land against an aggressor who attacks you, you shall sound short blasts on the trumpets, that you may be remembered before the Lord your God and be delivered from your enemies. (Num. 10:9)

Religious ceremonies are depicted elsewhere in the Bible. King Saul offers sacrifices to God before he heads out to battle against the Philistines (I Sam. 13:9). And when the Israelites go out to war against the Philistines, they take the Ark of the Covenant with them so that

7. The notion that God joins the Israelites in battle to deliver them from their enemies appears also in Judges 4:14 and Psalms 44:38. Also compare Numbers 14:42.
8. For an important discussion of the two types of revelation in Deuteronomy – the transcendental and the anthropomorphic – see Y. Knohl, "Biblical Faith: A Conversation with Yehezkel Kaufmann," in *Biblical Literature: Introductions and Studies*, ed. Tzipora Talshir (Jerusalem: Yad Ben Zvi, 5771), 155–156.
9. Many ancient nations were accustomed to dedicate these rituals to their gods of war: Ninurta, the Mesopotamian god of war; Anat, the Canaanite war goddess; and Anhur, the Egyptian war god.

they will prevail over their adversaries. In Deuteronomy, however, there are activities on the eve of battle that include addresses from the priests and magistrates, but there are no religious rites involved: no trumpets, no sacrifices, no Ark.

Here too, Moses initiates two parallel and seemingly conflicting processes. On the one hand, he refers to God moving about the military camp, and on the other hand, he removes all religious ritual from the military proceedings. We can understand why Moses does so if we return to our discussion of magic in part one. The tremendous fear that the people experience on the eve of war leads them to succumb to the temptation of magic and the illusion of control that magical rites afford. But the preparation for war that Moses wants is a religious experience devoid of magic. God fights for the people, but God is beyond their control.

And so instead of a religious ceremony on the eve of battle, Moses offers an address: "For it is the Lord your God who marches with you to do battle for you against your enemy, to bring you victory" (Deut. 20:4). This does not mean that the people's own soldiering is irrelevant or superfluous.[10] But one of the goals of Moses's approach is to have the people recognize that their military victories are not really their own. This is seen, of course, through witnessing miracles in battle, but Moses wants the people to see the hand of God even when their victories do not seem miraculous, and even when they do not directly experience them as divine.

When God struck Egypt with plagues, drowned Pharaoh's army in the sea, and fought on behalf of the people, the people did not fight, but merely looked on: "And when Israel saw the wondrous power which the Lord had wielded against the Egyptians, the people feared the Lord; they had faith in the Lord and His servant Moses" (Ex. 14:31). But the conquest of the Land of Israel will be different. This time, the people will not merely observe the military drama. They must head out into battle and conquer the enemy with their own blood and sweat and tears.

---

10. As we read in the book of Proverbs, "The horse is readied for the day of battle, but victory comes from the Lord" (21:31). The military must put forth its best effort, but victory depends on God.

Moses makes a difficult spiritual demand on the people. They must feel the same sense of awe and wonder during their conquest of Canaan that they felt during the Exodus from Egypt. But this time they will not witness divine victory as an open miracle. This time, they will have to actively identify God's presence.

JOY

The rebuke that appears in *Parashat Ki Tavo* contains a description of the future banishment of the Israelite nation from the Land of Israel as a consequence of their failure to serve God joyously.

> All these curses shall befall you; they shall pursue you and overtake you, until you are wiped out, because you did not heed the Lord your God and keep the commandments and laws that He enjoined upon you. They shall serve as signs and proofs against you and your offspring for all time, because you would not serve the Lord your God in joy and gladness over the abundance of everything. (Deut. 28:45–47)

The Israelites will lose what they had because they did not devote themselves to God "in joy and gladness over the abundance of everything." They did not rejoice when they had everything, and therefore what they had will be ruined. In the Bible, joy takes on an almost halakhic status.[11] The people are commanded to express joy in God's presence: "And you shall rejoice before the Lord your God with your sons and daughters and with your male and female slaves, along with the Levite in your settlements, for he has no territorial allotment among you" (Deut. 12:12).[12]

---

11. The rabbinic Sages institutionalized this emotion and converted it into a sacrifice: "And you shall rejoice in all types of joy – this teaches that it is required to bring a peace offering. It says here, 'And you shall rejoice' (Deut. 12:12), and it says there, 'And you shall rejoice on your festivals' (Deut. 16:14). Just as the joy there refers to a peace offering, so too does the joy here refer to a peace offering" (*Midrash Tanna'im* on Deuteronomy 26). Also: "Here it says 'joy' and there it says 'joy.' Just as the joy referred to there is a peace offering, so too here it signifies a peace offering" (Y. Bikkurim, chapter 2).
12. Also compare Deuteronomy 12:18–19: "These you must consume before the Lord your God in the place that the Lord your God will choose – you and your sons and

What is Deuteronomy's concept of joy? Why does the failure to feel joy result in the people's expulsion from the land? What is the meaning of rejoicing "before the Lord your God"? In Deuteronomy, joy is generally associated with generosity. For instance, Deuteronomy commands every person to take a tenth of his profits and enjoy them in Jerusalem.

> And spend the money on anything you want – cattle, sheep, wine or other intoxicant, or anything you may desire. And you shall feast there, in the presence of the Lord your God, and rejoice with your household. But do not neglect the Levite in your community, for he has no hereditary portion as you have. (Deut. 14:26–27)

According to Deuteronomy, joy is a person's enjoyment of the fruits of his labor, particularly when he shares those fruits with others, and especially with those who are weak.[13]

> On the holidays of Shavuot and Sukkot, too, joy is associated with generosity:

> You shall rejoice before the Lord your God with your son and daughter, your male and female slave, the Levite in your communities, and the stranger, the fatherless, and the widow in your midst, at the place where the Lord your God will choose to establish His name. (Deut. 16:11)

> After the ingathering from your threshing floor and your vat, you shall hold the Feast of Sukkot for seven days. You shall rejoice in

---

your daughters, your male and female slaves, and the Levite in your settlements – happy before the Lord your God in all your undertakings. Be sure not to neglect the Levite as long as you live in your land."

13. Is this the definition of joy according to the book of Deuteronomy? Or is it an instruction as to how people should channel their joy? We can understand the biblical verses in both ways. On the one hand, the feeling of joy in Deuteronomy is one of the humility that is expressed as generosity, and thus there is a commandment to rejoice. On the other hand, joy is an emotion which can also be an expression of pride; according to this understanding, the commandment to rejoice is not about experiencing joy, but about channeling our joy appropriately.

> your festival with your son and daughter, your male and female slave, the Levite, the stranger, the fatherless, and the widow in your communities. You shall hold a festival for the Lord your God for seven days, in the place that the Lord will choose; for the Lord your God will bless all your crops and all your undertakings, and you shall have nothing but joy. (Deut. 16:13–15)

Joy is expressed by means of generosity, which transforms joy from an emotion into an action. It is manifested by giving back to God what belongs to God, "each with his own gift, according to the blessing that the Lord your God has bestowed upon you" (Deut. 16:17).[14]

Generosity can be experienced as renunciation. A generous person relinquishes something of his own for the sake of someone else. But in the book of Deuteronomy generosity is not about renunciation, but rather about gratitude. This is a radically different understanding. Generosity out of joy is less a consciousness of giving than of receiving. A person who gives to the poor out of joy does not feel like he is giving up something of his own. By giving to others that way, he expresses his sense that what he has is a gift that he himself received; he is merely passing it on. The act of giving is not a renunciation of that which is his, but rather a declaration that what is ostensibly his was never really his in the first place.

The book of Deuteronomy does not challenge the legitimacy of private ownership. It is not a manifesto that regards all private ownership as a kind of theft. To the contrary, Moses defends private ownership. But from a psychological perspective, Moses says that the people should relate to their possessions as not exclusively theirs.

If we return to the passage of rebuke in *Parashat Ki Tavo* in light of this understanding of the nature of joy, we can now discern the ironic tone of the verse that explains why the people will be banished from the land: "Because you would not serve the Lord your God in joy and

14. Moreover, the recompense that a person receives for giving of the blessing that God bestows upon him is that God will bless him even more. See Deuteronomy 14:29 and 15:10. I am grateful to Noam Zion for his assistance with Jewish understandings of generosity.

gladness over the abundance of everything." Because the Israelites did not rejoice before God over everything that they received from Him, because they experienced all their conquests as theirs alone, they lost all that they had achieved and conquered.

THE BIBLE'S MISSING HOLIDAY

The Torah commands the remembrance of the Exodus from Egypt each year on Passover. And all generations following the wilderness generation must remember the wilderness period each year on Sukkot. We would expect that the most momentous historical event that took place after the wilderness period – the conquest of the land –would also merit a holiday. While the biblical story spans the Exodus from Egypt and the conquest of Canaan, the biblical calendar celebrates only the first half of that narrative. What happened to the missing holiday?

The truth is that there is – or was – such an effort. Joshua, who conquered Canaan, sought to incorporate the miraculous conquest of the land into the national memory.

> When the entire nation had finished crossing the Jordan, the Lord said to Joshua, "Select twelve men from among the people, one from each tribe, and instruct them as follows: Pick up twelve stones from the spot exactly in the middle of the Jordan, where the priests' feet are standing; take them along with you and deposit them in the place where you will spend the night.... This shall serve as a symbol among you: In times to come, when your children ask, 'What is the meaning of these stones for you?' you shall tell them, 'The waters of the Jordan were cut off because of the Ark of the Lord's Covenant. When it passed through the Jordan, the waters of the Jordan were cut off.' And so these stones shall serve the people of Israel as a memorial for all time."
> (Josh. 4:1–3, 6–7)

Just as Moses created a method to preserve the memory of the Exodus in the national consciousness, Joshua tries to create a parallel mechanism in order to implant the memory of the conquest in the national consciousness.[15] Moses succeeded: To this day, children ask their parents – in the words of the Passover Haggada – "What does all this worship mean to you?" But Joshua failed. Jews retell the story of the Exodus, but not the story of the conquest of the land.[16] The conquest is an important event in the history of the Jewish people, but it is not an event that the nation continues to celebrate. Power is not something of which to be unduly proud, nor is it something inherently sacred.

The great civilizations of the ancient world developed along rivers – the Nile, the Euphrates, and the Tigris. These river valley civilizations became great empires of Egypt and Mesopotamia. Both of these civilizations made power into a god.[17] The Torah suggests an alternative, but it is not the polar opposite. The Torah's response is not to preach asceticism.

---

15. Compare Exodus 12:25–26; 13:8–9; 13:14; and Deuteronomy 6:20–21.
16. Psalm 105 reflects a similar sensibility. The psalm begins with the verse, "Praise the Lord; call on His name. Proclaim His deeds among the peoples." The wondrous deeds that God performed throughout Jewish history must be proclaimed to the world. Following this opening, the psalm offers a survey of this wondrous history, with reference both to the patriarchs and to the Israelites' settlement in Egypt: "Then Israel came to Egypt; Jacob sojourned in the land of Ham. He made His people very fruitful, more numerous than their foes. He changed their hearts to hate His people, to plot against His servants" (vv. 23–25). Mention is made of the deliverance from Egypt and of some of the plagues: "He sent His servant Moses, and Aaron, whom He had chosen.... He turned their waters into blood and killed their fish. Their land teemed with frogs, even the rooms of their king" (vv. 26, 29–30). The miracles of the wilderness are also mentioned: "He spread a cloud for a cover, and fire to light up the night. They asked and He brought them quail, and satisfied them with food from heaven" (vv. 39–40). But after this detailed history, the psalm stops just at the entrance into the land, offering merely: "He gave them the lands of nations; they inherited the wealth of peoples." Elsewhere, the Bible tells a complete story of the Exodus from Egypt and the entry into Canaan, but demands that the Israelites remember only the first half of that narrative.
17. As we have seen, the Egyptian kings were regarded as gods, and the Mesopotamian kings, who were the representatives of God on earth, immortalized their power and heroism in monumental inscriptions that they left behind. See for instance William W. Hallo and K. Lawson Younger, Jr., eds., *Monumental Inscriptions from the Biblical World: The Context of Scripture*, vol. 2 (Leiden, Netherlands: Brill, 2003). On Egypt, see pp. 25, 27, 29–30, 37, 45. On Mesopotamia, see pp. 262, 279–280, 302, 336. Also see note 10 in chapter 2, above.

In this sense, the Torah is different from many religions and cultures that teach that people should avoid wealth and power because they lead to corruption.[18] For instance, a Christian legend tells the story of St. Francis, who read Jesus's harsh words to his disciples about the toxic effects of wealth. St. Francis felt as if Jesus were speaking directly to him, and he sold all his possessions and gave the proceeds to charity. Francis was not concerned primarily about the problem of poverty but about the problem of wealth. He strove to protect himself from the corrupting influence of power. But by means of the commandments, the Torah tries to create a society in which people can enjoy power and wealth without sullying their characters.

As with enjoying a daily cup of wine instead of a daily bottle, power does not necessarily corrupt, so long as it is used properly, in moderation.

18. This is, for example, part of the philosophy of Jainism and Buddhism, two outgrowths of Hinduism. Possessions and the desire for possessions are a source of suffering. A person should shun wealth and power if he wishes to attain nirvana, an end to suffering. The renunciation of the desire for power is called ahimsa. See Sunanda Shastri and Yajneshwar S. Shastri, "Ahimsa and the Unity of All Things: A Hindu View of Nonviolence," in *Subverting Hatred: The Challenge of Nonviolence in Religious Traditions* (New York: Macmillan, 1987): Ahimsa, vol. 1, pp. 152–153; Nonviolence, vol. 10, pp. 463–468. Wealth is frowned upon in Christianity, as well. The New Testament speaks out against wealth and the accumulation of material possessions because a wealthy person is not admitted into the "kingdom of heaven." See Luke 12:33–34; 18:22–24; Matthew 6:19–21; 19:21–24.

Chapter 7

The Moral Address

BECOMING A FREE PERSON

The Ten Commandments begin with an introduction: "I the Lord am your God who brought you out of the land of Egypt, out of the house of bondage" (Ex. 20:2). God introduces Himself to the people as their liberator. This is the only information that the people have about God – He frees slaves.

At Sinai, Moses enters into the fog, receives God's laws, and relays them to the people. From the first commandments that He transmits after the end of the public Revelation is the commandment to emancipate Hebrew slaves during the Sabbatical year.

> These are the rules that you shall set before them: When you acquire a Hebrew slave, he shall serve six years. In the seventh year he shall go free, without payment. (Ex. 21:1–2)

This commandment, which the people receive from Moses, is resonant of the first commandment they received from God. The first of the Ten Commandments is a description of God as a freer of slaves, and one of the first commandments given after Sinai is the injunction to free one's slaves. Is this just a coincidence?[1] Or are we supposed to infer that just as God is a liberating figure, so too are we commanded to create a liberating society? This ethic, which is only hinted at in Exodus, is made more explicit in Deuteronomy when Moses reiterates this commandment.[2]

> If a fellow Hebrew, man or woman, is sold to you, he shall serve you six years, and in the seventh year you shall set him free. When you set him free, do not let him go empty-handed. Furnish him out of the flock, threshing floor, and vat, with which the Lord your God has blessed you. Bear in mind that you were slaves in the land of Egypt and the Lord your God redeemed you. Therefore, I enjoin this commandment upon you today. (Deut. 15:12–15)

Unlike in Exodus, the injunction to emancipate slaves now has a rationale: The Israelites must emancipate their slaves every seven years because of the liberation from Egypt.[3] The nation that was liberated in the past is commanded to be a liberating nation in the present and in the future. The Exodus from Egypt is not just a nostalgic memory; it is a historical event that became a commandment. God liberated us from Egypt, and we need to be like God and liberate our own slaves.

---

1. Nahmanides writes in his commentary on Exodus 21:2: "'When you acquire a Hebrew slave' – the first line begins with a mention of the Hebrew slave because the freeing of the Hebrew slave during the seventh year recalls the Exodus from Egypt mentioned in the first commandment, as it is written, 'Bear in mind that you were slaves in the land of Egypt and the Lord your God redeemed you. Therefore, I enjoin this commandment upon you today' (Deut. 15:15)."
2. See also Leviticus 25:40–45.
3. The juxtaposition of the emancipation of slaves and the Exodus from Egypt also appears in Leviticus 25: "If your kinsman under you continues in straits and must give himself over to you, do not subject him to the treatment of a slave. He shall remain with you as a hired or bound laborer; he shall serve with you only until the Jubilee year. Then he and his children with him shall be free of your authority. He shall go back to his family and return to his ancestral holding, for they are My servants, whom I freed from the land of Egypt; they may not give themselves over into servitude.... For it is to Me that the Israelites are servants. They are My servants, whom I freed from the land of Egypt, I the Lord your God" (Lev. 25:39–42, 55).

It is interesting that the Hebrew slave is described in Deuteronomy as his master's brother. The Torah reads, "If a fellow Hebrew," and the term for "fellow" also means "brother." We previously encountered the metaphor of brotherhood in the verses about monarchy, in which the king is described as the citizens' brother: "Thus he will not act haughtily toward his fellows (brothers)" (Deut. 17:20). The metaphor of brotherhood is anti-hierarchical. We are all equal.

THE RETURN TO EGYPT

Moses warns the people that the plagues that struck Egypt may strike them, and when they do, the Israelites will find themselves in the same predicament as the Egyptians. In other words, Egypt is not just a thing of the past; it may become the future as well. It is not just the place we fled; it is also the place to which we are liable to return.

The aversion to Egypt is mentioned twice in Moses's address, first in the context of the prohibition on a future king acquiring too many horses: "Moreover, he shall not keep many horses or send people back to Egypt to add to his horses" (Deut. 17:16). It is mentioned again when Moses foretells that the people will become slaves: "The Lord will send you back to Egypt in galleys, by a route which I told you that you should not see again. There you shall offer yourselves for sale to your enemies as male and female slaves, but there will be no buyer" (Deut. 28:68). These two verses describe the return to Egypt, though this return is dependent on contradictory reasons. In the first verse, Moses describes a case in which the monarchy becomes too powerful, and in the second verse he describes the collapse of the monarchy altogether. Perhaps the Torah is saying that a person who seeks to rule like Egypt is liable to become a slave to Egypt instead.

The commandment to remember Egyptian bondage appears nine times in Deuteronomy[4] and four times in the rest of the Torah.[5] This commandment is almost always juxtaposed with the injunction to be sensitive to slaves, strangers, and anyone who is in a position of weakness: "You too must love the stranger, for you were strangers in the land

4. Deuteronomy 5:15; 6:12, 20–23; 7:18; 8:11–14; 15:15; 16:3, 12; 24:18, 22.
5. Exodus 13:3–16; Leviticus 19:34, 23:43; Numbers 15:40–43.

of Egypt" (Deut. 10:19). This verse actually contains two charges: First, do not be like Egypt; and second, be like the God who liberated from Egypt. The ideal of resembling God rather than the Egyptian overlords transforms the memory of bondage and liberation into a cornerstone of the Torah's message about power.

SHABBAT AND THE IDEAL OF LIBERATION

The Ten Commandments appear twice in the Torah. First, on the day they are given at Horeb, and second, on the day that Moses reviews them on the steppes of Moab. But Moses's review of the commandments is not an exact repetition.[6] The most significant difference between the two versions appears in the fourth commandment, which deals with Shabbat observance. This is how the commandment appears in Exodus:

> Remember the Shabbat day and keep it holy. Six days you shall labor and do all your work, but the seventh day is a Shabbat of the Lord your God: you shall not do any work – you, your son or daughter, your male or female slave, or your cattle, or the stranger who is within your settlements. (Ex. 20:8–10)

The first week of creation was God's week. He created for the first six days and rested on the seventh. In Exodus, God's week heralds humanity's week. Humanity is commanded to live a creative and productive life six days a week, and to rest on the seventh day – just like God. But this is not how Moses presents this commandment in Deuteronomy. When he reiterates the fourth commandment, he speaks of a very different kind of Shabbat.

> Observe the Shabbat day and keep it holy, as the Lord your God has commanded you. Six days you shall labor and do all your work, but the seventh day is a Shabbat of the Lord your God. You shall not do any work – you, your son or your daughter, your male

6. For a detailed comparison of the two versions, see Moshe Weinfeld, *The Ten Commandments and the Recitation of the Shema: The Evolution of Declarations of Faith* (Tel Aviv: HaKibbutz HaMeuchad, 5761).

> or female slave, your ox or your ass, or any of your cattle, or the stranger in your settlements, so that your male and female slave may rest as you do. Remember that you were a slave in the land of Egypt and the Lord your God freed you from there with a mighty hand and an outstretched arm. Therefore, the Lord your God has commanded you to observe the Shabbat day. (Deut. 5:12–15)

In Deuteronomy, the commandment of the Shabbat is incumbent upon the master, who is charged to free his slaves from all labor on that day so that they may rest as he does. In Exodus, the commandment was to rest; in Deuteronomy, the commandment includes the injunction to let others rest.[7] The Torah teaches that rest is not a privilege of status alone. All men and women are deserving of rest. Shabbat is the democratization of rest. On Shabbat, the social hierarchy collapses. Karl Marx maintained that a reshaping of the labor market would lead to equality among people. But in Deuteronomy, equality is to be found not in work, but in rest.

In Exodus, man recreates God's week of creation so as to resemble the Being at the top of the hierarchy, beyond the universe. In Deuteronomy, masters must let their slaves rest "so that your male and female slave may rest as you do." For six days people are permitted to rule over others, but one day a week all dominance is forbidden. And so more than Shabbat is a day without work, it is a day without domination.

In the Shabbat of Deuteronomy, too, man is compared to God, though not to a God who rests, but to a God who liberates: "Remember that you were a slave in the land of Egypt and the Lord your God freed you from there with a mighty hand and an outstretched arm; therefore the Lord your God has commanded you to observe the Shabbat day." People strive to transcend their human limitations by attaining power and control. But in Deuteronomy, man is compared to God not in his attainment of power, but in his renunciation of it.

In a previous chapter,[8] I focused on the strong influence of memory on personality. I discussed the injunction that a person in a

7. See Weinfeld, *Ten Commandments*, 68–69.
8. See chapter 5, "Protective Memory."

position of power must remember the period of his own powerlessness. The memory of enslavement and foreignness serves to counteract the psychological tendencies of a strong ruling power, and the commandment to observe Shabbat adds an important element that furthers this end. On account of Shabbat, a person in control of others is commanded not just to remember what it is like to be powerless but also to experience on a weekly basis a world without hierarchy. Power is corrupting because it causes a person to forget who he is. The commandment to remember periods of powerlessness and the commandment to observe Shabbat serve to stabilize people by reminding them who they really are. They strip themselves of all the power in which they have cloaked themselves and recognize their bare selves.

What can we learn from the Exodus from Egypt? According to Deuteronomy, the lesson that we are meant to glean from the Exodus is that we must aspire to resemble the God who took our people out of Egypt. Just as God liberated, we must free the Hebrew slave during the Sabbatical year; for one day each week, we must free all of those who work for us.

THE NEW SOCIAL FOCUS

The book of Leviticus instructs in the laws of various kinds of sacrifices. The Torah never explains the deep meaning of sacrifice, but the root word "*korban*," the Hebrew term for sacrifice, means closeness, suggesting perhaps that sacrifice brings the individual closer to God. The human act of renouncing and sacrificing a possession can bring a sense of intimacy with God. Deuteronomy proposes an alternative to this religious reality. According to Deuteronomy, sacrifices may be offered only in one place, and God does not even dwell in that place.[9] The book also omits many of the sacrifices described earlier in the Torah.

There is a third aspect of Moses's address: an emphasis on social consciousness.

9. There is also no mention in Deuteronomy of the showbread, the pleasant smell of the sacrifices, the Menora, or the libation vessels. See chapter 1, notes 38–39. Also see Weinfeld, *Deuteronomic School*, 191–224.

One of the ways to classify the various kinds of sacrifice is according to who eats them. The burnt offering, for instance, is not eaten at all; it is entirely burnt on the altar. The sin and guilt offerings, which are brought as atonement for sins, are partially eaten by the priests and partially burned on the altar. The eating of the sacrifice is crucial; if the priests fail to eat their part, then atonement is not achieved. When it comes to the peace offering, the circle widens further: It is not just the altar and the priests who consume these offerings, but the people bringing them as well. And it is specifically this type of sacrifice that Moses emphasizes in his final address.[10] The book of Deuteronomy makes marginal reference to those sacrifices that do not have a social component, but the sacrifices that Moses mentions in the greatest detail are those in which the people participate. Moreover, Moses stresses that the stranger, orphan, and widow must be included when the sacrificial meat is distributed.

> There you are to bring your burnt offerings and other sacrifices, your tithes and contributions, your votive and freewill offerings, and the firstlings of your herds and flocks. Together with your households, you shall feast there before the Lord your God, happy in all the undertakings in which the Lord your God has blessed you.... And you shall rejoice before the Lord your God with your sons and daughters and with your male and female slaves, along with the Levite in your settlements, for he has no territorial allotment among you. (Deut. 12:5–12)

The text nearly omits the sin and guilt offerings entirely, but it expounds at length on those sacrifices which may be shared with the weak. The Torah even repeats this commandment, though this repetition seems almost superfluous.[11]

---

10. See Weinfeld, *Deuteronomic School*, 211–212.
11. On the doubling of various sections of chapter 12, see Rofé, *Intro. to Deuteronomy*, 10–18. Also see Simeon Chavel, "The Literary Development of Deuteronomy 12: Between Religious Ideal and Social Reality," in *The Pentateuch*, ed. Thomas B. Dozeman, Konrad Shmid, and Baruch J. Schwartz (Tubingen, Germany: Mohr Siebeck, 2011), 303–326.

> You may not partake in your settlements of the tithes of your new grain or wine or oil, or of the firstlings of your herds and flocks, or of any of the votive offerings that you vow, or of your freewill offerings, or of your contributions. These you must consume before the Lord your God in the place that the Lord your God will choose – you and your sons and your daughters, your male and female slaves, and the Levite in your settlements – happy before the Lord your God in all your undertakings. Be sure not to neglect the Levite as long as you live in your land. (Deut. 12:17–19)

According to Deuteronomy, God does not dwell in the Temple and the sacrifices have only limited metaphysical significance. Nowhere in Deuteronomy is God described as receiving the sacrifices. Instead, Moses focuses on the social aspect of sacrifice. The absence of God from the Temple transforms the pilgrimage festivals. More than a time of encounter with God, they are a time in which the people congregate,[12] including the weakest members of society.[13]

> Then you shall observe the Feast of Shavuot for the Lord your God, offering your freewill contribution according as the Lord your God has blessed you. You shall rejoice before the Lord your God with your son and daughter, your male and female slave, the Levite in your communities, and the stranger, the fatherless, and the widow in your midst, at the place where the Lord your God will choose to establish His name. Bear in mind

12. The book of Deuteronomy also has echoes of the idea that the festivals are a time of communion with God. For instance, "When all Israel comes to appear before the Lord your God in the place that He will choose" (Deut. 31:11). And so perhaps we should say that Deuteronomy shifts the emphasis when it comes to festival observance, rather than offering a new understanding of the festivals.
13. I take issue with the claim that there is an absence of religious significance. There is religious significance that is not magical but educational: "So that you may learn to revere the Lord your God forever" (Deut. 14:23). That is, it is not just the weak members of society who are impacted; all those who bring the sacrifices may find their religious consciousness affected. See Rashbam's commentary on Deuteronomy 14:23.

> that you were slaves in Egypt and take care to obey these laws. (Deut. 16:10–12)

Deuteronomy offers a novel interpretation of Shavuot, as is revealed by a comparison to the description of the holiday in Leviticus. In Leviticus, following the counting of seven weeks, the commandment is to bring "an offering of new grain to the Lord. You shall bring from your settlements two loaves of bread as an elevation offering; each shall be made of two-tenths of a measure of choice flour, baked after leavening, as first fruits to the Lord" (Lev. 23:16–17). In Deuteronomy, at the end of seven weeks of counting the Omer, the commandment is to "rejoice before the Lord your God with your son and daughter, your male and female slave, the Levite in your communities" (Deut. 16:11). The offering of new grain and the elevation offering are not mentioned at all.[14]

Sukkot, too, becomes a holiday with communal significance in Deuteronomy.

> After the ingathering from your threshing floor and your vat, you shall hold the Feast of Sukkot for seven days. You shall rejoice in your festival, with your son and daughter, your male and female slave, the Levite, the stranger, the fatherless, and the widow in your communities. You shall hold a festival for the Lord your God seven days, in the place that the Lord will choose; for the Lord your God will bless all your crops and all your undertakings, and you shall have nothing but joy. (Deut. 16:13–15)

Here, the holy place is less of a site for encountering the divine and more of a site for encountering other people, especially the weak and the needy. Shabbat, too, is not just a time of imitating God's creativity and rest, but also a time of desisting from dominance. And so it

14. For an expansion of this comparison, see Kaufmann, *The Religion of Israel, from Its Beginnings to the Babylonian Exile* (Chicago: University of Chicago Press, 1960), 119–126.

is not just the holy place that takes on new meaning, but holy time as well. These new interpretations of central commandments reflect Deuteronomy's social bent.

The moral reconceptualization of Shabbat and of the Tabernacle paves the way to understanding a revolutionary theological process: the moral reconceptualization of God. The shift in emphasis from ritual to religion springs from a new understanding of God.

RESEMBLING GOD

There is a violent, intolerant side to the book of Deuteronomy. But in order to understand it properly, we first need to consider the book's tolerant and sensitive aspects, which inspired the leading scholar of Deuteronomy, Moshe Weinfeld, to call it "the humanist book of the Bible."

> Behold, the heavens to their uttermost reaches belong to the Lord your God, the earth and all that is on it! Yet it was to your fathers that the Lord was drawn in His love for them, so that He chose you, their lineal descendants, from among all peoples – as is now the case. (Deut. 10:14–15)

God rules over three levels of reality: the heavens, their uttermost reaches, and the earth. Everything is His, and yet He chose only Israel to love. This is one of the paradoxes of the Bible. The book of Deuteronomy makes it clear that God's choice of Israel does not signify that He is the God of Israel alone. He is a universal God who, paradoxically, chose just one nation. And the one nation that the God of all nations chose is commanded to emulate the universal God.

> And now, O Israel, what does the Lord your God demand of you? Only this: to revere the Lord your God, to walk only in His paths, to love Him, and to serve the Lord your God with all your heart and soul, keeping the Lord's commandments and laws, which I enjoin upon you today, for your good.... Cut away, therefore, the thickening about your hearts and stiffen your necks no more. For the Lord your God is God supreme and Lord supreme, the great,

> the mighty, and the awesome God, who shows no favor and takes no bribe, but upholds the cause of the fatherless and the widow, and befriends the stranger, providing him with food and clothing. (Deut. 10:12–13, 16–18)

How does one imitate the universal God? By being more universal. This is the significance of the commandment to love the stranger. A person must love even those who are not part of his or her national community.

There are real paradoxes inherent in these verses. Immediately after God is described as having chosen Israel from all the other nations, we are told that He does not show favor or take bribes. In the Torah, "showing favor" is a legal term referring to privileging one person over another in a courtroom situation. It is forbidden to allow feelings of closeness to sway one's objective judgment. God, according to the Torah, does not show favor. The Torah relates this injunction immediately after establishing that God's love is bestowed on Israel. This appears to be a contradiction. Does God treat Israel specially, or does God treat all people equally and fairly? Furthermore, the Torah goes on to assert that God is primarily sensitive not to His chosen people, but to the widow, orphan, and stranger. How then are we to understand the verses cited above?

In the book of Deuteronomy, God seems to be a distant God who did not come down to Sinai and never dwelled in the Tabernacle. He has no body and He cannot be represented, and therefore He can never be physically present. These are the theological principles that we focused on in previous chapters. But even though God cannot be visually represented, in these verses, Moses describes some of His attributes as being like human characteristics. God has no physical form, but He has feelings of love, concern, and compassion, and these feelings are incumbent upon human beings as well. For instance, the commandment to love the stranger stems not just from the memory of being strangers in Egypt, but also from the notion that God loves the stranger. Immediately after God is described as one who loves the stranger, there is the charge to love the stranger as well. Loving the stranger is thus a way of resembling God.

Exodus also describes God's attributes: "A God compassionate and gracious, slow to anger, abounding in kindness and faithfulness" (Ex. 34:6). The Sages explained that God is described as a moral being in order to teach a lesson. God is moral, and thus man must be moral: "Just as God is called compassionate and gracious, so should you be compassionate and gracious and give freely to all."[15] But these are the words of the rabbis. The book of Exodus itself does not present God as a role model. His attributes are described, but the commandment to imitate Him is never explicitly stated. In Deuteronomy, though, this charge is rendered clearly. Slaves must be freed from work on Shabbat because God freed Israel from Egypt, and human beings must love the stranger because God loves the stranger.[16] In order to draw closer to God, one must draw closer to other people. In order to be divine, one must be moral.

The book of Deuteronomy forbids any representation of God. But Deuteronomy offers another way to make God manifest, namely by adopting moral qualities that resemble the divine attributes. God resides in the heavens, but human beings can bring God down to earth – not by means of ritual, but by means of moral conduct. The distance between God and man cannot be bridged by means of religious ritual, but it can be bridged by means of social action. Social action is therefore a religious activity.

The turn toward social consciousness in the book of Deuteronomy is initiated by Moses, the greatest of all prophets. But this outlook will be further developed by several of Moses's spiritual heirs, the prophets of Israel.[17] For instance, Isaiah linked righteousness and holiness: "And the Lord of hosts is exalted by judgment, the Holy God proved holy by

15. *Sifrei, Parashat Ekev,* section 49.
16. Compare to Leviticus 19:33–34: "When a stranger resides with you in your land, you shall not wrong him. The stranger who resides with you shall be to you as one of your citizens; you shall love him as yourself, for you were strangers in the land of Egypt: I the Lord am your God." Here the commandment to love the stranger is described as a form of human sympathy, whereas in Deuteronomy it is described as a way of imitating God's compassion.
17. On the social role of the prophet, see Alexander Rofé, *Intro. to Biblical Literature,* 280–284.

righteousness" (5:16). For the prophets, righteousness becomes the new ritual. God is sanctified not by means of sacred rites, but by means of righteous acts. There is a notion that religion differs from ethics because religion deals with the relationship between man and God, whereas ethics deals with the relationship between fellow men. But Moses and the prophets of Israel repudiate this dichotomy, instead integrating religion and ethics.[18]

18. In addition to the new moral-social exegesis on the commandments that we find in Deuteronomy, we also find an amplification of the moral dimensions of these commandments, as the following examples attest. According to Exodus, Hebrew slaves must be freed after six years of servitude (Ex. 21:2–11). In addition to manumission, Deuteronomy commands the giving of gifts to the freed slave (Deut. 15:12–18). In Exodus, there is a commandment not to deceive the stranger (Ex. 22:20–23; 23:9). Deuteronomy adds the commandment to love the stranger (Deut. 10:19). In Exodus, there is a commandment to return a pledge to a lender (Ex. 22:25–26). In Deuteronomy, we find the additional prohibition against entering his home (Deut. 24:11).

Chapter 8

Moses's Three Concerns

Moses worries that his revolutions won't occur, that the one God will not remain the people's only God, and that the people will breach the covenant soon after they enter the land.[1]

Moses expresses his fears in three reflections that recur throughout his address:

1. What will happen when their prophet disappears? Moses has been the intermediary between God and the people, and now he worries that the Torah will not survive his death. He learned from the sin of the Golden Calf that when he disappeared for a brief time, the covenant was abrogated. Now he wonders if the people will continue to serve only God even after he, Moses, disappears forever.[2]

---

1. The idea that the Torah's laws are rules of conduct for life in the Land of Israel pervades the book of Deuteronomy. See, for instance, "And this is the instruction – the laws and the rules – that the Lord your God has commanded [me] to impart to you, to be observed in the land that you are about to cross into and occupy" (Deut. 6:1).
2. See the beginning of part one of this book.

2. What will happen when the period of isolation is over? Will the people keep serving God even after the transition from the wilderness to the land of Canaan, with all its cultural seductions? The Torah was given in the wilderness, and as Moses sees it, the wilderness has a great advantage: It is isolated and hence free of competing cultural influences from the outside world. Moses is not sure that the people's spiritual consciousness will survive the transition from the wilderness to Canaan.
3. Will power corrupt the people? Will the people's morality be impacted by the transition from a position of weakness to one of power? I have discussed this question at length, so I will now turn to the first two questions, beginning with Moses's most elemental fear: Will the covenant have a life after his own death?

TORAH WITHOUT INTERMEDIARIES

Moses's fear reflects the major challenge confronting the people: to fashion a religion that is not dependent on intermediaries. In part one of this book, we saw how Moses demands that the people ratify the covenant with God after he is gone. Following Moses's death and the entry into the land, the people are commanded to hold a ratification ceremony in the expanse between Mount Gerizim and Mount Ebal. This ceremony is the essence of what Deuteronomy seeks to accomplish, namely to reduce the dependence on intermediaries between humans and God. The book of Deuteronomy makes no mention of angels. Angels intercede in Genesis, Exodus, and Numbers, but not in Deuteronomy. We read in the book of Numbers:

> The Egyptians dealt harshly with us and our ancestors. We cried to the Lord and He heard our plea, and He sent an angel who freed us from Egypt. (Num. 20:15–16)

But when this story is repeated in Deuteronomy, the account is somewhat different:

> The Egyptians dealt harshly with us and oppressed us; they imposed heavy labor upon us. We cried to the Lord, the God of

> our fathers, and the Lord heard our plea and saw our plight, our misery, and our oppression. The Lord freed us from Egypt by a mighty hand, by an outstretched arm and awesome power, and by signs and portents. (Deut. 26:6–8)

In the version in Deuteronomy, the intermediary has been eliminated. God took the Israelites out of Egypt not by means of an angel, but with His outstretched arm. Moreover, it is not just the role of any intercessors that is eliminated in Deuteronomy, but also, in large part, the role of human agents.

Three figures are described as mediating between God and the people in the Bible: the king, the priest, and the prophet.

The King

The book of Deuteronomy strips the king of all of his religious functions. In the pagan world, the king was also the priest.[3] He was not only a political ruler but a religious presence as well. In Deuteronomy, the king is devoid of sanctity. He has no role in the cult, nor does he represent the people before God.

The Priest

The status of the priests as representatives of God is also downplayed in Deuteronomy. Deuteronomy reduces the significance of sacrifice and Temple worship, therefore also diminishing the status of those who bring sacrifices and serve in the Temple.[4] By contrast, in Leviticus, the priests

3. Part of the role of ancient Near Eastern kings was to lead the religious cult and to serve as high priest. See Liver, "King, Kingship," 1080–1085. Also see note 10 in chapter 2, above.
4. The diminished status of the priests is reflected in their proceeds. According to Leviticus, the tithes are "holy unto God" (Lev. 27:30) or given to the Levites (Num. 18:21–32). If the tither wishes to redeem his tithe with money, he must add a fifth of its value for *teruma*, which is given to the priests (Lev. 27:31). By contrast, the book of Deuteronomy teaches that the tithers eat their annual tithes in the Temple, alongside the Levite, who has no hereditary portion (Deut. 14:22–27). There is another tithe every three years which is eaten "at the gates," that is, wherever the farmers live. This replaces the second tithe and is designated for the local Levites, strangers, widows, and orphans. Moreover, the priests receive less of the sacrificial

carry out atonement ceremonies for the people, administering the sin and guilt offerings. Throughout Leviticus, we repeatedly find the phrase "The priest shall make expiation for him." Somewhat mysteriously, the priests are part of the atonement process.

Deuteronomy, however, makes no mention of these sacrifices. The only expiation ceremony mentioned in Deuteronomy – a ceremony that is not mentioned in the previous four books of the Bible – involves breaking a heifer's neck after a murdered body is discovered and the perpetrator is unknown. The priests and the elders of the town participate in this ceremony. Weinfeld has convincingly shown that it is the elders and not the priests who bring about expiation for the murder.[5]

> Then all the elders of the town nearest to the corpse shall wash their hands over the heifer whose neck was broken in the wadi. And they shall make this declaration: "Our hands did not shed this blood, nor did our eyes see it done. Absolve, O Lord, Your people Israel whom You redeemed, and do not let guilt for the blood of the innocent remain among Your people Israel." And they will be absolved of bloodguilt. Thus you will remove from your midst guilt for the blood of the innocent, for you will be doing what is right in the sight of the Lord. (Deut. 21:6–9)

The elders pray to God for atonement for the people, without intercession by the priests. Although the priests are present and the elders must wash their own hands in front of them, expiation is achieved by means of prayer, which is offered by the elders and not the priests.

In Deuteronomy, the priests are not intermediaries between God and the people, and there is no indication that they are any closer to God. The book blurs the line between the nation and the priests because

---

meat in Deuteronomy. They are given the inferior cuts, namely the shoulder, cheeks, and stomach. By contrast, Leviticus mandates that the priest be given the breast and the right thigh (Lev. 7:28–34; Num. 18:18). Also compare Numbers 18:17–18, which stipulates that the firstborns are gifted to the priest, with Deuteronomy 15:19–20, which states that firstborns belong to their masters. See Rashi's somewhat forced attempt to resolve this contradiction in his commentary on Deuteronomy 15:20.

5. See Weinfeld, *Deuteronomic School*, 199, 210–212.

prohibitions that apply just to the priests in the book of Leviticus apply to the entire nation in the book of Deuteronomy. Thus the sons of Aaron are commanded in Leviticus, "They shall not shave smooth any part of their heads, or cut the side growth of their beards, or make gashes in their flesh. They shall be holy to their God" (Lev. 21:5–6). The fact that this prohibition is addressed to the sons of Aaron suggests that it applies only to the priests. In Leviticus, the eating of an animal that has died of natural causes is also forbidden only to the priests,[6] but that is not the case according to Deuteronomy. The prohibitions are the same, but in Deuteronomy, they apply to all of Israel: "You are children of the Lord your God. You shall not gash yourselves or shave the front of your heads because of the dead, for you are a people consecrated to the Lord your God" (Deut. 14:1–2). This is true, too, of the prohibition against eating animals that died of natural causes: "You shall not eat anything that has died a natural death; give it to the stranger in your community to eat, or you may sell it to a foreigner. For you are a people consecrated to the Lord your God" (Deut. 14:21). The sanctity of the priests in Leviticus is thus extended to the entire nation in Deuteronomy,[7] blurring the social hierarchies.[8]

---

6. See Leviticus 22:1–2, 8: "The Lord spoke to Moses, saying: Instruct Aaron and his sons to be scrupulous about the sacred donations that the Israelite people consecrate to Me, lest they profane My holy name, Mine the Lord's.... He shall not eat anything that died naturally or was torn by beasts, thereby becoming unclean; I am the Lord." According to the book of Leviticus, animals that died naturally are prohibited to the priests but permitted to the people: "And the swine – although it has true hoofs, with the hoofs cleft through, it does not chew the cud; it is unclean for you. You shall not eat of their flesh or touch their carcasses. They are unclean for you" (Lev. 11:7–8). That is, if the meat of the animal is not forbidden, then it may be eaten regardless of how it died, even though the one who eats such an animal is rendered impure until nightfall: "If an animal that you may eat has died, anyone who touches its carcass shall be unclean until evening, anyone who eats of its carcass shall wash his clothes and remain unclean until evening, and anyone who carries its carcass shall wash his clothes and remain unclean until evening" (Lev. 11:39–40).
7. Full a full analysis, see Amnon Bezek, *Until this Day*, 129.
8. Although the priests have lost their role as mediators between the people and God, they receive other roles in Deuteronomy, such as priests and judges. See Deuteronomy 17:9, 18; 19:17; 21:5; 24:8; and 27:9.

In brief: Deuteronomy strips the world of angelic presences, rids the kings of their religious functions, and deprives the priests of their role as intermediaries between God and the people. But the attack on the notion that God has intercessors does not end here. It continues with the description of God's relationship with the final candidate for the role of His representative, namely the prophet.

The Prophet

Moses informs the people that in the future, prophets will rise from their ranks who will transmit the word of God. But they should regard these prophets with suspicion:

> If there appears among you a prophet or a dream-diviner and he gives you a sign or a portent, saying, "Let us follow and worship another god" – whom you have not experienced – even if the sign or portent that he named to you comes true, do not heed the words of that prophet or that dream-diviner. For the Lord your God is testing you to see whether you really love the Lord your God with all your heart and soul. Follow none but the Lord your God and revere none but Him. Observe His commandments alone and heed only His orders. Worship none but Him and hold fast to Him. As for that prophet or dream-diviner, he shall be put to death, for he urged disloyalty to the Lord your God – who freed you from the land of Egypt and who redeemed you from the house of bondage – to make you stray from the path that the Lord your God commanded you to follow. Thus you will sweep out evil from your midst. (Deut. 13:2–6)

The first commandment governing the relationship between the people and the person who is so bold as to prophesy is not to heed and obey him, but to regard him with caution. In his discussion of false prophets, Moses instills a deep suspicion in the consciousness of his listeners.

The commandment to obey the prophet appears only five chapters later:

> I will raise up a prophet for them from among their own people, like yourself. I will put My words in his mouth and he will speak to them all that I command him, and if anybody fails to heed the words he speaks in My name, I Myself will call him to account. But any prophet who presumes to speak in My name an oracle that I did not command him to utter, or who speaks in the name of other gods – that prophet shall die. (Deut. 18:18–20)

What happens when a true prophet arises and a particular citizen fails to obey him? Moses responds in the name of God, "I Myself will call him to account." In other words, the people do not have the authority to punish anyone who fails to obey the prophets. This punishment must be left to God. And so while God commands the people to kill a false prophet, they are not authorized to harm anyone who fails to listen to a true prophet. This is a striking asymmetry. A false prophet is killed, but a person who fails to listen to a true prophet is not subject to reproach. Moses's laws do not protect the false prophet, but they do protect from social or political sanction any person who fails to obey the true prophet.

The priest has no religious status, the priest's role is limited, and the prophet is under threat. And why? Because God communicates His will directly to His people, who are in any case very close to Him.

> Surely, this commandment which I enjoin upon you this day is not too baffling for you, nor is it beyond reach. It is not in the heavens, that you should say, "Who among us can go up to the heavens and get it for us and impart it to us, that we may observe it?" Neither is it beyond the sea, that you should say, "Who among us can cross to the other side of the sea and get it for us and impart it to us, that we may observe it?" No, the thing is very close to you, in your mouth and in your heart, to observe it. (Deut. 30:11–14)

God may be in the heavens, but His Torah is here on earth. Moreover, it is very accessible. There is no need for intermediaries. There is no need for anyone to cross the sea, ascend to the heavens, or bring God's word to man. These verses encapsulate one of the key messages of Deuteronomy: a person stands directly before God, without intermediaries. The phrase "the Lord your God" appears 234 times throughout the book. Moses's address, in addition to attacking and attenuating all intercessors, declares to man that God is his direct God and that God's Torah is accessible to everyone, "in your mouth and in your heart."

Moses is concerned about the challenge facing the people. He worries that his own disappearance will lead to the abrogation of the covenant.[9] But perhaps his disappearance is actually *part* of the covenant, which is meant to be a covenant without intercessors.

ISRAEL AND THE OTHER NATIONS

Of the three threats that endanger the people's loyalty to the covenant – the death of Moses, the lure of paganism, and the attainment of power – it is the lure of paganism that brings out the most violent streak in Deuteronomy. The Israelites who enter the land are commanded to destroy the local Canaanite cult, leaving no trace: "This is what you shall do to them: you shall tear down their altars, smash their pillars, cut down their sacred posts, and consign their images to the fire" (Deut. 7:5). And it is not just the Canaanite cult that must be eradicated, but also the Canaanites themselves. "In the towns of the latter peoples, however, which the Lord your God is giving you as a heritage, you shall not let a soul remain alive. No, you must proscribe them – the Hittites and the Amorites, the Canaanites and the Perizzites, the Hivites and the Jebusites – as the Lord your God has commanded you" (Deut. 20:16–17). This commandment appears more clearly and forcefully in Deuteronomy than in any of the preceding books of the Bible.[10]

---

9. See the beginning of part one of this book.
10. Compare to Exodus 23:20–23 and 34:11–16, where the Israelites are commanded to expel the Canaanites from the land. In Numbers 23:50–56, they are commanded to dispossess all the inhabitants of the land. But there are those who interpret the Hebrew word for "dispossess" as referring not to dispossession per se, but to destruction. See, for instance, the Behor Shor on this verse, as well as Ibn Ezra on Genesis 45:11 and Joshua 8:7. In Exodus, there is no commandment to destroy the Canaanites, but there is a description of this eventuality: "When My angel goes before you and brings you to the Amorites, the Hittites, the Perizzites, the Canaanites, the Hivites, and the Jebusites, and I annihilate them" (Ex. 23:23). The references in Deuteronomy are far harsher and more pronounced.

What is the source of this outburst of violence against non-Jews? It comes as a surprise, particularly because other verses in Deuteronomy display a very tolerant attitude. For instance, when the Israelites cross over into Esau's territory, God commands Moses to make sure that the people do not harm Esau's descendants.

> And charge the people as follows: You will be passing through the territory of your kinsmen, the descendants of Esau, who live in Seir. Though they will be afraid of you, be very careful not to provoke them. For I will not give you of their land so much as a foot can tread on; I have given the hill country of Seir as a possession to Esau. (Deut. 2:4–5)

God does not just protect the Israelites from other nations; He also protects other nations from Israel. Here is what God commands with regard to Lot's descendants:

> We then moved on, away from our kinsmen, the descendants of Esau, who live in Seir, away from the road of the Arabah, away from Elath and Ezion-geber, and we marched on in the direction of the wilderness of Moab. And the Lord said to me: Do not harass the Moabites or provoke them to war. For I will not give you any of their land as a possession; I have assigned Ar to the descendants of Lot as a possession. (Deut. 2:8–9)

As discussed earlier, the book of Deuteronomy occasionally contains digressions that read like parenthetical notes, and this is another of them. It describes the history of Esau's descendants and the struggles that led them to inherit their land. One interesting aspect of this note is the comparison the Torah draws between the history of Lot's descendants, known as the Moabites, and the national history of the Hebrews.

> It was formerly inhabited by the Emim, a people great and numerous, and as tall as the Anakites. Like the Anakites, they are counted as Rephaites, but the Moabites call them Emim. Similarly, Seir was formerly inhabited by the Horites, but the descendants

> of Esau dispossessed them, wiping them out and settling in their place, just as Israel did in the land they were to possess, which the Lord had given to them. (Deut. 2:10–12)

Although the Hebrews were taken out of Egypt by God and are destined to receive their land from Him, their story is not without parallel. There are other nations with similar histories.[11] God is not just the God of the Hebrews, but of all the nations, including those that do not worship Him. And why don't they? Moses has a surprising response. They worship the heavenly bodies because this is God's will.

> And when you look up to the sky and behold the sun and the moon and the stars, the whole heavenly host, you must not be lured into bowing down to them or serving them. These the Lord your God allotted to other peoples everywhere under heaven. (Deut. 4:19)

God created the luminaries – the sun, the moon, and the stars – in order to illuminate the world. But they do not just illuminate the world; they are also visible to human eyes. And thus the stars have tremendous magic, and it is hard not to succumb to the temptation to worship them. God permits the other nations to do so. It is only the Israelites who may not.[12]

FROM FEAR TO VIOLENCE

Since Deuteronomy is tolerant of the surrounding nations and their beliefs, how can we account for the outburst of violence against the Canaanites?

---

11. This motif is developed in the prophecy of Amos: "'To me, O Israelites, you are just like Ethiopians,' declares the Lord. 'True, I brought Israel up from the land of Egypt, but also the Philistines from Camphor and the Arameans from Kir'" (Amos 9:7).

12. According to an alternative explanation, the stars have a divine quality, and God gave them to the other nations. See Israel Knohl, *Biblical Beliefs: The Borders of the Biblical Revolution* [Hebrew] (Jerusalem: Magnes, 2007), 87–88; Knohl, "The Bible's Attitude Toward the Gods of Other Nations" [Hebrew], *Tarbiz* 64 (5754): 5–12; Alexander Rofé, *The Belief in Angels During the First Temple Period in Israel: In Light of the Biblical Tradition* (Jerusalem: 5729), 89–90.

The answer may be related to the connection between fear and violence. The fear of pagan influence is a catalyst for the violent treatment of these nations. The fear is that the people will enter the land and ultimately come to resemble the Canaanites. This fear stems from two sources: (a) the tremendous ambitiousness of the monotheistic vision and (b) a lack of faith in the people's spiritual ability to actualize this vision.

Moses knows that the monotheistic vision will be a daunting challenge to implement, especially in a pagan context. Monotheism does not just forbid the representation of God. It also suppresses God's intermediaries and drastically reduces the role of ritual in serving Him, while at the same time demanding total devotion to Him. How is it possible to devote oneself to a God who cannot be seen or represented?

Moses also knows that there is no real unity among the Israelites. They are human beings like everyone else. God chose them simply because He loved them, and love is irrational, arbitrary. "It is not because you are the most numerous of peoples that the Lord set His heart on you and chose you – indeed, you are the smallest of peoples. But it was because the Lord favored you and kept the oath He made to your fathers that the Lord freed you with a mighty hand and rescued you from the house of bondage, from the power of Pharaoh king of Egypt" (Deut. 7:7–8). This is the first time in the Torah that God's love for Israel is described. First we learn that God loves Israel. But Israel is chosen not because it is better than all people, but because of its commitment to an ancient covenant that God made with the people's forefathers.[13] They are committed to that covenant because they are loved.

This explanation is reiterated in Deuteronomy. It appears when Moses explains why God converted Balaam's curse into a blessing: "But the Lord your God refused to heed Balaam. Instead, the Lord your God turned the curse into a blessing for you, for the Lord your God loves you" (Deut. 23:6). It is because God loves the people, and not because

13. Ancestral merit is mentioned nearly thirty times in Moses's address: Deuteronomy 1:8, 35; 4:31, 37; 6:10, 18, 23; 7:8, 12–13; 8:1, 18; 9:5; 10:11, 15; 11:9, 21; 12:1; 13:18; 26:3, 15; 28:11; 29:12; 30:5, 20; 31:7, 20.

of any unique traits they possess.[14] This is a love without explanation or justification, an irrational love that survived the great national failures that Moses takes pains to recount: "Know, then, that it is not for any virtue of yours that the Lord your God is giving you this good land to possess, for you are a stiff-necked people" (Deut. 9:6).[15] God's love is not dependent on the beloved's characteristics. This is another important paradox that Deuteronomy proposes: God's love serves to highlight Israel's ordinariness.

The children of Israel are no different from other nations. And yet although they do not have any special nature, they are charged to create a special society. They must live by a religion and politics different from all other nations, even though they are, by nature, similar to all other peoples. How are they to succeed?

Moses does not believe in his people. He does not have faith that they will be able to enter Canaan and withstand the lure of the local cultures. Therefore, he charges the people to eliminate these cultures. They must engage in total warfare, "lest they lead you into doing all the abhorrent things that they have done for their gods and you stand guilty before the Lord your God" (Deut. 20:18). Moreover, the violence that the Torah commands is not just directed at other nations. It is also directed at any Jews who worship idols. Any "subversive city" must be destroyed (see Deut. 20:13–19), and anyone who worships idols must be killed, even if that worshipper is a member of Israel. The land of Canaan must be cleansed completely of paganism. Only then can an ordinary nation succeed in forging an extraordinary culture.

---

14. This love may also be understood as the faithfulness between the two parties in a covenant. See introduction, note 18, on ancient Near Eastern covenants. The phrase "treasured people," which appears three times in Moses's address (Deut. 7:6; 14:2; and 26:18), also seems to be derived from ancient Near Eastern treaties, where it is used to refer to the vassal state. The phrases "holy people" and "treasured people" are meant to attest to the exclusive covenant between God and Israel. For a discussion of the use of the word "treasured" in a letter dated from the thirteenth century BCE, written from the Hittite king to the Ugaritic king, see H. B. Huffmon and S. B. Parker, "A Further Note on the Treaty Background of Hebrew Yada," *BASOR* 184 (1966): 36–38. Also see Binyamin Oppenheimer, "The Semantics of *Segula*" [Hebrew], *Beit Mikra* 22:4 (Tamuz–Elul 5737): 431–437.
15. See also Deuteronomy 1:8; 4:20; 7:8; 10:15–16; 32:6, 18; 7:6; and 26:19.

The commandment to eliminate the inhabitants of the land is appalling to many modern readers, myself included. How are we to deal with the gulf between the dictates of the Torah and those of our conscience? There is no easy way out. This is not just a rift between ethical readers and an unethical text; it is a clash between two competing value systems. The Bible, which presents the values of its own time, is at odds with the modern values of many of its readers.

But the conflict between "then" and "now" only partially explains this rift. Because even in the text from "then," in Deuteronomy itself, we encounter a universalist moral sensibility. And so perhaps what is at play here is not just a conflict between an ancient text and modern readers, but a conflict within the ancient text itself. That is, there is not just a moral problem, but an underlying textual problem. How are we to reconcile the many expressions of universalist sensitivity in Deuteronomy[16] with the book's commandment to leave no soul alive from the seven Canaanite nations?

---

16. As we have discussed, the book of Deuteronomy seeks to cultivate sensitive human beings who renounce their control over weaker members of society, both within Israel and beyond. The text extends this sense of solidarity to those who are not members of the covenant. For instance, the temporary emancipation of slaves on Shabbat applies to the stranger as well as to the Hebrew. It is important to note that while the term used in Deuteronomy for stranger, "*ger*," also signifies "convert," that is not the connotation here. We know this from another verse in Deuteronomy: "You shall not eat any animal that has died a natural death. Give it to the stranger in your community to eat, or you may sell it to a foreigner. For you are a people consecrated to the Lord your God" (Deut. 14:21). That is, the Israelites are forbidden to eat such animals, but strangers (i.e., foreigners) may, because they are not obligated in the Torah's commandments. Even though the stranger is not part of Israel, the Torah mandates that he or she be treated with moral sensitivity. The Torah also reaches extraordinary ethical heights with regard to the law governing the treatment of fugitive slaves. According to the laws of the rest of the ancient world, such slaves must be returned to their masters, and one who harbors them is to be sentenced to death. The Torah changes the rules: "You shall not turn over to his master a slave who seeks refuge with you from his master. He shall live with you in any place he may choose among the settlements in your midst, wherever he pleases; you must not ill-treat him" (Deut. 23:16–17). In contrast to the dominant culture's punishment of anyone who harbors a slave, the Torah holds that it is a sin to extradite such a slave. This commandment follows on the heels of the laws of warfare, perhaps because it is so often the case that slaves take advantage of the chaos of war to flee to the enemy's territory.

The book of Deuteronomy envisions a religious revolution. It charges the people to engage in crushing violence so as to realize and defend this vision. Though it's not easy to admit, in this sense, Deuteronomy's revolution is similar to many other revolutions throughout history. Revolutions have a tendency to fly in the face of morality in order to establish a society that cultivates moral responsibility. Many great revolutions throughout history, which were outgrowths of moral ideas, involved very immoral acts.

INSTEAD OF A CONCLUSION: MORAL CONFUSION

The people are commanded to destroy all the local Canaanite cults – the statues, the altars, and the sacred posts. They must cleanse the land of idol worship, and of idol worshippers as well.

> When the Lord your God brings you to the land that you are about to enter and possess, and He dislodges many nations before you – the Hittites, Girgashites, Amorites, Canaanites, Perizzites, Hivites, and Jebusites, seven nations much larger than you – and the Lord your God delivers them to you and you defeat them, you must doom them to destruction: grant them no terms and give them no quarter. You shall not intermarry with them; do not give your daughters to their sons or take their daughters for your sons. For they will turn your children away from Me to worship other gods, and the Lord's anger will blaze forth against you and He will promptly wipe you out. Instead, this is what you shall do to them: you shall tear down their altars, smash their pillars, cut down their sacred posts, and consign their images to the fire. (Deut. 7:1–5)

> In the towns of the latter peoples, however, which the Lord your God is giving you as a heritage, you shall not let a soul remain alive. No, you must proscribe them – the Hittites and the Amorites, the Canaanites and the Perizzites, the Hivites and the Jebusites – as the Lord your God has commanded you.[17] (Deut. 20:16–17)

17. The commandment to wipe out the seven nations is paradoxically presented as part of a commandment to seek peace: "When you approach a town to attack it, you shall

The rabbis of the Talmud vitiated this commandment.[18] The Sages concluded that the Girgashites, Jebusites, Amorites and the other residents of Canaan have disappeared from the historical stage. The Assyrian king Sennacherib, who exiled the local nations, blotted out their identities. They no longer exist, and therefore there is no extant, viable commandment to wipe them out. But the circumvention of the commandment does not erase the verses, which remain part of the Torah. This is the eternal text of the Jewish people, a text that still inspires violence among an extreme minority, and which others read and shudder.

The commandment to obliterate the seven Canaanite nations is not the only commandment that gives rise to moral discomfort. The experience of reading the Bible involves an element of pain on account of the gulf between certain biblical verses and our consciences. How do we bridge the moral world of the reader and that of the Bible? There are many ways of answering this question, but for the time being, we can consider two familiar strategies: fundamentalism and anarchism.

---

offer it terms of peace. If it responds peaceably and lets you in, all the people present there shall serve you at forced labor" (Deut. 20:10–11). The underlying assumption is that it is forbidden to attack a city before first offering the enemy the option of surrendering. The classical commentators Rashi and Nahmanides debate whether the seven Canaanite nations are included in this injunction. According to Rashi, whose interpretation seems to be the plain meaning of the text, the offer of terms of peace does not apply to the Canaanites. "The Torah is speaking of a permissible [but not obligatory] war, as is explicit in the context of this section, 'Thus you will do to all the cities which are very far away from you' (Deut. 20:15)." By contrast, Nahmanides teaches that the offer of peace must be extended to the Canaanites as well: "But the call for peace applies even to obligatory war. It requires us to offer peace terms even to the seven nations [of Canaan], for Moses proclaimed peace to Sihon, king of the Amorites, and he would not have transgressed both the positive and negative commandments in this section, 'No, you must proscribe them' (20:17), and 'You shall not leave a soul alive' (20:16). Rather, the difference between them [i.e. obligatory and permissible wars] is when the enemy does not make peace and continues to make war. Then in the case of the 'cities which are very far off' (20:15), Scripture commanded us to 'put all its males to the sword' (20:13) and keep alive the women and male children, but in 'the cities of these peoples' (20:16) [i.e., the seven Canaanite nations, in the event they refuse the call to peace], it commanded us to destroy even the women and children." See *Ramban: Commentary on the Torah*, vol. 5, pp. 238– 239.

18. See Mishna Yadayim 4:4; Berakhot 28a.

1. *Fundamentalism*

The fundamentalist reading of the Bible is based on two beliefs: the belief in the total sanctity of the text, and the belief in the devaluation of the reader. When there is a conflict between the morals of the reader and the verses explicit in the Bible, the reader must submit to the verses. The fundamentalist reader is likely aware of his own moral conscience, but he prefers to quiet it. His own conscience and will are inconsequential. God's will, as reflected in the text, has absolute value. For such a reader, biblical verses do not conflict with the individual conscience. They replace it.

2. *Anarchism*

The response of the anarchist reader, who is an apologetic commentator on the text, is opposite to that of the fundamentalist. The anarchist reader bridges the moral gulf between his moral conscience and the Torah by a creative and sometimes ingenious reading of the text. He tries to show that the gulf only appears to exist. The text contains lofty values that are, incidentally, identical to her own.

This type of apologetic exegesis tends to be very spacious. It purifies lizards, rendering even the most unkosher animals suddenly kosher, and harmonizes moral contradictions. Unlike the fundamentalist reader, the anarchist reader does not allow the text to shape her conscience. Instead, she shapes the text to fit her conscience.

These two types of readers are united by their avoidance of conflict. They claim that the apparent tension between Torah and morality does not really exist. One type of reader maintains that any ostensible conflict stems from misguided morality, and the other type of reader maintains that any such conflict stems from misguided exegesis. And there is something else they both have in common: they both accept the total authority of the text, though one authority is literal and the other is figurative or metaphorical. Either the reader must fit the text or the text must fit the reader, but in either case harmonization is essential.

I'd like to propose that there is a third exegetical strategy, one that does not try to avoid tension but also does not dismiss the moral inconsistencies.

TO LIVE PERPLEXED

The perplexed reader is one who does not alienate himself from the text but also declines to compromise his moral values to accord with the text. The sanctity of Torah is important to him, but so is being true to his conscience. This person can endure the sometimes discomfiting paradox between conscience and creed.[19]

A few years ago, I celebrated Purim in a Jerusalem synagogue. Though I arrived late, I found one available seat, next to a well-known Jerusalem professor. I sat down and greeted the professor, "Happy holiday." He was quick to respond, "Purim is not a happy holiday. We are celebrating Jewish violence." The end of the Book of Esther describes an outburst of Jewish violence against the local populace. When he said the words "Jewish violence," his voice grew a bit louder, as if to compete with the din of the noisemakers all around us.

"But it was all in self-defense," I told him, in an attempt to defend the scroll's moral integrity. "The non-Jews were granted dispensation from King Ahasuerus to kill the Jews, and this dispensation was never revoked. Instead of being revoked, the king authorized the Jews to kill the non-Jews who rose up against them. If that's not self-defense, then I don't know what is."

The scholar questioned my moral reasoning. "I'll grant you that on the fourteenth of Adar, the Jews met violence with violence, but then they requested an additional day on which to massacre non-Jews. The king granted their request. And so there was another day of Jewish violence, one that is impossible to defend on moral grounds." As an apologetic reader, I might try to justify the second day, to say that this violence was also in self-defense, since it was also directed at those who sought to destroy the Jewish people. But I felt that such an argument would be in vain, since it was without any textual basis. And so I bit my tongue. I prayed quietly from my seat, embarrassed. At the conclusion of the Megilla reading, I hazarded to ask my seatmate one final question: Why

19. It is worth noting that the moral relativist has no issue here. Someone who believes that there are no absolute values but that values are subject to time and place can simply say that during biblical times it was customary to act a certain way, but that today such behavior is no longer appropriate. Such a person would not evaluate biblical values by our modern standards.

does he celebrate Purim in Jerusalem, where it is observed on the fifteenth rather than the fourteenth of Adar, thereby celebrating the violence that he himself cannot justify? After all, he could have opted to leave the city on the fourteenth of Adar and return after the holiday was over.

He looked at me and smiled. "If I did that, I wouldn't be able to sit in synagogue and suffer."

What are we to make of the additional day of Purim? Unlike apologetic readers, who will interpret the verses creatively so as to accord with their values, fundamentalist readers will simply argue that the text is right and one's moral qualms are subordinate.

But there are also those who sit in synagogue, read the text, and suffer. They are not prepared to forsake the text or to interpret it creatively, but they also don't want to compromise their values. These are the perplexed readers.

There is something surprising about this perplexity. Anyone who reads about the violence of the Hittites, Assyrians, or Romans and their wartime atrocities is not as likely to be unsettled. But when it is your own history, the response is more visceral. Perplexity comes of a sense of connection, and perhaps even of responsibility. Perplexed readers of the Bible are not those who turn their back on tradition. On the contrary, their response is highly moral, because it reflects their unwillingness to deny or disconnect from the past. Such an individual experiences the national past as if it is personal. The perplexed reader of the Bible is not learning history, but remembering it. History is something that happened to other people at another time; memory is what happened to us.

The fundamentalist and apologetic readers' desire for harmony is a desire to live in harmony with the tradition. But it may very well be that the experience of perplexity is the most traditional experience of all. Perplexed readers ascribe tremendous value to the holy text on the one hand, and to their morals and values on the other. Such readers do not reject the text, and the text does not reject them.

FROM THE PERPLEXED READER TO BIBLICAL PERPLEXITY

Question: How does a person dare to pit his or her own values against the holy text instead of surrendering to it? Answer: The source from which the individual draws inspiration not to submit to the Torah is the Torah itself.

The book of Amos opens with a prophecy of rebuke directed at the other nations of the ancient Near East.

> Thus said the Lord: "For three transgressions of Damascus, [even] for four, I will not revoke it, because they threshed Gilead with threshing boards of iron. I will send down fire upon the palace of Hazael, and it shall devour the fortresses of Ben-hadad. I will break the gate bars of Damascus and wipe out the inhabitants from the valley of Aven and the sceptered ruler of Beth-Eden, and the people of Aram shall be exiled to Kir," said the Lord. (Amos 1:3–5)

The sin of Aram-Damascus is its terrible violence during the war in Gilead. This is one of the first instances of what we now refer to as "war crimes." War is not an arena in which unbridled viciousness is permitted. War is an organized violent activity, but there are boundaries. The prophet continues to denounce the sins of various nations, all of which treat their enemies with gratuitous, excessive violence. The worst offenders are the Ammonites.

> Thus said the Lord: "For three transgressions of the Ammonites, [even] for four, I will not revoke it, because they ripped open the pregnant women of Gilead in order to enlarge their own territory. I will set fire to the wall of Rabbah, and it shall devour its fortresses, amid shouting on a day of battle, on a day of violent tempest. Their king and his officers shall go into exile together," said the Lord. (Amos 1:13–15)

The Ammonites savaged women and their unborn babies "in order to enlarge their own territory." Nations are capable of sinning. There are international crimes, and therefore there is also international law that to some extent regulates international relations. Morality is not just about a person's relationship to his community. A community also has moral obligations to other communities. Rabbi Abraham Joshua Heschel stressed that Amos's prophecy was the first time in which morality assumed the status of international law that was binding upon all nations of the world. As Heschel noted, universal moral law preceded all other official universal legislation.[20]

But there is a textual problem with the prophecy of Amos and all that it implies. If the Ammonites, Moabites, and Assyrians are charged with violating divine law, then they must be subject to it. Only if God commanded them with His laws can they be punishable for violating them. But when were they commanded? In his commentary on Genesis, Nahmanides answers that God punishes individuals for moral offenses even if they did not bear witness to Revelation,

> because violence is a sin that is known and widely publicized. Our rabbis have said (Sanhedrin 108a) that it was on account of the sin of violence that their fate was sealed. The reason for it is that the prohibition against violence is a rational commandment, there being no need for a prophet to admonish them against it.[21]

Prophecy is not a prerequisite for moral responsibility. This appears to be the lesson of the first crime in the Bible: Cain's murder of Abel. God condemned and punished Cain for his sin even though Cain

---

20. Abraham Joshua Heschel, *The Prophets* (New York: 1955), 38.
21. Nahmanides's commentary on Genesis 6:13, in *Ramban: Commentary on the Torah*, vol. 1, p. 109. Also see the commentary of the Rashbam (Rabbi Samuel ben Meir) on Genesis 26:5 and the commentary of Radak (Rabbi David Kimhi) on Psalms 107:11. On the naturalness and universality of morals, see Rabbi Yehuda HaLevi, *The Kuzari*, 2:48. The idea that biblical morality stems from human nature rather than revelation is developed extensively and compellingly by David Novak in his book *Natural Law in Judaism* (Cambridge University Press: 1998). The Netziv of Volozhin (Rabbi Naftali Zvi Yehuda Berlin) pointed to the natural morality – not dependent on revelation – that is found throughout the book of Genesis, and considered the possibility that a human being could misguidedly obey revelation while violating the natural moral order. This was the case with the Jews living during the Second Temple period, who were righteous and studied Torah but were not honest in their dealings with others (see Haamek Davar's introduction to the book of Genesis.) According to the Netziv, the Second Temple was destroyed not because the Jews violated the laws that God had revealed to them, but because they violated the divine will as it reveals itself in the human soul.

never received the commandment "Do not murder." One would think that without the revelation of a commandment, there can be no commandment; and if there is no commandment, there cannot be sin; and if there is no sin, there shouldn't be any punishment. But Cain sinned even though the commandment was never revealed to him, suggesting that when it comes to the foundations of morality, people are expected to know God's will intuitively.

Human conscience, then, is a site of revelation. This is why God decides to destroy Sodom and Gomorrah, whose inhabitants are immoral. It also explains the behavior of Abraham, who stands before God and criticizes Him directly: "Far be it from You to do such a thing, to bring death upon the innocent as well as the guilty, so that innocent and guilty fare alike. Far be it from You! Shall not the Judge of all the earth deal justly?" (Gen. 18:25). How does Abraham have the temerity to rebuke God? How can the Bible portray its hero as not just rebuking Israel, but as rebuking the God of Israel? Perhaps the answer is bound up in the reason that God shared with Abraham His intention to destroy Sodom in the first place: "For I have singled him out, that he may instruct his children and his posterity to keep the way of the Lord by doing what is just and right, in order that the Lord may bring about for Abraham what He has promised him" (Gen. 18:19). God tells Abraham of the imminent destruction of Sodom because Abraham is a just and righteous man. Justness and rightness are not expressions of human values. They are described as "the way of the Lord." When Abraham criticizes God with the words "Shall not the Judge of all the earth deal justly?" he is holding God to the standard of justice, a standard that is not human but divine.

Erich Fromm described Abraham's actions in Sodom as an example of radical humanism.[22] He argued that in Sodom, the individual stood before God and judged Him according to human values. The divine will was subjected to censure by the human conscience, and the hero elevated his conscience above the divine will. But it seems to me that Fromm erred. When Abraham stood before God on the eve of the destruction of Sodom, he did not pit his own values against the divine will. He rather

22. Erich Fromm, *You Shall Be As Gods* (New York: Holt, Rinehart and Winston, 1966).

pitted the divine voice within him against the divine voice outside him. He challenged the divine voice that had spoken to him from without by means of the divine voice that he experienced as his conscience. Sodom was the site of conflict between two different voices of God.

The magnificence of the Bible lies not just in its complexity, but also in its paradoxical inconsistencies. A person may at once heed and violate different expressions of the divine voice. The Torah intimates that one who silences the voice of conscience in order to heed the voice of Torah is actually being faithful to the Torah. After all, according to the Torah, God does not reveal Himself only through Torah, but to the human conscience as well. God speaks to man in two voices, through the text and the human conscience, and the perplexed reader is one who insists on submitting to neither of these voices. The perplexity that a person experiences in reading the Bible is a reflection of the Bible's perplexity. If we fail to experience this perplexity, then we are not apprehending the paradoxical spirit of the Bible.

Rabbi Abraham Isaac Kook wrote that the silencing of the conscience in the name of being God-fearing is not true fear of God:

> It is forbidden for fear of heaven to compromise one's natural morality, for then it would no longer be pure fear of heaven. The sign by which one can recognize pure fear of heaven is when the natural morality that is rooted in man's honest nature ascends by means of that fear of heaven to higher levels than it would have attained without it. But if there should be a fear of heaven, such that without its influence, life would tend to function better, and would actualize things beneficial to the individual and society, whereas with its influence, that actualizing power would diminish – such a fear of heaven is invalid.[23]

The conflict between commandment and conscience is not a conflict between the individual and the Bible, but an internal tension within

23. Rabbi Abraham Isaac Kook, *Orot HaKodesh*, part 3, introduction, section 11. Originally translated by Rabbi Bernard Caspar and Rabbi Reuven Ziegler in *Alei Etzion* 2 (5755).

the Bible. This tension is especially poignant in Deuteronomy. On the one hand, Deuteronomy is the epitome of biblical morality. It cultivates sensitivity to the weak, heightens our consciousness of the power of the strong, and shifts the spiritual emphasis from ritual to righteousness. On the other hand, it is also the most violent book in the Torah. How are we to reconcile the two? Perhaps no reconciliation is possible, or should be possible, because the perplexity that the reader experiences when encountering Deuteronomy is the perplexity of Deuteronomy itself.

Part Three

The Address That Entered the Land

Chapter 9

Introduction: The Address That Was Heard

It's been quite a few years since I delivered my first public lecture to a large audience. It was not easy. When I finished speaking, an older man came forward from the audience and approached me, sensing the frustration I was trying to conceal. He asked me what happened. I told him that based on the questions and reactions of the audience, it seemed they had misunderstood me. The man smiled in recognition. His response was cryptic. "Micah, don't you know that every lecture is in fact two different lectures?" When he saw that I didn't understand what he meant, he continued, "There is the lecture that you deliver before the audience, and then there is the lecture that the audience hears. Sometimes they are two different lectures entirely."

This book deals with Moses's two addresses: the address that he delivered, and the address that the people heard. The first two parts of the book focused on the former, and this last part will focus on the latter, that is, on how the ancient biblical nation of Israel – the nation of listeners – heard and assimilated Moses's address.

Moses's address featured two new and central ideas: the first is the de-emphasis on the Temple, and the second is the limitation on the power of the monarchy. These are both revolutionary ideas which grew out of the internalization of an even greater idea, namely the belief in one God. An emphasis on God's metaphysical greatness served to diminish the importance of Temple ritual and the trappings of kingship and to magnify the importance of morality and social consciousness.

Moses spoke to the people as they were poised to enter Canaan, so that their children would actualize these two ideas when they settled in the land. But did they assimilate Moses's address and realize his vision?

The continuation of Moses's story appears in the book of Joshua and concludes in the book of Kings. These books, which comprise the bulk of the historiographical sections of the Bible, describe the history of the people from the day they entered the land until the day they were expelled from it. The story does not end well. It begins with conquest and settlement, but it ends with expulsion and devastation.[1]

In the five books of Moses there are two preeminent stories that shape Jewish consciousness. The first is the story of Abraham, who heard a voice – the voice of God – and, in its wake, left his home and his homeland in Aram Naharaim (Mesopotamia) and went to the land of Canaan. The second is the story of the children of Israel, who raised their voices – voices of wailing heard by God – which led to the beginning of their journey from Egypt to Canaan. The Torah is the story of two exoduses, one from Mesopotamia and the other from Egypt. While the rest of the world was magnetically drawn to these great civilizations, the heroes of the Torah set their steps in the opposite direction.

The end of II Kings relates how King Zedekiah, the last king of Judah, abrogated his vassal treaty with the king of Babylon and rebelled against him. In response, the Babylonian king Nebuchadnezzar besieged Jerusalem, destroyed it, and exiled most of the inhabitants of

1. Biblical scholars claim that the fingerprints of the authors of Deuteronomy are evident throughout the historiographical books. It is no surprise, they say, that there is such a deep ideological affinity between the content of Moses's speech and the stories of the attempts to bring his words to fruition. For further elaboration, see the appendix.

Judea to Babylonia.[2] Nebuchadnezzar appointed Gedalia ben Ahikam to govern the small community remaining in Judea, but he was assassinated. The last of the Jews in the Land of Israel, fearing Babylonian retaliation, fled to Egypt.[3] And so the story that began with leaving Babylon and fleeing Egypt ends with both returning to Babylonia and fleeing to Egypt.

The Bible appears to be a story of failure. It ends right where it begins. The Hebrews did not succeed in creating an alternative to the great civilizations of the ancient world but were instead absorbed into them. Much of the Bible can be read as an attempt to explain this failure. What caused it? The Bible offers various answers. One answer is suggested by the historiographical books (Joshua–Kings), and another by the prophetic books (Isaiah–Malachi).

According to the historiographical books, the Jewish nation failed because of idol worship, which reached its peak during the reign of King Menashe. The nation that abandoned its God was in turn abandoned by its God. The prophetic books add that the people were also guilty of moral depravity, which is what led to social collapse.

This is one of the differences between Joshua–Kings and the prophetic books. Whereas the stories in the former refer almost exclusively to idolatry, the latter emphasize the moral degeneration of the Jewish people in biblical times.[4] In Joshua, Judges, and Kings, the focus is on the significant role played by the kings in leading the people to idolatrous practices.[5] The prophets instead point to society's moral blindness. Amos, Isaiah, and Jeremiah cry out that the degeneration stems from privileging Temple ritual over the moral obligation to the poor, humble, and disempowered.[6] One prophetic stream blames the institution of monarchy and the other blames the institution of the Temple.

2. II Kings 25.
3. II Kings 25; Jeremiah 42–44.
4. This is Yehezkel Kaufmann's illuminating distinction. See Kaufmann, *The Religion of Israel* (Jerusalem: Bialik Institute, 5724), vol. 1, 31–43 and vol. 3, 9–10.
5. See, for instance, I Kings 14:7–9. The kings are described as doing "what was displeasing to the Lord" eighteen times throughout the books of Kings.
6. See Isaiah 1:23, Jeremiah 7:4–6, and Amos 3:3–5.

JOSHUA AND SOLOMON

The Bible is really one continuous narrative that begins in Genesis and concludes in II Kings. It begins with Creation and ends with the exile of the Jewish people to Babylonia. In between, the children of Israel descend to Egypt, are liberated from bondage, wander in the wilderness, return to Canaan, and conquer and settle the land. The story is spread out across nine books, containing some 150,000 words and comprising about half of the Bible.

Deuteronomy is situated at the middle of these nine books. It is preceded by Genesis, Exodus, Leviticus, and Numbers, and followed by Joshua, Judges, Samuel, and Kings. (Samuel and Kings were each originally one book; they were divided only later.) It is positioned in the middle of this great dramatic narrative, preceded by the Exodus from Egypt and the wilderness wanderings, and followed by the conquest and settlement of the land.[7] Deuteronomy not only revisits and interprets what preceded it, but it also prefigures later Jewish history. Two figures, Joshua and King Solomon, engage in a kind of dialogue with Moses's final address. It is impossible to understand them fully without analyzing their relationship to Moses and his final words.

There is a major difference between Joshua and Solomon. Joshua represents the total realization of Deuteronomy's vision. Solomon, I will argue, abrogates Moses's instructions in Deuteronomy.

7. In a groundbreaking book on biblical philosophy, Yoram Hazony convincingly demonstrates that the historiographical books are the backbone of all biblical literature. See Yoram Hazony, *The Philosophy of Hebrew Scripture: An Introduction* (Cambridge: Cambridge University Press, 2012).

Chapter 10

Joshua and Moses

THE MISSING END OF THE BIBLE

Moses's life is interrupted. He dies before he completes his mission.

And it is not just Moses's life that is cut short, but also the book of Deuteronomy. Deuteronomy draws to a close after the children of Israel conquer Sihon and Og, but before they conquer Canaan, and after Moses instructs them on how to enter the land, but before they actually enter. Deuteronomy documents only the prelude to the story that is related in Joshua. The book of Joshua thus serves as the missing ending to the book of Deuteronomy, and concludes when the entire generation that conquers the land has died out.

> Israel served the Lord during the lifetime of Joshua and the lifetime of the elders who lived on after Joshua, and who had experienced all the deeds that the Lord had wrought for Israel. (Josh. 24:31)

The final verses of the book of Joshua describe the death of the generation that heard the last address of Moses. The book of Joshua, then, is about Moses's audience, the generation that entered the land and sought to implement Moses's vision. While the book of Deuteronomy ends with the death of the deliverer of the address, the book of Joshua ends with the death of its audience.

This is represented symbolically in the text by the motif of Joseph's bones. The book of Exodus relates that the children of Israel left Egypt carrying Joseph's bones with them.

> And Moses took with him the bones of Joseph, who had exacted an oath from the children of Israel, saying, "God will be sure to take notice of you: then you shall carry up my bones from here with you." (Ex. 13:19)

But Joseph's burial is not described until the end of Joshua.

> The bones of Joseph, which the Israelites had brought up from Egypt, were buried at Shechem, in the piece of ground that Jacob had bought for one hundred *kesita* from the children of Hamor, Shechem's father, and which had become a heritage of the Josephites. (Josh. 24:32)

The verses that conclude the book of Joshua are like those that conclude the story of the Exodus from Egypt. Only now, after the conquest and settlement of the land, does the curtain come down on this chapter in Jewish history with the act of burying Joseph's bones in Canaan.

Perhaps it is not surprising, then, that there is a theory that the Torah originally consisted of not five books but six,[1] i.e., that early versions of the Torah began with Genesis and concluded with Joshua. We

1. This idea, known as the Hexateuch Theory, dominated biblical studies from the end of the nineteenth century until the middle of the twentieth, and endures to this day. For a comprehensive analysis of the ways of dividing the books of the Bible and the early prophets, see the following collection of articles: T. B. Dozeman, T. Romer, and K. Schmid, eds., "Pentateuch, Hexateuch, or Enneateuch?" *SBL* (Atlanta), 11–93. For an overview of the literature on this subject and a discussion of the Hexateuch Theory, see Thomas Romer's article, "Many Books (teuchs): Pentateuch, Hexateuch, Deuteronomic History, or Enneateuch?" pp. 29–32, 39–42. Also see A. Graeme Auld, *Joshua, Moses and The Land* (Edinburgh: T&T Clark, 1980), 1–3, 19–23. And see S. Achituv, "Joshua with an Introduction and Commentary" [Hebrew], *The Bible for Israel*, ed. M. Greenberg and S. Achituv (Jerusalem: Magnes, 1996), 4–9.

can hear echoes of this notion in rabbinic literature: "Had Israel not sinned, only the five books of Moses and Joshua would have been given to them, because Joshua records the disposition of the land among the tribes" (Nedarim 22b). The Sages refer to the five books of Moses, plus Joshua, as a composite unit that might have constituted the entire Bible.

MOSES *DID* LEAD THE ISRAELITES INTO THE LAND

The book of Joshua opens with a reference to Moses: "After the death of Moses the servant of the Lord, the Lord said to Joshua son of Nun, Moses's attendant" (Josh. 1:1). Moses is referred to as "the servant of the Lord" and Joshua, by contrast, is described as "Moses's attendant." But when the book concludes with the death of Joshua, things have changed: "After these events, Joshua son of Nun, the servant of the Lord, died at the age of 110 years" (Josh. 24:29). By the end of the book, Joshua is referred to in the same way that Moses was at the beginning of the book.

Joshua undergoes this metamorphosis not because he liberates himself from his role as Moses's attendant, but because he continues to serve Moses faithfully even after Moses's death. How is it possible to serve someone who is no longer alive? By obeying the dictates in the book that he left behind. Joshua's obedience to Moses is apparent in the following three ways:

1. *God Quotes Man*

The book of Joshua begins with a revelation in which Joshua hears the following words:

> But you must be very strong and resolute to observe faithfully all the Torah that My servant Moses enjoined upon you. Do not deviate from it to the right or to the left, that you may be successful wherever you go. Let not this book of the Torah cease from your lips, but recite it day and night so that you may observe faithfully all that is written in it. Only then will you prosper in your undertakings and only then will you be successful. (Josh. 1:7–8)

Joshua's first private revelation refers to Moses and quotes from Moses's final address.[2] Joshua is commanded to obey and remain faithful to Moses's Torah: "Do not deviate from it to the right or to the left" (Josh. 1:7). This echoes Moses's words in Deuteronomy: "Thus he will not act haughtily toward his fellows or deviate from the commandment to the right or to the left, to the end that he and his descendants may reign long in the midst of Israel" (Deut. 17:20). Moreover, God commands Joshua to study Torah night and day – "Let not this book of Torah cease from your lips, but recite it day and night" (Josh. 1:8) – another echo of Moses's address: "Let it remain with him and let him read in it all his life, so that he may learn to revere the Lord his God, to observe faithfully every word of this Torah as well as these laws" (Deut. 17:19).

Although it is generally man who quotes God, in the revelation to Joshua it is God who quotes man. God's instructions to Joshua are clear and simple: He must devote himself wholeheartedly to Moses's Torah and follow it his entire life. What is God saying to Joshua? That he may be Moses's successor, but he is not his replacement. The moment Joshua assumes the mantle of leadership, he must recognize that he is beholden to another leader.

2. *Conquest as Moses's Commandment*

The land of Canaan is conquered in three stages. First Joshua's army conquers Jericho and the Ai, taking control of Givon and the Hivite cities. They thus take over the middle of the country, cutting off the north from the south. From the base they establish in the central hill country, they move on to the second stage of the war – the southern offensive. Then they attack the north.

Once the army has gained control of the middle of the country, Joshua goes to Mount Gerizim and Mount Ebal and conducts the ceremony that Moses commanded. Joshua fulfills Moses's dictate, writes

2. For a comparison between the books of Joshua and Deuteronomy, see Elie Assis, *From Moses to Joshua and from Miracle to Nature* [Hebrew] (Jerusalem: Magnes, 5765), 12–15, 43–44, 50–51.

his address on the stones, brings a peace offering, and reads the words of the covenant, including the blessing and the curse.

> And there on the stones, he inscribed a copy of the second Torah [Deuteronomy] that Moses had written for the Israelites. All of Israel – stranger and citizen alike – with their elders, officials, and magistrates, stood on either side of the Ark, facing the Levitical priests who carried the Ark of the Lord's covenant. Half of them faced Mount Gerizim and half of them faced Mount Ebal, as Moses the servant of the Lord had commanded them of old, in order to bless the people of Israel. (Josh. 8:32–33)

Joshua reads all of Moses's words without omitting anything.

> After that, he read all the words of the Torah, the blessing and the curse, just as is written in the book of the Torah. There was not a word of all that Moses had commanded that Joshua failed to read in the presence of the entire assembly of Israel, including the women and children and the strangers who accompanied them. (Josh. 8:34–35)

Not only does Joshua read all of Moses's Torah aloud, he also obeys it all. For instance, the cities that Joshua conquered were proscribed in accordance with Moses's dictates:

> Joshua captured all those royal cities and their kings. He put them to the sword; he proscribed them in accordance with the charge of Moses, the servant of the Lord.... Just as the Lord had commanded His servant Moses, so Moses had charged Joshua, and so Joshua did. He left nothing undone of all that the Lord had commanded Moses. (Josh. 11:12, 15)

Joshua proscribed the inhabitants of the land, put the kings to death, and then disposed of their bodies in accordance with Moses's instructions.

> After that, Joshua had them put to death and impaled on five stakes, and they remained impaled on the stakes until evening. At sunset, Joshua ordered them taken down from the poles and thrown into the cave in which they had hidden. (Josh. 10:26–27)

3. *Addressing the People as Moses Commanded*

When the fighting ended, Joshua approached the two and a half tribes who had requested to settle on the eastern side of the Jordan. He certified that they did all that had been commanded. These tribes – Reuven, Gad, and half the tribe of Menashe – entered the land girded for war, showed their solidarity with the rest of the tribes and fought for them and alongside them. Now, having fulfilled their obligations, they were granted permission to return to the other side of the Jordan.

Joshua says: "You have observed all that Moses the servant of the Lord commanded you" (Josh. 22:2). The same tribes who told Joshua at the beginning of the book that they would be loyal to him as they were loyal to Moses now hear Joshua tell them that even when they were being loyal to Joshua, it was in fact truly Moses whom they were serving.

This motif recurs throughout Deuteronomy, and it reflects an attempt to portray the period of Joshua's leadership as an extension of Moses's tenure.[3] Joshua physically led the Israelites in conquering the land, but in another sense, the leader was really Moses – and Moses's Torah. Moses was left behind at Mt. Nevo, but the words that he transmitted to the people accompanied them into the land. Ironically, while the people did not always listen to Moses in his lifetime, they did hearken to his Torah after his death.

In Joshua's two parting addresses to the people before his death, he sought to extend Moses's influence to subsequent generations. First he gathered the leaders and reminded them of Moses's final address:

3. Assis, *From Moses to Joshua*, 17–20, 52–53.

> But be most resolute to observe faithfully all that is written in the book of the Torah of Moses, without ever deviating from it to the right or to the left. (Josh. 23:6)

If the people dedicate themselves to Moses's Torah, then all of the success they were met with prior to Joshua's death will continue to accompany them once he is no longer with them. But if they do not adhere to Moses's Torah, then their successes will become failures, their victories will become defeats, and they will be destroyed.

> The Lord has driven out great, powerful nations on your account, and not a man has withstood you to this day. A single man of you would put a thousand to flight, for the Lord your God Himself has been fighting for you, as He promised you. For our own sakes, therefore, be most mindful to love the Lord your God. For should you turn away and attach yourselves to the remnant of those nations – to those who are left among you – and intermarry with them, you joining them and they joining you, know for certain that the Lord your God will not continue to drive these nations out before you; they shall become a snare and a trap for you, a scourge to your sides and thorns in your eyes, until you perish from this good land that the Lord your God has given you. (Josh. 23:9–13)

Joshua does not ask the people to be loyal to him, but to be loyal to Moses. Just as the real source of authority in Joshua's lifetime was Moses's Torah, so too the people are charged to remain faithful to Moses's Torah after Joshua's death.

This message is reflected in the words of the talmudic Sage R. Shimon bar Yoḥai, who relates that when God revealed Himself to Joshua, Joshua was studying Deuteronomy: "The book of Deuteronomy was a banner for Joshua. At the time when God revealed Himself to him, He found him sitting with the book of Deuteronomy in his hand" (Genesis Rabba 6:9). Joshua, then, was Deuteronomy's loyal emissary to the world.

FROM OBEYING TO IMITATING MOSES

Joshua did not just subordinate himself to Moses's Torah, but to the image of Moses as well. Throughout the book of Joshua, there is a clear attempt to portray Joshua as a kind of second Moses.[4] For instance, in preparation for receiving the Torah at Mt. Sinai, Moses commanded the people to sanctify themselves for three days. Similarly, on the eve of their entry into the land, Joshua instructed the people to sanctify themselves for three days. Even God repeats the same activities for Moses and Joshua: God splits the Sea of Reeds for Moses and dries up the Jordan for Joshua. Moreover, Joshua merited to experience revelation through an angel, very similar to the revelation of the angel to Moses at the burning bush. The angel that appears to Joshua echoes, almost word for word, the angel who appeared to Moses: "Remove your sandals from your feet, for the place where you stand is holy" (Josh. 5:15).[5]

The repetition of motifs from Moses's life during Joshua's life reaches its climax in the parting address that Joshua delivers, like Moses before him. Both the content and the context of Joshua's speech resemble that of Moses. Moses delivered his address after the victory over Sihon and Og, but before the conquest of the land. Joshua delivers his address after most of the land has been conquered, but before the conquest has been completed. Moses used his address as a means of capitalizing on the victory over Sihon and Og to strengthen the people's faith that they would continue to win.

> I also charged Joshua at that time, saying, "You have seen with your own eyes all that the Lord your God has done to these two

4. For a literary analysis of the figure of Joshua as compared to that of Moses, see Yair Zakovitch, *The World of the Bible: Joshua*, 16–18; Shmuel Achituv, "Joshua with an Introduction and Commentary" [Hebrew], *The Bible for Israel*, ed. M. Greenberg and S. Achituv, 37–39 and the commentary on Joshua 1, p. 71; Alexander Rofé, "Hosea ben Nun in the History of Biblical Tradition" [Hebrew], *Tarbiz* 73:3 (Nisan–Sivan 5764), 333–364; Hartmut N. Rosel, *Joshua* (Leuven: 2011), 17–18; and Assis, *From Moses to Joshua*, 17–20, 52–53.
5. Compare to Exodus 3. Also see Y. Zakovitch, *On the Concept of Miracles in the Bible* [Hebrew] (Tel Aviv: Misrad HaBitahon, 5747), 108.

> kings; so shall the Lord do to all the kingdoms into which you shall cross over. (Deut. 3:21)

Joshua employs the very same rhetorical device. He tells the people that just as they have been victorious until this point, so will they continue to win.

> You have seen all that the Lord your God has done to all those nations on your account, for it was the Lord your God who fought for you....The Lord your God Himself will thrust them out on your account and drive them out to make way for you, and you shall possess the land as the Lord your God promised you. (Josh. 23:3–5)

Joshua is charged to conquer the land and divide it up among the tribes. Moses anticipated both of these tasks: He conquered the portion of the two and a half tribes and divided the land among them. The book of Joshua's summary of all of Joshua's conquests begins with Moses's conquests.[6] Likewise, prior to describing Joshua's division of the land, the book of Joshua describes Moses's division.[7] Moses's conquest and division of the land thus served as a model for Joshua.

The Talmud says, "Moses's face was like the sun; Joshua's face was like the moon" (Bava Batra 75a). Although the rabbis may not have been aware of it, the astronomical knowledge we have today renders this ancient midrash an even more fitting description of the relationship between Moses and Joshua. The light of the moon, as we know, is merely a reflection of the light of the sun; the moon has no light of its own. Joshua obeyed Moses's Torah and emulated Moses. But was there anything unique about Joshua? Did he submit himself entirely to Moses's example, creating himself in Moses's image? To answer this question, we turn now to the story of the second battle of the Ai.

6. See Joshua 12:1–6.

7. Ibid. 13:1–14.

JOSHUA AND THE BATTLE OF THE AI

The story of Joshua's second battle to conquer the Ai, following the failure of the first battle, is a tale of military strategy. Joshua received the battle plan through divine revelation. He concealed part of his army behind the Ai. Then he marched at the head of the rest of the troops and crossed before the Ai, luring its inhabitants from the city in pursuit. When Joshua saw that the inhabitants of the Ai had abandoned their city for the sake of the chase, he signaled to the waiting contingent to emerge from its hiding place, fall upon the empty city, and set it aflame. He gave the order by raising his javelin.

> The Lord then said to Joshua, "Hold out the javelin in your hand toward the Ai, for I will deliver it into your hands." So Joshua held out the javelin in his hand toward the city. As soon as he held out his hand, those waiting in ambush came rushing out of their station. They entered the city and captured it, and they swiftly set fire to the city. (Josh. 8:18–19)

Here too, we find a parallel between Moses and Joshua. Moses brought the plagues upon Egypt by raising his staff in the air: "So Moses held out his rod toward the sky" (Ex. 9:23).[8] Joshua lifts his javelin into the air, wreaking havoc on the Ai as Moses wreaked havoc on Egypt.

But this time the analogy is more complex. Joshua's hand, which held the javelin, was not lowered until the end of the battle. "Joshua did not draw back the hand with which he held out his javelin until all the inhabitants of the Ai had been exterminated" (Josh. 8:26).[9] This, too,

---

8. Also see Exodus 10:13, 22.
9. This verse is missing from the Septuagint. Scholars are divided as to whether this verse appeared in the masoretic text and was excised from the Septuagint because of its miraculous nature, which is inconsistent with the book's rationalism, or whether this verse did not appear in the masoretic text but was added at a later point in order to emphasize God's role in the battle. On the former view, see Assis, *From Moses to Joshua*, 154–155, notes 54 and 57. On the latter view, see Zakovitch, *Concept of Miracles*, 112–113; Y. Amit, "Joshua's Javelin (Joshua 8:18, 26)" [Hebrew], *Bible and Ancient Near East Studies Annual*, 5–6 (5741–5742), 14; and L. Mazor, "The Story of the Victory Over the Ai (Joshua 8)" [Hebrew], in *The Bible in the Eye of its Interpreters: A Book in Memory of Sarah Kamin*, ed. S. Yafet (Jerusalem: Magnes, 5754), 94–97.

is reminiscent of Moses. The first battle fought by the people who left Egypt was against Amalek.[10] The Torah relates that when Moses raised his hand, the people would prevail, and when Moses lowered his hand, Amalek would prevail (see Ex. 17:11). But it was Joshua who actually fought against Amalek while Moses stood on the hill with his hands up.

> Then, whenever Moses held up his hand, Israel prevailed, but whenever he let down his hand, Amalek prevailed. But Moses's hands grew heavy, so they took a stone and put it under him and he sat on it, while Aaron and Hur, one on each side, supported his hands. Thus his hands remained steady until the sun set. And Joshua overwhelmed the people of Amalek with the sword. (Ex. 17:11–13)

This juxtaposition offers a fresh perspective on the relationship between Moses and Joshua. Joshua does not just become a second Moses, standing on the hill and looking out over the battle; he also continues in the role of the young Joshua who fought on the battlefield. Joshua does not overwrite his own role so as to resemble Moses. Rather, he combines his role as warrior with Moses's presiding role. He continues being Joshua while also taking on the role of Moses.

IS JOSHUA EVEN GREATER THAN MOSES?

We have considered Deuteronomy's perspective on monarchy, i.e., that only if the king is aware that he is not truly in power will his reign prosper and endure. Now we will see that Joshua represents the perfect fulfillment of this paradox.

Near the beginning of the book, God informs Joshua that He is about to elevate him in the eyes of the people by drying out the Jordan before all of Israel: "The Lord said to Joshua, 'This day, for the first time, I will exalt you in the eyes of all of Israel, so that they shall know that I will be with you as I was with Moses (Josh. 3:7). This great miracle will exalt the status of Joshua, but this is not how Joshua presents it to the people:

10. See articles by Amit and Zakovitch as cited in the previous note.

> By this you shall know that a living God is among you, and that He will dispossess for you the Canaanites, Hittites, Hivites, Perizzites, Girgashites, Amorites, and Jebusites. The Ark of the Covenant of the Sovereign of all the earth is advancing before you into the Jordan. (Josh. 3:10–11)

The miracle that God says will glorify Joshua instead is described by Joshua as the glorification of God. Perhaps this is some sort of redress: In the dramatic story at Meribah, God instructed Moses to draw water miraculously from the rock so as to sanctify God's name. But instead, Moses and Aaron characterized the miracle as one which they themselves had performed.[11] The sin on account of which Moses was not permitted to enter the land is thus redressed in the miracle by which Joshua enters in his stead.

The consequence of Joshua's demurral is explicit: "On that day, the Lord exalted Joshua in the sight of all of Israel, so that they revered him all his days as they had revered Moses" (Josh. 4:14). When Joshua shunned honor, honor caught up with him.

This is the secret of Joshua's success. He is a leader who merits to receive honor because he rejects it. In the miracle in which the sun stands still at Gibeon, perhaps the climactic moment in Joshua's biography, we find the same pattern with a surprising twist.

> Joshua addressed the Lord ... and he said in the presence of the Israelites: "O sun, stand still at Gibeon, and O moon, in the Valley of Ayalon!" And the sun stood still and the moon halted, while a nation wreaked judgment on its foes. (Josh. 10:12–13)

---

11. Numbers 20:11–12. Nahmanides, in his commentary on Numbers 20:8, cites R. Ḥananel, "who wrote that the sin consisted of their saying, 'Shall we get water for you out of this rock?'" R. Ḥananel comments that Moses's sin lay not in what he did, but in what he said. He spoke in first person plural ("Shall we get water?") instead of in third person ("Shall He [God] get water?"). This suggests that Moses attributes the miracle to himself and Aaron, which is the reason he was punished. The same reading is offered by Rabbi Yosef Bechor Shor and by modern commentators. See Jacob Milgrom's discussion on the matter: J. Milgrom, *Numbers: The JPS Torah Commentary* (Philadelphia: JPS, 1990), 165, 448–456.

A miracle occurred: The sun stood still and the day was extended so as to allow Joshua to finish triumphing over the enemy.

> Neither before nor since has there ever been such a day, when the Lord acted on words spoken by a man, for the Lord fought for Israel. (Josh. 10:14)

The Bible states that the miracle performed for Joshua was unique. This is a startling assertion, suggesting that Joshua's miracle was of a different – and perhaps superior – quality to those of Moses.[12] But what was so unprecedented about the miracle of the sun at Gibeon? "The Lord acted on words spoken by a man" (Josh. 10:14).[13] Every other biblical miracle comes about when man heeds a divine order. For instance, when God tells Moses to cast down his staff, the staff becomes a snake. When God tells Moses to strike the sea, the sea splits. But in the case of Joshua at Gibeon, the miracle happens when God listens to man. Joshua, who forfeits his own power in Moses's presence, merits that God forfeits His power in his presence.

COLLECTIVE SINS

Prior to their entry into the land, the people sinned and complained. All of this changed after the conquest of Canaan. Joshua's tenure was a period of loyalty, obedience, and national and religious uplift. The people were faithful to Joshua and to God. Joshua did not run after power, and

---

12. We can find an echo in the Talmud's statement in Sota 13b: "And whom have we greater than Moses...let it suffice (*rav*) for you – you have a *rav*, and who is it? Joshua."

13. There are many commentaries on this short and puzzling verse, which seems to intimate that Joshua surpassed Moses. See, for instance, Dan Alshich's interpretation of Joshua 10:14–43, where he quotes the Talmud's statement in Avoda Zara 25a that the sun stopped for three individuals: Moses, Joshua, and Nakdimon ben Gurion. Alshich notes that in Moses's case, God performed this miracle not for Moses's sake, but because the exigencies of the moment demanded it. In Nakdimon's case, God performed this miracle on account of Nakdimon's power of prayer. But in Joshua's case, God performed this miracle merely on account of words that Joshua spoke to God. And this is why the miracle in Moses's day and the miracle in Nakdimon's day – those before and after – were not comparable.

so power ran after him. He was responsible for the fulfillment of all that Moses had commanded with his final words.

It was a successful time, but not a perfect one. The book of Joshua also contains one significant stumble – the story of a great sin that was met with painful punishment. This was the sin of Achan, the open wound of the book of Joshua. If the majority of the book represents the fulfillment of Deuteronomy's vision, this chapter represents the fulfillment of Deuteronomy's admonishments: Anyone who thinks that his success is his own will be robbed of that success.

As we read in Joshua, the people set out to conquer the Ai, but they lose. Thirty-six soldiers are killed. Joshua rips his clothes in mourning and asks God why they were defeated. God responds that the spoils of Jericho had been explicitly forbidden to them; Jericho was supposed to be preserved for God alone. But one man, Achan, ignored the ban and raided the spoils, leading to the collective punishment of the nation, the defeat at the first battle with the Ai.[14]

This story raises a recurrent question throughout the Bible. Abraham asked God why He kills the righteous along with the wicked (Gen. 18:23). Moses asked God a similar question: "When one man sins, will You be wrathful with the whole community?" (Num. 16:22). And this question also emerges from the story of Achan. How can it be that when only one person sins, the whole nation is punished?

A close reading of God's words suggests that this is not the right question. Rather, when Achan sinned, the whole nation sinned as well. God remonstrates: "Israel has sinned! They have broken the covenant by which I bound them. They have taken of the proscribed and put it in their vessels. They have stolen; they have broken faith!" (Josh. 7:11). The punishment was collective because the sin was collective. This is apparent from the strange and surprising wording of the opening verse of this chapter:

> The Israelites violated the proscription: Achan son of Carmi son of Zabdi son of Zerah, of the tribe of Judah, took of that which was proscribed, and the Lord was incensed with the Israelites. (Josh. 7:1)

---

14. See Joshua 7:1–5.

The boundary between the individual and the collective is blurred and indistinct. Who sinned, the nation ("the Israelites violated the proscription") or Achan ("Achan…took of that which was proscribed")? The issue is one of collective responsibility.

The notion of collective responsibility may come as a surprise, given Deuteronomy's respect for the individual. Deuteronomy's laws emphasize the importance of safeguarding private property. Unlike Marxist theory, Moses's final address does not claim that all private property is theft. By contrast, Moses defends private ownership.[15] But there is a difference between private ownership and "private sin." The Torah is not opposed to economic privatization, but it is opposed to ethical privatization. The individual's sin does not exist in isolation from society, and sometimes a sin is attributed to the collective.

The story of Achan is a prime example, as we learn from Pinchas, the grandson of Aaron the priest. The context is the book of Joshua, where Pinchas rebukes the two and a half tribes who settled on the opposite side of the Jordan for having built an altar.

> Is the sin of Peor, which brought a plague upon the community of the Lord, such a small thing to us? We have not cleansed ourselves from it to this very day, and now you would turn away from the Lord! If you rebel against the Lord today, tomorrow He will be angry with the whole community of Israel. (Josh. 22:17–18)

Pinchas tells the wayward tribes that when God punishes, He punishes collectively. Therefore, Pinchas says, the sin of the two and a half tribes

---

15. This is apparent from the tenth commandment in the book of Exodus (20:14). Alexander Rofé demonstrates that the book of Deuteronomy contains several laws that emphasize the prohibition on violating private property. See Deuteronomy 19:14; 23:25–26; 24:10–11; and 27:17. One particularly interesting example is the tenth commandment as it appears in Deuteronomy (5:18). In Exodus, the commandment is stated as "You shall not covet…you shall not covet," whereas in Deuteronomy it is stated as "You shall not covet…you shall not crave." Moses expounds on the tenth commandment in his address, noting that it is forbidden not just to covet, but also to crave, that is, even to think about coveting. See Alexander Rofé, "The Tenth Commandment and the Laws of One's Fellow" [Hebrew], in *An Introduction to Deuteronomy* (Jerusalem: Academon, 5748), 110–126.

is also the sin of all of Israel. He invokes the episode with Achan. When Achan sinned, the whole nation was punished. Pinchas says, "When Achan son of Zerah violated the proscription, anger struck the whole community of Israel; he was not the only one who perished for that sin" (Josh. 22:20).

Pinchas's message is that God views the sin of the few as the sin of the many. Society is responsible for preventing its members from sinning. If it does not, the entire society will be punished along with them. The failure to prevent sin is itself a sin. There are no innocent bystanders; everyone is implicated.

Why was it such a transgression to take from the spoils of Jericho? Jericho was not conquered by a military offensive, but rather by a religious ceremony. The Israelites surrounded the walls of Jericho for seven days. They were led not by warriors but by the priests and the Ark of the Covenant. The walls did not fall on account of sophisticated weaponry or military strategy, but on account of the blowing of shofars. On the seventh day, after the Israelites circumambulated the walls seven times and blew on their shofars seven times, the walls fell and the city was destroyed. Perhaps this is why the Israelites were forbidden from plundering the city. It was not they who conquered the city, but God. When Achan took from the spoils, he was expressing that Jericho belonged not to God, but to the people. As we will see, Achan gave voice to a notion that many of the Israelites harbored, namely that the victory in Jericho was *their* victory. Achan's sin was a sin of the entire nation.

THE POWER OF THE STORY

In order to get a sense of the mood of the people following the victory in Jericho, we need to take a step backward and return to the days of Joshua's youth. Joshua was one of the twelve spies sent to scout out the land of Canaan. He was also one of the only two spies who did not participate in telling terrifying stories about the land. The remaining ten spies did just that: "The country that we have traversed and scouted is one that devours its settlers. All the people we saw in it are men of great size. We saw the Nephilim there – the sons of giants – and we looked like grasshoppers to ourselves, and so we must have looked to them" (Num. 13:32–33). The people heard the word "Nephilim" and grew weak of spirit.

How did the people know what the ten spies were referring to? It was on account of an ancient myth that is referenced in the sixth chapter of Genesis. The Bible describes the Nephilim, created from the union of the sons of the gods and the daughters of man. When the spies returned from their scouting expedition and reported that these mythical figures indeed walked the land, the Israelites grew frightened and their courage flagged.

Forty years later, two of the spies sent to Jericho as part of the preparations to enter the land did not gather much by way of military intelligence. The knowledge they supplied to Joshua focused rather on the general mood in Canaan. Rahav told the spies what the inhabitants of the land thought of the Israelites. The spies conveyed this information to their leader. In essence, though, the information that the spies gathered was information about the people of Israel, and not about the inhabitants of Canaan. For the first time the people learned about the image that the Canaanites had of them, and the stories they told about them.

> For we heard how the Lord dried up the waters of the Sea of Reeds for you when you left Egypt, and what you did to Sihon and Og, the two Amorite kings across the Jordan, whom you doomed. When we heard about it, we lost heart, and no man had any more spirit left because of you. (Josh. 2:10–11)

The inhabitants of Canaan, so Rahav informed the spies, were terrified of Israel and would not dare to set out against them in battle. They had heard stories about the splitting of the Sea of Reeds and the Israelites' victories against Sihon and Og. They would not be so bold as to confront the flesh-and-blood heroes of these tales.

Now it is the Israelites who are the new mythical heroes. The author of the book of Joshua quotes Rahav, who explains that the inhabitants of Canaan heard rumors about the Israelites, and these rumors have terrified them: "When all the kings of the Amorites on the western side of the Jordan, and all the kings of the Canaanites near the sea, heard how the Lord had dried up the waters of the Jordan for the sake of the Israelites until they crossed over, they lost heart, and no spirit was left in them because of the Israelites" (Josh. 5:1). In other words, the war to conquer the land was not supposed to happen. Joshua's army was supposed to be met with immediate and total surrender.

But if the war was not supposed to happen, why did it? If the inhabitants of the land were supposed to surrender to the Israelite army, why didn't they? The answer may be related to the people's defeat in the first battle of the Ai. When the inhabitants of the Ai defeated the Israelites and killed thirty-six of Israel's soldiers, they did not just overcome Joshua's army, they also subdued their own fears. The image of the legendary, intimidating Israelites was shattered. The first battle of the Ai signified a major turning point in the book of Joshua. This was the battle in which the inhabitants of the land no longer despaired of the possibility of defeating the Israelites.

Following the defeat at the Ai, Joshua cries out to God:

> Joshua said, "Ah, Lord God, why did You lead this people across the Jordan only to deliver us into the hands of the Amorites, to be destroyed by them? If only we had been content to remain on the other side of the Jordan." (Josh. 7:7)

What bothers Joshua? He does not cry on account of his lost soldiers. He understands that war has a price. He bemoans the rumors that will spread on account of this defeat: "When the Canaanites and all the inhabitants of the land hear of this, they will turn upon us and wipe out our very name from the earth. And what will You do about Your great name?" (Josh. 7:9).

Joshua wants to fulfill Moses's military vision. Moses says in Deuteronomy that the inhabitants of the land will flee from the Israelites because they will be terrified on account of what they have heard about them. "This day I begin to put the dread and fear of you upon the peoples everywhere under heaven, so that they shall tremble and quake because of you whenever they hear you mentioned" (Deut. 2:25). The fear that the stories about the Israelites instill in the inhabitants of the land is supposed to deter them from war. But the defeat at the Ai, attributed to the sin of Achan, destroyed the perception of Moses's people as impregnable.

This brings us back to our original question: How did Achan's sin give voice to a collective sentiment on account of which the people were all punished so severely?

THE FAILURE OF THE CONCEPT

The Israelites went to battle against the Ai after the victory in Jericho. As they had done with Jericho, they sent spies to the Ai, who reported back as follows:

> Not all the troops need go up. Let two or three thousand men go and attack the Ai. Do not trouble all the troops to go up there, for the people there are few. (Josh. 7:3)

The spies suggested that Joshua need send only two or three thousand troops to conquer the Ai. But we know that in the second battle of the Ai, Joshua sent more than 35,000 troops. How could the spies have thought that a city that could only be defeated by tens of thousands of troops would submit to just two or three thousand? It seems that the report of the spies spoke less to the military capability of the Ai than to the morale of the people at that point. Following the victory in Jericho, the people – and the spies among them – believed that they would be able to defeat the Ai almost effortlessly. The erroneous intelligence relayed to Joshua reflects the national mood – the people were drunk on their victory in Jericho. The ease with which Jericho was conquered led to a national ego trip which resulted in an inaccurate interpretation of the military intelligence, causing a terrible loss. For modern readers, this story may sound painfully all too familiar.

If on the eve of the battle of Jericho, the Israelites understood that the inhabitants of the land believed the myths about them; on the eve of the battle on the Ai, they themselves came to believe in these myths. This bring us back to the power paradox: When the people believed with total certainty that they would win, they lost instead.

This is essentially a second and opposite version of the original story of the spies. The sin of the first set of spies, in the wilderness, was lack of confidence. The sin of the second set of spies, in the Ai, was overconfidence.

Achan took from the spoils, essentially declaring that they belonged to him rather than to God. But he was not alone. The entire people experienced a sense of inflated national morale in the wake of the victory at Jericho. They regarded this victory as their own. This was a heretical response, because the victory in fact belonged to God. And so in this sense, the entire people took from the proscribed spoils.

The episode with Achan is the open wound of the book of Joshua. Joshua is described as being immune to haughtiness. He credits God with all of his accomplishments, and all his actions are in line with Moses and his Torah. He defers to his predecessor, obeys his Torah, and devotes himself wholeheartedly to God. Consequently, he is met with success, prosperity, and power. Joshua embodies the idea that someone who experiences his power as not being his own will merit to retain power. Throughout his book, there is just one instance of the opposite syndrome, and that is the episode at the Ai. When the people of Israel believed that their power was their own, that power was taken from them. When they believed that they could not possibly lose, they lost. But otherwise, the book chronicles Joshua's exemplary response to the spiritual challenges posed by success.

Chapter 11

A National and Religious Climax

The historiographical books of the Bible chronicle the two major challenges that confronted the Jewish people living in their land – the national challenge and the religious challenge.

The national challenge was to forge unity. The book of Judges relates how the nation failed in its attempt to bring about solidarity among the tribes, and the book of Kings describes the failure to preserve a united kingdom.

The religious challenge is the challenge of maintaining total devotion to the God of Israel. Throughout the Bible the nation is repeatedly tempted to serve other gods – sometimes in addition to God, and sometimes in place of God.

Only in the period of Joshua does the nation meet both of these challenges. The book of Joshua concludes with two events that reflect this success: the encounter with the two and a half tribes, and the covenant sealed at Shechem. The encounter with the two and a half tribes underscores the extraordinary national unity of the time, and the covenant at Shechem shows the spiritual strength of the people.

THE TWO AND A HALF TRIBES

The story of the two and a half tribes begins after the Israelites have defeated Sihon king of the Amorites and Og king of the Bashan in Moses's day. The tribes of Gad and Reuben were pleased with the territory they had conquered on the eastern side of the Jordan and wanted to settle there. Moses listened to their request but responded with a firm no.

> Moses replied to the Gadites and the Reubenites, "Are your brothers to go to war while you stay here? Why will you turn the minds of the Israelites from crossing into the land that the Lord has given them? That is what your fathers did when I sent them from Kadesh-barnea to survey the land. After going up to the wadi Eshkol and surveying the land, they turned the minds of the Israelites from invading the land that the Lord had given them. (Num. 32:6–9)

Moses was concerned that the tribes, like the ten spies before them, were avoiding battle on account of their fear. But the leaders of the tribes explained that they were proposing not that they stay behind, but that they first lead the people in their conquest of the land and only then cross back over the Jordan. They showed that they were being driven not by fear but by their territorial preference.

> And we will hasten as shock troops in the vanguard of the Israelites until we have established them in their home, while our children stay in the fortified towns because of the inhabitants of the land. We will not return to our homes until every one of the Israelites is in possession of his portion. (Num. 32:17–18)

This is an expression of national solidarity. The two and half tribes assure Moses that they will not enjoy their territorial portion until all the tribes have received theirs. And this time, Moses is persuaded.[1]

> Moses said to them, "If you do this, if you go to battle as shock troops at the instance of the Lord, and every shock fighter among you crosses the Jordan at the instance of the Lord, until He has dispossessed His enemies before Him and the land has been subdued at the instance of the Lord, and then you return – you shall be clear before the Lord and before Israel, and this land shall be your holding under the Lord. (Num. 32:20–22)

The solidarity of these tribes is evidenced once again during Joshua's day. At the conclusion of the fighting, Joshua tells the two and a half tribes that they are released from their oath and may return to their territory on the other side of the Jordan. The tribes do so – they cross back over the Jordan and settle in their land. But they also do something else there – they build an altar.

> When they came to the region of the Jordan in the land of Canaan, the Reubenites and the Gadites and half the tribe of Menashe built an altar there by the Jordan, a great conspicuous altar. (Joshua 22:10)

When the Israelites hear about this altar, they respond aggressively:

> A report reached the Israelites: the Reubenites, the Gadites, and half the tribe of Menashe have built an altar opposite the land of Canaan, in the region of the Jordan, across from the Israelites. When the Israelites heard this, the whole community

1. I should qualify this statement by noting that I have chosen to quote from the version of the story that appears in Numbers, rather than Deuteronomy. The book of Deuteronomy does not revisit the entire story, and it leaves out this notion of solidarity. The entire suggestion is presented as coming from Moses. See Deuteronomy 3:16–20.

> of the Israelites assembled at Shiloh to make war on them. (Josh. 22:11–12)

The two and a half tribes fought on behalf of their fellow tribes, and now their fellows want to fight them. But just before a civil war breaks out, a delegation arrives in an attempt to persuade the two and a half tribes to abandon their alternative place of worship. The head of this delegation is Pinchas son of Elazar son of Aaron the priest. These tribes explain why they built an altar, and they manage to win over Pinchas and the rest of the emissaries. The members of the delegation came to persuade the two and a half tribes, but it was they who left persuaded. What was the explanation they were given?

> We did this thing only out of our concern that, in times to come, your children might say to our children, "What have you to do with the Lord, the God of Israel? The Lord has made the Jordan a boundary between you and us, O Reubenites and Gadites; you have no share in the Lord!" Thus your children might prevent our children from worshipping the Lord. So we decided to provide a witness for ourselves by building an altar – not for burnt offerings or other sacrifices, but as a witness between you and us, and between the generations to come. (Josh. 22:24–27)

The two and a half tribes are concerned that the geographical distance between themselves and the rest of Israel will lead to an erosion of national solidarity. They worry that the rest of the nation will not view them as an integral part of the nation serving God. Their motivation for erecting the altar is not to offer sacrifices but rather to express their national and religious solidarity with the other ten tribes dwelling in the land.[2] The altar is not the cornerstone of a new religion cut off from the

2. See R. Goldstein, "Joshua 22:9–34: The Priestly Story from the Period of the Return to Zion," *Bible and Ancient Near Eastern Studies Annual*, vol. 13 (5762): 57–61; S. Achituv, "Joshua with an Introduction and Commentary" [Hebrew], *The Bible for Israel*, ed. M. Greenberg and S. Achituv, 353–354; and Richard D. Nelson, *Joshua: A Commentary* (Westminster: John Knox Press, 1997), 249.

rest of Israel, but rather a symbol of unity. This incident epitomizes the national solidarity that distinguished Joshua's tenure.

THE COVENANT AT SHECHEM

In the book of Joshua, the people reach not only a national apex but also a religious one. At the end of the book the Israelites gather at Shechem and declare their unwavering commitment to God.[3] The spiritual exaltation of the people at Shechem is the climax of Joshua's parting words to the people.

Like Moses, Joshua ends his life with a series of parting addresses. The first address deals with Joshua's interpretation of the conquest. The conquest was an unquestionable military success. Joshua defeated many of the inhabitants of the land, subdued their kings, and crippled their armies.

> You have seen all that the Lord your God has done to all those nations on your account, for it was the Lord your God who fought for you. (Josh. 23:3)

Joshua's first statement is that all of his successes were not really his. He tells the people that it wasn't really they who conquered the land. Everything came from God. Joshua expresses gratitude to God for all the miracles of the past. Then he turns to the future:

> See, I have allotted to you, by your tribes, the territory of these nations that still remain, and that of all the nations that I have destroyed, from the Jordan to the Mediterranean Sea in the west. The Lord your God Himself will thrust them out on your account and drive them out to make way for you, and you shall possess their land as the Lord your God promised you. (Josh. 23:4–5)

---

3. Alexander Rofé and others have proposed that the covenant in chapter 24 of the book of Joshua is not a renewal of the prior covenant, but an alternative to the covenant at Sinai and Moab from the Efrati school. See Rofé, "Gathering at Shechem," 17–25.

Then Joshua offers a warning:

> For your own sake, therefore, be most mindful to love the Lord your God. For should you turn away and attach yourselves to the remnant of those nations – to those who are left among you – and intermarry with them, you joining them and they joining you, know for certain that the Lord your God will not continue to drive these nations out before you; they shall become a snare and a trap for you, a scourge to your sides and thorns in your eyes, until you perish from this good land that the Lord your God has given you. (Josh. 23:11–13)

This is the essence of Joshua's first address. If the people want to continue to prevail, then they must remain faithful to God.

Joshua's second address is delivered at Shechem, where he does not just survey the history of his own tenure, but also the history of the Jewish people.

> Then Joshua said to all the people: "Thus said the Lord, the God of Israel: In olden times, your forefathers – Terah, father of Abraham and father of Nahor – lived beyond the Euphrates and worshipped other gods. But I took your father Abraham from beyond the Euphrates and led him through the whole land of Canaan and multiplied his offspring. I gave him Isaac, and to Isaac I gave Jacob and Esau. I gave Esau the hill country of Seir as his possession, while Jacob and his children went down to Egypt. (Josh. 24:2–4)

Then Joshua enjoins the people:

> Now, therefore, revere the Lord and serve Him with undivided loyalty. Put away the gods that your forefathers served beyond the Euphrates and in Egypt, and serve the Lord. Or, if you are loath to serve the Lord, choose this day which ones you are going to serve – the gods that your forefathers served beyond the Euphrates, or those of the Amorites in whose land you are settled – but I and my household will serve the Lord. (Josh. 24:14–15)

Joshua seems to be reviewing the people's history so as to remind them of their pagan roots, which, he implies, have not been completely extirpated. Joshua entreats the Israelites to liberate themselves from their idolatrous history and serve God alone.

In his first address, Joshua was essentially instructing the people to continue in the monotheistic ways that had led them to so much recent success. In his second address, he charges them to liberate themselves from their ancestors' sins.

Joshua's commentary on early history lays the foundation for his next act as leader. He makes a covenant between the people and God which is intended to cut off the people from their pagan past. At Shechem, the people are liberated from their past and they refashion their national story.

Shechem marks the third covenant between the people and God. The first was made at Horeb[4] and the second at Moab.[5] In the biblical literary tradition, the covenant with God seems to be in need of renewal every few generations. But the new covenant does not exactly repeat the prior ones, because at Shechem, for the first time, the covenant is voluntary. It is not forced upon the people, but chosen by them.

> Joshua said to the people: "You will not be able to serve the Lord, for He is a holy God. He is a jealous God; He will not forgive your transgressions and your sins. If you forsake the Lord and serve alien gods, He will turn and deal harshly with you and make an end of you, after having been gracious to you. But the people replied to Joshua, "No, we will serve the Lord!" Thereupon Joshua said to the people, "You are witnesses against yourselves that you have by your own act chosen to serve the Lord." "Yes, we are!" they responded. (Josh. 24:19–22)

The Sages of the Talmud contend that this voluntary element was absent from the covenant at Horeb, which was forced upon the people.

4. Deuteronomy 4:24–28.
5. Ibid. 28:39–30:20.

> And they stood under the mount. R. Abdimi ben Ḥama ben Ḥasa said: This teaches that the Holy One, blessed be He, overturned the mountain upon them like a cask and said to them, "If you accept the Torah, it is well and good; if not, there shall be your burial." R. Aḥa b. Jacob observed: This furnishes a strong protest against the Torah. (Shabbat 88a)

One of the great medieval philosophers, Rabbi Hasdai Crescas, offered a commentary on this midrash. In what way, he asks, did the Jews not have free will at Horeb? He responds that the dramatic backdrop to the Revelation at Sinai – the fire, the lightning, the resounding voice of God – did not leave those standing at the foot of the mountain with any free choice. The drama of the event left them in a state of shock, which was followed by ecstatic fervor.[6]

The absence of free choice at Horeb gave rise to a fundamental question. If the people did not voluntarily agree to the covenant, how could it have been binding? The Talmud explains that the people ultimately accepted the covenant of their own volition during the time of King Ahasuerus. The story told in the Book of Esther does not include revelation, prophecy, or obvious divine intervention. It was thus an opportunity for the Jews to accept Torah from a place of calm rationality rather than ecstatic fervor. On Purim the Jews chose Torah freely and were not swept up in the drama of revelation.

> Said Raba: Yet even so, they reaccepted it in the days of Ahasuerus, for it is written, "They [the Jews] confirmed and took upon themselves," that is, they confirmed what they had accepted long before. (Shabbat 88a)

But the Sages did not have to fast-forward to the time of Ahasuerus in order to find a consensual covenant binding the nation. Nor did they have to base this covenant on a somewhat far-fetched midrash on the words "They confirmed and took upon themselves" (Est. 9:27). The covenant at Shechem in the book of Joshua works just as well. Like the

6. Rabbi Hasdai Crescas, *The Light of God*, article 2, rules 5, 6.

covenant in the time of Ahasuerus, it was a covenant without a backdrop of miracles and divine revelation. The people embraced God with full spiritual freedom.

The Ukrainian-born Jewish writer Micah Josef Berdichevsky (1865–1921) proposed that we view the covenant at Shechem – the covenant of Gerizim, as he called it – as the foundational covenant of the Jewish people. The covenant at Gerizim has several advantages over the covenant at Horeb. First, as Berdichevsky notes, the covenant at Gerizim was sealed in Israel rather than in exile, and by those who settled the land rather than those who were landless.[7] Second, at Horeb, nearly immediately after the end of the revelation, the covenant was abrogated with the sin of the Golden Calf. At Shechem there was no revelation, and the people committed themselves to the covenant without following it with a grievous sin. And as we have already noted, the covenant at Gerizim was made out of free choice, and not out of coercion. From Exodus through Deuteronomy, the Israelites are described as the chosen people; in Joshua, for the first time, they are the choosing people.

The end of the book of Joshua is also the high point of the book, and perhaps the high point of the entire Bible. The Bible describes two major challenges confronting the Israelite nation: the challenges of national solidarity and religious devotion. The book of Joshua concludes with a national climax with the account of the two and a half tribes, and a religious climax with the covenant at Shechem. But there is also sadness. The period following Moses's death was also the only time when Moses's vision was realized on such a broad scale.

THREE REASONS FOR THE COLLAPSE OF ANCIENT MONOTHEISM FOLLOWING THE DEATH OF JOSHUA

The book of Deuteronomy contains the last words of a pessimist.[8] After forty years of leading the Israelites through the wilderness, Moses has lost faith in his people. He is certain that they will breach the covenant.

---

7. M. J. Berdichevsky, *Sinai and Gerizim* (Tel Aviv: 5722).
8. Moses's address explicitly gives voice to his pessimism only at the end of Deuteronomy, but it is implicit throughout the entire book. It is reflected in the angry and threatening tone of much of Moses's address. Even so, biblical scholar Yoshi Fargeon

> For I know how defiant and stiff-necked you are. Even now, while I am still alive in your midst, you have been defiant toward the Lord; how much more, then, when I am dead! Gather to me all the elders of your tribes and your officials, that I may speak all these words to them and that I may call heaven and earth to witness against them. For I know that, when I am dead, you will act wickedly and turn away from the path that I enjoined upon you, and that in times to come, misfortune will befall you for having done evil in the sight of the Lord and vexed Him by your deeds. (Deut. 31:27–29)

The book of Joshua is a counterpoint to Moses's pessimism. The people are not wicked, and they do not turn away from the correct path. But does this mean that Moses's pessimistic prophecy was wrong?

The high note on which the book of Joshua ends does not last long. After Joshua and his generation have died, the people relapse into their characteristic destructive behavior patterns.

> Joshua son of Nun, the servant of the Lord, died at the age of 110 years and was buried on his own property, at Timnat-heres in the hill country of Ephraim, north of Mount Gaash. And all that generation were likewise gathered to their fathers. Another generation arose after them, which had not experienced the deliverance of the Lord or the deeds that He had wrought for Israel. And the Israelites did what was offensive to the Lord. They worshipped the Baalim and forsook the Lord, the God of their fathers, who had brought them out of the land of Egypt. They followed other gods, from among the gods of the peoples around them, and bowed down to them; they provoked the Lord. (Judges 2:8–12)

---

contends that the pessimism of the end of the book signifies a turning point, and it is a consequence of the divine revelation to Moses that took place in the Tent of Meeting prior to Moses's death: "The Lord said to Moses: You are soon to lie with your fathers. This people will thereupon go astray after the alien gods in their midst, in the land that they are about to enter. They will forsake Me and break My covenant that I made with them" (Deut. 31:16).

Moses was concerned not about the first generation settling in the land, but about their descendants: "When you have begotten children and children's children and are long established in the land" (Deut. 4:25). And as Moses predicts, Joshua's generation fulfills his Torah, and the subsequent generation does not.

What accounts for the spiritual decline following Joshua's death? The Bible offers three explanations:[9] the end of the era of miracles, the end of the war to conquer the land, and the end of the confederation. These three explanations describe the end of Joshua's tenure and the end of a biblical era.

1. *The End of the Era of Miracles*

Joshua's generation was the last generation to experience God's miracles firsthand.

> Israel served the Lord during the lifetime of Joshua and the lifetime of the elders who lived on after Joshua, and who had experienced all the deeds that the Lord had wrought for Israel. (Josh. 24:31)

This verse, one of the last of the book of Joshua, is virtually repeated at the beginning of the book of Judges. Joshua and the elders are described as a generation who "witnessed all the marvelous deeds that the Lord had wrought for Israel" (Judges 2:7). This serves as background to the Bible's description of the next generation.

> Another generation arose after them, which had not experienced the deliverance of the Lord or the deeds that He had wrought for Israel. (Judges 2:10)

9. These are not the only explanations, of course. One could add, for instance, the death of Joshua. In the second part of this book we saw that Moses was concerned that the covenant with God would not outlive him. The verses describing the death of Joshua (Judges 2:8–12) speak to a connection between the death of Joshua and the people's return to idolatry.

The transition from Joshua's generation to the next was traumatic. The new generation had not experienced miracles, and their behavior seems to have suffered.

> And the Israelites did what was offensive to the Lord. They worshipped the Baalim and forsook the Lord, the God of their fathers, who had brought them out of the land of Egypt. (Judges 2:11–12)

Apparently, loyalty to God required God's public manifestation. The period of miracles did not conclude with the death of Moses and the entry into the land; the conquest of the nation was also miraculous. The walls of Jericho collapsed without any human contact (Josh. 6:20), stones fell from the sky on the descent from Beit Horon (Josh. 10:11), and the sun stood still in the sky at Gibeon (Josh. 10:12–13). But once the land was conquered, the manifest miracles – those in which God violates the laws of nature – virtually ceased. For as long as the Israelites could witness God's actions with their own eyes, they remained faithful to God. But when the era of manifest miracles came to an end, the people's loyalty waned.

Monotheism could not endure the transition from manifest to concealed miracles.

2. *The End of the War*

After establishing their position on the mountain, the Israelites launched two major offensives. The first was against the cities of the south, including Jerusalem. The second was against the northern kings, led by Hazor. "For it was the Lord's doing to stiffen their hearts to give battle to Israel, in order that they might be proscribed without quarter and wiped out" (Josh. 11:20).

As He had done to Pharaoh in Egypt, God removed free will from the kings of the nations living in the Land of Israel, goading them to war. Perhaps the Torah is suggesting that if these kings had not gone out to war against Israel, then Israel would not have gone out to war against them and would not have conquered their cities or the neighboring ones. God hardened Pharaoh's heart so as to slow the Exodus from Egypt, but

He hardened the hearts of the Canaanite kings in order to accelerate the pace of the conquest. After these two battles, apparently other cities did not mobilize to fight Israel, and as a result, the Israelites did not initiate a war against those surviving inhabitants of Canaan. Most of the land was conquered by Israel in wars which Israel had not initiated. The war ended without the Israelites having fully conquered the land. The transition to the generation after Joshua signified not just the end of the era of manifest miracles, but also the end of the era of conquest.

There is a link between the premature, incomplete conclusion of the war and the spiritual decline of the people. Perhaps, once the Israelites began serving other gods, they could no longer conquer their enemies. The cessation of conquest was a punishment for unfaithfulness.

> Then the Lord became incensed against Israel, and He said, "Since that nation has transgressed the covenant that I enjoined upon their fathers and has not obeyed Me, I for My part will no longer drive out before them any of the nations that Joshua left when he died." (Judges 2:20–21)

Since the nation worshipped pagan gods, God would no longer deliver the pagan nations of the land into their hands.

There is another explanation for the connection between the end of the war and the resumption of idolatrous practices, and it comes from Deuteronomy: the failure to conquer the remainder of the Canaanite nations was not a punishment, but it was rather the sin itself.[10] As Moses had commanded in Deuteronomy, the erasure of the other nations of the land was necessary because otherwise the Israelites would be influenced by them and would come to worship their gods.

> No, you must proscribe them – the Hittites and the Amorites, the Canaanites and the Perizzites, the Hivites and the Jebusites – as the Lord your God has commanded you, lest they lead you into

10. And there is a third explanation that appears in the book of Judges, according to which the survival of some of the Canaanite residents was not a punishment but a trial: "For it was in order to test Israel, to see whether they would faithfully walk in the ways of the Lord as their fathers had done" (Judges 2:22).

> doing all the abhorrent things that they have done for their gods and you stand guilty before the Lord your God. (Deut. 20:17–18)

The end of the war transformed the nature of Israel's relationship with the inhabitants of the land. During a period of war, the Israelites were naturally averse and hostile to their enemies and to their cultures. But when hostilities ended, the repugnance also eroded. The covenant of peace with the inhabitants of the land led to the abrogation of the covenant with God.

3. *The End of the Confederation*

The end of the age of miracles diminished the appeal of serving God, and the end of the war increased the appeal of the Canaanite gods. Monotheism was put to the test. Without manifest miracles to glorify God in the people's eyes, and without a fierce struggle against the Canaanite nations that served to repel the people from their gods, the spiritual consciousness of the Israelites was no longer insulated from the lure of paganism.

There is a third, more political basis for the spiritual decline of the people. Joshua's death did not just mark the end of the period of miracles and warfare; it also marked the period in which the Israelite political confederation dissolved. Ancient monotheism failed to survive the political change that came about with the death of Joshua.

At Mount Sinai, the Israelites were commanded to leave the mountain. "The Lord our God spoke to us at Horeb, saying: You have stayed long enough at this mountain. Start out and make your way to the hill country of the Amorites" (Deut. 1:6–7). Immediately following the revelation, in which God commanded the people to begin moving toward the Promised Land, Moses tried to create a new political order. He set up the administrative backbone of society by strengthening the positions of the leaders of the tribes.

> Pick from each of your tribes men who are wise, discerning, and experienced, and I will appoint them as your heads. You answered me and said, "What you propose to do is good." So I took your

> tribal leaders, wise and experienced men, and appointed them heads over you: chiefs of thousands, chiefs of hundreds, chiefs of fifties, and chiefs of tens, and officials for your tribes. (Deut. 1:13–15)

Each tribe had its leaders and judges, and Moses was the leader of all the tribes. In effect, the Israelites in the wilderness were organized into a political confederation.

When Joshua took over from Moses, he inherited the political structure of the confederation of tribes and left it intact. But Joshua did not appoint a successor. When he died, each tribe had a leader, but there was no head over all the tribes. The confederation dissolved and what ensued was a period of intertribal conflict in which "there was no king in Israel; everyone did as he pleased" (Judges 21:25).[11]

11. This phrase also appears in Judges 17:6. This was the period of the horrible story of the idol of Micah and the concubine on the hill. See the story of Micah, which begins with the words "In those days, there was no king in Israel" (Judges 18:1).

Chapter 12

The Riddle of King Solomon

SOLOMON – THE UTOPIA

King Solomon's reign is depicted as the golden age of Jewish biblical history. The Midrash on the book of Exodus divides biblical history into three generations, from Abraham to Zedekiah, the final king of Judah.

> The moon begins to shine on the first of Nisan and goes on shining until the fifteenth day, when her disc becomes full. From the fifteenth until the thirtieth day, her light wanes, until on the thirtieth it is not seen at all. So too with Israel: there were fifteen generations from Abraham to Solomon.... When Solomon appeared, the moon's disc was full, for it says, "And Solomon sat upon the throne of the Lord as king" (I Chr. 29:23).... Thus the disc of the moon was at its fullest. From then on, the kings began to diminish in power. (Exodus Rabba 15:26)

Just as the moon has period of darkness and illumination, so too does Jewish history. The period of King Solomon was the brightest period, analogized to a full moon. After him, the light diminished. Solomon's reign was the climax of the biblical period. And the book of Kings indicates that this was how Solomon saw it as well.

> He stood, and in a loud voice blessed the whole congregation of Israel: Praised by the Lord who has granted a haven to His people Israel, just as He promised, not a single word has failed of all the gracious promises that He made through His servant Moses. (I Kings 8:55–56)

The ancient promises have been realized. The dream has come true.

And this is not just Solomon's position, but also the position of the author of his story.

> All the days of Solomon, Judah and Israel from Dan to Be'er Sheva dwelt in safety, everyone under his own vine and under his own fig tree. (I Kings 5:5)

We are used to hearing these words as the promise of a future era. The book of Leviticus reads, "You shall dwell securely in your land" (Lev. 26:5) and the prophet Micah describes the redemption as a period in which "every man shall sit under his vine or fig tree" (Mic. 4:4). But the author of the book of Kings invokes these images to describe not a utopian future, but the current historical reality.

Solomon possessed three great virtues: wisdom, architectural prowess, and great faith.

SOLOMON'S WISDOM

In Exodus, Jethro advises Moses not to judge the people all by himself. He counsels him to institute a hierarchical system of adjudication, with chiefs of thousands and chiefs of hundreds.

> You shall also seek out from among all the people capable men who fear God, trustworthy men who spurn ill-gotten gain. Set these over them as chiefs of thousands, hundreds, fifties, and tens, and let them judge the people at all times. Have them bring every major dispute to you, but let them decide every minor dispute

> themselves. Make it easier for yourself by letting them share the burden with you. (Ex. 18:21–22)

The leaders of the nation need to be God-fearing, trustworthy, and uncorrupted – all moral and religious criteria. Note that no mention is made of any intellectual qualifications.

In Deuteronomy, when Moses returns to this episode, there is no mention of Jethro as having offered this advice. Moreover, Moses describes the leaders of the people differently. This time, they must be wise.

> So I took your tribal leaders, wise and experienced men, and appointed them heads over you: chiefs of thousands, chiefs of hundreds, chiefs of fifties, and chiefs of tens, and officials for your tribes. (Ex. 1:15)

Here, the judges are not characterized as God-fearing, trustworthy, and uncorrupted; instead, they are called "wise and experienced." Moreover, the privileging of wisdom as a criterion for leadership extends to the king as well. The king in Deuteronomy is not described as a military hero who leads the people out in battle, but as a wise man who studies Torah.

> When he is seated on his royal throne, he shall have a copy of this Torah written for him on a scroll by the Levitical priests. Let it remain with him and let him read in it all his life, so that he may learn to revere the Lord his God, to observe faithfully every word of this Torah as well as these laws. (Deut. 17:18–19)

And it is not just the leaders who are charged to be people of the book. Here is how Deuteronomy describes the relationship of the other nations of the world with Israel:

> See, I have imparted to you laws and rules, as the Lord my God has commanded me, for you to abide by in the land that you are about to enter and occupy. Observe them faithfully, for that will be proof of your wisdom and discernment to other peoples, who

> on hearing of all these laws will say, "Surely, that great nation is a wise and discerning people." (Deut. 4:5–6)

Deuteronomy expresses great reverence for both the Torah and the nation of Israel. The strength of the Torah lies in the wisdom of its laws, and the strength of the nation lies in the wisdom of its members.

King David and his son King Solomon have different foundational narratives.[1] David is heroic; Solomon is wise. Each undergoes an experience that transforms the way the people regard him. For David, this experience is the victory over Goliath in the Elah Valley. For Solomon, it is his adjudication in the case of the two mothers arguing over the remaining live baby. Following David's victory over Goliath, the people go out with timbrels and sing, "Saul has slain his thousands; David his tens of thousands" (I Sam. 18:7). Following Solomon's ruling in the case of the baby, the Bible relates that "when all Israel heard the decision that the king had rendered, they stood in awe of the king, for they saw that he possessed divine wisdom to execute justice" (I Kings 3:28). And so the event that invested David with the authority to rule was an extraordinary heroic feat, and the event that invested Solomon was an extraordinary feat of wisdom.

Solomon is described as the wisest man in his generation.

> Solomon's wisdom was greater than the wisdom of all the Kedemites and than all the wisdom of the Egyptians. He was the wisest of all men: wiser than Ethan the Ezrahite and Heman, Chalko, and Darda the sons of Mahol. His fame spread among all the surrounding nations. He composed three thousand proverbs, and his songs numbered one thousand and five. He discoursed about trees, from the cedar in Lebanon to the hyssop that grows out of the wall, and he discoursed about beasts, birds, creeping things, and fish. (I Kings 5:10–13)

---

1. The Midrash on Song of Songs attempts to find more parallels between the two figures: "Whatever is stated about one is stated about the other." See Song of Songs Rabba 1:1.

Solomon's metaphors were brilliant. As king, he was a marvel, and emissaries came to Jerusalem from all over the world to witness his sagacity: "Men of all peoples came to hear Solomon's wisdom, sent by all the kings of the earth who had heard of his wisdom" (I Kings 5:14).

Solomon fulfilled Moses's dream of a wise leader famous for his wisdom.[2] His reign represents the manifestation of Moses's final address.

SOLOMON'S CONSTRUCTION PROJECT: THE PLACE OF GOD'S CHOOSING

Deuteronomy proscribes the offering of sacrifices in any place not chosen by God. There is not only a chosen people, but also a chosen place. But Deuteronomy does not specify the location of that place.[3] This enigma is solved only several hundred years later, in King David's time, when it is revealed that God chose Jerusalem as His dwelling place. And the designation of Jerusalem as an actual physical location takes place only in the days of David's son, who builds the Temple there.

There are twenty-one references throughout Deuteronomy to "the place of God's choosing."[4] Some of those verses also mention that in this place, God will cause His name to dwell.[5] The king who made it happen was Solomon: "And so I propose to build a House for the name of the Lord my God" (I Kings 5:19). In addition to his wisdom, Solomon became famous for his magnificent construction projects. Solomon devoted seven years to building a great and glorious home for the God of Israel.

SOLOMON'S FAITH

God is great. Moses describes Him as "the great, the mighty, and the awesome God" (Deut. 10:17). He stands at the apex of existence, "for the Lord your God is God supreme and Lord supreme" (Deut. 10:17).

2. For a discussion of the development of the motif of wisdom in the figure of King Solomon, see Simon J. DeVries, *I Kings: Word Biblical Commentary*, vol. 12, 2nd ed. (1985), 73–77.
3. See chapter 1, note 27.
4. Deuteronomy 12:5, 11, 14, 18, 21, 26; 14:23–25; 15:20; 16:2, 6–7, 11, 15–16; 17:8, 10; 18:6; 26:2; 31:11.
5. Deuteronomy 12:5, 11; 14:23; 16:2, 11; 26:2.

He is not just above everything, but everything belongs to Him: "Look, the heavens to their uttermost reaches belong to the Lord your God, the earth and all that is on it!" (Deut. 10:14). One of the aspects of God's greatness is His remoteness. "Look down from Your holy abode, from heaven, and bless Your people Israel and the soil You have given us, a land flowing with milk and honey, as You swore to our fathers" (Deut. 26:15).

Moses exalts God and sets Him at a distance, which is somewhat in contrast to the descriptions of God in the other books of the Bible. The idea that God is not present in the Temple is one of the major developments in the history of Israelite faith, and it is central to Deuteronomy's theology.

And what about Solomon? The building of the Temple was the focus of Solomon's royal agenda. There is more about the construction of the Temple than about Solomon's wisdom.[6] After Solomon finished building the Temple, he assembled the people for a dedication ceremony. Here was the king who had finally built a dwelling place for God. It was the opposite, apparently, of everything Moses stood for in Deuteronomy. Or was it?

During the festive high point of the dedication ceremony, Solomon delivered an address that was essentially a prayer. In that prayer, perhaps to the surprise of his listeners (and his readers), Solomon raised doubts as to whether God would indeed dwell in the Temple. "But will God really dwell on earth?" (I Kings 8:27). God will not be contained by the Temple, Solomon declares, because "even the heavens to their uttermost reaches cannot contain You – how much less this House that I have built!" (I Kings 8:27). Solomon avers that the entire cosmos cannot contain God, and certainly not this House being built in His honor.

Solomon's prayer bespeaks a paradox.[7] Deuteronomy both concentrated all worship in the Tabernacle and, at the same time, claimed that God does not dwell only in the Tabernacle. The book

6. The building of the Temple and its vessels is described in I Kings 5:6 until 6:27, as well as in 7:13–51. The wisdom of Solomon is described several times in various contexts. See I Kings 2:6, 9; 3:12, 28; 5:9–14, 21, 26; and 10:4, 6–8, 23–24.

7. For a honing of this paradox, compare I Kings 8:13 to the verse quoted above. Solomon declares that he built a House for God to dwell in and then immediately points out that it cannot contain Him.

of Deuteronomy glorifies the place of God's choosing while at the same time removing God from it. Solomon does the same thing – he builds a House for God and denies the idea that it is the physical House of God.[8]

Solomon's attitude toward sacrifice is also resonant of Deuteronomy. Solomon does not refer to sacrifices at all in his speech. Rather, he says, the essence of Temple activity is prayer, not sacrifice. The founder of the Temple, an institution whose primary activity is sacrificial worship, views it primarily as a synagogue.[9]

There is something confusing about the idea that God has a House and consumes sacrifices, since the monotheistic God of the Bible is a transcendent God. And yet it seems that this is not a problem that readers have with the Bible, but a problem within the Bible itself. Those sections of the Bible that glorify the Temple are the very same sections that remove God from it. This is the case both with Deuteronomy and with Solomon's prayer.

Solomon – in his wisdom, his construction projects, and his faith – represents the fulfillment of the theology of Deuteronomy, with all its complexities and sensitivities.[10]

---

8. Biblical scholarship emphasizes the connection between Deuteronomy and Solomon's prayer. According to some scholars, this prayer was a later addition that came from the Deuteronomic school, responsible for the ideology that led to the composition of Deuteronomy. These scholars contend that the paradox evident in Solomon's words is a product of the synthesis of different sources. See Moshe Weinfeld, "The Turning Point in the Concept of God and Ritual in the Book of Deuteronomy" [Hebrew], *Tarbiz* 31:1 (Tishrei 5722): 10–12. Also see chapter 1, note 39.
9. Immediately after this prayer, Solomon offers 22,000 cattle and 120,000 sheep and goats. Moreover, Solomon sacrifices them himself, as if he were a priest. It seems that the contradiction between his prayer and his sacrifices heralds many other contradictory aspects of his nature, which we will discuss below.
10. This emerges not just from Solomon's removal of God from the Temple, but also from his emphasis on God's unity and uniqueness. The book of Deuteronomy is the first book of the Bible that proclaims God's uniqueness: "It has been clearly demonstrated to you that the Lord alone is God; there is none beside Him" (Deut. 4:35). Moses's statements are echoed in Solomon's public address: "O Lord God of Israel, in the heavens above and on the earth below there is no god like You" (I Kings 8:23). Moses attests that God has demonstrated that He alone is God. Solomon goes even further, contending that demonstrating the uniqueness of God is

THE DOWNFALL

But for all his promise, the monarchy of Solomon ends in deep disappointment. The end of his reign was a period of rampant idolatry.

> King Solomon loved many foreign women ... from the nations of which the Lord had said to the Israelites, "None of you shall join them and none of them shall join you, lest they turn your heart away to follow their gods." To these did Solomon cling to love [them]. He had seven hundred royal wives and three hundred concubines, and his wives turned his heart away.... Solomon did what was displeasing to the Lord and did not remain loyal to the Lord like his father David. At that time, Solomon built a shrine for Chermosh the abomination of Moab ... and he did the same for all his foreign wives who offered and sacrificed to their gods. The Lord was angry with Solomon because his heart turned away from the Lord. (I Kings 11:1–9)

Although Solomon built a House for God, he also built houses for gods. The king who fulfilled the biblical vision was also the king who repudiated the biblical covenant.

Solomon's most egregious sin appears explicitly only at the end of his royal biography, and so it may seem that Solomon was a good

incumbent upon the people: "And may these words of mine, which I have offered in supplication before the Lord, be close to the Lord our God day and night, that He may provide for His servant and for His people Israel, according to each day's needs, to that end that all the peoples of the earth may know that the Lord alone is God; there is no other. And may you be wholehearted with the Lord our God, to walk in His ways and keep His commandments, even as now" (I Kings 8:59–61). When the Queen of Sheba arrived, she told the king of the reports she had heard about him: "When the Queen of Sheba observed all of Solomon's wisdom, and the place he had built, the fare of his table, the seating of his courtiers, the service and attire of his attendants, and his wine service, and the burnt offerings that he offered at the House of the Lord, she was left breathless. She said to the king, 'The report I heard in my own land about you and your wisdom was true'" (I Kings 10:4–6). His wisdom was famous, his building project was famous – and what about his faith? The Bible states only that Solomon aspired to publicize God's uniqueness throughout the world.

and God-fearing king for most of his life and only at the very end fell into the traps of his many wives and made Jerusalem a center of idol worship. But while Solomon's sin is mentioned only at the end of the story, it did not just happen at the end of his life. It had its origins in the earliest days of his reign. Here is the first verse that describes his royal undertakings after he eliminated his opponents and established his sovereignty:

> Solomon allied himself by marriage with Pharaoh king of Egypt. He married Pharaoh's daughter and brought her to the City of David until he had finished building his palace and the House of the Lord and the walls around Jerusalem. (I Kings 3:1)

As soon as Solomon became king, he married the daughter of Pharaoh. The verses at the end of the story of Solomon's life, which describe his descent into idolatry, begin with mention of this woman: "King Solomon loved many women in addition to Pharaoh's daughter – Moabite, Ammonite, Edomite, Phoenician, and Hittite women" (I Kings 11:1). What is mentioned at the end of the text is alluded to at the beginning. Pharaoh's daughter, who is mentioned at the beginning of the Bible's account of his life, is the source of his ultimate undoing.[11] This is a message familiar from Deuteronomy, which states why a king may not have too many wives: "lest his heart go astray" (Deut. 17:17). The verses that conclude the story of Solomon are an echo of that:[12] "He had seven

11. It is not just Pharaoh's daughter who is mentioned at the beginning and end of the Bible's account of Solomon's life. There are several symmetries between chapters 3 and 11, as Yoshi Fargeon pointed out to me. These symmetries demonstrate that the seeds of Solomon's downfall were planted early on in his reign. For instance, in I Kings 3:1–4, we are told about Solomon's project of building the Temple, and in 11:7–8, we learn of the shrines he built for Chermosh and Molech. In 3:4, we learn of the thousands of sacrifices he offered, and in 11:3, we learn of his hundreds of wives and concubines. In 3:5, God appears to Solomon at Givon, and in 11:9, God turns away from Solomon because of his idolatrous practices.
12. Moshe Weinfeld argues that the law of kingship was intentionally worded as an echo and contrast to Solomon's sin. Weinfeld contends that the law that appears in

hundred royal wives and three hundred concubines, and his wives turned his heart away" (I Kings 11:3).

And that is not all. The book of Deuteronomy states that the king is forbidden from amassing too many horses: "Moreover, he shall not keep many horses or send people back to Egypt to add to his horses, since the Lord has warned you, 'You must not go back that way again'" (Deut. 17:16). A passion for horses will return the people to Egypt, which was famous for its horses and horse-drawn chariots. The book of Kings even numbers Solomon's equine assets: "Solomon had forty thousand stalls of horses for his chariotry and twelve thousand horsemen" (I Kings 5:6). He also built cities to accommodate all his horses and chariots: "Solomon assembled chariots and horses. He had fourteen hundred chariots and twelve thousand horses, which he stationed in the chariot towns and with the king in Jerusalem" (I Kings 10:26). We even learn – as if to emphasize his acquisitiveness – where they came from: "Solomon's horses were procured from Egypt and Keveh, from which the king's dealers would buy them at a fixed price" (I Kings 10:28).

Solomon also violates the third prohibition in Deuteronomy, that of amassing too much silver and gold.

> The weight of the gold which Solomon received every year was 666 talents of gold, besides what came from tradesmen, from the traffic of the merchants, and from all the kings of Arabia and the governors of the regions. King Solomon made two hundred shields of beaten gold – six hundred shekels of gold to each shield – and three hundred bucklers of beaten gold – three minas of gold to each buckler. The king placed them in the Lebanon forest house. (I Kings 10:14–17)

Solomon made Jerusalem a city of gold: "All King Solomon's drinking cups were of gold, and all the utensils of the Lebanon forest house were of pure gold. Silver did not count for anything in Solomon's

---

Deuteronomy 17:14–20 may be ancient, but its wording in Deuteronomy was directed against Solomon. See Weinfeld, *Deuteronomic School*, 168–169.

days" (I Kings 10:21). He had many horses, many wives, and much gold. By systematically violating all the Deuteronomic laws of kingship, he became the antithesis of the ideal king described by Moses.

In Solomon's time, the biblical promises were all realized, but the biblical commandments were all violated. King Solomon at once represents the fulfillment and abrogation of the Torah.[13]

13. Bible scholars sought to resolve the tension inherent in the figure of Solomon by shifting it from the psychological to the historical plane. Instead of viewing Solomon as a bundle of contradictions, they viewed the text as an amalgam of sources. They argued that the description of Solomon as a successful king and as the fulfillment of the Torah's vision of kingship is ancient, whereas the negative portrayal of Solomon is a later addition by the Deuteronomic editors. See Simon J. DeVries, *I Kings: Word Biblical Commentary*, vol. 12, 2nd ed. (1985), xxvi–xxvii, and see above, note 8.

Chapter 13

The Tyranny of Idolatry

THE RABBINIC CRITIQUE OF KING SOLOMON

> R. Shimon bar Yoḥai said: The book of Deuteronomy went up and prostrated itself before the Almighty and said before Him, "Sovereign of the Universe, You have written in the Torah that a testament of which part is canceled is wholly canceled. King Solomon seeks to remove the letter *yod* from the Torah." The Holy One, blessed be He replied, "Solomon and a hundred like him will pass away, but a *yod* in you will never pass away." (Song of Songs Rabba 5:11)

In this richly imagined passage, the book of Deuteronomy complains to God about King Solomon. It is one of several midrashim that focuses on what was rotten in Solomon's kingdom. If we judge by the portrayal of Solomon in various midrashim, there is no tension, no balance between good and evil, just a whole lot of evil.

Here is another example:

> "Solomon loved the Lord" – for four years, until he began building the Temple. But once he began building the Temple – "He married Pharaoh's daughter and brought her to the City of David,"

> which is to say, "This city has aroused My anger and My wrath from the day it was built" (Jer. 32:31). (*Yalkut Shimoni*, I Kings 3, section 172)

According to this radical midrash, Solomon's love for God did not endure once he married Pharaoh's daughter and began building the Temple. The construction of the Temple was not an expression of love of God, but the beginning of the end of this love, which lasted only four years.

In another midrash, the Sages describe a party for Pharaoh's daughter during the dedication of the Temple: "There were two celebrations, one for the building of the Temple and one for Pharaoh's daughter" (Leviticus Rabba 12:5). "And the revelry on account of Pharaoh's daughter exceeded that of the Temple" (Numbers Rabba 10:4). That is, at the same time that Solomon spoke of the unity of God in his address and his prayer, he was profaning that unity with Pharaoh's daughter. Another midrash states that from God's perspective, the seeds of the Temple's destruction were sown when the Temple was first constructed: "At that moment, it entered His mind to destroy Jerusalem" (Leviticus Rabba 12:5).

Several midrashim venerate King Solomon. But in others,[1] Solomon's sins overwrite and cancel out his accomplishments. Let us turn from the Midrash back to the Bible and draw out the subtext of the biblical story, a harsh critique of the tyranny of the Bible's utopian king.

THE SIN OF TYRANNY

Solomon turned Jerusalem into a center of idolatrous worship when he built temples for his many wives. But the link between Solomon's construction enterprise and his sinfulness does not end there. In his architectural vision lay another, even greater sin: tyranny.

Solomon needed cedar trees for the construction of the Temple. He made an agreement with the Phoenician kingdom of Tyre to supply

1. For a summary of the various rabbinic attitudes toward Solomon, along with a collection of all the rabbinic sources that deal with him, see Gilad Sasson, *King and Commoner: The Sages' Attitudes Toward King Solomon* [Hebrew] (Tel Aviv: Resling, 5773), 163–172.

the trees. And to cut all this timber, he needed tens of thousands of workers, at least half of whom were Israelites, as the book of Kings relates.

> The Lord had given Solomon wisdom, as He had promised him. There was friendship between Hiram and Solomon, and the two of them made a treaty. King Solomon imposed forced labor on all of Israel. The levy came to thirty thousand men. He sent them to the Lebanon in shifts of ten thousand each month; they would spend one month in the Lebanon and two months at home. Adoniram was in charge of the forced labor. (I Kings 5:26–28)

Solomon also needed stones and other raw materials, which required tremendous amounts of manpower – a total of 150,000 men: "Solomon also had seventy thousand porters and eighty thousand quarriers in the hills" (I Kings 5:29). He appointed 3,300 supervisors responsible for driving the workers. They were "in charge of the work and supervised the groups doing the work" (I Kings 5:29).

Throughout Solomon's lifetime, there is no mention of a single word of complaint from the populace. But then Solomon died, and Rehoboam succeeded him. He came to the city of Shechem to make a treaty with the people, only to discover that the northern tribes were none too pleased, since they remembered the harsh labor they had endured under King Solomon: "Your father made our yoke heavy. Now lighten the harsh labor and the heavy yoke which your father laid on us, and we will serve you" (I Kings 12:4). This is the first time that we are explicitly told of the public reception of Solomon's building projects. The tribes had experienced Solomon's reign as a period of harsh labor, and they asked Rehoboam to relieve that yoke. Rehoboam returned after a few days with the following response: "My father flogged you with whips, but I will flog you with scorpions" (I Kings 12:11). This is a son's testimony about his father. He affirms to the northern tribes, and in so doing he reminds the readers of the text that Solomon imposed a heavy yoke on the people.

The northern tribes, who were never at peace during Solomon's reign, did not merely voice their protest. Their bitterness led to a rebellion, which ultimately split the kingdom, with Jeroboam son of Nebat ruling over the kingdom that broke rank. The repressed aggression of the northern tribes that broke out during Rehoboam's reign was at least in part a delayed response to King Solomon.

The Bible describes, as is its wont, two parallel accounts of sin and punishment. According to one, the kingdom split on account of Solomon's many wives and idolatrous practices. Solomon betrayed God, and so the kingdom was torn in two. But according to the other account, Solomon's sin was the imposition of forced labor on his people, which embittered them and drove them to rebellion. Was Solomon sinning against God or against humanity? Was he guilty of the sin of idolatry, or the sin of tyranny? The book of Kings integrates these two accounts, which stem from the same source: Solomon's ambitious building enterprise. He built shrines to other gods – a project that symbolizes his abandonment of God – and in so doing, he imposed forced labor on his subjects. In this sense, his sin against God and his sin against humanity were one and the same.

SOLOMON'S WORST SIN: SELF-AGGRANDIZEMENT

Solomon built temples for his wives' gods, a Temple to the God of Israel, and a palace for himself. It was this latter project that was most important to him. He devoted seven years to the building of the Temple (I Kings 6:38), and almost twice as many years – thirteen – to the building of his own palace: "And it took Solomon thirteen years to build his palace, until his whole palace was completed" (I Kings 7:1).

The results were commensurate. The dimensions of the Temple were "60 cubits long, 20 cubits wide, and 30 cubits high" (I Kings 6:2). These are relatively modest proportions when compared to Solomon's palace, whose entryway alone was 100 cubits long, 50 cubits wide, and 30 cubits high (I Kings 7:2). Solomon's home was significantly larger than the home he built for God.[2] He did not just devote more time to the building of his own home; he also gave himself significantly more space.

2. We do not know the size of Solomon's home or his palace. But from the dimensions of the Lebanon forest house (1,250 meters), which may have served as the entryway to the palace complex, we can gain a sense of the size of the palace. There are some who suggest that the Lebanon forest house served as the Jerusalem arsenal, based

One aim of religious architecture is to awaken feelings of human insignificance in the face of the divine. Instead, Solomon's projects elevated man above God. The forced labor that Solomon imposed was for his own aggrandizement. His throne was made of ivory, and his cutlery was made of gold. It was a kingdom of splendid opulence.

Solomon lived before the biblical prophets Amos, Hosea, Ezekiel, Isaiah, and Jeremiah, who spoke out with moral fervor against the excesses of powerful kings. These prophets began to appear only two hundred years after Solomon. And so the prophetic rebuke of Solomon's building enterprise that we would expect to find does not appear in the Bible. Nonetheless, it is not difficult to imagine how it would have sounded. A king very similar to Solomon, named Uzziah, would later arise in Judah. He was a strong and successful king who, like Solomon, built enormous complexes. According to the book of Chronicles, he was guilty of the sin of excessive pride and was punished with leprosy.

> When he was strong, he grew so arrogant he acted corruptly; he trespassed against his God by entering the Temple of the Lord to offer incense on the incense altar. The priest Azariah, with eighty other brave priests of the Lord, followed him in and, confronting King Uzziah, said to him, "It is not for you, Uzziah, to offer incense to the Lord, but for the Aaronite priests, who have been consecrated, to offer incense. Get out of the Sanctuary, for you have trespassed; there will be no glory in it for you from the Lord God. Uzziah, holding the censer and ready to burn incense, got

---

on the verse from Isaiah (22:8), "to the arms in the forest house." Archaeologists have suggested that the Lebanon forest house was built in accordance with the Mesopotamian and Syrian palace model known as Bit-hilani. Parts of the description of the building's construction as it appears in I Kings 7:2–6 are not sufficiently clear. Noga Hareuveni suggests that it had four cedar columns, which supported hewn branches, and the whole room was surrounded by copper mirrors. Whether or not he is correct, there is no doubt that it was an impressive structure, since it is mentioned again in I Kings chapter 10 (verses 17 and 21) as a symbol of Solomon's wealth and wisdom. See "The Lebanon Forest House," *Biblical Encyclopedia*, vol. 2, columns 80–81; Hareuveni, "The Lebanon Forest House," *Beit Mikra* 7:3 (Tevet 5723): 42–45; D. Ussishkin, "King Solomon's Palace and Building 1723 in Megiddo, *Israel Exploration Journal* 16:3 (1966), 174–186.

> angry, but as he got angry with the priests, leprosy broke out on his forehead. (II Chr. 26:16–19)

The successful and arrogant king who built these impressive edifices incited the wrath of the prophet Isaiah. The second chapter of Isaiah is devoted to the rebuke of Uzziah's architectural enterprise:

> Their land is full of silver and gold; there is no limit to their treasures. Their land is full of horses; there is no limit to their chariots. And their land is full of idols; they bow down to the work of their hands, to what their own fingers have wrought. (Is. 2:7–8)

The prophet describes a period of wealth and opulence, followed by the descent into idolatry. The land is full of gold, horses, and ultimately idols. Isaiah's criticism of the people's descent into idolatry is not just theological, but also psychological: this wealthy society's fatal flaw was its arrogance.

In part one, we considered the prophetic understanding of the relationship between arrogance and idolatry. Idolatry is a sophisticated form of self-worship. Isaiah, too, describes the worshippers of idols as those who "bow down to the work of their hands, to what their own fingers have wrought" (Is. 2:8). The only way to root out idolatry is to confront this arrogance: "But man shall be humbled and mortal brought low.… Man's haughty look shall be brought low, and the pride of mortals shall be humbled. None but the Lord shall be exalted on that day" (Is. 2:9–11).

Abraham, according to a midrash, destroyed his father's idols as part of his crusade against idolatry.[3] Isaiah contends that the shattering of idols begins with the shattering of arrogance. The problem is not just the physical representation of the god, but the person's aspiration to be a god himself. "For the Lord of hosts has ready a day against all that is proud and arrogant, against all that is lofty – so that it is brought low" (Is. 2:12). The great day on which God will put an end to human arrogance will be the day when he will suppress idolatry. "On that day, men

3. Genesis Rabba, *Noaḥ* 58:38.

shall fling away... the idols of silver and the idols of gold that they made for worshipping" (Is. 2:20).

When the prophet describes the symbols of man's idolatrous arrogance, he focuses on large-scale works of human construction.

> For the Lord of hosts has ready a day against all that is proud and arrogant... against every soaring tower and every mighty wall. (Is. 2:12–15)

These words are directed at Uzziah, the arrogant, successful king who glorified himself with edifices of magnificent proportions. But Isaiah's criticism of Uzziah could have been just as easily leveled at King Solomon. In Solomon's kingdom, silver, gold, and horses were in abundance, as were idols. The king's construction of soaring towers and mighty walls gave expression to human arrogance. If, according to Isaiah's criteria, any building that glorifies man is idolatrous, then Solomon was certainly guilty of this sin.

THE KING WHO RULED TOO MUCH

Solomon, who may have been intentionally portrayed as the mirror image of Pharaoh, was a king who ruled without restraint.[4] He did not just subject his people to forced labor, but also crushed the tribal political structure that preceded him. The Bible describes the sophisticated bureaucratic system he instituted in order to recruit laborers and materials from the people and to harness them in service of his building project.

> These were his officials... Azariah son of Natan, in charge of the prefects.... Solomon had twelve prefects governing all of Israel, who provided food for the king and his household. Each had to provide food for one month in the year. (I Kings 4:2–7)

4. See note 10, below, on the contrast between Solomon and Pharaoh. Also see Batsheva Brosh, "The Contribution of the 'Chronological Shift' to the Shaping of the Figure of Solomon and the Figure of Hezekiah" [Hebrew], *Beit Mikra* 53:2 (5768): p. 10, note 21.

The greater the project, the more elaborate the bureaucracy. Solomon divided the nation into twelve administrative districts, each governed by a prefect responsible for collecting taxes. The twelve districts corresponded not to the twelve tribes, but to the twelve months: each district was responsible for supplying food for the king and his household during one month of the year. The district borders were not identical to the tribal borders. Rather, each district contained parts of various tribes. The prefects thus usurped the tribal rulers, and the king thereby replaced local bottom-up tribal rule with an administration enforced from above.

Prior to the rise of monarchy, each tribe had a leader, but there was no leader over all the tribes. The founding of the monarchy converted the tribes into a political collective with a common ruler. But Solomon changed this structure as well. Solomon's desire to reign, which led to the construction of idolatrous shrines, also led to the political dismantling of the tribes.

WAS SOLOMON PHARAOH?[5]

The ancient Egyptians erected enormous pyramids to memorialize their pharaohs.[6] And there is something Egyptian about Solomon's national building project, which effectively enslaved his people. The text is full of hints of his Egyptian tendencies, particularly when it comes to his various building projects.[7] His home, too, was enormous and opulent, and Solomon subjected many citizens to forced labor in

5. For a more extensive discussion of the parallels between Pharaoh and Solomon, see Amos Frisch, "Solomon's Reign in the Book of Kings" [Hebrew] (PhD diss., Bar-Ilan University: 1986), 99–101. Also see Hanan Gafni, "The Monarchy of Solomon: The Failure and its Causes" [Hebrew], *Megadim* 31 (Alon Shevut, 5760): 87–94.
6. See preface, note 1.
7. The archaeological evidence also points to a connection between the architecture of Solomon's time and ancient Egyptian architecture. As D. Milson has shown, the buildings dated to Solomon's reign in Hazor, Gezer, and Megiddo were built according to Egyptian proportions. See D. Milson, "The Design of the Royal Gates at Megiddo, Hazor, and Gezer," *Zeitschrift des Deutschen Palastina-Vereins*, Bd. 102 (1986): 87–92. Scholars debate, however, whether these structures indeed date back to Solomon's time. See Y. Finkelstein and N. A. Silverman, *David and Solomon* [Hebrew] (Tel Aviv: Bar-Ilan, 5766), 253–259.

order to build it.[8] And so Solomon's Egyptian tastes were not limited to his choice of wife. [9]

The mention of Pharaoh's daughter awakens certain associations. The last time the Bible mentioned Pharaoh's daughter, she was rescuing a Hebrew baby floating in an ark in the Nile, an act which in turn brought about the liberation of the Israelites from bondage. Now Pharaoh's daughter appears again. Of course, she is another daughter of another Pharaoh. But if the previous Pharaoh's daughter was responsible for saving the people from bondage, this time she is the cause of their bondage. The people are once again subjected to forced labor, this time so as to build her home.

In addition to the connection to Pharaoh's daughter, Solomon also had a connection with the king of Egypt himself, who gave him the city of Gezer as a present.

> Pharaoh king of Egypt had come up and captured Gezer. He destroyed it by fire, killed the Canaanites who dwelt in the town, and gave it as dowry to his daughter, Solomon's wife. So Solomon fortified Gezer. (I Kings 9:16–17)

Pharaoh conquered a city and killed off its inhabitants, and then Solomon rebuilt it.[10] He rebuilt not just Gezer, but also many garrison towns.[11] The reference to Solomon's garrison towns is a direct and traumatic echo of the garrison towns that the Israelites built as slaves to Pharaoh in Egypt.

> So they set taskmasters over them to oppress them with forced labor, and they built garrison cities for Pharaoh: Pitom and Raamses. (Ex. 1:11)

8. See I Kings 7:8–11.
9. Solomon's idolatry and tyranny are associated with Pharaoh's daughter, and the rabbis also associate his wealth with her. See Sanhedrin 21b.
10. Amos Frisch contends that these verses contain an implicit critique of Solomon. Whereas Solomon did not trouble himself with exterminating every last inhabitant of Canaan, Pharaoh complied with the laws of war articulated in Deuteronomy (7:2; 13:17; 20:16). See Frisch, "Solomon's Reign in the Book of Kings" [Hebrew] (PhD diss., Bar-Ilan University: 1986), 57.
11. See I Kings 9:19.

Solomon was also the first Israelite king who placed overlords and taskmasters over the people,[12] responsible for conscripting people into forced labor.

At the beginning of part two, we considered Moses's warning to the Israelites not to become like the Egyptians. Moses cautions the people that the greatest danger that threatens those who fled Egypt is that they will one day make their land into another Egypt. They are charged to build a society that is the antithesis of the one that they fled. This society must aspire to social consciousness, not arrogant opulence; to limited monarchy, not absolute monarchy; and to liberation, not bondage.

But Solomon enlisted the people in forced labor for the sake of building his home, a home for Pharaoh's daughter, the city that Pharaoh had conquered, and various garrison towns. These are all strong textual hints that contribute to a sense of déjà vu. We cannot help but be reminded of Egyptian bondage. Only this time, the people do not need to return to Egypt, because Egypt has returned to them.

12. Ibid. 1:5, 28, 30 and 12:18.

Chapter 14

The Art of Renunciation?

SOLOMON'S WISDOM

During Solomon's reign, all the biblical promises – and warnings – came to fruition. The relationship between the various aspects of Solomon's nature is not paradoxical, but causative. Solomon received from God the gift of great wisdom, which led him to acquire silver, gold, horses, and wives, and that in turn drove him to idolatry. In other words, it was his success that brought about his downfall. Moses cautioned about this problem in Deuteronomy – the problem of success. But Solomon did not know how to deal with his own success. He became its victim.

It all began with a divine revelation. God asked Solomon to make a wish. Solomon, who was just starting out as king, asked for wisdom. The people were numerous, and in order to succeed as their ruler, he needed tremendous wisdom. God was impressed not just by what Solomon requested, but also by what he did not request. He did not ask for power, wealth, or honor. Instead of asking for qualities that would serve him well, he asked for qualities that would enable him to serve the people well. God, in response and in recompense, gave Solomon both what he requested and what he did not request. He gave him wisdom, wealth, power, and honor.

> And God said to him, "Because you asked for this – you did not ask for long life, you did not ask for riches, you did not ask for the life of your enemies, but you asked for discernment in dispensing justice – I now do as you have spoken. I grant you a wise and discerning mind; there has never been anyone like you before, nor will anyone like you arise again. And I also grant you what you did not ask for – both riches and glory all your life – the likes of which no king has ever had. (I Kings 3:11–13)

The biblical verses indicate that Solomon requested what he already had. Even prior to this divine revelation, Solomon was described as exceedingly wise. His father David said to him, "For you are a wise man" (I Kings 2:9). But the wise Solomon asked for wisdom because he understood the tremendous advantage of wisdom over folly. It seems that only someone who already has wisdom can appreciate the value of wisdom, which may bring with it many other advantages.[1]

And perhaps Solomon learned something else, too, from this first divine revelation. He renounced wealth and honor, and therefore he received them. The principle that things belong to the one who renounces them informed his deliberation in the case of the two mothers who came before him fighting over a single baby, each claiming it was hers. Solomon knew to give the baby to whichever woman was prepared to renounce it:

> But the woman whose son was the live one pleaded with the king, for she was overcome with compassion for her son. "Please my Lord," she cried, "Give her the live child; only don't kill it!"...Then the king spoke up. "Give the live child to her," he said, "and do not put it to death. She is its mother." (I Kings 3:26–27)

This seems to be the fulfillment of the principle that Solomon learned from his first divine revelation. There, he renounced wealth and honor

1. The privileging of wisdom over wealth is a notion that appears in the book of Proverbs, which is attributed to King Solomon. See Proverbs 3:13–18 and chapter 8.

and merited both. Now here, the mother renounces the baby and then merits to receive it. This is the essence of Solomon's wisdom.

SOLOMON AND JOSHUA

Everything Solomon did was on a grand scale. He composed three thousand fables, wrote 1,005 poems, offered one thousand sacrifices, bedded one thousand women, received 666 talents of gold a year (I Kings 10:14), and had forty thousand horse stables and twelve thousand chariots. He was a man who wanted everything without renouncing anything. This is how we must understand his compromises, too. He gave the baby to the woman who renounced it, just as he renounced wealth and then attained it, and just as his advisors counseled his son to cede some power in order to preserve his authority. Solomon, it seems, adopted a strategy of renunciation so as not to have to renounce anything. These are the virtuous politics of the wisest of men.

Solomon may be compared to Joshua, both of whom were rulers who had an intimate but complex relationship with Moses's final speech. Joshua emulated Moses and obeyed his commandments. He continued to be a devoted disciple even after the death of his teacher. He was less Moses's heir than his successor; his leadership was essentially a continuation of Moses's leadership. It is the student who concedes to his teacher who is exalted above that teacher. It was he who obeyed his teacher who merited to have God to listen to him: "The Lord acted on words spoken by a man" (Josh. 10:14).

Joshua and Solomon are similar in this sense. They both merited power because they renounced it. As we learned in Deuteronomy, a king will merit to remain on his throne only if he internalizes the notion that his kingdom is not really his. When he comes to believe that he is entitled to his power, it will be taken from him. Both Joshua and Solomon manage to remain in power. But the similarities end there.

Joshua's renunciation was part of the fabric of his being, whereas Solomon's renunciation was merely a political tactic. Joshua renounced power and therefore merited it. Solomon renounced power so as to gain more power. For Joshua, power was a consequence of renunciation. For Solomon, power was the motivation for renunciation. Joshua fled from honor, and so honor pursued him. Solomon fled from honor so that honor would pursue him. That which was an authentic spiritual act for Joshua was a political tactic for Solomon. The gestures appear similar, but they are qualitatively different.

That is why Joshua succeeds and Solomon fails. During the final revelation that Solomon merits to receive, God tells him, "Because you are guilty of this – you have not kept My covenant and the laws which I enjoined upon you – I will tear the kingdom away from you and give it to one of your servants" (I Kings 11:11). Solomon, a king who ruled without any sense of restraint, must watch as the borders of his kingdom are contracted. He wanted more than he had, and he received much less than he had. He was a victim of his own success.

The Babylonian Talmud cites a particularly pointed midrash that describes the curtailment of Solomon's reign:

> Reish Lakish said: At first, Solomon reigned over the higher realms, as it is written, "Then Solomon sat on the throne of the Lord as king" [I Chr. 29:23]. Afterward, he reigned only over the lower realms, as it is written, "For he had dominion over all the region on this side of the river, from Tifsah even to Gaza" [I Kings 5:4]. Rav and Samuel explain this verse in different ways. One says: Tifsah was situated at one end of the world and Gaza at the other. The other says: Tifsah and Gaza were beside each other, and just as he reigned over these, so did he reign over the whole world. But eventually, his reign was restricted to Israel, as it is written: "I, Kohelet, have been king over Israel" [Eccl. 1:12]. Later, his reign was confined to Jerusalem alone, as it is written, "The words of Kohelet, son of David, king in Jerusalem" [Eccl. 1:12]. And still later, he reigned only over his couch, as it is written, "Behold it is the litter of Solomon; sixty mighty men are about it" [Song. 3:7]. And finally, he reigned only over his staff, as it is written, "This was my portion from all my labor" [Eccl. 2:10]. (Sanhedrin 20b)

And so according to Reish Lakish, Solomon started out as ruler over the higher realms, then ruled over the lower realms, and then his kingdom was contracted to Israel alone. Next, he ruled only over Jerusalem, and finally, just over his own staff.

Chapter 15

The Failure of the Israelites

TOO MUCH GOVERNANCE VS. LACK OF GOVERNANCE

Joshua and Solomon were chosen as two means of examining what I referred to as Moses's second address, namely the address that the people received in the generations following Moses's death. The book of Deuteronomy offers the promise that if the children of Israel will fulfill Moses's instructions to them on the eve of their entry into the land, then they will merit to remain in the land. If they do not follow the directives, they will be exiled from the land. Joshua fulfilled Moses's dictates; Solomon did not. After Solomon died, everything began to fall apart.

It started with a revolt. The revolt against Solomon's son was, in actuality, a revolt against Solomon. All of the grievances that had built up in Solomon's day broke out during his son's lifetime. The kingdom split into Israel and Judah, a northern and southern kingdom. There were long periods of hostility and civil war between the kingdoms, which weakened them both.

This was the climate during the reigns of Asa and Baasha and Jehoash and Amaziah, but the internecine hatred reached its climax during the time of Ahaz king of Judah and Pekah son of Remaliah king of Israel. Pekah made a treaty with Rezin king of Aram to attack the kingdom of Judah. The members of the kingdom of Israel and the Arameans united against the residents of Judah in the south. Ahaz king of Judah appealed to Tiglath-Pileser, the king of Assyria, to come to his aid. The Israelite kingdoms often involved foreign nations in the struggles between them.

The consequence was dire. Within a single generation, the Assyrians gained control over the northern kingdom and exiled its inhabitants. The southern kingdom was left unscathed, but several generations later, its inhabitants were exiled too – this time by the Babylonians. The civil war weakened both kingdoms and contributed to their decline. This process began after Solomon's death, but it was the result of his rule.

Solomon's reign was a full moon, the climax of the Bible's narrative. But the light began to fade after his death. The man who wanted the most powerful kingdom was responsible for the division and decline of that kingdom. The desire for too much governance led to a total loss of governance – Deuteronomy's paradox of power.

THE PERIOD OF THE JUDGES

The opposite of too much governance during Solomon's reign was insufficient governance during the period of the Judges.[1]

During the era of the Judges, Israel did not have a king. The nation was confronted with the challenge of how to preserve intertribal solidarity without a single leader over all the tribes. There were those who persuaded members of one tribe to kill and be killed for the sake of members of other tribes. Otniel son of Kenaz, for instance, a member of the southern tribe of Judah, led the tribes in battle against Cushan Rishathaim, the king of Aram, a distant northern threat.[2] There was some intertribal solidarity, but that was the exception.

1. The book of Judges does not unfold chronologically. For instance, the story of the hill concubine features the figure of Pinchas the son of Elazar the son of Aaron the priest, who was a contemporary of Moses and Joshua. That is, a story that appears at the end of the book of Judges actually takes place at the beginning of this historical period. See Yaira Amit, *The Book of Judges: The Art of Composition* (Jerusalem: 5752).
2. Many biblical scholars regard this story as a later addition to the biblical text that served to glorify the tribe of Judah. Others maintained that the story has authentic Mesopotamian roots. See A. Malamat, "Cushan-Rishathaim and the Decline of the Near East Around 1200 BCE," in *Journal of Near Eastern Studies* 13:4 (October 1954): 231–242.

In the book of Judges, the term "judge" generally refers to a charismatic leader who is never formally appointed but manages to deliver Israel through force of personality and with the help of God's spirit. If a judge is a leader, then the last judge, Samson, was quite an unorthodox one. He was a leader without followers and without national support. He delivered Israel from the Philistines not by enlisting the manpower of the Israelites, but by dint of his own brute force. At the end of the story when Samson found sanctuary within the territory of the tribe of Judah, the members of the tribe extradited him to his Philistine pursuers.[3] At the time, intertribal solidarity was at a low ebb. The last leader in the book of Judges was not really a judge. After him, the situation only deteriorated, since there were no judges at all.[4]

The reason for the moral and national deterioration at the end of the period of the Judges is stated explicitly and repeatedly: "In those days there was no king in Israel; every man did as he pleased" (Judges 17:6; 21:25; see also 18:11).[5] That is, the reason for the moral, religious, and ultimately national collapse was the absence of a king. The implication is that if there were a king ruling over all the tribes, there would not be such violent tension among them. If there were a sovereign national ruler, the nation would be united and strong.

The book of Samuel follows Judges. There is a natural transition from the failed attempt to live without monarchy to the beginning of the royal dynasty. But this attempt also fails. After seventy-three years of a united kingdom, that kingdom split following Solomon's death. The period of the Judges ended in failure because there was no king, and the period of Solomon ended in failure because there was too much kingship.

3. See Judges 15:10–13.
4. The story of the statue of Micah is a mockery of a society that has lost its way and fallen into a kind of religious syncretism, where might means right. The story of the hill concubine is even worse than mockery. It is a rebuke to a society that has lost all sense of sexual morality. The stories that conclude the book of Judges involve idolatry, sexual immorality, and bloodshed. The only time there is any display of national solidarity, a tragedy occurs. The Israelites unite not against a foreign enemy, but against one of their own, the tribe of Benjamin.
5. On the development and significance of this verse, see S. Talmon, "In Those Days There Was No King in Israel" [Hebrew], *World Congress of Jewish Studies* 5:1, 135–144.

Is there a middle way between the anarchy that divided the nation during the period of the Judges and the tyranny that oppressed the nation during the period of the monarchy? The answer is yes – it is the way that Moses described in the book of Deuteronomy.

The laws of kingship in Deuteronomy establish the need for monarchy, but also the need for the king to remember that he does not have total power. This is not the anarchy of the period of the Judges, because there is a king. But it is also not the tyranny of the period of Pharaoh and Solomon, because there are limits placed on the monarchy. The notion of limited power sounds obvious to the modern Western ear, which is accustomed to the separation of powers, but in the biblical period, it was revolutionary. The idea that the ruler has power but is limited in that power is one of the Bible's major contributions to Western political tradition.

The problem is that even though the law of kingship in Deuteronomy influenced Western civilization, it did not sufficiently influence Jewish civilization in biblical times. Moses's final address, at least from a political perspective, is an address that was not truly heard. Israelite life in the wake of the book of Deuteronomy led to a loss of Deuteronomy's legacy.

THE RELIGIOUS MODEL THAT FAILED

Moses proposed a new kind of politics and a new approach to religion. We have focused primarily on the evolution of his political ideas, which were fulfilled in Joshua's time, forsaken during the period of the Judges, and trampled by King Solomon. Moses's political model did not last very long. But what about his religious model? Did his notion of a religion that requires total devotion without all-consuming ritual worship succeed? Did a religion that privileges morality above ritual take root in the Land of Israel?

In the biblical books between Joshua and Kings, there is no clear answer to this question, because the narrative focuses on political leaders and not religious priests. The early prophetic books from Judges to Kings deal primarily with the political collapse rather than the religious challenge. But the later prophetic books of Isaiah, Jeremiah, Ezekiel, Hosea, and Amos cry out against a society that subordinates morality to ritual worship. As Hosea put it succinctly, "For I desire loving-kindness, not sacrifice" (Hos. 6:6). Isaiah gave voice to this message in the famous first chapter of his prophecy.

> "What need have I of all your sacrifices?" says the Lord. I am sated with burnt offerings of rams, and suet of fatlings, and blood of bulls, and I have no delight in lambs and he-goats. That you come to appear before Me – Who asked that of you? Trample My courtyards no more. Bringing obligations is futile; incense is offensive to Me. (Is. 1:11–13)

God rejects sacrificial worship because it has become the focal point of religious life, instead of social consciousness and morality.

In one of Jeremiah's great addresses, which he delivers inside the Temple, the prophet criticizes the Jews' distorted relationship with the Temple. His address suggests that the Temple is to blame for the people's disregard for the weak members of society – the stranger, the orphan, and the widow. How could the Temple have led to such a negative development? Jeremiah describes the people's religious failures as follows:

> Thus said the Lord of hosts, the God of Israel: Mend your ways and your actions, and I will let you dwell in this place. Don't put your trust in illusions and say, "The Temple of the Lord, the Temple of the Lord, the Temple of the Lord are these. No, if you really mend your ways and your actions; if you execute justice between one man and another; if you do not oppress the stranger, the orphan, and the widow; if you do not shed the blood of the innocent in this place; if you do not follow other gods, to our own hurt – then only will I let you dwell in this place, in the land that I gave to your fathers for all time. See, you are relying on illusions that are of no avail. Will you steal and murder and commit adultery and swear falsely, and sacrifice to Baal, and follow other gods whom you have not experienced, and then come and stand before Me in this House which bears My name and say, "We are safe"? Safe to do all these abhorrent things! (Jer. 7:3–10)

The people have fallen sway to the false rhetoric of the mantra "The Temple of the Lord, the Temple of the Lord, the Temple of the Lord," which gives them a false sense of security.[6] They ascribe magical properties to the Temple, as if meticulous attention to ritual detail will enable them to manage their fate. The prophets preached that if the people did not develop a social consciousness, the Temple would be destroyed; but the people were so convinced that Temple worship would protect them that they ignored the prophetic warnings and society continued to deteriorate. This sense of immunity caused the people to believe that they could continue acting as they were. On account of the people's faith in the Temple, the Temple was destroyed.[7]

In summary: The kingdom fell apart and the Temple was destroyed because both were too highly regarded. Moses envisioned a religious life that was not entirely defined by Temple worship, and a political life that was not entirely caught up in the trappings of monarchy. He proposed a politics free of tyranny and a religion free of magic. His proposal may have been accepted in theory, but it was disregarded in practice. After a few hundred years it became clear that the people were unable to fulfill this vision. A religion and politics that were not a means of control remained an unrealized biblical dream.

---

6. A nation that had come to believe that destruction was impossible responded violently to Jeremiah's prophecy, which predicted just that, as we find in chapter 26 (verses 8–9): "And when Jeremiah finished speaking all that the Lord had commanded him to speak to all the people, the priests and the prophets and all the people seized him, shouting, 'You shall die! How dare you prophesy in the name of the Lord that his House shall become like Shiloh and this city be made desolate, without inhabitants?'" On the political relationship between Jeremiah and his contemporaries, see Benjamin Lau, *Jeremiah: The Fate of a Prophet* (Jerusalem: Maggid, 2013).
7. Jeremiah tells the people that anyone who uses the Temple as a means of atonement and an excuse to keep sinning is spurning the Temple: "'Do you consider this House, which bears My name, to be a den of thieves? As for Me, I have been watching,' declares the Lord" (Jer. 7:11). The belief in the power of the Temple to automatically achieve atonement constitutes a debasement of the Temple.

Afterword

The Book of Deuteronomy and the Renewal of Judaism

THE BOOK OF DEUTERONOMY AND EXILE

The revolutionary idea of the book of Deuteronomy was realized in many respects after the destruction of the Temple. The transition from Temple to study house, and from sacrificial worship to prayer, took place during the rabbinic period.[1] The great Jewish drama, the move from ritual to text, began with Moses's address on the steppes of Moab and became a reality at the rabbinic court in Yavneh.

This is the irony of the book of Deuteronomy: The book has a clear agenda, namely to enable the people to maintain a proper and healthy sense of priorities so they can remain in the land and avoid exile. But Moses's words were not heeded. The Temple became the center of

1. As Weinfeld notes, Deuteronomy provides fixed liturgy for those who bring a broken-necked calf, those who offer tithes, and those who bring first fruits. Weinfeld showed that our liturgy today was strongly influenced by Deuteronomy. See Weinfeld, "The Biblical Origin of the Shabbat and Festival Amida" [Hebrew], *Tarbiz* 65:5 (Tamuz–Elul 5756): 547–563. Also see Weinfeld, *Deuteronomic School*, 43.

religious life, the monarchy became too powerful, uncontrolled and unaccountable, and the study of Torah was not organically integrated into the lives of the people. Moses's warnings were realized. The people were exiled from the land.

Without monarchy or the Temple, learning became the center of Jewish life. Moses's injunctions, whose purpose was to avoid exile, were fulfilled in exile. The exiles did not overvalue the Temple or the monarchy. They could not, because they had neither. They understood that in the absence of these institutions, the Torah and its study were the only guarantees of Jewish survival. Without Torah, the people would disappear in exile.

THE BOOK OF DEUTERONOMY AND ZIONISM

Of course, Jewish history did not end with the destruction of the Jewish Temple and the dispersion of the Jewish people. Zionism arose. The people were returned to their land and Jewish sovereignty was restored. Jews became once again powerful and prosperous. The nation for which Deuteronomy was written had now been reinvented. And so I have tried to heed the words of Moses's last address not just as a Jew, but also as a third-generation Israeli.

The relationship between modern Israelis and the Bible is complicated and sometimes fraught, marked by periods of affinity and estrangement.[2] The Zionism that sought to rescue the Jews also sought to transform them. David Ben-Gurion, for example, dreamed of a transformation that would be not just geographical but also textual.[3] As he saw it, the return to the Land of Israel also signified a return to the Bible, which he hailed as the "book of books" that the Jewish people had given to the world.

---

2. Anita Shapira and Uriel Simon contend that secular Zionism, which was devoted to the Bible during its early generations, abandoned the Bible in the 1970s. See Shapira, *The Bible and Israeli Identity* [Hebrew] (Jerusalem: 5766), 23–27. Also see Simon, "The Status of the Bible in Israeli Society: From National Midrash to Existential Peshat" [Hebrew], *Yeriot* 1 (Orna Hess: 5759).
3. See David Ben-Gurion's letter to Nathan Rosenstreich in Shapira, *Bible and Israeli Identity*, 133–135.

This is a tragedy of Zionism: Over time, the Bible was abandoned. The generation that founded the state lived and breathed the Bible, walked the land with it, studied it and taught it. This is true, to an extent, of the next generation as well. But the passion for the Bible dissipated in the third generation of the state, and as Uriel Simon put it, "The aspiration to attain mastery in Scriptures has given way to unabashed ignorance."[4] In mainstream secular Zionist society, the Bible has fallen from glory.

In a recent interview on Israeli radio, a young Israeli author was asked why he and his generation are not interested in the Bible. The author responded that "the Bible is the book of the religious." Although today his response may sound reasonable, it would have dumbfounded the Israeli founding fathers such as David Ben-Gurion, Berl Katznelson, and Yitzhak Tabenkin. For them, the Bible was not a religious book, but just the opposite. It was the text they invoked when they rebelled against the religious world of Eastern European *ḥeder* and yeshiva, where the great stories and themes of the Bible were subordinated to Talmud study and the mastery of halakhic minutiae. But in the last generation something went awry,[5] the inspirational force of the Bible dissipated, and it became just another "religious book."

Were we to attempt an interim summary of the Zionist enterprise, it would look something like this: it succeeded politically and geographically, but it failed textually. Zionism brought millions of Jews from exile to the Land of Israel, but it did not give the Bible the stature that Ben-Gurion had envisioned. Instead, Zionism forsook the Bible.

---

4. "The Bible has been marginalized and is no longer at the center of the cultural arena; it has lost its magic. A new generation has arisen that does not feel obligated to be immersed in the canonical national literature.... and pride in the Bible's greatness has given way to alienation from it." See Simon, "Status of the Bible," 7.
5. Several answers have been offered to the question of what went awry and what caused this change in the status of the Bible in secular Zionist society. Anita Shapira claimed that one of the reasons that the Bible lost its stature was because it was appropriated by the settler movement. See Shapira, *Bible and Israeli Identity*, 25–27. By contrast, Uriel Simon argued that the downfall of the Bible was a result of the collapse of all the major ideologies that nurtured Zionism. In the absence of these major ideological movements, there was no place for a major text to serve as their foundation. See Simon, "Status of the Bible," 24.

Moses directed the Book of Deuteronomy to a nation on the brink of power. But when that nation came into power in the modern age with the creation of the State of Israel and was poised more than ever before in Jewish history to heed and actualize its message, the book was forsaken. Is this a painful irony of Jewish history? Has Moses's parting address been fated not to be realized by those for whom it is most immediate and urgent?

THE BIBLE'S SECOND CHANCE

Religious Israelis, particularly those who identified as religious Zionists, began returning to the Bible in droves in recent decades. A process that began in the seventies and gained momentum in the eighties and nineties led to a shift in the intellectual discourse in the religious Zionist world. In a considerable number of yeshivot, the Bible began to receive more attention, sometimes even at the expense of Talmud study. Anita Shapira pointed out that it all happened simultaneously, starting after the Six-Day War. Just when secular Israelis began abandoning the Bible, the members of the religious Zionist camp began returning to it.[6]

The biblical connotations of the Six-Day War were different from those of the War of Independence. When David Ben-Gurion read aloud the Declaration of Independence and described the Land of Israel as the birthplace of the Bible, he knew very well that the state he was proclaiming was located only in the near vicinity of the majority of the biblical drama. Shechem, Hebron, and Jerusalem – sitting on the land of the forefathers and foremothers – were all outside the borders of the new State of Israel. The full return to the birthplace of the Bible only took place nineteen years later. In June 1967, in six days of war, the world of religious Zionism was reborn. The war bestowed two bounties upon the religious Zionists: they celebrated a wondrous victory that was regarded as a miracle of biblical proportions, and they gained access to the land of biblical memory. The balance of the modern biblical miracle and the ancient biblical land sparked biblical fervor in the religious Zionist camp.

And the Bible played a political role as well. When rabbis and leaders of religious Zionism advocated the settlement of the greater

6. Shapira, *Bible and Israeli Identity*, 25–27.

Land of Israel, they returned to and quoted the Bible. The use of the Bible to justify modern Jewish sovereignty on ancient land was not their own invention, however. In 1937, David Ben-Gurion told the British Peel Commission that the real basis for Jewish sovereignty in Palestine was not the Balfour Declaration. "The Bible is our mandate," he pronounced. The members of the religious Zionist camp echoed Ben-Gurion when they invoked the Bible as justification for sovereignty over all parts of the ancient Land of Israel – over Shechem, over Hebron, and over Jerusalem.

It seems that throughout the history of Zionism, the Bible was invoked to justify the new Jewish sovereignty over the land. But is that the role that the Bible intended for itself? I hear the answer of the book of Deuteronomy, and the answer is no.

Moses's last address is not a justification for sovereignty but an appreciation of its dangers. More than the book justifies sovereignty, it offers guidance on how to safeguard against its excesses. The book of Deuteronomy is far more than a justification of Jewish power. Deuteronomy envisions and articulates a society that is not undermined and corrupted by that power.

Israel's Declaration of Independence avers that that the state "will be based on freedom, justice, and peace as envisaged by the prophets of Israel." But it is a sad fact that the biblical nation of Israel never realized the vision of those prophets. In invoking the prophetic vision, the Declaration of Independence expresses an aspiration to fulfill this vision for the first time in Jewish history. Modern Israelis are charged to create a Jewish state that does not repeat the sins of the biblical nation. Modern Israel is supposed to be a state whose religion does not give rise to illusions of control, but rather allows people to accept the healthy constraints upon control.

The prophetic books deal in large part with the dangers of power and so may be less relevant to a powerless people. The Zionism that revived Jewish sovereignty simultaneously rendered the ancient biblical addresses more compelling than ever before. Perhaps it is fitting, then, that in recent decades more and more young people – whether they identify as secular, religious, or neither – are being drawn to the Bible and other Jewish texts. It is too early to judge the lasting impact of this phenomenon. But it may be that now, in the third generation of the State of Israel, Deuteronomy's moment has come. If so, then it will be not just a great moment for Deuteronomy, but a great moment for Zionism as well.

Zionism and Deuteronomy complement one another. Zionism gave Jews power, and Deuteronomy teaches how to manage that power. The biblical story, as we have seen, chronicles the abrogation of the biblical vision. And the Zionist enterprise, which is still underway, seeks to succeed where the Bible failed. Zionism, then, is the Bible's second chance.

Appendix

Who Wrote the Book of Deuteronomy?

Part 1

According to Academic Scholarship

My working assumption in writing this book was that Moses was the author of the series of addresses that appear in the book of Deuteronomy. Many of the traditional Jewish commentators, as well as many academic scholars, take issue with this assumption. Most rabbis attribute Deuteronomy to God, and most academics attribute the book to a group of sages in King Josiah's court. Neither group attributes the book to Moses. They do not accept Deuteronomy's own identification of its author.

In the first part of this appendix, I will present my rationale for reading Deuteronomy as Moses's final address on the eve of the people's entry into the land, and not as a product of the seventh century BCE. In the second part, I will make the case for my decision to read the book as Moses's final words, and not as a dictation from God.

The Authority of the Community of Readers

The consensus among academic scholars is that Deuteronomy was not spoken by Moses, but written by a group of sages during the period between King Hezekiah and King Josiah. According to this understanding, the majority of the book was written in the seventh century BCE – more than four hundred years after the Israelites entered Canaan.

The question of who wrote Deuteronomy is an interesting one, but I gave myself license not to discuss it in my book because I am concerned with the theology and philosophy of Deuteronomy, and not with its history; the philosophy of the book is not dependent on the question of authorship.[1] My exegetical method is literary and synchronic. I read the book as the book itself asks us to read it, as an address that Moses delivers on the eve of the people's entry into the land. I am not a Bible scholar. My interest is philosophical. I believe that great books come into the world bound up in certain assumptions, and accepting these assumptions at face value is a condition for understanding their worldview.

But there is another, more important reason that I've adopted this way of reading the text. I wanted to read Deuteronomy the way Jews have read this book for generations. Throughout Jewish history, Jews have believed that Moses spoke these words and wrote the book of Deuteronomy. In following suit, I am basing myself on an idea that was first clearly articulated by Ahad Ha'am (Asher Tzvi Ginsburg, 1856–1927) in his seminal article about Moses.[2]

---

1. See Heschel, *God in Search of Man*, 258: "The philosophy of religion's concern is not whether the Pentateuch was written down in its entirety during the forty years of Israel's sojourn in the desert, but rather to understand the meaning and the validity of the claim that the will of God reached the understanding of man, and that the Pentateuch is a mirror of God's reaching man.... The essence of our faith in the sanctity of the Bible is that its words contain that which God wants us to know and fulfill. How these words were written down is not the fundamental problem. This is why the theme of biblical criticism is not a theme of faith, just as the question of whether the lightning and thunder at Sinai were a natural phenomenon or not is irrelevant to our faith in Revelation."
2. Rabbi Abraham Isaac Kook also referenced this idea during that period in his book *Eder Hayekar* (1906), p. 39: "Many have thought that the main basis of the Oral Law's existence has been the nation's acceptance of our Sages' greatness and holiness.... But the eternal basis of our commitment is only the nation's acceptance of it into its way of life throughout the generations.... It is certain that the practical fulfillment of the Written Law requires no less, in terms of its national basis, than the Oral Law and rabbinic enactments... for its basis is the divine importance found in this nation.... This includes the oral side of the written – that is, the acceptance of

Ahad Ha'am on Moses

Ahad Ha'am wrote that Moses was essentially a real figure, even if he never existed. His double image as liberating hero and law-giving prophet shaped the Jewish nation and Western civilization more than any other historical figure. This is the case regardless of whether Moses was a real flesh-and-blood person who played a role in history.

Ahad Ha'am distinguished between the historical Moses and the archaeological Moses. Questions about the archaeological Moses include who Moses really was and to what extent the Bible is based on a true story. Questions about the historical Moses include the nature of this figure who has played such a role in Jewish (and non-Jewish) consciousness. Ahad Ha'am wrote that one can doubt the existence of the archaeological Moses, but not the historical Moses:

> Not every archaeological truth is also a historical truth. Historical truth is that, and that alone, which reveals the forces that go to mold the social life of mankind. Every man who leaves a perceptible mark on that life, though he may be a purely imaginary figure, is a real historical force; his existence is a historical truth. And on the other hand, every man who has left no impress on the general course of life, be his concrete existence at a particular time never so indisputable, is only one of the millions, and the truth contained in the statement that such a one existed is a merely literal truth, which makes absolutely no difference, and is therefore, in the historical sense, no truth at all...
>
> And so when I read the Haggadah on the eve of Passover, and the spirit of Moses the son of Amram, that most supreme of heroes, who stands like a pillar of light on the threshold of our history, hovers before me and lifts me out of this netherworld, I am quite oblivious of all the doubts and questions propounded by non-Jewish critics. I care not whether this man Moses really

---

the nation as a whole and its divine benefit that it is evident to all. And this serves to silence every heretic and destroyer, even the greatest advancers of biblical criticism." (Translation courtesy of VBM: The Israel Koschitzky Virtual Beit Midrash, https://etzion.org.il/en.)

> existed; whether his life and his activity really corresponded to our traditional account of him; whether he was really the savior of Israel and gave his people the law in the form in which it is preserved among us; and so forth. I have one short and simple answer for all these conundrums. This Moses, I say, this man of old time, whose existence and character you are trying to elucidate, matters to nobody but scholars like you. We have another Moses of our own, whose image has been enshrined in the hearts of the Jewish people for generations, and whose influence on our national life has never ceased from ancient times till the present day. The existence of this Moses, as a historical fact, depends in no way on your investigations. For even if you succeeded in demonstrating he was not such a man as we supposed, you would not thereby detract one jot from the historical reality of the ideal Moses – the Moses who has been our leader not only for forty years in the wilderness of Sinai, but for thousands of years in all the wildernesses in which we have wandered since the Exodus.[3]

The book of Deuteronomy purports to convey Moses's final address. This is how Jews and non-Jews have understood the book for generations, and I rely on the weight of their authority in my own choice to read Deuteronomy in this way. Deuteronomy consists of Moses's last words as they have been inscribed in our consciousness. My book, to invoke Ahad Ha'am's terminology, is a book about the historical Moses, and not about the archaeological Moses.

De Wette's Hypothesis

One of the major conventions of biblical criticism came out of the doctorate of Wilhelm Martin Leberecht de Wette (1780–1849), written and published when he was just twenty-four years old. De Wette argued that Moses did not write the book of Deuteronomy; it was rather the product

3. Ahad Ha'am, "Moses," in Leon Simon (trans. & ed.), *Selected Essays of Ahad Ha'am* (New York: Atheneum, 1970; reprint of Jewish Publication Society, 1912, 1939), 308–309.

of an author close to King Josiah at the end of the seventh century BCE. The book was intended to serve as a source of inspiration and authority for the king's religious reforms.[4]

According to II Kings (chapter 22), King Josiah instituted a major renovation of the Temple in the eighteenth year of his reign (622 BCE). While the workers were busy with the repairs, the priest Hilkiah entered the Temple and discovered a book that he referred to as a "book of Torah." Hilkiah handed the scroll to Shaphan, the king's scribe, who read it to the king. The king was quite taken by the scroll and, inspired by it, he revolutionized his kingdom. He eliminated all idol worship and destroyed the shrines in Judea and Israel where sacrifices were offered outside of the Temple confines.

De Wette claimed that the book referred to as a "book of Torah" was Deuteronomy. He based this claim in part on the fact that the phrase "book of Torah" does not appear at all in the first four books of Moses, and is mentioned several times in Deuteronomy.[5] Moreover, de Wette argued that the king and his associates did not "find" the book, but rather, they wrote it. He noted that only in Deuteronomy do we find mention of the prohibition on ritual worship outside the Temple,[6] and only King Josiah – of all the figures who appear in the Prophets and

4. W. M. L. de Wette, *Dissertatio Critic-Exegetica qua Deuteronomium a Priorobus Pentateuchi Libris Diversum*, Aluis Cuiusdam Recentioris Auctoris opus esse Monstratur, Jena 1804. De Wette offers a critical exegetical reading in which he demonstrates that Deuteronomy is different from the previous four biblical books and is the product of a single later author. This claim was made earlier by the church fathers, but de Wette added a significant insight, as I will discuss. See H. H. Rowley, *Studies in Old Testament Prophecy* (Edinburgh: T&T Clark, 1957), 163, note 28.
5. See, for instance, Deuteronomy 28:61; 29:20; 30:10; and 31:24, 26. For more on the phrase "book of Torah," see Schwartz, "The Torah," 163.
6. Biblical critics compared Deuteronomy's law of centralized worship with the priestly law (from the priestly school) that appears in Leviticus 17:1–9, according to which it is forbidden to offer sacrifices anywhere, except at the entrance to the Tent of Meeting. The major difference between the priestly law and the law in Deuteronomy is that according to the former, no cattle or sheep may be sacrificed outside the Tent of Meeting, whether for ritual worship or eating. But Deuteronomy permits sacrificing cattle and sheep outside the Temple for the sake of eating (see Deut. 12:15, 20–21). See B. Oppenheimer, "On the Question of Centralized Worship in Israel," *Tarbiz* 28:2 (5719): 138–140.

the Writings – enforced this prohibition.[7] Gideon, Samuel, and Elijah all built altars outside of the Temple.[8] The Bible does not depict them as sinning, but as engaging in legitimate and even desirable religious activity. How can it be that the heroes of the Bible are not aware of a biblical prohibition? De Wette therefore argued that this prohibition – and Deuteronomy itself – was not part of the Bible as they knew it. Perhaps Elijah and Samuel were not regarded as violating one of the Torah's laws because there was no such law in their time, until it was renewed by Josiah.

The academic community readily adopted and elaborated on de Wette's theory.[9] Scholars who followed de Wette added that the book discovered in Josiah's time was not the full book of Deuteronomy,[10] but an earlier and shorter version of it.[11] According to another corollary

7. The concentration of worship had been attempted before Josiah's time by his great-grandfather Hizkiya, as we will see. But Hizkiya did not act based on a law written in a book.
8. See Judges 6:24; Samuel 1:7, 17; and I Kings 18:31–32.
9. For a presentation of de Wette's theory and its reception, see Alexander Rofé, *Intro. to Biblical Literature*, 58–60, and E. Nicholson, *The Pentateuch in the Twentieth Century* (Oxford: 1998), 5–6, 15–17.
10. See M. D. Cassuto, "Deuteronomy," *Biblical Encyclopedia*, vol. 2, 15, pp. 609–619.
11. This contention is based primarily on the repetitions and interruptions in the flow of the verses. For instance, there are two different openings to Moses's address in Deuteronomy, 1:1 and 4:44–45, which has led to the hypothesis that a new opening was later appended to the "original" version. Between the address that appears in chapters 1–3 and the address that appears in chapters 5–26 is a middle section, consisting of chapter 4, which seems to be independent. This section seemingly unnecessarily repeats some of that which precedes and follows it. More importantly, it contains language and ideas that are thought to be later, such as, "It has been clearly demonstrated to you that the Lord alone is God; there is none besides Him (4:35) and "Know therefore this day and keep in mind that the Lord alone is God in heaven above and on earth below; there is no other" (4:39). These verses sound strikingly similar to Deutero-Isaiah: "I am the Lord and there is none else; besides Me, there is no god. I engird you, though you have not known Me, so that they may know, from east to west, that there is none but Me. I am the Lord and there is none else" (Is. 45:5–6, and see verse 14). Chapter 40 and onward in Isaiah are thought to be dated to the middle of the sixth century BCE, the Persian period. See Rofé, *Intro. to Biblical Literature*, 231–232. This is the source of the hypothesis that Deuteronomy was reworked during the Persian period. Another major criterion for distinguishing among the different historical strata of Deuteronomy is

added to de Wette's theory, the ideas that comprise Deuteronomy date to a period earlier than King Josiah's reign, since Hizkiya – who preceded Josiah by about one hundred years – also prohibited all religious worship outside of the Temple.[12]

The following consensus began to emerge: During the period between Hizkiya and Josiah, a new stream of thinking developed that promoted new ideas about the nature of the Jewish religion. These ideas were recorded in an earlier version of the book of Deuteronomy, which consisted mainly of the list of laws in chapters 12–28. This stream of thinking was influenced by northern teachings that the sages brought with them when they migrated to Judea after the destruction of Samaria.

These revolutionary ideas continued to develop until the destruction of the Temple.[13] The book of Deuteronomy, this academic consensus maintains, is the multigenerational product of a group of revolutionary sages who were active in the Judean kingdom prior to and following the destruction of the Temple, when the book reached its final form.[14]

The literary output of the group of sages responsible for Deuteronomy's religious revolution included other books as well. This group is responsible for significant portions of the historiographical books from Joshua to II Kings. The book of Deuteronomy describes Moses's vision for the nation entering the land, and the historiographical

---

the language. We often find the regular Deuteronomic language juxtaposed with priestly language, as in the phrase "the blood is the life" which appears in Deuteronomy 12:23 (compare to Leviticus 17:11, 14). Scholars attribute the synthesis of priestly and Deuteronomic language to a much later stage, to the return of the Babylonian exiles. On the complex structure of Deuteronomy, see Nelson, *Deuteronomy*, 2–5. On the dating of the various historical strata of Deuteronomy, see Rofé, *Intro. to Deuteronomy*, 66–71. On the synthesis of priestly and Deuteronomic language as a chronological marker, see Y. Knohl, *The Silent Temple*, 91, note 126 and pp. 95–96. Also see R. Goldstein, "Joshua 22:9–34: A Priestly Book from the Period of the Return to Zion," *An Annual for Biblical and Ancient Near Eastern Studies*, vol. 13 (5762): 47.

12. See II Kings 18:3–7.
13. This understanding is accepted by most biblical critics today. It is presented in one of the most up-to-date commentaries on the book of Deuteronomy, R. D. Nelson's *Deuteronomy*, 6–9.
14. See Rofé, *Intro. to Biblical Literature*, 67–70.

books describe the story of the nation that entered the land. The group of sages responsible for this book, known as the "Deuteronomic school," both formulated the vision and described the attempt to realize it.[15]

Of course, this brief overview does not reflect the full complexity of the academic discourse about Deuteronomy. I wrote my book from a philosophical perspective, not a historical one.

The Philosophy vs. the Dating of Deuteronomy

The philosophical discussion in *The Last Words of Moses* does not resolve the question of the dating of Deuteronomy, but perhaps it can add one piece to the puzzle. There is a gap of several hundred years between the period when the book of Deuteronomy purports to have been written and the date that academic scholars associate with the text. If Moses delivered his address on the eve of the people's entry into the land, then the book can be dated to the twelfth century BCE. But if it was written during the period of King Josiah, then it can be dated to the end of the seventh century BCE. The problem that emerges from this gap in time takes on new meaning when considered in light of Deuteronomy's own sense of time.

We considered the sense of time in Deuteronomy in the context of the discussion of the power and significance of memory.[16] We saw how Moses uses the power of memory in order to make the past present. We saw how Moses challenges the people to overcome the gap between the generation he is addressing and the previous generations. He turns to the children of those who left Egypt as if they themselves were the ones who fled. Moses, who is of course aware of the generational gap, enjoins the people to ignore it. According to Moses's sense of time, the generation that received the Torah at Sinai and the generation that entered the land are one and the same. We have also seen that Moses does not distinguish between past and present in his address. He artificially erases the past and the future so that all time collapses into the present.

> To the end that He may establish you this day as His people and be your God, as He promised you and as He swore to your fathers,

15. Weinfeld, *Deuteronomic School*, 1–8.
16. See chapter 5, "Protective Memory."

> Abraham, Isaac, and Jacob, I make this covenant, with its sanctions, not with you alone, but both with those who are standing here with us this day before the Lord our God and with those who are not with us here this day. (Deut. 29:12–14)

Moses makes this covenant with all the generations – all are present. According to Deuteronomy, gaps in time do not render anyone less present.

It is not just all the generations that collapse into a single one. All the days also collapse into a single "today." This is one of the most powerful motifs in Deuteronomy.[17] Moses's address is delivered "today," the laws are transmitted "on this day,"[18] and the entry into the land takes place "on this day."[19] Moses knows that the entry into the land will not take place until a few weeks later.[20] But for him, the future, too, takes place "today." In Deuteronomy, all the generations are the same, and all time is the present.

If so, what is the sense of time in Deuteronomy? The theology of the book assumes that there is a gap between the objective and subjective experiences of time. Time is in motion, but an individual has the power to experience the past and future as a continuous present.

In this sense, de Wette's hypothesis, which seeks to distinguish between the generation in which the book of Deuteronomy was written and the generation to which it is addressed, contradicts Deuteronomy's own sense of time, in which past and future collapse into a single day. The days on which the speech was heard, written, and read are all a single day.[21]

---

17. The phrase "today" as a reference to the day that Moses delivers his final address repeats sixty-three times throughout Deuteronomy: 1:10, 39; 2:25; 4:4, 8, 20, 26, 38–40; 5:1–3; 6:6, 24; 7:11; 8:1, 11, 18–19; 9:1, 3; 10:13; 11:2, 8, 13, 26–28, 32; 12:8; 13:19; 15:5, 15; 19:9; 26:16–18; 27:1, 4, 9–10; 28:1, 13–15; 29:3, 9, 11–12, 14, 17; 31:2, 21, 27; 32:46.
18. Deuteronomy 4:8, 26, 40; 5:1–3; 6:6; 7:11; 8:1; 11:2, 13, 26–28, 32; 13:19; 15:5; 19:9; 26:16, 18; 27:1, 9–11; 28:1, 13–15; 29:9–14, 17; 30:2, 8, 11, 15–19.
19. Deuteronomy 2:18; 4:20, 38; 9:1–3.
20. See, for instance, Deuteronomy 27:2; 31:21.
21. Heschel, *Heavenly Torah*, 670: "We must distinguish between factual truths and eternal verities. Every fact depends on time, and when its time has passed, the fact disappears. Yet there are moments that are like eternity, and what happens in them transcends time. The passage of time brings forgetfulness; the present moment makes

In other words: The book purports to have been written at a certain point in time, but at the same time, its message is trans-historical. Hence de Wette's assumption, which challenges what is written in Deuteronomy, does not challenge the book's message.

The Future of Deuteronomy

The tremendous significance of Deuteronomy does not stem from its conception of the past but from its reshaping of the past in a way that decidedly influenced the future. This is a book that managed to transform the Jewish people and Western civilization, not when it was read critically, but when it was read in line with the book's own guidelines for how it ought to be read, i.e., as Moses's final address.

There is great value in this approach. For someone who reads Deuteronomy as the book itself intends to be read, its words were spoken neither in the twelfth century BCE nor in the seventh century BCE. They are spoken today.

---

us forget the moment past. Two moments in time cannot coexist. They crowd each other out. But the opposite is the case with eternity, for there is no forgetting at the throne of glory, and for God, past, present, and future come simultaneously. So the giving of the Torah happened in the past as a factual truth, but endures as an eternal verity. God's voice, as it emanated from Mount Horeb, was never muted.... Said Ben Zoma: It is not written, 'On that very day,' but rather, 'On this very day.' Each day that you busy yourself with Torah, you may say, 'On this day I received it from Sinai.' Moreover, it says: 'The Lord your God commands you this day' (Deut. 26:16)."

Part 2

According to Jewish Tradition

A Human Book Attributed to God

The book of Deuteronomy is written in a very different style from the preceding books. Exodus, Leviticus, and Numbers speak in God's voice. The phrase "The Lord spoke to Moses and said" appears again and again before the presentation of laws and commandments. The book of Deuteronomy, by contrast, begins with: "These are the words that Moses addressed to all Israel" (Deut. 1:1).

Most of the book is written in the first person and is narrated from Moses's perspective. The receiving of the Ten Commandments, for instance, is described as follows in Exodus: "When He finished speaking with him on Mount Sinai, He gave Moses the two Tablets of the Covenant" (Ex. 31:18). Deuteronomy reads, "And the Lord gave me the two tablets of stone" (Deut. 9:1). The account in Deuteronomy is personal.

This is not a story about Moses. It is a book in which Moses tells about what happened to him.[1] It is not biography, but autobiography.

Autobiography, too, has its own exegetical tradition. I have tried to remain faithful not just to the reading guidelines that are present in the Bible, but also to the multigenerational Jewish conversation about it.

1. There are exceptions to this rule. See Deuteronomy 31:14, 16; 32:48; and 34:4.

And so I cannot ignore the most important Jewish commentary on Deuteronomy – the Bible itself. At some point long ago, it was decided that Deuteronomy would be included in the five books of Moses. The inclusion of Deuteronomy in the Torah is the first commentary on the book. The meaning of this commentary is clear: Moses's words are part of the divine Torah. The book of Deuteronomy is a divine book.

This is the height of the tension, and the essence of Deuteronomy's great paradox. It is a book with a human voice that merited inclusion in a divine work.

"To Speak as If of His Own Accord"

The laws governing how a Torah scroll must be written do not admit to any difference between the book of Deuteronomy and the four books that precede it. These laws are very strict: A Torah scroll that is missing a single letter, or has an additional letter, is invalid.[2] According to these laws, the omission of a single letter from Moses's address is equivalent to the omission of a single letter from any other book of the Pentateuch.

Jewish law, which does not differentiate between the status of the fifth book of the Bible and the four books that precede it, does emphasize the difference in status between the five books of Moses and the biblical books that follow – the Prophets and the Writings. There is a hierarchy of holiness: It is forbidden to place a book of the Writings on top of a book of the Prophets, and it is forbidden to place a book of the Prophets on top of the five books of Moses. "And the five books of Moses may be placed on top of the books of the Prophets and the Writings. But the Prophets and Writings may not be placed on top of the five books of Moses."[3]According to Maimonides, this hierarchy is rooted in the different sources of these books. Only the five books of Moses are divine.[4] Although the prophets transmitted God's word, it

2. *Mishneh Torah, Sefer Ahava, Hilkhot Tefillin UMezuza VeSefer Torah* 10:1.
3. Ibid. 10:5.
4. The unique status that Jewish tradition accords to the five books of Moses is reflected in their monopoly on legislation. The prophetic books, for instance, do not have the authority to legislate new laws that are binding on the people. The prophets can exhort the people to keep the laws given in the Torah, but they cannot develop laws of their own. As Maimonides argues in the *Mishneh Torah*: "It is clear and explicit

was through the lens of their own personalities and worldviews. Moses's prophecy alone[5] represents God's will in its most pure and unadulterated form.[6] We find a clear expression of this notion in Maimonides's assertion that the laws that appear in the books of the Prophets and the

---

in the Torah that it is [God's] commandment, remaining forever without change, addition, or diminishment.... This teaches that a prophet can no longer add a new precept [to the Torah]. Therefore, if a person will arise, whether Jew or gentile, and perform a sign or wonder and say that God sent him to add a mitzvah, withdraw a mitzvah, explain a mitzvah in a manner which differs from the tradition received from Moses, or if he says that the mitzvot commanded to the Jews are not forever, but rather were given for a limited time, he is a false prophet. He comes to deny the prophecy of Moses" (*Sefer HaMadda, Hilkhot Yesodei HaTorah* 9:1, trans. Eliyahu Touger, 2010). On Maimonides's different relationship to the Bible in *The Guide for the Perplexed*, see part two of my book *Maimonides and the Book That Changed Judaism*.

5. Maimonides's unequivocal position, which appears in his introduction to the Mishna and in *Hilkhot Yesodei HaTorah* in the *Mishneh Torah*, is not the only view on this matter. For a discussion of Maimonides's position and opposing stances, see E. E. Urbach, "Law and Prophecy," in *The World of the Sages* [Hebrew] (Jerusalem: 5748), 21–49.
6. This belief is based on the following verses, in which God says to Miriam and Aaron, "Hear My words: When a prophet of the Lord arises among you, I make Myself known to him in a vision; I speak with him in a dream. Not so with My servant Moses – he is trusted throughout My household. With him, I speak mouth to mouth, plainly and not in riddles, and he beholds the likeness of the Lord" (Num. 12:6–8). This belief was also expressed by the Sages, as evidenced by a midrash (*Yalkut Shimoni*, Lev. 247:432) that states that all the prophets saw through seven lenses, whereas Moses saw through a single lens. The rabbis go on to suggest an alternative, namely that all the other prophets saw through a dirty lens, whereas Moses saw through a polished lens. This belief is also reflected in Maimonides's *Mishneh Torah*: "What is the difference between Moses's prophecy and that of all the other prophets? [Divine insight is bestowed upon] all the [other] prophets in a dream or vision. Moses, our teacher, would prophesy while standing awake.... [Divine insight is bestowed upon] all the [other] prophets through the medium of an angel. Therefore, they perceive only metaphoric imagery and allegories. Moses our teacher [would prophesy] without the medium of an angel... there was no metaphor. Rather, he would perceive the matter in its fullness, without metaphor or allegory. The Torah testifies concerning him [Num. 12:8]: '[I speak to him...] manifestly, without allegory.' His appreciation of prophecy would not be through metaphor, but through open revelation, appreciating the matter in its fullness" (*Sefer HaMadda, Hilkhot Yesodei HaTorah* 7:6, trans. Eliyahu Touger, 2010).

Writings are of the same status as the laws instituted by the Sages, which in turn are ranked below the laws that appear in the Torah.

Implicit in all these laws is that premise that the belief in the divinity of the Torah requires us to believe that every word and letter in it is the product of divine revelation, as the Talmud mandates:

> "Because he has despised the word of the Lord" [Num. 15:31] – This refers to one who maintains that the Torah is not from Heaven. And even if he asserts that the whole Torah is from Heaven, except a particular verse, which he maintains was not uttered by God but by Moses himself, he is included in "because he has despised the word of the Lord." (Sanhedrin 99a)

The Talmud asserts that every verse in the Bible is divine; Moses recorded these verses, but they do not originate with him. These claims are unqualified and unequivocal. But how do they accord with the very human and autobiographical style of Deuteronomy?[7] Rabbeinu Baḥya (1255–1340) tried his hand at explaining the disparity between faith in the divinity of the Torah and the personal style in which Deuteronomy is written:

> And know that the rebukes in this section were stated in Moses's words, but Moses did not speak them of his own accord, since we have as received tradition that all of the Torah ... was written by Moses from the mouth of the Almighty ... that is, to speak as if of his own accord, since he accorded his wisdom with that of the Holy One, blessed be He.[8]

---

7. The earliest commentary to refer to Deuteronomy as the word of God and not as Moses's words was found at Qumran in the Temple Scroll. See Yigal Yadin, *The Temple Scroll* (Jerusalem: The Society for the Study of the Land of Israel and its Antiquities, The Archaeological Institute of Hebrew University, The Shrine of the Book, Jerusalem: 5736). Alternatively, see the publications of the Dead Sea Scrolls, DJD: E. Puech, DJD XXV, plates VI–VIII, 85–114. For a discussion and explanation of the scroll, see Moshe Weinfeld, "The Temple Scroll" or "Torah for the King," *Bible and Ancient Near Eastern Studies Annual*, vol. 3 (5739): 214–237. For more on the description of Deuteronomy as God's word, see the introduction to this book.
8. Rabbeinu Baḥya on the Torah, Deuteronomy 29:6 (*Parashat Nitzavim*).

Rabbeinu Baḥya explains that even though the rebukes of Deuteronomy were written as if they originated with Moses, they did not. Rather, the book of Deuteronomy is written as if it were all attributed to Moses so as to teach of the depth of Moses's identification with the word of God.

Abaye's Words

But not everyone accepted Rabbeinu Baḥya's view. There was one talmudic Sage, Abaye, who concluded that, based on its narrative style, Deuteronomy must be a human text.[9] Referring to the litany of curses in Deuteronomy, Abaye asserted, "Moses uttered them of his own accord." This distinction was relevant to the laws of how this passage must be chanted. Is it permitted for the person chanting from the Torah to stop in the middle of these rebukes? According to Abaye, it is forbidden to stop in the middle of the passage of rebuke that appears in Leviticus, but one may stop in the middle of the parallel passage in Deuteronomy.

> Said Abaye: This rule was laid down only for the curses in Leviticus, but in the curses in Deuteronomy, a break may be made. What is the reason? In the former, Israel are addressed in the plural and Moses uttered them on behalf of the Almighty; in the latter, Israel are addressed in the singular and Moses uttered them of his own accord. (Megillah 31b)

According to Rashi's interpretation of this passage, it is forbidden to interrupt the curses in Leviticus because the person who stops in the middle seems as if he is recoiling from the curses, and it is forbidden to recoil from God's word. The implication of Rashi's statement, then, is that it is permitted to interrupt the curses in Deuteronomy because they are not God's word.

An awareness of the human aspect of the book of Deuteronomy is also reflected in the methods of biblical exegesis. Talmudic literature establishes that one of these methods is "proximity of passages." That is, the student of Torah may draw conclusions about one passage in the Torah from an adjacent passage, even if those passages are not related

9. For an overview of the talmudic sources, see Heschel, *Heavenly Torah*, 452 ff.

in terms of their content. There were some Sages who took issue with this methodology and argued that proximity did not necessarily reflect any meaningful implicit connection between biblical passages, but even these Sages permitted this exegetical method when it came to the book of Deuteronomy.

> R. Joseph said: Even he who does not base interpretations on the proximity of biblical passages anywhere else does base them on the passages in Deuteronomy, for R. Judah who does not elsewhere base any interpretations on textual proximity does base such interpretations on the Deuteronomic text. (Yevamot 4a)

The book of Deuteronomy was different from the rest of the Bible, and it was permitted to employ the method of proximity of passages to expound upon it. One of the explanations given for the exception made for Deuteronomy is that the first four books are divine, and so we cannot draw any conclusions from the order of the passages. The divine Torah does not necessarily unfold chronologically. But Deuteronomy is based on a human lecture, and it is organized according to human logic, so there is significance and intentionality to the order in which its passages appear.

This is the interpretation offered by one of the great European sages of the twelfth century, Rabbi Eliezer ben Natan, known as the Raavan:

> Because the entire Torah was stated by the Almighty and has no chronological order, but Moses arranged Deuteronomy chapter after chapter specifically so that it could be interpreted.[10]

Were we to learn about the status of Deuteronomy from the laws governing the writing of Torah scrolls, we would conclude that Deuteronomy is no different from the other books of the Bible. But were we to learn about the status of Deuteronomy from the laws of how Torah is chanted or its methods of exegesis, we would discover that there were those sages

10. *Responsa of the Raavan*, responsum 34.

who regarded Deuteronomy as a different sort of text – as a book spoken not by the Almighty, but by Moses.

On Reconciling Abaye's Statement

Abaye's take on Deuteronomy's words is categorical: "Moses uttered them of his own accord." Abaye was the head of the yeshiva at Pumbedita and one of the greatest Babylonian Sages. His opinion could not be disregarded. Nearly all of the conversations about Deuteronomy's provenance make reference to Abaye's statement.

Here are three examples of attempts to reconcile Abaye's statement about Deuteronomy with the reigning consensus regarding the divinity of the entire Torah.

1. *Rabbeinu Ḥananel's Addition*

Students of the Talmud are familiar with Rabbeinu Ḥananel ben Ḥushiel, an eleventh-century rabbi and Talmudist, from his commentary on Moed, Nashim, and Nezikin, which appears in the margins of the Vilna edition of the Babylonian Talmud. Rabbeinu Ḥananel understood Abaye as follows: "Moses uttered them of his own accord – to be written." That is, all of Moses's address was authored by the Almighty, but it was Moses's initiative to record it.

2. *The Tosafot*

Like Rabbeinu Ḥananel, the *Tosafot* added words to the talmudic text in order to clarify its hidden meaning: "Moses uttered them of his own accord – with the holy spirit." According to the *Tosafot*, Abaye was not suggesting that Moses was the author of Deuteronomy. Rather, Deuteronomy also came from God, though not directly. It was transmitted though a divinely inspired Moses.

3. *The Maharal*

According to the Maharal of Prague (Rabbi Judah Loew ben Bezalel), the book of Deuteronomy is no different from the other four books of Moses. All came from the Almighty. Abaye's words refer to the way in which God's words were transmitted, not to the nature of their source:

> This does not mean, God forbid, that Moses would say anything on his own initiative, not even one letter.... Every word said in the Torah – though it was Moses who said it – even so, it is as if God said the entire Torah, for so God decreed and commanded. God would put the words in his mouth, as it is written with regard to the Ten Commandments, "As Moses spoke, God answered him in a voice" (Ex. 19:19). God would place the words in his mouth. But in Deuteronomy, Moses spoke on his own, like a messenger who speaks what he was commanded by the one who sent him, and this is what the Sages meant when they said that the curses in Deuteronomy were spoken by Moses on his own, meaning that God did not put the words directly into his mouth.[11]

The Vilna Gaon (Rabbi Elijah ben Shlomo Zalman Kremer, 1720–1797) expressed a similar notion.

> The first four books were heard as God's voice coming up, as it were, from Moses's throat – unlike Deuteronomy, in which Israel heard the words of this book just as they heard later prophets who came after Moses. The Holy One, blessed be He, would speak to the prophet one day and on the next day, the prophet went forth to tell his prophecy to Israel.[12]

According to these three explanations, the source of Moses's address was divine revelation. According to Rabbeinu Ḥananel, only the act of writing was Moses's initiative; according to the *Tosafot*, the revelation in Deuteronomy was transmitted through a divinely inspired human prophet; and according to the Maharal, the revelation was reported in Moses's address, but it did not take place at the moment that the address was delivered. These three explanations reconcile Abaye's statement with the widespread understanding of the divinity of the Bible. The Bible and

11. The Maharal of Prague, *Tiferet Yisrael*, chapter 43.
12. Quoted by the Maggid of Dubno (Rabbi Jacob ben Wolf Kranz), *Ohel Yaakov*, Deuteronomy.

all its letters are divine, and Abaye – one of the pillars of the Oral Torah – does not undermine this understanding.

But why do we not simply assume that Abaye disagrees with the prevailing consensus? We can answer this question with help from Rashi, who comments on Abaye's statement in the Talmud. Rashi explains that Abaye noted the stylistic difference between the curses in Leviticus and the curses in Deuteronomy. In Leviticus, God speaks in the first person, whereas in Deuteronomy, Moses speaks of God in the third person. Rashi does not try to reconcile Abaye's statement with the dominant opinion; he simply clarifies it. Rabbi Menachem Mendel Kasher (1895–1983), the author of the *Torah Shlema*, wrote that even though Rashi does not say so, his view accords with that of the *Tosafot*, who hold that Moses spoke the words of Deuteronomy through the holy spirit. As Rabbi Kasher put it, "We can say that Rashi held like this even though he doesn't say it explicitly, since this is known and clear to all."

How did Rabbi Kasher know what Rashi meant? Because it is "known and clear to all." That is, since everyone knows that the Torah is divine, Abaye also knew it, and Rashi knew that Abaye knew it. Rabbi Kasher's words capture the intuition that lies at the heart of all attempts to explain Abaye's statement, namely a sense that it is impossible that Abaye could have meant what he seemed to be suggesting.

On Not Reconciling Abaye's Statement

Even so, not all commentators tried to reconcile Abaye's statement with the rabbinic consensus. Rabbi Isaac Alfasi (known as the Rif, 1013–1103) ruled that it is permitted to interrupt the chanting of the curses in Deuteronomy, based on Abaye's theological explanation. He quoted Abaye without trying to justify his stance.[13]

Nahmanides, too, was not afraid to consider the possibility that Deuteronomy was not the product of revelation. In his commentary on

13. See the Rif's commentary on Megillah 11a. It is interesting to note that Maimonides, too, ruled in accordance with Abaye, though he did not quote Abaye's reasoning. See *Mishneh Torah, Sefer Ahava, Hilkhot Tefilla UVirkat Kohanim* 13:7.

Deuteronomy 1:1, he writes that Moses delivered his address on his own initiative and of his own accord. He bases his argument on Deuteronomy 1:5: "Moses undertook to expound this Torah." The word "undertook," according to Nahmanides, suggests personal initiative.

> And the meaning of "Moses undertook" [*ho'il Moshe*] is that Moses undertook to explain the Torah to them. This is said to inform us that Moses saw fit to do so although God had not yet commanded him, related to the expressions, "Be willing [*ho'il*] and tarry all night" (Judges 19:6), "Would that we had been willing [*ho'alnu*] and dwelt beyond the Jordan" (Josh. 7:7), and also many others. (Nahmanides, commentary on the Torah, Deut. 1:1)

But even Nahmanides does not believe that the laws in Deuteronomy reflect ideas that Moses came up with on his own.

> It is stated that "Moses addressed the Israelites in accordance with the instructions that the Lord had given him for them" (Deut. 1:3), this being an allusion to the commandments that he would tell them in this book that have not been mentioned thus far in the Torah. And it says that these commandments were exactly as God commanded him; he did not add to or subtract from what he had been commanded. (Nahmanides, commentary on the Torah, Deut. 1:1)

The book of Deuteronomy contains laws that were not stated previously, but even so, Nahmanides asserts that they too are divine. This is what Moses meant by the words "in accordance with the instructions that the Lord had given him for them" (Deut. 1:3). According to Nahmanides, the address was human but the commandments were divine.

The clearest articulation of this notion comes from Rabbi Haim ben Attar (1743–1696) in his commentary the *Ohr HaḤayim*. He does not try to reconcile the personal style of Deuteronomy with its inclusion in the biblical canon, nor does he try to reconcile Abaye's statement with the reigning consensus. Instead, he explains it:

> They said that the curses in Deuteronomy were spoken by Moses of his own accord, and even when he went back and interpreted God's previous statements, he was not commanded to do so, but did so of his own accord.... Thus it says, "These are the words" (Deut. 1:1), meaning that these alone are the words which Moses spoke on his own initiative, as opposed to the other four books in which Moses did not utter as much as one letter on his own, for the words that came from the mouth of God came in their precise form without any change, even so small as the addition or subtraction of one letter on his own, for the words that came from the mouth of God came in their precise form. (*Ohr HaḤayim*, Deut. 1:1)

The *Ohr HaḤayim* uses the human opening of Deuteronomy to defend the divinity of the previous four books of the Torah. But in so doing, he accepts the humanity of Deuteronomy and takes Abaye's statement at face value: Deuteronomy was spoken by Moses of his own accord.[14]

There is a tension between the style in which Deuteronomy is written and its biblical context. And there is a tension between Abaye's statement and the reigning consensus about Deuteronomy's divine source. Many have tried to resolve these tensions, but some accepted them at face value. Together, they are part of Judaism's multigenerational tradition of exegesis.

The Beginnings of the Oral Torah

There have been many attempts to bridge the gap between the human and the divine aspects of Deuteronomy, but I found the words of Don Isaac Abrabanel to be the most compelling. According to Abrabanel, Moses indeed wrote Deuteronomy, but God approved of all that Moses wrote and included it in the Torah, such that Moses's human words received divine authorization.

14. The belief that Moses wrote part of the Torah is expressed in the talmudic discussion about the authors of the various books of the Bible: "Moses wrote his own book and the sections on Balaam and Job" (Bava Batra 14b). For a brief summary of the development of this notion and further bibliographic references, see Schwartz, 163. Also see Heschel, *Heavenly Torah*.

> For Moses spoke these words of his own accord, and the divine wisdom commanded that it be written in the scroll like the other parts of the Torah.[15]

The conclusion that the book of Deuteronomy is a human book invested with divine authority enables a new way of thinking about the status of the Oral Torah, as noted by Rabbi Zadok HaKohen of Lublin (1823–1900):[16]

> And this is the beginning of Moses's Torah, which is the Oral Torah, and as they said, "Moses uttered these words of his own accord," and as it is written, "Moses undertook to expound this Torah."[17]

According to Rabbi Zadok, the book of Deuteronomy is the first book of the Oral Torah. It is the human part of the divine Torah, and therefore it serves to represent the Oral Torah within the Written Torah. This is a fascinating insight because it paves the way to a new understanding of the nature of the Oral Torah. Within the rabbinic tradition, there is a deep-rooted attempt to blur the distinction between the Written Torah and the Oral Torah by means of the assertion that everything that the Sages established was previously dictated to Moses on Sinai. According to this understanding, the distinction between the Written and Oral Torah is merely halakhic and not metaphysical.

Rabbi Zadok turns this equation on its head. Instead of asserting that the Oral Torah is divine, he asserts that part of the Written Torah is human. The Oral Torah is not a divine work expressed through human voices, but rather a human work that receives divine authorization. This

---

15. See Abrabanel's commentary on Deuteronomy 1:1. Abrabanel attributes the laws in Deuteronomy directly to God.
16. Rabbi Tamir Granot made the connection between the positions of Abrabanel and Rabbi Zadok HaKohen. See his article, "These Are the Words...," VBM: The Israel Koschitzky Virtual Beit Midrash, https://etzion.org.il/en/tanakh/torah/sefer-devarim/parashat-devarim/devarim-these-are-words%E2%80%A6.
17. *Pri Tzadik*, Deuteronomy 1.

is of course a very significant inversion, since most of Jewish tradition as we know it is based on the Oral Torah.[18]

The relationship between the first four books of the Torah and the fifth can serve as a model for Jewish tradition as a whole – a tradition that unites God's word as spoken to man and man's divinely authorized word.

18. See the article by Rav Avia HaCohen, "Rabbi Tzadok HaKohen of Lublin and the Development of the Oral Torah," *Mishlav* 35 (Winter 5760).

The fonts used in this book are from the Arno family

Maggid Books
The best of contemporary Jewish thought from
Koren Publishers Jerusalem Ltd.